EMPIRES
IN THE **SUN**

EMPIRES
IN THE SUN

THE STRUGGLE FOR THE MASTERY OF AFRICA

LAWRENCE JAMES

PEGASUS BOOKS
NEW YORK LONDON

Empires in the Sun

Pegasus Books Ltd
148 West 37th Street, 13th Floor
New York, NY 10018

First Pegasus Books paperback edition May 2018
First Pegasus Books hardcover edition August 2017

ISBN: 978-1-68177-731-3

10 9 8 7 6 5 4 3 2 1

Printed in the United States of America
Distributed by W. W. Norton & Company, Inc.

To Peter Rycraft

In thanks for all he taught me

CONTENTS

ILLUSTRATIONS

PREFACE

This book is about the transformation of Africa during the nineteenth and twentieth centuries, when almost the entire continent became a part of Europe's global empires. It is a story of power struggles between nations and between rulers and the ruled. Change generated conflict, since it was imposed from above by foreigners who called it progress and believed that it would benefit them and their African subjects. Some agreed, cooperated with the invaders and flourished, while others resisted. Wars of conquest and pacification dragged on for over a hundred years and only ended with the Italian subjugation of Abyssinia in 1936. War had always been endemic in Africa, but the Europeans brought with them all the latest advances in military technology. Throughout the early period of conquest machine-guns gave their forces an immense advantage and during the 1920s and 1930s the Spanish, French and Italians deployed bombers, tanks and mustard gas against Moroccans, Libyans and Abyssinians. Nonetheless, incompetent European generals occasionally evened out the odds.

Foreigners also fought each other for control of the land in Africa. The continent was drawn into both world wars, in which Germany and then Italy lost their colonies. Over a million Africans volunteered or were conscripted to fight and many found themselves campaigning on distant fronts. During the Second World War, black soldiers from Britain's colonies fought the Japanese in Burma, and Algerians and Moroccans served alongside French forces against Germans in Italy and Western Europe. Veterans returned home proud, puzzled and angry. They had been told that they were risking their lives for universal freedom and a better world, but for the time being the imperial order remained entrenched in Africa.

The post-1945 dismantlement of the empires coincided with a new contest, the Cold War, and Africa was again drawn into a struggle between outsiders. Its protagonists, the United States and the Soviet Union and their allies, funded and armed nationalist movements and new, independent states and the Kalashnikov became the dispenser of power. The upshot was over forty years of intermittent wars in every corner of the continent, which was swamped with modern Russian and American weaponry. Percipient Africans recognised a new 'scramble' for their continent, undertaken as part of a global struggle between democratic capitalism and Communism. Ideological labels masked what turned out to be cynical and ruthless bids for political and economic power. When handling Africa's new rulers, each side adopted the principle that 'he may be a son of a bitch, but he's our son of a bitch'. Fragile democracies perished, dictators flourished and wars proliferated. Millions died, many from famines.

Conflict is one theme of this book; the other is reciprocity. In its broadest sense this concept was a constant feature of attitudes towards Africa and its people. Strange as it may seem, Charles de Gaulle, Mussolini, Cecil Rhodes and Nikita Khrushchev believed that their countries had something of value to offer Africans. The nature of this gift had first become apparent during the period of conquest, partition and annexation, roughly between 1830 and 1914. Then, British, French, German and Italian imperialists had convinced themselves and their countrymen that they were sharing the moral, cultural, scientific and technical benefits of Europe's intellectual and industrial revolutions. The French coined the expression *mission civilisatrice* to describe this mass export of the eighteenth- and nineteenth-century Enlightenment. Catholic and Protestant churchmen concurred: conversion of the heathen was integral to Africa's entry into the civilised world. While engineers built railways, missionaries preached the Gospel.

This dual partnership of physical and spiritual regeneration was appropriate for Africa, which in the popular imagination was depicted as a 'dark' continent. It was as yet largely unexplored and inhabited by peoples whose lives seemed to be so darkened by ignorance and superstition that they had failed to master their environment. This was a gross simplification, but it became rooted in the European consciousness and its consequences would have a baleful effect on how Africans were imagined and treated. If history represented an onwards and upwards march of mankind – and this was widely accepted during the age of empires – then why had some people fallen behind? Was this the upshot of complex external circumstances, or was it genetic? The latter explanation suggested that there was a biological and unchangeable hierarchy of races: modern racism had its roots in Europe's imperial experience. Multiple proofs of the capacity and ingenuity of the African mind did not lay the ghost of inherited inferiority. Neither did the vehement claims of the missionaries that all souls were equal before God.

Delivering the fruits of the European Enlightenment to Africans was more than a one-way exercise in ambitious philanthropy: Africans had something to give in return. It was widely imagined that they were sitting on vast, undiscovered lodes of minerals and were surrounded by forests and swathes of fertile land ripe for rubber, fruit and coffee plantations. Africa's hitherto underused resources would be exploited and the continent integrated into the global network of industry and trade. Its entry would be assisted by white settlers who would bring with them efficient and scientific methods of farming to grow food for European markets. Native labour was abundant and cheap and the African would spend his wages on the products of European industries, or so the theory went.

Like the subjugation of his homeland, transforming the African into a biddable worker and consumer was an interminable struggle, not least because imported economic systems disrupted or eliminated old ones. Advocates of reciprocity tended to forget that African society and customs, like those of Europe, had evolved to satisfy local needs and conditions. Nevertheless, there was abundant evidence that the African was keen to wear imported cotton from Lancashire and ride bicycles made in Birmingham.

Above all, the new Africa needed stability and order. These required new laws, new administrative systems, armies, police forces, taxation and the active participation of Africans. Greater and lesser native rulers usually retained their authority under supervision, and a new class of largely mission-educated Africans emerged to undertake the humbler chores of administration. Accommodations were made with local customs. Despite the protests of the missionary lobby, the Kenyan government refused to outlaw female circumcision. In Morocco, French officials tolerated the sale of potentially lethal local medical remedies, although they hoped that they would disappear once Moroccans discovered the effectiveness of European drugs. Of greater significance were the accommodations agreed between the British and the French and local Muslim princes and clergy. The former promised to respect Islam and the latter agreed to cooperate with their new rulers; some theologians argued that European victories over Muslim armies reflected the will of Allah to which the faithful had to submit.

There were no compromises over slavery. With varying degrees of determination, the imperial powers pledged themselves to rid Africa of slavery and slave-trading which, by the middle of the nineteenth century, was mostly undertaken by Arabs. They and their African auxiliaries were well armed and organised and operated on a large scale across much of East Africa and the regions bordering on the Sahara. Estimates of their victims run into millions. By the first decade of the twentieth century, Britain, France and Germany had all but suppressed this trade, which has attracted far less historical attention than its Atlantic counterpart. I have attempted to redress this imbalance.

The issue of slavery is still contentious and touches on other moral and emotional questions that arose from the imperial period in world history. Fifty years after the dissolution of the European empires, Africans and Asians are still drawing attention to the iniquities of alien regimes and some are clamouring for retrospective compensation, although it is uncertain how, if at all, it could be quantified and to whom it should be paid. Modern concepts of 'genocide' and 'war crimes' are invoked to describe what previous generations had labelled as atrocities. They did occur everywhere, most notably in the Belgian Congo, which was run as a purely business enterprise to fill the pockets of King Leopold II of Belgium. There are also complaints about the appropriation of land in those African regions that were settled by Europeans, nearly all of whom were farmers. Save in Algeria, their numbers were tiny compared with those who emigrated to North America and Australasia.

The final part of this book looks at decolonisation, the process by which colonies secured independence and African rule superseded European. Liberation movements were a consequence of the concept of reciprocity insofar as the extension of civilisation included educating Africans and introducing them to European philosophies and political ideals. Among them were democracy and notions of individual freedoms that were part of the British and French political traditions.

After 1945, both countries accepted the principle of independence for their African colonies, but believed that its attainment might take up to thirty or forty years, perhaps longer. American pressure and Cold War expediencies forced Britain and France to accelerate the process. African impatience led to armed struggles. The Algerian struggle led to one of the bloodiest wars ever fought in Africa, with at least a million casualties.

What happened in Algeria during the 1950s and, to a lesser extent, in Kenya confirmed earlier fears that the racial nature of colonial warfare was morally corrupting to the point when Europeans deteriorated into savagery, even madness. I have discussed this disturbing subject in Chapter Twelve. Elsewhere, I have examined other moral aspects of imperialism, in particular the ways in which ordinary people were persuaded to view Africans. These include the 'human zoos' of the turn of the nineteenth century, which were as much part of the imperial phenomena as mission schools and measures to control malaria.

Throughout this book, I have tried to avoid retrospective morality and its present-day repercussions. They regularly surface: most recently there has been a bad-tempered debate as to whether the statue of Cecil Rhodes should be removed from Oriel College, Oxford, which had benefited from his generosity. Debates over whether imperial rule was a blessing or a curse invariably end up by telling us what we already know. Good men can do bad things and bad men can do good things, and propensities towards virtue and vice are fairly evenly distributed in all races. Moreover, speculation as to what would have happened if there had been no foreign intervention in Africa is little more than indulgent fantasy. It is the purpose of history to explain why people behaved in the way they did, what they hoped to achieve and what were the consequences. They are still with us, and I hope that this book will add to our understanding of the forces that created modern Africa.

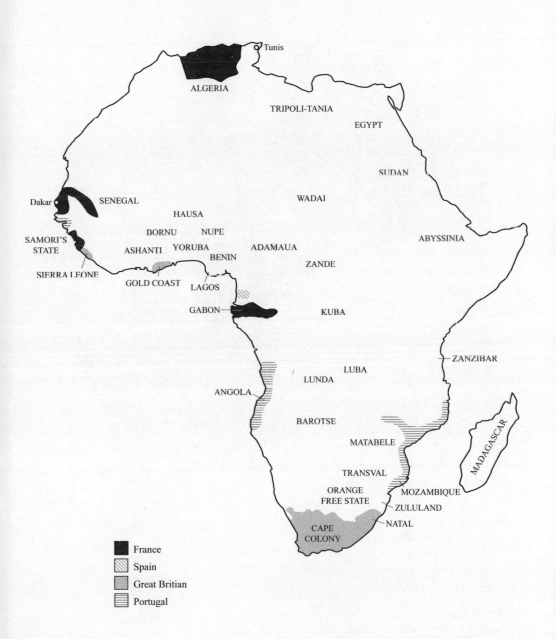

c. 1850

Tunis

ALGERIA

TRIPOLI-TANIA

EGYPT

SUDAN

WADAI

Dakar SENEGAL

HAUSA

BORNU NUPE

SAMORI'S
STATE

ASHANTI YORUBA ADAMAUA

SIERRA LEONE

BENIN

GOLD COAST

LAGOS

GABON

ZANDE

KUBA

ABYSSINIA

ZANZIBAR

LUBA

LUNDA

ANGOLA

BAROTSE

MATABELE

TRANSVAL

ORANGE
FREE STATE

CAPE
COLONY

MOZAMBIQUE

ZULULAND

NATAL

MADAGASCAR

■ France
▨ Spain
▨ Great Britian
▤ Portugal

1914

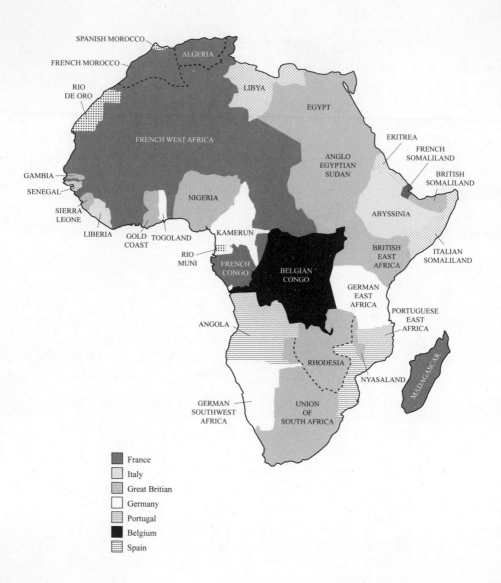

SPANISH MOROCCO

FRENCH MOROCCO

RIO DE ORO

ALGERIA

LIBYA

EGYPT

FRENCH WEST AFRICA

GAMBIA

SENEGAL

SIERRA LEONE

LIBERIA

GOLD COAST

TOGOLAND

KAMERUN

RIO MUNI

FRENCH CONGO

NIGERIA

ANGLO EGYPTIAN SUDAN

ERITREA

FRENCH SOMALILAND

BRITISH SOMALILAND

ABYSSINIA

BRITISH EAST AFRICA

ITALIAN SOMALILAND

BELGIAN CONGO

GERMAN EAST AFRICA

PORTUGUESE EAST AFRICA

ANGOLA

RHODESIA

NYASALAND

MADAGASCAR

GERMAN SOUTHWEST AFRICA

UNION OF SOUTH AFRICA

France

Italy

Great Britian

Germany

Portugal

Belgium

Spain

1945

SPANISH
MOROCCO (Sp)

MOROCCO (Fr)

IFNI (Sp)

RIO (Sp)

TUNISIA (Fr)

ALGERIA (Fr)

LIBYA (FR UK)

EGYPT

ERITREA (UK)
FRENCH
SOMALILAND

BRITISH
SOMALILAND

FRENCH WEST AFRICA

FRENCH
EQUATORIAL
AFRICA

ANGLO-EGYPTIAN
SUDAN

GAMBIA (UK)

PORT GUINEA

SIERRALEONE
(UK)

LIBERIA

TOGOLAND (Fr)

GOLD
COAST
(UK)

TOGOLAND (UK)

CAMEROONS (Fr)

RIO MUNI (Sp)

NIGERIA
(UK)

CAMEROONS (UK)

ETHIOPIA

ITALIAN
SOMALILAND

CAMBINDA (Port)

RUANDA-
URUNDI
(Belg)

BELGIAN
CONGO

UGANDA
(UK)

KENYA
(UK)

TANGANYIKA
(UK)

NYASALAND
(UK)

ANGOLA
(Port)

NORTH
RHODESIA
(UK)

SOUTH
RHODESIA
(UK)

MOZAMBIQUE
(Port)

MADAGASCAR (Fr)

SOUTH WEST AFRICA
(SA)

BECHUANALAND
(UK)

UNION
OF
SOUTH AFRICA

SWAZILAND (UK)

BASUTOLAND (UK)

1990

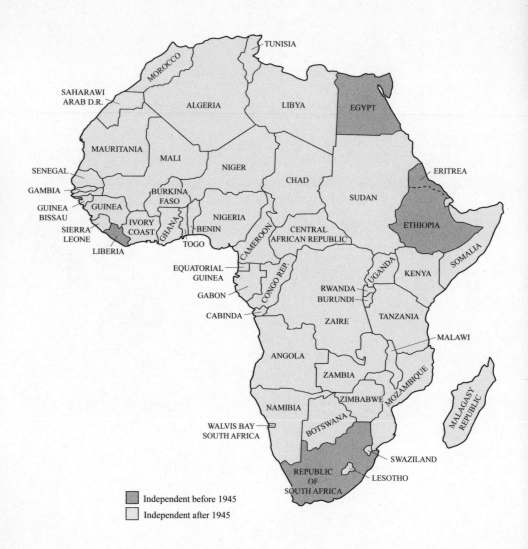

TUNISIA

MOROCCO

SAHARAWI ARAB D.R.

ALGERIA

LIBYA

EGYPT

MAURITANIA

MALI

NIGER

CHAD

SUDAN

ERITREA

SENEGAL

GAMBIA

GUINEA BISSAU

GUINEA

BURKINA FASO

SIERRA LEONE

IVORY COAST

GHANA

BENIN

TOGO

LIBERIA

NIGERIA

CAMEROON

CENTRAL AFRICAN REPUBLIC

ETHIOPIA

SOMALIA

EQUATORIAL GUINEA

GABON

CONGO REP.

CABINDA

UGANDA

KENYA

RWANDA

BURUNDI

ZAIRE

TANZANIA

MALAWI

ANGOLA

ZAMBIA

MOZAMBIQUE

MALAGASY REPUBLIC

NAMIBIA

ZIMBABWE

BOTSWANA

WALVIS BAY

SOUTH AFRICA

SWAZILAND

REPUBLIC OF SOUTH AFRICA

LESOTHO

■ Independent before 1945

□ Independent after 1945

PART ONE
1830–1881

1

Mission Civilisatrice:
Europe and Africa in 1830

I

On 14 June 1830 a French battle fleet hove to off Algiers and shelled the city. Infantrymen in bright-red trousers, blue jackets and shakoes waded ashore, clambered over its battered defences and fought their way through its burning streets. Algiers fell and patriots in Paris went wild: France had recovered its ancient glory and its soldiers had confirmed their legendary courage. *Le Constutionnel* excited its readers with the tale of how a badly wounded *voltigeur** had refused to leave the front line for treatment and rushed into the fray. His bravery was in a good cause, for, as the paper proclaimed: 'The standard of France and of civilisation flies over the walls of Algiers and over the wreckage of ancient Barbary.'

'Algiers is ours, women, eunuchs, dey and people', announced *Le Figaro*. Fittingly for a satirical journal with a disreputable reputation, it conjured up the scenes that followed French soldiers breaking into the dey's seraglio. 'It was wonderful to see the plump odalisques lying in the arms of *voltigeurs*.' The pious attributed the triumph to the hand of God; King Charles X and his court attended a thanksgiving mass; and one overheated cleric declared the capture of Algiers as a victory over 'an implacable enemy of the Christian Universe', Islam.[1] Frenchmen of the Left celebrated the overthrow of the dey, an oriental despot, as striking a blow for liberalism.

The events in Algiers and the reactions of Frenchmen set the pattern and tone for over a hundred years of European conquest in Africa. Superior, modern fleets and armies prevailed; the *Journal des Débats Politiques et Littéraires* reported how the 'nomads and desert plunderers'

---

* Sharpshooter.

fled in terror at the first sight of the French battleships. There was plenty of crowing in the same vein in 1936, when, in the final imperial war of conquest in Africa, the Italian press described Abyssinians fleeing in panic from tanks and aeroplanes.

Technical inequalities reflected moral ones. In Algiers the forces of light had overcome those of darkness: the dey of Algiers had been a cruel tyrant, his subjects were barbarians and many were slave traders and pirates. Their city was also a place of sensual temptations, which excited soldiers and newspaper readers. So too was Abyssinia. Mussolini's legions blatantly announced themselves as the seducers of Africa when they marched into battle singing the jaunty 'Faccetta Nera, bell'Abissina', which addressed a young native girl:

> *Dusky little face*
> *Lovely Abyssinian Damsel*
> *For the hour is near*
> *When we will be*
> *At your side.*

II

The metaphor of empire as a form of seduction has much to recommend it insofar as it suggests possession, usually by force or threat, and exploitation. This is what followed the fall of Algiers: its hinterland was conquered piecemeal and the way opened for what Frenchmen boasted was their *mission civilisatrice*. Its first phase was depicted by the artist Horace Vernet, who was commissioned by King Louis-Philippe in 1837 to decorate a gallery dedicated to the 'fruits of colonisation'. One frieze showed French NCOs drilling Algerian recruits, engineers building roads and soldiers tilling fields.[2] Vernet used a neoclassical style, which was appropriate since the scenes called to mind Roman colonisation in North Africa nearly two thousand years before.

Over the past 300 years, similar activities had been undertaken on a vast scale by French, Spanish, Portuguese and British colonists in North and South America. The British were well on the way to subjugating India, and the Dutch had established themselves in Java. Yet Europe's empire builders had hitherto conspicuously neglected Africa, where the European presence had been confined to slave-trading ports on its western shores. A few thousand Dutch settlers (Boers) occupied the region beyond Cape Town and provided supplies and provender for European merchantmen on their passage to and from India and the Far East. Most of these vessels were British, which was why, in 1806, Britain annexed the Cape. The world's leading maritime and commercial nation could not tolerate such a strategic and commercial asset to be owned by foreigners.

Trade with Africa had long flourished. Slaves were the largest commodity, shipped from the west coast to the sugar and tobacco plantations of the Americas. Arabs dominated the equally large and profitable slave trade in North and East Africa. Their hunting grounds were the southern fringes of the Sahara and the East African hinterland as far as the Great Lakes. Caravans of captives trudged northwards across the desert to the slave markets in Algiers, Tunis and Tripoli to be sold and, in many cases, exported to Turkey and its Balkan provinces. Zanzibar was the centre of the East African trade whose market was principally Arabia. Africa's other exports were gold, spices, palm oil and ivory: elephants died in thousands to satisfy the swelling demand for billiard balls in aristocratic saloons and keys for pianos in bourgeois parlours. Imports were dominated by mass-produced textiles, alcohol, metal wares and firearms, for which there was always a seller's market.

By 1830 old patterns of trade were changing. In 1807 Britain had outlawed the slave trade and successive governments spent the next sixty years persuading other powers to do likewise. British warships intercepted slavers and impounded their cargoes in East and West African waters and the Atlantic. In 1833 Parliament banned slavery in all British territories, which was why escaped Tunisian slaves fled to the British consulate.

Britain's crusade against slavery coincided with the heyday of the Industrial Revolution, in which she was still far ahead of her rivals, France and the German states. Manufacturers were hungry for new markets and sources of raw material, and Africa appeared to possess both. At the close of the eighteenth century Sir Joseph Banks, the explorer, naturalist and luminary of the recently formed African Association, warned that 'If Britain did not "possess" itself of the "Treasures" of Africa', then rival nations would. On the eve of Mungo Park's second expedition up the Niger in 1803, Banks urged the explorer to discover from the 'ignorant savages' the exact source of gold dust that had been found in the sediments of the river's estuary.[3]

Industrial Britain had useful and attractive goods for African consumers. In the 1820s British explorers in the Sahara presented local rulers with telescopes, finely honed Birmingham steel knives and scissors and, most welcome of all, modern guns. A pocket compass and a brace of richly inlaid blunderbusses given to the Sultan of Sokoto represented not just the goodwill of King George IV, but the wonders of British technology. A generation later, fireworks, a magic lantern, a magnetic battery and musical boxes were used by Sir Samuel Baker to impress the natives of Equatoria.[4]

The exploration of Africa had hitherto been fitful. Over the past two and a half thousand years the continent had been visited by the Phoenicians, Greeks, Romans, Arabs, Portuguese, British and French. Their revelations were a compound of fact, conjecture and fantasy, with the latter two predominating. There were persistent tales of a Christian prince (Prester [Presbyter] John) who ruled over a vast empire hidden in the heart of the continent, and equally persistent rumours of mass cannibalism, with human flesh on sale in urban markets. A sixteenth-century Capuchin missionary-cum-explorer horrified his readers with accounts of the 'Jagas', a Congolese tribe of cannibals whose men preferred the flesh of their mistresses and whose women prized that of their lovers. According to the reviewer of a history of African exploration published in 1817, these tales were the fabrication of a 'monkish dolt'. Africans, the writer continued, 'are invariably more mild and harmless, in proportion as they recede from the coast'.[5] The findings of recent explorers had exploded some of the old myths about Africa but, the reviewer regretted, two-thirds of the continent remained uncharted, with 'its grandest features distorted, or vaguely traced, or left incomplete'. Ignorance was now in full retreat. As part of their wider inquiries into the mechanisms and secrets of the natural and human universe, savants of the eighteenth-century Enlightenment had turned their attention to Africa. By 1830 more and more missing pieces of the African jigsaw were being found and slotted into place.

Geographical knowledge was fundamental to the opening up of Africa. It was also power, for it gave Europeans a template for future economic penetration and conquest. A French chart of what was then known of Africa published in 1845 was decorated with a vignette of a French officer showing the map to Africans, whose reaction is a mixture of incomprehension and amazement.[6] The foreigner knew more of their lands than they did: he could go wherever he wished, utilising rivers, mountain passes and avoiding natural obstacles.

Intruders still faced formidable barriers. Yellow fever, malaria, heat exhaustion and various gastro-enteric distempers attacked white men who attempted to penetrate the tropical forests and bush of sub-Saharan Africa. The West African coast was notorious as the 'white man's grave', and for good reason. In 1841, 80 per cent of the sailors who served on British expeditions up the Niger became infected by fevers. Of the seventy-four French missionaries sent to Senegal between 1844 and 1854, twenty died from local maladies and nineteen were invalided home soon after their arrival. During the French Algerian campaign of 1846, 7,000 soldiers died of sickness compared to just over a hundred killed by their enemies.[7]

III

At this stage, it is worth pausing to examine briefly the continents of Europe and Africa on the eve of the period of conquest and occupation. Future events in Africa would become interwoven with political, economic and social developments in Europe. The decision to invade Algeria in 1830 was taken by Charles X to raise the flagging prestige and popularity of the Bourbon dynasty. In Britain, the strategic concerns of the Admiralty, commercial lobbies and the all-powerful anti-slavery movement dictated policies towards Cape Colony and naval bases in West Africa. Equally influential were the men on the spot who enjoyed a considerable leeway in taking decisions. It could not have been otherwise, since it took ninety days for a steamer carrying orders from London to reach Cape Town.

In theory, British and French administrators on Africa's frontiers were answerable to ministers in London and Paris and, through them, to elected Members of Parliament and the National Assembly. These institutions distinguished both countries from the rest of the Continent, where power rested with hereditary princes and whomever they chose to advise them. These absolutist rulers were the beneficiaries of

the Vienna Settlement of 1815, which ended over twenty years of intermittent and destructive war that had been triggered by France's efforts
to export its revolution. The conservative spirit of the ancien régime
permeated these autocracies: paternalist princes exalted obedience,
quietism and piety as public virtues and royal power was supported by
their respective churches.

Post-Napoleonic Europe was dominated by two empires: the Austrian, which encompassed northern Italy and most of central Europe,
and the Russian, which was embarking on an ambitious expansionist programme in Central Asia. Neither empire had any interest in
Africa.

A third empire, the Ottoman, did. It straddled south-eastern
Europe, Turkey, the Middle East and North Africa and was beginning
its slow journey from stagnation towards disintegration. The authority
of the Sultan in Constantinople was splintering: Serbia broke free from
his grip in 1815, Greece nine years later (assisted by Britain, France and
Russia), and Egypt, Tunisia and Algeria were already virtually independent states. In 1843 Cyrenaica (eastern Libya) fell into the hands
of the Sanussi, an ascetic Muslim brotherhood that secured control
over the tribes of the interior and enforced a civil peace and rigorous
orthodoxy.

Britain and France were ideologically distinct from the old imperial
powers of Europe; they were liberal states that had broken free from
the political and intellectual straitjacket of the ancien régime. Each
was the offspring of popular revolution: the Glorious Revolution of
1688–9 and the French of 1789. These had laid the foundations of the
liberal ideology: individual liberty, freedom of conscience and expression, free-market capitalism and government by consent. Assemblies
elected by richer citizens decided the laws and daily governance of
Britain and France. They were not yet democracies in a modern sense,
but both countries were gradually enlarging their electorates.

Liberalism was gaining ground across Europe, particularly among
the professional and commercial middle classes, intellectuals and
writers. Liberals dominated the embryonic Polish, Italian, Hungarian
and German national movements, which were seeking to create new
states united by language, culture and popular sentiment. Nationalism
challenged the multinational Austrian, Russian and Ottoman empires,
but it also fostered tribal sentiments, notions of racial superiority and

a sense of national destiny. These would become prime ingredients in the new imperialism that emerged later in the century.

IV

The ethnographic and political map of Africa was complex and often incomprehensible in its diversity. The continent was a vast collection of polities with different languages, laws, religions and social structures. When Europeans attempted to make sense of it, they naturally made comparisons with their own systems and ideas. David Livingstone characterised the polities of the Zambezi basin as patriarchal 'and, according to the temperament of the Chief, despotic or guided by the elders of the tribe'.[8] Absolutism and a diluted liberalism rubbed shoulders in Africa.

Like his contemporaries, Livingstone identified the tribe as the basic political unit of Africa, but the bonds that held it together were often hard to fathom. How did one define the Ibo of southern Nigeria? They lived in small, autonomous villages which were often at odds with each other, spoke different dialects and had no collective name for themselves. Outsiders detected the threads of a common culture, language and lineage, but the collective term 'Ibo' was the invention of their later rulers, the British.[9]

Kingship, where it existed, was more readily understood. Like the Christian autocrats of Europe, many African monarchs enjoyed divine approval, even ancestry. Again like their European counterparts, they wore gorgeous regalia on public occasions, advertised their prestige by richly clad retinues, and were treated with flattering servility.

The façade of power and its rituals encouraged comparisons between European and African princes. The King of Dahomey and the Asantehene of the Asante appeared to be absolute rulers of centralised states with large armies, including the famous female regiment (Amazons) of Dahomey, and treasuries filled by the profits of slave-trading. This omnipotence was deceptive. Asantehenes ruled over a confederation of small communities with the guidance of local councils, including village 'Young Men's Associations'. Checks and balances existed elsewhere. A council drawn from craft guilds and their kinsmen (who also held the offices of state) guided the Yoruba kings of Nigeria. Ancient customs, religious traditions and law bound the African ruler as they did the European.

There was abundant evidence of hierarchies of races and tribes. When in 1835 Sir Benjamin D'Urban, the Governor of Cape Colony, criticised the Xhosa paramount chief Hintsa Ka Khawuta for his ill-treatment of the Fingoes (Mfengu), he replied: 'Are they not my dogs?' A British traveller in the western Sahara observed that the Arab ladies of Fezzan despised Negresses, despite their being 'not a half shade darker than themselves'. Another explorer heard Arabs dismiss the blacks of Borku and Waday as 'savages of the worst description'. 'We have guns', declared one Arab ruler, and this alone made his people superior to men armed with spears and bows and arrows.[10]

Beyond the Sahara, West Africa and the hinterland of Cape Colony the nature of African societies was only vaguely understood. There was, however, plentiful evidence to indicate the prevalence of endemic, localised struggles for survival between states, tribes and clans. At stake were fertile land, livestock and the right to extract protection money from the caravans of traders that passed through tribal lands. This tribute underwrote the loyalty of the warriors of the Chaga chiefs, whose tribesmen occupied the slopes of Mount Kilimanjaro. African warfare was expected to pay for itself.

The history of Africa, like that of Europe, had been one of continual shifts in balances of power and the expansion and contraction of states. Poland had been a recent, classic example: within thirty years it had been transformed from being an independent kingdom to three provinces of its neighbours Prussia, Russia and Austria. Between 1810 and 1830, the South and Central American empires of Spain and Portugal had been overturned by local nationalist uprisings, leaving their mother countries impoverished backwaters.

A similar pattern of growth and decay marked African history, which included the fragmentary narratives of vanished supremacies. One was the commercial empire of Zimbabwe, which imploded at some unknown date in the fifteenth century. Its rise and fall are unrecorded, for Africans remembered rather than wrote down their history. All that remains are the ruins of a great city so sophisticated that European archaeologists imagined that it could only have been built by Arabs or (a wild guess, this) Phoenicians! Written Arab sources touch on the richness and splendour of the inland empire of Ghana on the western edge of the Sahara, which collapsed in the early thirteenth century. Revealingly, two modern states adopted the names Zimbabwe and Ghana after independence.

At the beginning of the nineteenth century two African states were extending their territory by large-scale wars of conquest, the Egyptian in the north and the Zulu in the far south. In 1820 Khedive Muhammad Ali began the piecemeal conquest of the Sudan and within twenty years had overrun most of its northern provinces. Khartoum, already a major focus for the slave trade, became the capital of a new and still-expanding Egyptian empire. Over a tenth of its 15,000 inhabitants were soldiers, for resistance was common and stubborn.

The war ground on, and to finance it the Egyptians squeezed taxes from the Sudanese, which provoked further uprisings. Sudan was the springboard for further expansion southwards, with the ultimate aim of making Egypt the dominant power in East Africa. Successive khedives fielded European-style armies: Egyptian peasant conscripts were commanded by European mercenary officers, armed with imported modern artillery and rifles and supplied by Nile paddle steamers.

Zulu soldiers fought with traditional weapons and, led by Shaka, they created an empire in South Africa. He was a military genius and tactical innovator whose disciplined impis relied on the assegai, a variant of the traditional spear. He died in 1828 after over a dozen years of ruthless warfare in which he absorbed the Zulu clans into a kingdom that covered over 10,000 square miles and supported an army of 20,000 warriors. The success of Africa's Napoleon and the courage of his fighting men captured the imagination of Europeans, but, like the French emperor, Shaka wreaked havoc on his own people and their neighbours. His campaigns produced famines and disruption as uprooted tribes fled from his armies.

Across eastern and Central Africa there was a scattering of predatory and fissile petty states, created by local warlords and financed by selling slaves to Arab dealers. Their chiefs were encountered by European explorers from the 1850s onwards, whose accounts of their ferocity and enterprise contributed to the impression of vast areas of Africa as convulsed by perpetual anarchy. Memories of wars, slave raids and conflicts remained in the African historical consciousness for generations, although recollections of their exact causes were forgotten or only partially remembered.

V

Reports of endemic violence confirmed the commonplace European perception of Africa as a 'dark' continent. This metaphor of darkness conveyed two meanings. One, less and less applicable after 1830, was geographical and covered those diminishing areas that were still unexplored. The other darkness was that of the human soul which set the African apart from the rest of humanity. For various reasons which scientists and philosophers were endeavouring to fathom, the Negro had somehow been isolated from the mainstreams of progress and civilisation. According to current interpretations of world history, there was a vibrant and superior European civilisation, and there were Arab, Indian, Persian and Chinese civilisations which had become ossified and decadent.

So far as it was known, there was no African Taj Mahal or Forbidden City. Why this was so had perplexed Europe's men of reason during the eighteenth century. The answer seemed to lie in a genetic intellectual deficiency. The naturalist Linnaeus classified the Negro as 'phlegmatic', 'ignorant' and ruled by caprice. According to the philosopher David Hume, the Negro's intellectual attainments were those of a parrot, and John Wesley regarded his flaws as evidence of man's capacity for moral degeneration.[11]

At least by implication, Wesley allowed the black man a lifeline of regeneration and salvation, which was an acknowledgement of the Christian belief that all men had been created by God and shared a common ancestry. Yet the Negro's lineage was tainted by the myth of Ham. According to Genesis, he had spied on his father Noah coupling with his mother and the outraged patriarch had sentenced Ham and his descendants to eternal servility as a punishment. Their black skins were indelible evidence of their forefather's wickedness. This fairy story had far-reaching and horrendous consequences. It was transmitted from Judaism to Christian and Islamic theologies, both of which invoked it as evidence of a divine sanction for slavery.

Notions of African inferiority gained a shallow legitimacy from the more lurid reports of early explorers and European residents in Africa, many of whom were employed in the slave trade. These tales crept into scientific literature: the *Encyclopédie*, first published in 1751, accused the natives of the Ivory Coast of debauchery, a lack of belief in the afterlife, and described African political structures as 'bizarre', 'despotic' and based solely on passion. The African spurned reason and the upshot was the 'ferociousness, cruelty, perfidy, cowardice [and] laziness' which characterised all black races. Moreover, Negro minds were prey to witchcraft and superstition, as, for that matter, were those of the peasantry of remote and backward regions of Europe. In 1840 the islanders of St Kilda, for example, slaughtered a Great Auk in the belief that it was a witch.

Interior darkness was announced by outward appearances. A child's story book published in France in 1837 described the horror of the hero when he first meets Negroes: 'they seemed hideous, I would have thought of them as monkeys of the worst species, if their bodies, which had no clothes, had not human form'.[12] The Christian European psyche had traditionally connected whiteness with sanctity, virtue and honour, whereas blackness was associated with evil in all its manifestations.

The fabricated moral genetics that weighed so heavily against all black races were being questioned. A visitor to Fezzan in the 1790s wondered whether the lethargy of its citizens was not a consequence of heredity but the result of tyranny, poverty and a diet of dates and 'a kind of farinaceous pap'.[13] The plight of the African was neither preordained nor immutable: it was the product of many complex historical and cultural factors that could be changed.

By 1800 the cockeyed notion that the African's deficiencies were hereditary and irredeemable was being challenged by two increasingly influential movements, Romanticism and Evangelical Christianity. Their followers would have endorsed Wordsworth's assertion that 'we all have one human heart'. Romantics insisted that the Negro possessed feelings like the rest of mankind and these made him part of the human race. He deserved sympathy, assistance and the chance to enjoy those universal birthrights, liberty and happiness. Evangelicals believed that his conversion to Christianity would complete his felicity.

The optimistic view of the African's future was supported by much of the new literature of exploration. Mungo Park was struck by the decency and kindness of the people he met on the banks of the Niger, including a woman who fed and cared for him when he had fallen sick. His short stay in Sokoto in 1824 convinced Hugh Clapperton, a naval officer, that its inhabitants were 'civilised, learned, humane and pious'. Their intelligence and conduct dispelled all preconceptions about 'naked savages, devoid of religion, and not far from the condition of wild beasts'. A British officer newly arrived at the Cape thought the Xhosa were 'the finest formed people I ever saw . . . models of the human form in its most perfect form'.[14]

2

'Sold just like chickens': Slavery
and the Slave Trade

I

Slavery and the slave trade were vast but not immovable obstacles to progress in Africa; they skewed economic and social development, and were a constant cause of wars. This was a view fervently held in Britain, less so in France. It was rejected by the reactionary Catholic empires of Spain and Portugal, where slavery and slave-trafficking were tolerated until the last quarter of the nineteenth century. Arab and African slavers insisted that they were engaged in a historically legitimate, economically necessary and rewarding enterprise. 'All he cared about was business' was the folk memory of Rashid Masidi, a late-nineteenth-century Swahili slave dealer who operated in what is now Tanzania.*[1] Market forces and high profit ratios trumped all other considerations and the slavers were ready to fight to uphold them.

The Islamic conscience was untroubled by slavery. Salme Sayyid, the daughter of Sultan Sayyid al-Busaidi of Zanzibar, assumed that all slaves enjoyed a good life: 'they have no care themselves, and their welfare is always studiously looked after'.[2] As we shall see, this was a misconception. What mattered to Salme was the fact that her father and elder brother Sultan Madjid received a levy from the price of every slave sold in the Zanzibar market. Like everyone else who stood to lose from the slave trade, the Al Busaidi sultans bitterly resented Britain's efforts to abolish it. In 1854 Sir Richard Burton discovered that Britain was the most hated European nation in Somaliland because of its naval war against the slave trade. Zanzibari Arabs called the outstandingly vigilant HMS *Lyra* 'el shaleen' (the devil).

The feelings of the slave trade's victims were seldom recorded.

* Swahilis were of mixed Arab and African descent.

Senegalese folk memories of late-nineteenth-century slave raids give an impression of permanent insecurity in areas where armed gangs of kidnappers terrorised villages.[3] Yet in one part of the Congo basin villagers welcomed the slavers, to whom they sold their bad hats, including witches' and thieves'.[4] There is no reason to disbelieve that the joy of liberated slaves described in anti-slavery literature was not heartfelt, though bewilderment and even despair followed after released men and women found themselves stranded on an alien shore without employment.

An officer on HMS *Wasp* wondered what fate awaited the young female slaves, rescued by his ship and put ashore at Mahé on the Seychelles, a British colony. Similarly in Sierra Leone, where victims of the Atlantic trade had been settled since the late eighteenth century. Here and elsewhere the British government relied on missions to provide accommodation and work. Missions close to the naval base in Gabon also resettled slaves rescued by French warships.

II

Before turning to the largely British efforts to eradicate the slave trade, it is useful to pause and examine its extent and nature. The far from perfect statistics of the slave trade, which give a rough but valuable impression of its magnitude, do much to explain the determination of the vested interests that justified it, and why it took so long to eliminate. The calculus of the slave trade is also a salutary reminder that it was a multiracial activity that enriched not just Europeans, but also Arabs, Turks, Egyptians and Africans.

Until the beginning of the nineteenth century the Atlantic was the largest sector of the trade. In 1800 there were 2 million slaves in Brazil, 900,000 in the United States and 800,000 in Spanish America, all of whom had West or East African ancestry. Most worked on cotton, sugar and tobacco plantations, which supplied a largely European market.

Like every other capitalist undertaking, the slave trade was subject to the laws of supply and demand and political pressures. The rapid expansion of cotton production in the southern states of America after 1820 led to a growing demand for slaves, with 100,000 being imported annually during the mid-1840s. In 1861 politics abruptly intervened:

the outbreak of the Civil War terminated the import of slaves via Cuba into the Confederacy, and the Union blockade strangled cotton exports. The slack in cotton-growing was taken up by Egypt, which required a yearly quota of between 30,000 and 35,000 African slaves to meet new production requirements. Some were drafted from the cotton fields into the Egyptian army. In 1863, Khedive Ismail hired out several hundred as mercenaries to serve with Napoleon III's forces in malarial regions of Mexico during the Emperor's ill-fated attempt to annex the country.[5]

In defiance of British warships and international treaties signed by Portugal, 50,000 slaves were covertly transported from Angola and Mozambique for labour in the Brazilian coffee plantations between 1846 and 1850.[6] They were among the last victims of the Atlantic slave trade, whose scale and atrocities are well known in Britain and America thanks to exhaustive research that continues to add to a sense of ancestral moral guilt in both countries.

The literature on African slavery is selective and imbalanced since it largely ignores the Arab–African slave trade. In scale it equalled – probably surpassed – its Atlantic counterpart and, in some regions, it persisted until the early twentieth century. During the 1860s between 60,000 and 100,000 slaves from northern Mozambique and modern Tanzania were passing through Zanzibar for shipment to Arabia and the Persian Gulf.[7] At the same time, more than half of Zanzibar's 230,000 inhabitants were slaves working on plantations and in Arab households.

During the 1870s up to 30,000 slaves from Abyssinia and the southern Sudan were yearly shipped by dhows across the Red Sea to Arabia. These regions also supplied women and eunuchs for the slave markets of Egypt and Turkey. Totals for the far more extensive Saharan slave trade are difficult to assess. British consuls estimated that about 5,000 a year were being sold in Tunis during the 1850s after having been driven overland from what are now Mali, Niger and Northern Nigeria. In 1855 1,000 were shipped from Tunis to Ottoman-ruled Crete and a few were sold to buyers in Albania, then a Turkish province. African slavery penetrated the fringes of Europe.

The torments endured by victims of the Arab-controlled slave trade equalled those of its Atlantic counterpart. One rare first-hand account was taken from Saaba Fula, who was purchased by a French explorer,

Victor Largeau, at the slave market in Ouargla in south-eastern Algeria in 1877. Saaba was between sixteen and eighteen years old and had been kidnapped by Arab raiders scouring villages on the banks of the Upper Niger. Her father and brothers were murdered, and she and her mother were forced to trudge nearly a thousand miles northwards across the Sahara. The slave caravan travelled by night to avoid the heat, but many slaves died from hunger, dehydration and fatigue. Saaba's mother was one: she 'followed me for a long time, wailing and crying, but all of a sudden I did not hear her any more. I think the Arabs killed her.' On arrival in Ouargla, Saaba was put up for sale with a dozen other girls in blue cotton robes. Largeau described them standing or crouched, 'their eyes lowered and full of tears'. He paid 650 francs (about £60) for Saaba, who 'sobbed violently', remembering that she had been told that Frenchmen ate Negroes. Then, 'pulling herself together, she bid farewell to her companions and followed me with a firm step'.[8] Unbeknown to her, she had been liberated. She had been doubly fortunate, for losses during the cross-desert treks were between one and two-thirds.

Precise figures for the localised, indigenous African slave trade are impossible to obtain. Nevertheless, some measure of its scale can be gained from the fact that during the twenty years after the French occupation of Timbuktu in 1894, half a million former slaves drifted back to their homelands to the south.[9]

The arithmetic of the indigenous and Arab slave trade speaks for itself. Yet there has been an extraordinary historical amnesia among the descendants of those who participated in it. The collective moral shame and regret felt by subsequent generations of Europeans and Americans have never been shared by Turks, Egyptians and Arabs.

III

The statistics show us how deeply embedded slavery had become in the economies of large parts of Africa. This was why British philanthropists convinced themselves that slavery was a barrier to social and economic progress. Overturn it and the way would be open for a far-reaching economic revolution. 'Legitimate' trade in such commodities as palm oil, timber and the unknown mineral ores thought to exist somewhere in the continent's mountain ranges would create new and untainted sources of wealth. It was an attractive proposition: Africans would prosper and use their new profits to buy British goods.

This was the vision of David Livingstone. When he was not exploring southern and Central Africa and teaching the Gospels to their inhabitants, he was urging the British nation to step up its efforts in the struggle against slavery. Nothing less than the wholesale regeneration of the continent was at stake, for, as Livingstone repeatedly predicted, the end of slavery would mark the arrival of a golden age of stability and general prosperity. In 1854 he foresaw the Zambezi crowded with steamers passing to and fro with cash crops and cargoes of British textiles and metal wares.

Livingstone was idolised by the British public and by the end of his life was an international figure. This was why, when he 'disappeared' in northern Tanzania in 1866, the *New York Herald* hired Henry Morton Stanley to find him whatever the cost. Livingstone was a working-class Scottish lad who, through application and perseverance, had qualified himself as a physician and a clergyman. He personified the Victorian ideal of active, manly Christianity. His faith was fervent and practical, and he was as brave as one of the many lions he had had to contend with during his expeditions. His travel books were bestsellers, he lectured and preached across the country and his message, based on his experiences, commanded attention. Livingstone's eyewitness accounts of slave raids, with images of distraught mothers and terrified children, touched the hearts of his audience. Above all, his insistence that 'Christianity, Civilisation and Commerce' were the remedies for Africa's maladies entered the British political consciousness. Livingstone taught his own and later generations that Africans could be saved from themselves.

To an extent, Livingstone was preaching to the converted insofar as the popular anti-slavery movement was already embedded in Britain's political culture. In the late eighteenth century public opinion had been mobilised against the British slave trade, which as we have seen was outlawed in 1807, and against slavery in Britain's colonies, which became illegal in 1833. Two great political victories were the prelude to a new contest: the final destruction of the international slave trade. This was the goal of the largely middle-class missionary and anti-slavery lobbies, which had enormous political clout.

Slavery was repulsive to the British. It was a denial of that personal liberty which they had won for themselves in the seventeenth century, when one radical insisted that 'the poorest hath a life to live as the greatest-he'. Individual freedom defined national character. The battle hymn of eighteenth-century triumphalism, 'Rule, Britannia!', declared that 'Britons never will be slaves'. British freedom had gone hand in hand with the remarkable progress made by the nation since it had encouraged individuals to foster their natural talents and advance themselves. It was right and proper, therefore, for this beneficial freedom to be extended to all people everywhere.

By contrast to the 'freeborn' Briton, the slave was a degraded creature, stripped of his humanity, unable to determine his own or his family's future and denied any outlet for his inborn abilities. 'A slave is a *Person* perverted into a *Thing*', wrote Coleridge. Everyone employed in the slave trade became morally tainted. The man who held another as a chattel and sold him forfeited his own humanity. The economist Adam Smith observed that: 'There is not a negro from the coast of Africa who does not . . . possess a degree of magnanimity which the soul of his sordid master is often scarce capable of receiving.'

The literature which graphically described the cruelties and humiliations inflicted on slaves was profoundly disturbing. It could not have been otherwise in a country in which an epitaph of 1799 in Dorchester Abbey described how a lady of clearly Romantic inclinations had died 'a martyr to excessive sensitivity'. One wonders how she would have reacted to Mungo Park's poignant account of his encounter with an impoverished Nigerian mother forced to stay alive by offering her own child to a slaver: 'Good God, thought I, what must a mother suffer before she sells her own child.'

The mid-Victorians were the heirs in spirit of the Romantic and Evangelical movements, and as such had a passionate empathy with the helplessness and misery of the slave. The mechanics of the slave trade were repugnant to a people that set a high store by decency and human dignity. The reactions of the august proconsul Sir Bartle Frere as he walked through the Zanzibar slave market in 1873 were typical:

The examination of the women was still more disgusting. Bloated and henna-dyed old debauchees gloated over them, handled them from head to foot before a crowd of lookers-on, like a cowseller or a horse-dealer, and finally when one was apparently satisfactory, buyer and seller and woman all retired behind a curtain of the shed to play out the final examination.

Here was fuel for a moral outrage that transcended political and religious loyalties and was felt in all levels of society. In 1824, Britain's official policy towards slavery and the slave trade had been summarised by the Tory Foreign Secretary George Canning when he told the Commons that the struggle against slavery was 'a matter of right, of humanity [and] of morality' and that its success would transform for the better 'an entire class of our fellow creatures'. His sentiments held true for the rest of the century and were a source of immense national pride. Another crusader against slavery, Lord Palmerston, saw Britain's willingness to take up the cudgels against it as an expression of a superior national 'character'.

Britain was the friend of the weak and the oppressed and a nation deeply aware of its collective Christian duty. In 1859 Samuel Wilberforce, Bishop of Oxford ('Soapy Sam'), reminded Liverpool businessmen that they were part of a nation upon which 'the blessings of God had been showered', and for that reason alone were obliged to do good in the world. Older and newer concepts of Britain's global humanitarian duty fused and, after the occupation of Egypt in 1882, would make it easy for politicians and journalists to whip up support for annexationist policies in Africa.

British diplomats persuaded Russia, Prussia, Austria and France to outlaw the slave trade at the Vienna Congress in 1815, and afterwards the French navy deployed a small slave squadron in West African waters. Slavery had been abolished in all French colonies by the First Republic in 1794, was restored by Napoleon in 1802 and finally outlawed by the Second Republic in 1848. For the next fifty or so years this ban was laxly and haphazardly enforced. Not only was the French attitude towards slavery often casual, but there was a feeling in some quarters that the Negro was somehow temperamentally fitted for it. General Louis Faidherbe, who was appointed Governor of Senegal in 1854, remarked that 'one would never think of enslaving Arabs for they would assassinate their master'.[10]

French views about slavery were by-the-way. Britain's counted, for it was the richest nation in the world, it dominated international trade and was well on the way to become the world's banker. It was no

coincidence that after a decade of prevarication, Khedive Ismail bowed
to British diplomatic pressure and set about suppressing the Egyptian
and Sudanese slave trade in 1877. There was little else he could have
done, for his state was slithering into insolvency and Britain was one of
his largest and most impatient creditors. On balance, it was preferable
to keep British goodwill and forfeit the 10 per cent tariff he collected
for every slave sold in Egypt.

Britain also resorted to force to get its way over slavery. It had a
preponderance of global naval power and from 1807 onwards successive
governments committed the Royal Navy to a war against slavers in the
Atlantic and Indian oceans. These operations were costing £700,000 a
year in the 1850s and involved, on average, the deployment of twenty-
five warships on the Africa station.

IV

Britain's diplomatic offensive against the slave trade was a slow and
frustrating struggle. Between 1820 and 1882 the Foreign Office signed
thirty treaties with individual states, each of which pledged to ban
the trade. Backsliding was common, not least because the will or the
means of enforcement were lacking. Spain, Portugal and the Ottoman
Empire were the worst offenders. In 1840 the Sultan explained to Lord
Ponsonby, the British Ambassador, that while he conceded that Britain
was superior in science, the arts and war, he rejected utterly the notion
of its moral superiority.[11] For him this rested on the Quran, but, like
other rulers bent on sidestepping Britain's demands for the abolition of
the slave trade, the Sultan knew that it was the cement of his empire's
economy.

Slavery was also essential to the economies of large parts of West
Africa. An African slave worked in his master's fields, tended his livestock and undertook the drudgery of everyday household chores for
his wife. The stock of domestic slaves required constant replenishment
since women held in slavery tended not to have children.

The wealth generated by slavery was a key factor in African politics.
Fortunes were amassed by the indigenous entrepreneurs and invested
in the soldiers and modern weaponry that were necessary to establish and defend their hunting grounds. In many respects these private
armies were like the 'militias' recruited and armed by the modern

warlords of West and Central Africa: they ruled competitive warrior-slave states that were in perpetual conflict. These turf wars intensified as the market for slaves was dislocated by British naval activity. Some outlets managed to stay open: with the connivance of the Portuguese authorities, a dwindling number of slavers operated out of Mozambique in the 1880s. Blind eyes were turned elsewhere: in 1888 a British warship patrolling the Indian Ocean intercepted fifteen French-registered dhows carrying slaves.

The slave trade was a ladder for ambitious chiefs to climb in order to raise their status and extend their power. The West African kingdoms of Dahomey and Lagos had grown rich and powerful during the eighteenth and early nineteenth centuries by providing slaves to European dealers. By 1850 both states were under growing pressure from Britain, but distance prevented this from being exerted inland; the southern fringes of the Sahara and the interior of East Africa as far as the Great Lakes continued to provide the raw materials for the slavers.

The last area was home to José de Andrade, the son of a chief and a Goan girl, who carved out a virtually independent state in western Mozambique during the 1870s and 1880s based entirely on his income from slaving. He procured modern firearms and his forces scoured the neighbouring regions for slaves, who were driven to the coast and surreptitiously shipped from Portuguese ports to Brazil and Cuba. Andrade was a terrifying figure: local folklore claimed that when he spotted vultures circling near his village he would order the killing of a man or woman to satisfy their hunger. His nickname was 'Kanyemba' ('the ferocious').[12]

Kanyemba's career was paralleled by that of his contemporary Al-Zubayr Rahma Mansur, a Cairo-based businessman whose activities were centred on Khartoum. During the 1870s he controlled a 1,000-strong army that trawled for slaves in the south of the Sudan and, like Andrade, he behaved as if he was the ruler of an independent state. Khedive Ismail's belated efforts to prohibit the slave trade made Al-Zubayr's position precarious. The suppression of slaving in the Sudan triggered an inflation of slave prices in Cairo. On average his agents smuggled about 1,000 slaves a year to Egypt, paying £8 each for them in Khartoum. By 1877 prices in Cairo ranged between £100 and £200 for black males and up to £1,000 for comely Abyssinian girls, who were favoured as concubines by Egyptian army officers. Those slaves purchased for domestic service were called 'talking animals' by their owners and given names that emphasised their degraded status. Muslim claims that slaves were treated with kindness were empty. Also on sale in Cairo were white Circassian female slaves abducted on the Turko-Russian frontier, who commanded prices as high as £10,000.[13]

In 1877 Khedive Ismail appointed Colonel Charles Gordon as Governor-General of the Sudan with a mandate to terminate the slave trade. A fervent and single-minded Evangelical, Gordon Pasha shared with Cromwell a belief that he was a soldier chosen by divine providence to accomplish God's will. Al-Zubayr's operations were one of his first targets, and in July 1879 he defeated his army and had his son, Sulayman, executed. But Gordon's campaign soon petered out, a casualty of Egypt's financial crisis and the outbreak of the Mahdist revolt in the Sudan.

Al-Zubayr and Kanyemba were sharks, but there were plenty of small fry chasing profits from the slave trade. Among them were the African gangs that preyed on the scattered villages around Souroudou-gou (Burkina Faso) in the 1880s, ambushing families, killing the father and carrying of his wife and children, who 'were sold just like chickens'.[14] During periods of famine violence was not needed, for parents were willing to sell their offspring to buy food.

V

Naval vigilance and diplomatic persistence were Britain's weapons in the war against men like Andrade and Al-Zubayr. In West and East Africa, warships blockaded suspected slave ports; landing parties attacked and demolished the forts that defended them and the barracoons where slaves were imprisoned; and patrolling men-o'-war intercepted slavers. There were plenty of legal wrangles, since the French and American governments were prickly about British warships stopping and searching their merchantmen.

The Treasury paid £5 in bounty money for each slave liberated. This head money was divided among the crew according to rank: after four years' successful patrolling in the Atlantic, an able seaman on HMS *Waterwitch* received £178, a chief petty officer £528 and the captain £2,600.[15] This was ample compensation for duties performed in a region where the death rate from disease hovered between 5 and 10 per cent. A scrap with a slaver was a welcome break from tedious weeks cruising; in 1840 a midshipman aboard HMS *Pickle* wrote to his mother of his excitement as his ship closed with a slave ship off the Cuban coast:

> How glorious! Seeing one's name in the papers for something of that sort. Should you not like it, dearest Mama? I was sharpening my sword in the most butcher like manner in the chase. It was delightful to see how eager our men were to get up with her.[16]

The eradication of the Atlantic slave trade required the cooperation of the rulers of coastal states. British consuls extracted promises from them to outlaw the transit of slaves through their territories, but many refused to forfeit a valuable source of income. King Kosoko of Lagos was a persistent recidivist and at the end of 1851 Palmerston, the Foreign Secretary, decided he needed to be taught a lesson. 'Barbarous African chiefs', he declared, should not be allowed to interrupt 'the accomplishment of a great purpose'. The island withstood one bombardment and amphibious assault, but the second succeeded. Shrapnel and incendiary Congreve rockets did the trick (their unintentionally erratic course convinced their victims that they were somehow being guided towards their targets), and Kosoko fled from his burning capital. His successor, the biddable Atikoye, came ashore with the marines and bluejackets. The Union Jack was hoisted and 300 schoolchildren from an inland mission sang 'God Save the Queen'.

Lagos and its inland dependencies came under British control. The island became an ancillary base for the slave squadron and an outlet for the export of palm oil, a morally acceptable commerce which, it was hoped, would replace slaving. The annexation was justified at home on humanitarian grounds, although there were parliamentary misgivings about the future expenses of a new colony. A dilemma had emerged: was it possible to eliminate the slave trade by maritime coercion and diplomatic arm-twisting, or would ultimate success depend on occupying territory? Annexations involved long-term expenditure and were, therefore, anathema to those Whigs and Liberals attached to the principle of cheap government and low taxes. In the early 1860s there were parliamentary stirrings over the funding of a string of West African coastal forts and dependencies. Some had been acquired from Denmark over the previous fifty years, and all were seen as strategic assets in the war against the slave trade. The humanitarian imperative prevailed, but the debate was a reminder that at this date there were strong political reservations about British acquisitions in Africa.

VI

The same balance of naval coercion and diplomatic persuasion was initially applied to the campaign against the East African slave trade. This was dominated by the sultanate of Zanzibar, a mercantile state that had been founded by the Omani prince Sultan Sayyid al-Busaidi in the 1820s. He was a dynamic businessman with a Midas touch, and worked closely with Indian capitalists to create a commercial empire in East Africa. It eventually encompassed the coastal littoral, and rested on the profits of the slave trade. In 1870 between 100 and 300 slaves were sold daily in the Zanzibar market and the Sultan took a percentage of each transaction. Some slaves stayed in Zanzibar to work the clove plantations, which contributed £190,000 to the island's economy in 1879. Al-Busaid signed trade treaties with Britain, America and France, but took care to stay on the right side of Britain, the predominant naval power in the Indian Ocean.

By the early 1870s the future of Zanzibar looked uncertain. A hurricane destroyed Sultan Barghash's fleet at anchor in 1872, and he was unnerved by recent Egyptian encroachments in Uganda and on the Red Sea. To make matters worse, his British patrons were becoming increasingly impatient with his evasiveness on the matter of the slave trade; one diplomat complained about his use of the 'exasperating arts of the East' to forestall coming to a decision. Reports of Barghash's procrastination angered two parliamentary inquiries in 1870 and 1871 and they concluded that the time had come for rigorous arm-twisting.

In June 1873 the Sultan caved in and agreed to ban the slave trade. A squadron of British warships that was standing by offshore had helped to concentrate his mind. The anti-slavery lobby in Britain was jubilant and the Prime Minister, William Gladstone, was overcome by the news that an Anglican cathedral was to be built on the site of the old slave market.* A cruiser remained permanently stationed in Zanzibar

---

* Gladstone's zeal was that of a convert. His family money came from West Indies plantations and in the early 1830s he defended slavery in the Commons.

harbour as a base for landing parties and Kilwa, one of the slavers' chief outlets, was placed under a tight blockade.

Barghash's renunciation of the slave trade was a victory, but a limited one. Gladstone's government had fallen into a trap that would ensnare its successors: it took at face value an African ruler's pretensions to sovereignty over regions that he lacked the capacity to control. When missionaries complained to the Sultan in 1882 about slave raiders abducting twenty-nine converts from the Masasi (Tanzania) mission, he was 'polite' but 'did not help us'. Even if, and this is doubtful, he had the will, Barghash lacked any effective police or military force with which to engage the slaving parties that ranged over the areas under his nominal rule.

Britain's more or less single-handed war against the slave trade had achieved remarkable success. Between 1810 and 1864 the Royal Navy had liberated 150,000 slaves. By the latter date the Atlantic trade (now deprived of the American market) was fast withering away; and a hard but not fatal blow had been inflicted on the Indian Ocean trade. There remained the interior African trade, protected by remoteness and sympathetic local regimes, which, as the experience in the Sudan in the late 1870s had shown, could only be destroyed by superior force. In 1876 the Asantehene Mensa Bonsu told a Methodist missionary that his kingdom could not survive without slavery.[17]

The eradication of slavery would bring economic dislocation to many areas and could only be achieved by the extension of European hard power far inland, possibly involving conquest and occupation. For the time being this was not contemplated by Britain. France was the only power making incursions into Africa and the destruction of the slave trade was not one of its motives.

3

'Ethiopia shall soon stretch out her hands to God': Missionaries

▬▬▭

I

Christian missions multiplied across Africa during the nineteenth century and transformed the spiritual and moral climate of the continent. The sense of purpose, fervour and physical and mental stamina of the missionaries was astonishing and sometimes moving. Their ambition was the conversion of the entire continent and the results were remarkable: in 1800 there were a few thousand Christians in Africa whereas a hundred years later the total was approaching 15 million.

Most of the missionaries were British, French, Americans, Germans and Scandinavians who were supplemented and followed by African converts. Just as the pioneer settler transformed the barren wilderness into fruitful farmland, the missionary prepared the soil by uprooting the weeds of superstition and clearing away the rocks of ignorance. The seeds of faith were then sown and nurtured to produce a harvest of souls saved for Christ and destined for eternal, celestial life.

The missionaries brought with them the denominational and sectarian divisions of European Christianity. They also, unwittingly, helped create further schisms, for Africans quickly began to follow their own consciences and devise their own interpretations of the Scriptures; some sought to define a specifically African deity. Such theological speculation disappointed those missionaries who had dreamed that Christianity might unite the continent. What it did accomplish was the creation of a growing body of educated Africans hungry for knowledge and often critical of the political status quo.

Saving the African soul was a catalyst for another fundamental and far-reaching cultural revolution. Hitherto-spoken languages were transposed into written ones which used the Latin alphabet so that Africans could read the Scriptures for themselves. The newly literate could also study the knowledge and wisdom of Europe; the African could and would now read Descartes and Darwin as well as Deuteronomy.

Lessons in English and French mission schools were taught in those languages and prize pupils were sent to study in European and American universities. Many missionaries were also doctors who introduced European methods of diagnosis and treatment. Traditional remedies and magical nostrums were in retreat, although their practitioners yielded ground stubbornly and many still have their followers today. Africa had hosted small-scale Christian missions since the sixteenth century, and was home to two ancient Christian faiths, the Coptic Church of Egypt and the Abyssinian Church, which shared some of its theology. Since European churches were exclusive and competitive, missionaries considered Abyssinian Christians fair game for conversion, which led to tensions. The Emperor Tewedros expelled the Catholic mission on his accession in 1855, accusing its clergy of subversion and meddling in Abyssinian politics. Protestants remained welcome, because their printed Amharic Bibles allowed the Emperor's subjects to read the Scriptures in their own language.[1] Shrewder African rulers wondered whether the missionaries were the advance guard of Britain and France, and they were not entirely mistaken. In the 1870s the Superintendent of Methodist missions in West Africa looked forward to an alliance between the British authorities and the churches to overthrow the slave trade as well as to advance Christianity.[2] It was no coincidence that missions flourished in those parts of southern Africa that were under British control. In the 1870s the Natal government encouraged the growth of self-supporting mission villages by exempting them from the hut tax and (briefly) the poll tax. In return for such favours, the missionaries fostered that quietism which had always been such a strong feature of European Christianity. One black African preacher in Zululand urged his congregation to pray for Queen Victoria, her magistrates and the Zulu royal family.[3]

Missionaries were, inevitably, drawn into native politics. In the small state of Thaba-Nehu on the border of the Orange Free State and Basutoland (Lesotho), Anglican and Methodist missionaries backed rival claimants to the throne in the early 1880s. The Anglican candidate, Samuel Moroka, was toppled in a coup and shot while hiding in a mission lavatory. His successor, the Methodist-backed Tshipinate, rewarded his allies with a gift of 2,900 acres of land. Prudently, he also donated 2,500 acres to the Anglicans together with £50 for a school.[4] These shenanigans worried the government of the Orange Free State, which occupied and annexed Thaba-Nchu on the grounds of preserving regional stability.

II

Tension and turmoil were unavoidable, since African converts had to break with their collective past. Their new faith required the public rejection of ancient gods, tribal religious and social rituals and festivals, and traditional explanations of the universe and an individual's place in it. Old usages begat new sins, most notably polygamy. The theatre of religion changed: out went the traditional dances and throbbing drums and in came the restrained but often awesome rites of the Christian mysteries. Catholics and Anglicans enjoyed an advantage here. Some converts tried to blend old and new ways, which upset missionaries, who were always on the lookout for signs of recidivism. After their lessons had ended, boys at a mission school in Sierra Leone in the 1830s celebrated their freedom by drumming, singing and performing somersaults. Their teacher admonished them, telling them that their time was better spent in Bible-reading.[5]

It was not just the demonisation and suppression of fun that irritated Africans. As the wave of missionary activity gathered momentum, it filled the elite with political misgivings. In 1876 the Asantehene Mensa Bonsu refused to allow the Gold Coast (Ghana) Methodist mission to establish schools and missions for his subjects. The king was vehement: 'It is your religion that has ruined the Fanti country, weakened their power and brought down the high man to the level of the low man.'[6] Missions and schools would, he was convinced, undermine his throne and dilute the warrior spirit of his people. Recent history had shown how his 'weakened' Fanti neighbours had been unable to resist British encroachments on their independence.

Bonsu's contemporary, the Zulu King Cetshwayo, was more accommodating, once telling an Anglican missionary that he liked all missions. His fondness was tempered by apprehension, for he reminded the clergyman that 'we follow the customs of our forefathers'. Among them was compulsory military service in the royal impis and, like the Asantehene, the king feared that conversion would subvert the fighting spirit of his young men. 'These boys are soldiers . . . by becoming Christians they become lost to me.' Converted women, it seems, became cussed wives who refused to accept their traditional lot. As one henpecked husband declared: 'You are our cattle and ought to obey us.'[7]

Another powerful monarch, King Lobengula of the Ndebele, was astonished when George Knight-Bruce, the Bishop of Bloemfontein, requested permission for Christian teachers to instruct his subjects. 'Why did I want to teach his dogs?' he asked. The king could understand white men coming to his country to hunt game or to look for gold, but not to teach. What, he asked, would be taught and why?[8] Lobengula's suspicions were shared by white employers in Bloemfontein, who objected to native boys attending mission schools.[9]

Christianity in Africa was a profoundly disruptive force. Missionaries demanded the eradication of ancient customs such as polygamy and male and female circumcision, and denounced all forms of magic and the invocation of spirits as satanic. As he steeled himself to the task of setting up a mission in up-country Sierra Leone in 1868, Joseph Turpin knew that he had to change the mindset of people who 'trust in greegrees [magical talismans] and other charms, and believe in witchcraft and other superstitions, or are worshippers of snakes, idols and evil spirits'.[10] What anthropologists would later reveal as expressions of deeply rooted beliefs and reactions to the human condition that had evolved over centuries were dismissed by the missionaries as evidence of the human capacity for sin and error.

Just what Turpin was up against was discovered by Charles Yorke, a missionary in East Africa, when he visited the sickbed of a prospective female convert. He was horrified to encounter a shaman and find a 'pepo' (wooden doll) with its limbs broken off and its loins covered by 'a dirty rag' placed by a tray of maize. He rebuked the invalid: 'You have heard me preach *uganga* [sorcery] is wrong . . . you have heard the word of God.' He reminded her that she had accepted Christianity, was seeking baptism and wished 'to go heaven'. Yorke then confronted the shaman: 'You are trying to kill her soul and send her to hell.' 'It is our custom', the man replied. It was devilry, riposted the missionary, who warned the woman that if she resorted to *uganga*, she would 'at the last day be cast into hell fire'.

Yorke comforted her and promised that God alone could expel the demon that she imagined had caused her sickness. Afterwards, he told the local chief that his people were doing evil.[11] The terror of the Last Judgement had, so it seemed, trumped traditional spells. Conversion often boiled down to a contest between different forms of magic. It was made easier when tribes such as the Yoruba of Nigeria believed in a single, supreme being.

Whether or not they were monotheists, Africans remained deeply attached to the culture that had grown out of their old religions. James Laing, who worked among the Zulu of Natal in the 1840s, was frequently disheartened by displays of recidivism. A chief's son whose adoption of European clothes indicated his imminent conversion joined in rain-making ceremonies, consulted sorcerers and beat his wife. There were clashes of loyalty over the annual circumcision rituals, which traditionally marked a boy's coming of age. Laing condemned this rite of passage into adulthood as 'unmanly', but his congregation thought otherwise and stayed away from church during the period when the ceremonies were being performed. Worst of all, converts gladly joined in wars against the British and their neighbours.[12]

What the missionaries saw as backsliding was defended on purely cultural grounds. In 1882, Methodist prohibitions on 'dancing and nakedness' provoked one councillor to a South African Christian chief to assert: 'we have a right to do as we like with our own . . . what the piano and violin are to the Englishman the *intojane* [female puberty rites] dances are to us'.[13]

Additional problems were created by the probing logic of potential converts. One Xhosa argued that if, as the missionary claimed, the soul was spirit rather than matter, then how could it burn in hellfire? Another asked why, if God loved the world, did he not send rains when they were needed?[14] Acute questioning of this kind by Zulus compelled John Colenso, Bishop of Natal, to conclude that the first five books of the Old Testament were riddled with fancies and fabrications. Prudently, given the warrior ethos of the Zulus, he also insisted that Jehovah's multiple injunctions to the Israelites to wage war mercilessly were incompatible with the divine nature. A scandalised Anglican establishment rallied behind the fable of Noah's ark and declared Colenso a heretic. The Bishop had been perceptive and far-sighted. Africans were intelligent enough to recognise the many inconsistencies in the Old Testament and tackling them led many to develop their own, home-grown and often idiosyncratic theologies.

III

Colenso also raised orthodox hackles by his toleration of polygamy, one of the commonest obstacles to conversion. Polygamy created two wider, fundamental questions. Should missionaries turn a blind eye to some local customs in order to swell the numbers of conversions? Or should they be unbending in their orthodoxy because a faith diluted or compromised was shallow and worthless? This was the line of Bishop Jean-François Allard of the Oblates of Mary Immaculate, whose stubbornness on polygamy won him so few converts among the Zulus in the 1850s that he moved his mission to Basutoland.

An opposite view was held by Father Lieberman, founder of the Saint-Coeur de Marie order, who asked his missionaries to 'lay aside the mores and spirit of Europe and become Negroes with the Negroes'.[15] This was a risky path. One wonders what Lieberman would have made of the flexible attitudes in mid-century Senegal where black and mixed-raced worshippers heard Mass, left the church and then turned towards Mecca to say Muslim prayers.[16]

Christianity could always count on one great advantage over the faiths it aimed to displace: modern medicine. A trained doctor, Livingstone was known as *Ngaka* (healer) across southern Africa, and he believed that one of the outstanding features of civilisation was the ability to perform 'surgical operations . . . without pain'.[17] European medicine was then making enormous headway in understanding the nature of contagion and disease and their treatment. This was why, during a typhoid epidemic in Zanzibar, the royal family consulted a European rather than Arab or Swahili physicians.

The alternative was the female fortune-teller whose diagnostic method was to throw small shells, pebbles, broken glass and coins in the air, examine the pattern they made after they fell, and deduce from it whether the patient would live or die.[18] African medicine rested on a belief that all sicknesses had a supernatural origin and could only be treated by charms or the appeasement of malevolent spirits, often by animal sacrifice. Even Europeans were occasionally taken in. Boer women living deep in the interior and far from doctors resorted to this

sort of jiggery-pokery to help induce childbirth, swallowing a mixture of brandy and powdered clay-pipe bowls prescribed by Khoikhoi
midwives. Of course, folk medicine still persisted in backward areas of
Europe and it has its adherents today.

Missionary medicine had the great advantage that it worked. Minor
triumphs of modern medicine proved its superiority over magical nostrums, and helped redeem souls. One missionary in South Africa in
the 1860s removed cataracts and tumours and sewed up wounds, and
was rewarded by the conversion of grateful patients. For some Bantu-
speakers, the missionary's promise of 'everlasting life' was confused
with the 'life' and 'health' provided by his cures.

IV

Translated Bibles, scalpels and quinine were paid for by the churches
of Europe and the missionary societies their congregations funded.
They were rich and formidable organisations and a political force to be
reckoned with in France and Britain. The journal of the Société de la
Propagation de la Foi had a circulation of 100,000 at a time when the
Orléanist and Bonapartist monarchies were making strenuous efforts
to secure Catholic support.

In Britain, the politically ascendant middle classes threw themselves into mission work. Wealthy men gave freely. The 'Great Zambesi
Meeting' held in London in 1859 to raise money for the recently founded
Oxford and Cambridge Mission to Central Africa collected £20,000.
A further £11,000 was received after a similar meeting in Manchester
during which donors had heard Bishop Wilberforce appeal to their
piety and patriotism: 'Let England be true to England's mission, let her
understand that it is hers to teach her people to love Christ.' France too
was blessed and entrusted to undertake God's work. In 1873 the Bishop
of Avignon told the Lyons branch of the Société de la Propagation
de la Foi that its purpose was 'eminently patriotic . . . It speaks above
all with the name of God, that of France.'[19] Chosen nations were the
interpreters and instruments of the divine will.

The British and French missionary movements ran powerful and
persuasive propaganda machines. Sermons, pamphlets and public
rallies stirred Christian consciences and reminded the devout of their
duty to convert the heathen. Most important of all in terms of how

Europeans regarded Africans was the missionary movement's fundamental belief that they were the children of God. For all his vices (extensively described in missionary literature), the African possessed that divine spark which, once kindled, would allow him to enter the Christian world and redeem his soul. The final, hopeful line of the missionary anthem 'From Greenland's Icy Mountains' promised a new world to which the 'Creator in bliss returns to reign'.

This millennium would embrace a political and economic rebirth. In 1854, a summary of missionary progress among the Yoruba in southern Nigeria praised their 'spirit of independence and generosity', and predicted that their conversion would prepare them to emerge as 'a fine and noble nation'. Moreover – and this would have pleased the businessmen among the missions' sponsors – Yoruba chiefs believed that the missionaries were the 'servants' of Queen Victoria and had asked her for instruction in the 'mechanical arts' and 'agriculture' so that they could learn how to treat sugar, rum and tobacco for the market. George Bruce-Knight was more forthright when he argued that a Christian education would purge the Ndebele 'of their slavish qualities of lying and cowardice, and some add, thieving' and turn them into 'an intelligent nation'.*[20]

Yet for all their optimism, missionaries were constantly frustrated by disappointing rates of conversion. Six priests taught a class of eight boys and seven nuns taught twenty girls in one mission school in Gabon in the 1860s.[21] At the same time in Cape Colony and Natal missionaries were grumbling about a trickle of conversions. James Laing, whose Natal church could hold 200, never had a congregation of more than fifty and in one year he had a single baptism.[22] Laing persevered, although some of his colleagues wondered whether a greater tolerance towards local customs might speed the flow of converts. As we have seen, Bishop Colenso reached this conclusion and was swiftly ostracised. An orthodox take-it-or-leave-it attitude was clearly not working. A less arrogant and more sympathetic approach might be more fruitful, which was why Charles Lavigerie dressed his White Fathers in a version of Arab dress rather than the traditional soutane. He also encouraged his missionaries in East Africa to purchase slaves, who were

* The Ndebele were no cowards: in 1893 and 1896 they charged headlong into rifle and machine-gun fire in defence of their homeland.

freed, converted and taught medicine in the White Fathers' schools. The British Consul in Zanzibar disapproved, accusing the Catholics of tacitly condoning slavery. In all areas high hopes were placed on the creation of a cadre of literate African converts who would be ordained and sent out to preach to their own people in their own language. In 1871 one East African missionary reported sixty boys undergoing training and one 'with little aptitude for learning' who became the missionary's houseboy, sparing him the annoyance of having to employ 'heathen and Mohammedan servants'.[23] The brightest alumni of Anglican missions were sent to St Augustine's College in Canterbury with a £60 annual allowance paid by church collections; pious children were asked by their Sunday schools to give a penny a week.

Creating a body of African missionaries soon paid dividends in terms of converts. An African preacher had a rapport with his people; he was one of them and not a stranger who held their customs in contempt. Many of Africa's new clergy began thinking for themselves, and their consciences led them away from mainstream theology and observances. In particular, the African Christian wanted to understand what his place was in what was then a white Christian cosmos. Some clue as to his identity and the spiritual future of his continent was found in the thirty-first verse of Psalm 68: 'Ethiopia shall soon stretch out her hands to God.'

Ethiopia was taken to mean all of Africa, and the statement seemed to promise that it was destined to turn to God. But which God? Some South African converts believed that they had discovered 'Thixo', a black deity whose adherents would take revenge on the whites for the murder of the son of their god.[24] Whatever his colour, an African god would have been delighted by the joyful exuberance and uninhibited praise of his black worshippers. These were evident among the congregation of one mission church in Bloemfontein in 1871, where a somewhat perturbed minister noticed a black woman who 'gave expression to her emotion in large sobs and sighs'.[25]

The genesis of what would later be called the 'Ethiopian' Protestant churches was under way. They first flourished in southern Africa, a region where missions were heavily concentrated and where Europeans were politically dominant. A spiritual awakening was the prelude to the political and social transformation of Africans, concluded Alan Gibson, a Methodist missionary based in Natal in the early 1880s.

'There are no forces in the world so levelling ... as education and Christianity', he observed. They prompted the educated convert to consider his place in the scheme of things. His 'history and tradition' had taught him 'that he has a prior right in the soil to the white man'. He had become conscious of his latent abilities, understood that 'all authority comes from God' and believed that 'there is in God's sight an inherent brotherhood of men'. 'Perhaps', Gibson added, he had 'caught mutterings of socialism and communism which come from European lands'. The seeds of Christianity planted in the African soil were about to yield some unexpected crops.

There were, inevitably, occasions when missions found themselves compelled to fill political vacuums. In the late 1870s, the missions at Blantyre and Livingstonia on the southern shores of Lake Nyasa acted as magistrates and lawmakers in an area where the Portuguese authorities enjoyed the pretensions of overlordship, but no power. The missionaries stepped in: they tried criminals, flogged the guilty, banned alcohol and sent a body of armed converts in pursuit of a predatory local chief. The Church of Scotland was scandalised and warned its servants that they were in Africa to redeem souls, 'not [to lay] the foundations of a British colony or a small state'.[26] The Livingstonia mission responded with a request for a British consul, and it was not long before he was asking the Foreign Office for a gendarmerie to uphold his authority. Those Africans who had feared that the missionaries were paving the way for European rule were not entirely mistaken.

4

White Man's Countries I:
Razzia: The Conquest of Algeria

In the summer of 1851 General Aimable Pélissier laid siege to the oasis town of Laghouat 250 miles south of Algiers. He was a hard, professional soldier with a working-class background, and had spent the past twenty years campaigning in Algeria. His photograph, taken a few years later during the Crimean War, shows a burly, bristly-moustached figure spilling out of his uniform; one British officer likened him to a 'coal heaver'. Algerians called him 'the devil', and with good reason, for five years before he had ordered fires to be lit at the mouths of caves near Dahra, where about 500 Arab fugitives had taken refuge. All, including women and children, were choked to death.[1]

Laghouat had to be punished by 'une terreur salutaire' for its support of an uprising led by a messianic Muslim holy man. Pélissier's artillery shelled the town, which was then stormed by his infantry, who fought their way through the streets, looted, demolished houses and uprooted gardens. A quarter of Laghouat's 4,000 inhabitants were massacred. Most of the survivors fled their ruined homes, leaving behind 400. Among them was a band of orphans who lived by begging from the French garrison and brushing the officers' boots.

This operation was called a *razzia*. Its components were the obliteration of buildings, the slaughter or theft of livestock, the destruction of crops and the looting of anything portable. The *razzia* was designed to implant abject fear and remained a permanent feature of French rule: Algerians knew that resistance would always be met with extreme violence.

Four mosques were demolished in Laghouat, one of which was converted into a church. Its first Mass was conducted by the Abbé

Jacques Suchet, who told his military congregation that 'In conquering Algeria, this new France . . . you do the work of God.' 'The sword of France', he continued, 'was like a cross, that shines throughout this country like a radiant star which will shed light . . . by banishing the crescent, the lugubrious night of sleep.'[2]

The ghastly events in Laghouat were repeated many times during the conquest and pacification of Algeria, and the Abbé's sermon offers us a clue as to why. For patriotic Frenchmen, opposition to their nation's *mission civilisatrice* was a perverse obstruction of an inexorable and beneficial force of history. Devout Catholics saw the war as a revival of the crusading traditions of St Louis. Once again, France was the champion of Christendom.

II

The war in Algeria had begun in 1830 and dragged on into the early 1880s, when there were still sporadic, localised uprisings which were officially dismissed as 'banditry'. Mass uprisings were rare, for the Algerians were divided by tribe and clan (blood feuds were common) and so unity proved elusive and, when it was achieved, brittle. The Arabs were, therefore, forced to fight a partisan war of attrition. Large-scale fighting did occur in the 1840s when 100,000 men (one-third of the army) were deployed against Abd al-Kadir. He was France's most determined adversary, part holy man and part tribal leader, whose charisma united the tribes. Al-Kadir was finally overcome in 1847, captured and exiled; French officers were struck by his noble bearing and dignity.

France's overall strategy was simple: a slow, systematic and piece-meal advance southwards from the coastal plains into the mountains of the hinterland. It was a gruelling war of marches, often in intense heat, punctuated by ambushes, skirmishes, the occasional pitched battle and the inevitable *razzias* inflicted on communities that had aided the rebels.

Philip Kearney, an American cavalry officer eager for adventure, joined one of the punitive expeditions in 1839 and recorded that mixture of long periods of discomfort and tedium punctuated by the brief excitement of combat that would become the pattern for all white soldiers in Africa. For this young fire-eater, a fight was exhilarating: 'The report of the musketry, the smoke wreathing about you, the uniforms of the French, the wild costume of the Arabs . . .'[3]

Conscripts bore the brunt of the fighting. They served seven years and were chosen by lottery, but wealthy parents were allowed to hire substitutes. Kearney was impressed by the courage and 'nonchalance' of the French soldier, whose deadliest foes were local diseases, chiefly waterborne. Invalids followed the columns in litters, and the American was distressed by the 'wan and ghastly cheeks' of dying men who knew they would never see their homes and families again.[4] This sight was all too common, for nearly all the 7,000 men who died in the later campaigns against Al-Kadir were the victims of cholera and typhoid.[5]

Kearney also met a new type of soldier, the thrusting careerist who was chasing promotion by commanding locally recruited troops. He had attached himself to one of these units, the Chasseurs d'Afrique, and he was struck by the appearance of his commanding officer, Commandant Bascarin. His head was shaved and polished in the Arab fashion; he had a long, thin, drooping moustache, smoked a hookah and sipped sherbet. Bascarin and his horsemen wore a dashing equivalent of Arab dress, as did their infantry equivalent, the Zouaves. These troops were permitted to retain some of their military customs, such as collecting the ears of their dead enemies. The Algerian regiments, together with the Foreign Legion, comprised the Armée d'Afrique, which was commanded by French officers. They considered themselves as men apart, distinguished by an excess of the traditional French martial élan and panache and an almost mystical ability to win the admiration and loyalty of their Arab soldiers. Officers who took the greatest risks in battle and survived were believed to possess *barraka*, a form of supernatural protection bestowed by Allah.

Fluent in Arabic, these specialist officers formed the nucleus of the Bureaux Arabes that had been founded in 1844 to oversee the administration of the tribal regions. They studied local customs and history and prided themselves on an arcane ability to penetrate the Arab mind. In the process, many came to respect their subjects, but their prime objective was always to encourage and reward collaboration.[6]

The mentality and methods of the Armée d'Afrique were shaped by the nature of the Algerian battlefield. Terror and ruthlessness were seen as necessary and, some claimed, were already endemic to the region.

In fact the *razzia* and the philosophy behind it had their origins in the Peninsular War between 1808 and 1814, when Napoleon's commanders had applied them against Spanish guerrillas. It was a veteran of that campaign, Marshal Jean-de-Dieu Soult, who, as Minister of War in the 1830s, ordered commanders to employ the tactics of terror. Killing civilians was 'hideous' and 'abhorrent', the Minister admitted, but 'in Africa it is war itself'. In Algeria, as in Spain, the massacre of civilians was fundamental.* The enemy had not just to be defeated in battle, he had to be utterly vanquished, humiliated and beggared, which, of course, was the purpose of the *razzia*.[7]

Soult's ideas were transmitted to his subordinates. Thomas-Robert Bugeaud, another Napoleonic veteran, who was commander-in-chief in the 1840s campaigns against Al-Kadir, followed them, but with some pragmatic misgivings. If too many Arabs were killed, he feared, there would be a shortage of labour for the immigrant settlers who were now arriving in droves. Such considerations did not trouble those members of the National Assembly who were demanding a war of extermination. Their clamour and that of the press reached the front line. Kearney noticed how commanders always had an ear open for public criticism that was invariably provoked by newspaper reports hinting at a lack of the aggressive spirit expected of French generals.

Telegraph lines between Algiers and Paris conveyed news of the progress of French armies. Other new technologies were quickly applied to the war and the firepower of French forces increased as it progressed. The Minié rifle, with a range of up to 800 yards, appeared in the early 1850s and in the next decade breech-loaders were introduced which had nearly twice the range. In the same period exploding shells replaced cannonballs and grapeshot, and in the early 1870s Algerian insurgents faced the fire of the *mitrailleuse*, a proto-machine-gun which could fire several hundred rounds in a minute.

The Arabs relied on muzzle-loaders and had few cannon, although Kearney was impressed by the marksmanship of the Kabyle tribesmen. The imbalance of weaponry was reflected in the enormous casualties

---

* Soult was a soldier of good fortune who had a knack of making himself useful to whoever was in power. He successively served the French Republic, Napoleon, the restored Bourbons, Napoleon again (he was at Waterloo), the Bourbons after 1815 and finally the Orléanist monarchy.

suffered by the Arabs. Algerian losses between 1830 and 1875 have been calculated at 825,000, a figure that includes deaths from starvation, the inevitable by-product of the *razzia*. A further 800,000 Algerians were believed to have died as a result of the famines of 1867 and 1868, a total that must have included the thousands of victims of land seizures. At the time the country's native population was thought to be about 2.5 million.[8]

III

The immediate reasons for the conquest of Algeria were embedded in recent French history and older notions of national self-esteem. Nineteenth-century France was mesmerised by that heady abstraction, *La Gloire*. Napoleon had been its latest and greatest embodiment: his genius for war had (briefly) made France master of Europe and convinced his own and later generations that winning wars was part of their national birthright. Memories of high taxes, conscription, mass casualties and the foreign invasions of 1814 and 1815 faded. The Napoleonic era was reinvented as a heroic age in which France had enjoyed unprecedented and well-deserved greatness. *La Gloire* may have been eclipsed at Waterloo, but its comforting afterglow remained.

The three dynasties that ruled France between 1815 and 1870 exploited *La Gloire* for all it was worth to win popular support. The reactionary Bourbon Charles X, his liberal successor the Orléanist Louis-Philippe and the Bonapartist Napoleon III promised peace. Yet, paradoxically, they were uncomfortably aware that their subjects would judge them by their ability to enhance *La Gloire* by winning wars. It could no longer be found on the battlefields of Europe, for at the Vienna Congress the great powers had confined France to its old frontiers.

The only alternative was overseas expansion. Charles X remembered how Napoleon had attempted to conquer Egypt and in 1811 had been contemplating the seizure of Algiers. An internal political crisis in 1830 prompted the king to revive Napoleon's plan and so dampen down criticism of his rigid absolutism. A swift, spectacular victory in the grand Napoleonic style would disarm the opposition. The reverse occurred. Two weeks after Algiers fell the king was toppled by a revolution, and Louis-Philippe took the throne with promises of a more liberal regime. To the delight of French satirists, Charles X set off for exile in Dorset at the same time that Husain, the Dey of Algiers, began his in Naples.

Henceforward, French domestic politics were entwined with the history of Algeria. Charles X had reawakened his countrymen's appetite for *La Gloire* and his successors appreciated that its satisfaction would pay political dividends. In 1831 Soult announced that the war in Algeria would continue. 'Absolutism dreamed of this conquest as a means of suppressing liberty', he declared; 'Victorious liberty will keep it as trophy captured from absolutism.'[9] The conquest picked up a fresh, politically driven momentum. The pursuit of *La Gloire* initially proved expensive: between 1831 and 1840 French taxpayers disgorged 341 million francs to pay for the annexation of Algeria's coastal regions, whose annual revenues were then a twentieth of that sum. Louis-Philippe's sons joined the forces in Algeria, proving the warrior mettle of their dynasty, and victorious generals were given titles in the old Napoleonic manner. Bugeaud was created Duc d'Isly after his defeat of Al-Kadir at Isly in 1844. Officers loved a war that offered them adventure, medals, promotion, plunder and extra allowances that doubled their pay.[10] This had been Soult's idea, and shows how well he understood the minds of his subordinates. The other ranks were not so lucky, although mobile brothels were attached to the columns that trudged through the Algerian uplands.

IV

The French imperial project in Algeria was far more than just an exercise in national and dynastic vanity. Its ultimate and astonishingly ambitious objective was to absorb Algeria into France, and to fill it with European colonists who would become French citizens and contribute to the nation's wealth. Ardent Catholics hoped that this process might include the mass conversion of Muslims. For the military authorities it was the equivalent of thrusting a stick into a hornets' nest, since the history of resistance had proved the power of Islam to unite Algerians. Islam was, therefore, treated with caution and sensitivity.[11]

In other areas an uncompromising approach was adopted: French became Algeria's official language, French syllabuses were taught in schools, French law was paramount and the day-to-day governance of the country was placed in the hands of French administrators, all of whom were soldiers or ex-soldiers.

France became Algeria's landlord. Its sovereign rights rested on conquest and were applied to legitimise the confiscation of Arab land, some but not all of whose owners had resisted the invaders. By 1870, 1.9 million acres had been expropriated and sold, leased or rented to French, Italian, Maltese, Spanish and Greek immigrants.[12]

The inflow of settlers rose sharply: they totalled 8,000 in 1833, 109,000 in 1847 and 385,000 in 1881. Most were the urban paupers, unskilled labourers and peasants who had scraped a precarious living in regions of thin soil and overpopulation. The incomers were familiar with the climate, and the smallpox, cholera and typhus they encountered in Algeria were endemic in their homelands. Many immigrants were desperately poor and malnourished. When he inspected a batch of new arrivals, Bugeaud was appalled by their shabbiness and sickly appearance and feared that they would give Arab sheiks an unfavourable impression of French manhood. These scarecrows, he assured them, were Prussians.[13]

Economic migrants were joined by large numbers of unwanted and potentially dangerous Frenchmen and women. The survivors of the failed uprisings of 1832 (the one depicted in Victor Hugo's *Les Misérables*) and 1834 were transported to Algiers, and there was a further expulsion of dissidents, chiefly working-class Parisians, after the revolutions of 1848 and 1849. Before their departure, these veterans of the Paris mob were told that they would be given land and with it the chance to become productive and therefore useful citizens. Similar arguments were advanced in contemporary Britain to justify the deportation of criminals to Australia. Three thousand diehard republicans and a further 14,000 Parisian workers were banished to Algeria after Napoleon III's coup d'état in December 1851. This political cleansing was repeated by the Third Republic after the suppression of the Paris Commune in 1871. Communist deportees rubbed shoulders with ultra-patriotic Frenchmen and women from Alsace and Lorraine who preferred a new life in Algeria to the continuation of their old one under German rule.

Willing and unwilling immigrants were given an exclusive national identity. In 1834 all Algerians were declared French subjects and in 1865 French citizenship was opened to every Arab who repudiated Islam.

The government alleged that Muslims were disqualified from membership of an enlightened and liberal society by a mindset that was closed to reason and fearful of modernity. By contrast, the faith and traditions of Algeria's Jews made them responsive to French values and so they were naturalised en masse in 1870.[14] According to the official mind, a Sicilian farmer or a Spanish wine-grower possessed an innate capacity to relish the wit of Voltaire, respect the Rights of Man and appreciate the operas of Offenbach. All were seen as beyond their Arab labourers, which ruled out future assimilation.

V

Algeria had undergone a revolution, imposed from above; but what had France gained from its conquest? The historic energy and courage of its soldiers were confirmed and the battlefields of Algeria had been rungs on the ladder of promotion for many officers. Victories in Algeria added to national prestige and reinforced the army's claim that it embodied the spirit of the nation. In July 1870, on the eve of France's declaration of war on the German Confederation, *Le Figaro* proclaimed: 'L'armée française c'est la nation française.' Most Frenchmen, in particular those on the Right, strongly agreed. Within three months the Germans had defeated France, whose army — geared to fighting disorganised and ill-armed Arabs — failed the test of fighting a modern war against a European adversary. The government of the new Third Republic was compelled to surrender Alsace and Lorraine, *La Gloire* was again in eclipse and Frenchmen and women suffered one of the worst traumas in their history.

France had, at least in its own eyes, acquired moral stature in Algeria. The columns of soldiers that criss-crossed the hills and valleys were the advance guard of the *mission civilisatrice*. It was widely agreed that French civilisation was superior to all others. It was synonymous with what, in 1870, one newspaper called the nation's self-evident 'grandeur et prospérité', and its components were universal suffrage, industrial and scientific progress and artistic, musical and literary genius.[15]

How did this civilisation translate to Algeria and who benefited? Defenders of the *mission* stressed that it was providing the colony with the vital prerequisite of progress: civil peace. This was the line that had been taken by a general in his address to an assembly of tribesmen in the newly submitted town of Mascara in July 1845. These 'new subjects of France' were promised security: caravans would no longer be plundered by brigands, merchants would not be kidnapped and ransomed, and everyone's property would be safe. Universal prosperity would inevitably follow.[16]

Algerians may have been removed from harm's way, but they did not enjoy most of Algeria's new wealth, which flowed into the pockets of the immigrants, who had much of the most fertile land. Nor did the Arabs share the fruits of French culture. In 1879 *écoles supérieures* were established, but sixty years later Muslims accounted for a mere 97 of their 2,000 pupils.[17] The cultural and intellectual genius of France was sparingly disseminated, and then only to the offspring of the *colons* and *pieds-noirs*, as the settlers came to be called.

There were valuable economic gains for France. The *colons* introduced capitalist farming and viticulture, both wholly dependent on French markets. By 1880, France bought 90 per cent of Algeria's exports. Wine from the newly planted Algerian vineyards dominated, supplying France with 7.5 million gallons a year, nearly all of which was blended with local products for the cheap, everyday *vin ordinaire*.

Algeria became the first modern European colony in Africa. It generated wealth for France, and fulfilled a useful social function by transforming some of the troublesome underclass of the big cities into yeoman farmers. Men and women who had defended the barricades would, it was hoped, join other immigrants and become part of a prosperous community of independent farmers. Its members formed a middle layer in an imported social order with a largely military ruling elite above them and an Arab majority below. The *colon* looked to the authorities to protect him, for he feared the Arabs, many of whom had been dispossessed in order to provide him with his livelihood. Assimilation was, therefore, impossible and future tension inevitable.

The nature of the French conquest of Algeria had baleful consequences for both countries. It had created a hierarchical settler class which depended on an embattled army and administration. Violence was the accepted reflex action towards any form of dissent and opposition. This was a fact of life, and one not confined to Africa: after the suppression of the 1848 uprisings, the revolutionaries accused 'African' generals of using the brutal methods applied in Algeria to the Parisian working class.[18] The same official terror was employed by generals with an African background on an even greater scale during the 1871 Paris Commune.

5

White Man's Countries II:
'I am a chief and master': South Africa

Two photographs explain why Britain occupied South Africa and devoted so much energy and treasure to keeping it. The first, taken in the 1870s, shows a horse-drawn cart laden with bales of blankets woven in Witney about to begin a journey that will carry them to London for distribution to home and foreign markets. Some consignments went to Cape Colony, where many indigenes, men and women, were eager to wear the warm Witney blanket with its brightly coloured stripes rather than the traditional *kaross*, a mantle made from animal skins.

Africans paid for their mass-produced clothing with another novelty, cash, which they had earned as servants, farm labourers and artisans. As consumers and employees of white settlers native people across the colony were becoming integrated into a global economy still dominated by British exports.

The second photograph, taken in the 1890s, shows the anchorage at Simon's Bay, nearly thirty miles south of Cape Town. In the foreground are three gunboats, HMSs *Griper*, *Gadfly* and *Tickler*, cocksure names that convey a capacity to harass, irritate and sting Britannia's foes. In the foreground one can glimpse quays and derricks. These were part of a large complex of storehouses, dockyards, arsenals, coal bunkers and workshops which provisioned, armed and refurbished the warships of the Africa station.

These two photographs reveal the two fundamental and complementary foundations of British power: commerce and maritime supremacy. The prosperity of industrial Britain relied on open access to markets and resources worldwide. This required a preponderance of sea power: the Royal Navy protected the world's seaways and Britain's overseas assets and investments. Maritime supremacy was also essential for the security of Britain's expanding but widely scattered territorial empire. By 1850 Britain had gained mastery over India, and a steady flow of British emigrants were colonising Canada, Australia and New Zealand.

Ruling the waves required a network of bases, sentinels that guarded the world's major seaways. Simon's Bay lay astride the confluence of the Atlantic and Indian oceans; all ships bound to and from Europe to Asia and the Far East passed through Cape Town. Nearly all were registered in London. The British Merchant Navy was the largest in the world: in 1870 it totalled nearly 4,000 ships, 90 per cent of which were sail-powered. This fact meant that the Cape route retained its importance even after the opening of the Suez Canal in 1869, which could only be used by steamships and at a high cost to their owners.

II

In strategic terms ownership of the Cape was advantageous, but in political terms it turned out to be a liability. Its white and black population, having lived for years under a torpid Dutch administration, suddenly found themselves under masters who were determined to govern actively and stamp British values on the new colony. The British imperial mind, shaped by experiences in India, was obsessed by stability, forever nervous about the dangers of porous or ill-defined frontiers and intensely jealous of other sources of local power, which had to be either neutered or removed. Collaborators were warmly embraced, although there was a tendency among British officials to exaggerate the power of the greater chiefs over their subordinates and subjects. The long-term aim of the rulers of the Cape was the creation of a tranquil colony under humane, British laws, and a passive population that would take advantage of the civil peace to enrich themselves.

Few of the Cape's whites wanted any part in the new order. They were the descendants of Dutch, German and French Protestants who had begun settling in the region in the seventeenth century. They soon identified themselves as indigenous and took the name Afrikaner. Most Afrikaners – or Boers (from 'boer', Dutch for farmer) – were pastoral farmers, egalitarian in spirit, conservative in thought, and guided by an austere Calvinism that cast them as a chosen people like their fellow agriculturalists, the Jews of the Old Testament. One issue above all others divided the Boers from the British: the treatment and legal rights of the colony's black population. Afrikaner views on this subject rested on the Book of Genesis: in return for compliance to His will, God had given the Afrikaners absolute mastery over the Negro race, who were the descendants of Ham, condemned by Jehovah's diktat to perpetual servility. The Old Testament conveniently sanctioned economic necessity, for the Afrikaner economy relied on slave labour.

Britain saw the black man in a different light: he was a subject of the Crown with the same legal rights as an Englishman. The laws of the Cape and later Natal were those of Britain. They rested on the premise that 'There shall not be in the eye of the law any distinction of colour, origin, race or creed' and the 'protection of all law . . . shall be extended impartially to all alike'.[1] What this meant in practical terms was explained to newly arrived British settlers in 1825, who were informed that the natives were 'no longer insulted, robbed, or shot'.[2] Safeguarded by impartial laws, black South Africans could be guided towards a better life under a benevolent paternalist administration. It regarded them as childlike, with an infant's capacity for good and evil, but with the right balance of fairness and firmness they could be turned into tractable and industrious subjects.

Missionaries took a close and critical interest in the day-to-day application of humane principles by the government. Moreover – and this weighed heavily on the official mind – the missionaries could mobilise the influential philanthropic lobbies at home who were always ready to protest against any injustice, maltreatment or exploitation.

Social and cultural affinity between the Boers and their rulers was impossible. British officers and bureaucrats were recruited from a largely patrician elite who despised the Boers as a graceless and curmudgeonly people wedded to an archaic view of the world and their place in it. A British writer who visited the Cape in the late 1820s summed up the opinions of his countrymen when he described the 'perfect specimen of the boor' as a 'phlegmatic, indifferent [and] large lump of apathy'. At the same time, British settlers were officially urged to do all in their power to bring 'civilisation' to both Africans *and* Boers.[3]

The concept of racial parity before the law was anathema to the Boers, and they objected strongly whenever the authorities intervened in relations between masters and slaves. Sparing the *sjambok* would spoil the child.* Leniency and indulgence would lead to the nightmare of a native rebellion. 'Flames of devastation' would engulf the homes of the Boers, one wrote in 1826, adding revealingly that 'our wives and daughters . . . will in a libidinous manner be persecuted by our slaves with rape and defloration'.[4]

Friction between the Boers and the British intensified and, from the mid-1820s onwards, small parties of Afrikaners began to slip across the northern and eastern frontiers of the Cape to escape what they considered an intolerable racial policy. Matters came to a head in 1834 with the abolition of slavery. In the next ten years a trickle of emigrants became a torrent, with some 14,000 Boers heading into the hinterland in search of independence and the freedom to do as they wished with their own. The fugitives called themselves 'Voortrekkers'. Some went to Natal, which the British annexed in 1843 on security grounds, but the bulk shifted deep inland. The history of the Afrikaner diaspora confirmed their covenant with God. It was an epic of endurance, faith and battles fought against the odds. Although a number of the initial groups of voortrekkers were defeated by Zulu and Ndebele impis, Boer stamina and willpower overcame every obstacle. Ndebele and Zulus attacked the intruders and were trounced, the latter crushingly at the Battle of Blood River in December 1838. Just under 500 riflemen defended a laager (circle) of wagons against twenty times their number of Zulus, who were repelled with huge losses.

God was on the side of the Boers and rewarded them with two new homelands, the Transvaal and Orange Free State, both republics with minimalist administrative systems and elected assemblies. The borders of these new states were drawn by Britain, which recognised their independence in the early 1850s.

III

The Boer problem had solved itself, at least for the time being, leaving the imperial authorities free to pacify the Xhosa of the eastern Cape and the Zulu kingdom of Natal. It was an unquiet region, the victim of the demographic aftershock that had followed the growth of the Zulu

* The *sjambok* was a rhinoceros-hide whip. It was the traditional instrument of severe correction and was used by the police until the end of the apartheid era.

kingdom at the beginning of the century. Shaka's conquests had uprooted tribes, herded them southwards and placed pressure on grazing
land in areas where intertribal conflict was already endemic.

Xhosa resistance to British governance was persistent and there were
five Frontier wars between 1818 and 1878. Like the Boers, the Xhosa
resented an intrusive imperial government bent on changing their
traditional way of life and encouraging European settlement. After the
1835 war, the Attorney General of the Cape detected a 'foolish notion
of nationality' among the rebels that had convinced them that they
had a right to own the land. They were also infected by an 'envy at the
prosperity and industry' of the white colonists. New settlements and
farms were regularly attacked and destroyed.

The Xhosa were masters of bush warfare. They moved nimbly and
often imperceptibly, waging a war of ambushes in a rugged terrain of
hills, rivers and narrow ravines with which they were familiar. For the
British soldier it was a hostile landscape full of hidden terrors. Thomas
Scott, a former labourer who served with the 12th (Suffolk) Regiment,
recalled an attack of diarrhoea during a patrol in 1850: 'I was taken very
bad and had to fall out two or three times going on in the worst part of
the wood. And I was rather afraid but I soon fell in again'.[5]

Scott's commanders were often at their wits' end as to how to overcome elusive and tenacious enemies. General Sir Harry Smith (Governor of the Cape between 1847 and 1852) vented his frustration when
he damned the Xhosa as 'savages . . . whose extermination would be a
blessing'. He swallowed his bile and added that 'my study and exertions
shall be for their reformation, improvement and consequent happiness'.
The British liberal conscience (or fear of how Parliament and the press
might react to massacres of the Xhosa) prevailed. Nonetheless, Smith
demanded utter submission. Once he placed his foot on the neck of a
defiant chief and declared: 'You are a dog . . . I am a chief and master
and this way I shall treat the enemies of the Queen.'

Bringing the Xhosa to heel was the task of British regular troops.
They were volunteers from the margins of society. Soldiering was a
career of desperate resort for petty criminals, casual and unemployed
workers and the destitute. Ireland was full of such creatures, which was
why Irishmen made up over a third of the British army in 1840. Another
area of rural deprivation, the Scottish Highlands, was also a fruitful
source of recruits. Highland troops had a reputation for the hardiness

and grit necessary for colonial campaigns and were frequently deployed against the Xhosa.

The upper class led the lower into battle. Officers were, by definition as well as birth, gentlemen, and before 1871 their families paid for their commissions. Officers were expected to show exemplary and inspiring courage and, when not fighting, they relaxed in the manner of a country squire, attending balls, drinking and gambling in their messes and hunting. It was widely believed, probably correctly, that soldiers admired sporting officers with a devil-may-care spirit. For many officers, particularly those with thin private resources, colonial campaigns were a stepping stone to well-paid civilian posts in the administration. Sir Harry Smith was a veteran of the Peninsular War, the Anglo-American War of 1812, the 1835 Frontier War and the 1845–6 Anglo-Sikh War. From the beginning, like the French, British empire-building in Africa was the business of career soldiers.

Local auxiliaries under European command supplemented British forces. These included the excellent Cape Mounted Rifles, a multi-racial unit recruited from Europeans, Khoikhoi and Cape coloureds (men of mixed blood). Fingoes – more formally the 'Mfengu' – comprised the bulk of the native irregulars and proved enthusiastic soldiers. 'Fingoes' was a generic name given to several distinct groupings of associated clans who fled Shaka. They had been displaced by Zulu expansion, and were loathed by the Xhosa as competitors for land.

The British protected the Fingoes and, as a bonus, gave them the chance to even scores with their enemies. They were skilful scouts and bush fighters who treated war as a chance to make money. British commanders condoned the traditional methods of waging war and so Xhosa villages were plundered and their livestock impounded. After one skirmish in 1877 the Fingoes seized 3,500 head of cattle and 'a vast quantity of miscellaneous loot'.[6] Collaboration was profitable, as it would be in later British campaigns everywhere in Africa.

Some Fingoes were armed with obsolescent firearms. As in Algeria, the conquerors enjoyed superior firepower. During the 1877–8 Kaffir War British forces were armed with breech-loading Martini rifles with a range of over 800 yards, a new model of rocket and Gatling machine-guns.

Xhosa independence crumbled under intermittent hammerings. The authority of their chiefs was diluted as magistrates were appointed to enforce the British laws that were superseding the Roman code of the Dutch and native custom. Defiant or obstructive chiefs were deported to Robben Island which, nearly a hundred years later, would be home to another Xhosa, Nelson Mandela.

Unbowed Xhosa turned to rumours and prophecies to confound their enemies. The outbreak of the Crimean War in 1854 led to tales of an impending landing by the Russians, who would liberate the Xhosa. Two years later, a prophetess, Nongqawuse, called on the Xhosa to slaughter all their cattle, a sacrifice that would be the prelude to the extinction of the Europeans and the dawn of a golden age. She and her fellow soothsayers were believed, and 400,000 cattle were killed. This calamity coincided with a drought that caused 15,000 deaths and drove thousands to seek work in other areas of the Cape. Wars, an outbreak of collective insanity, a famine and demographic disruption had broken the Xhosa and prepared them for integration into the new imperial order.

IV

One feature of the Xhosa millennium had been the abolition of money. It was the often bewildering lubricant of the nascent capitalist economies of the Cape and Natal. Both were agrarian colonies, which attracted a limited flow of British immigrants, including Cecil and Herbert Rhodes, the sons of a Hertfordshire parson, who tried but failed to establish a cotton plantation. By 1880, Natal had a white population of 17,000 and a native population of 300,000 that had grown steadily over the past fifty years despite wars and famines. Nonetheless, the settlers were forever moaning about labour shortages.

Natal's pioneers were seeking opportunities to prosper that had been denied them at home, or to recover lost fortunes. George Russell, a ship's mate, settled in the colony in 1850 after his family had been ruined by speculation in railway shares. As in Algeria, the colonial authorities had assumed ownership of all unoccupied or confiscated lands. Rents for Crown land were between sixpence and a shilling an acre, and one 13,000-acre farm in Natal was available for an annual rent of £30.[7] Private and corporate capital funded the colonists' ventures, for the government demanded proof of individual solvency before agreeing leases.

Economic growth depended on a constant supply of semi- and unskilled labour. Settlers were continually moaning about the lack of labourers, and in response the authorities began to hire Indian workers. From the time the first batch of 300 indentured Indian labourers arrived in Natal in 1860, a total of 6,445 men, women and children arrived over the next six years. More came later to form the nucleus of South Africa's Indian community.

Each black worker was paid in cash and had to adapt himself to the discipline of tightly regulated employment. It was an irritating innovation that required the natives to take on board the bewildering concept of time as it was understood in an industrial society. Hitherto, they had laboured from sunrise to sunset, but when sugar cane was being harvested they were compelled to work at night to process the crop. At Pietermaritzburg a cannon was fired at eight every morning as a summons to work. A local poet spoke for many when he grumbled about being 'bullied by sir o'clock'.[8]

Masters expected submission and hard graft from their workforce. Among the Xhosa phrases in a book sold to settlers in the 1860s were 'You are obstinate' and 'I shall take your blanket.' Slackness and insubordination were punished by local magistrates with powers to sentence offenders to hard labour and flogging. Theoretic equality under the law was not a licence for laziness. The *sjumbok* was supplemented by the sermon, for missionaries preached the Protestant ethic of industriousness and thrift. Many natives heeded these appeals and sought to make their way upwards in the new economic world. During the 1860s and 1870s there was an upsurge in the demand for mission education and, where it was not available, enterprising white shopkeepers offered classes in English at two shillings and sixpence a month.[9]

Shepherding the natives of Natal into the modern, capitalist world was the job of Sir Theophilus Shepstone, Secretary for Native Affairs between 1856 and 1877. He was an exemplary proconsul, upright and busy, and his experience as a commander of native levies convinced him that he had an acute insight into the African mind. Sensibly, he followed the Burkean principle that societies were delicate organisms that evolved naturally in accordance with their needs.

Shepstone, therefore, insisted that 'chieftainship and tribalism' had to be adapted to work in the imperial interest. He believed that 'violent measures' would never eradicate 'barbarism' or 'commend civilised ideas to barbarous races'.[10] His conclusions accorded with the widely held European assumption that the historic path to civilisation was marked by four stages based on economic activity. Hunting was superseded by pastoral farming, which in turn was replaced by growing crops. Then came manufacturing and trade, the features of civilisation as exemplified by Victorian Britain.

Compromise was always infinitely preferable to coercion. This was why Shepstone rejected the missionaries' clamour for the abolition of polygamy which, in the words of one, was 'a system of slavery, involving as it does, the bartering of women for cattle'. Shepstone demurred and treated polygamy as integral to a native society and a culture that rested on male domination. Its abuses were corrected by existing social mechanisms. 'If a man beats a woman', argued Shepstone, 'he is entitled to punish her, but somehow he usually gets the worst of public opinion which is against cruelty to women.' He was supported by Bishop Colenso, who thought that the termination of polygamy would shatter Zulu family life.[11] The issue was resolved by an agreement reached in 1869: henceforward, polygamous marriages had to be registered by magistrates and a tax was levied on the bride's dowry.[12]

Natal needed all the revenue it could get, for Britain expected its colonies to be self-supporting, with the Treasury footing the bill for local garrisons and then only grudgingly. Hut taxes were the prime source of income and were an important reason why it was imperative to engage as many natives as possible in the cash economy. The labour market expanded dramatically in the 1870s in response to a wider economic revolution. It had been triggered by the discovery of diamonds in 1867 in the district around what later became Kimberley. The diamond rush attracted over 10,000 diggers (including 120 blacks), who staked mostly small claims that provided jobs for over 30,000 migrant black workers from the surrounding regions. A large number were paid with rifles, which they carried back to their villages. Small operators were soon bought up by big corporations financed by City capital.

Within a decade diamonds transformed the Cape from a colonial backwater struggling to make ends meet into a thriving state with a modern infrastructure. Investment flowed in: between 1874 and 1885 £20 million was raised to finance the extension of the colony's railway network and the modernisation of its harbours. White immigration soared from 12,000 during the 1860s to 47,000 in the next decade. The demand for black labour outstripped the supply and workers had to be recruited in Mozambique.

The new prosperity of the Cape was a key factor in Britain's political plans for the future of the region. In 1872 it was granted self-government, with an elected assembly like those already successfully established in Canada and the Australian states. Whitehall wanted South Africa to adopt the Canadian model with the creation of a South African union of the Cape, Natal, the Transvaal and Orange Free State. With its white population of nearly a quarter of a million, diamond revenues and investment potential the Cape would be the keystone of a new dominion. The response of the Boer governments was lukewarm: seen from the veld the proposed federation looked like a device to stifle Afrikaner independence and advance British supremacy.

V

Proposals for South Africa's political future had to be shelved in 1876. For the next four years the Transvaal, Natal and Zululand were convulsed by a sequence of wars. There was the final Xhosa rebellion, a contest for land between the Transvaal and the neighbouring kingdom of Sekhukhune I of the Bapedi, and a British invasion of Zululand. From a white perspective, a combination of a rebellion and the belligerence of two formidable independent states looked dangerously like a concerted effort to reverse the spread of European power.

Yet the challenges were uncoordinated and, in the case of the Zulus, existed only in the imagination of nervous soldiers and officials – who did, however, welcome the upheavals as an opportunity to eliminate once and for all independent states with strong rulers. Like Shaka, Sekhukhune was bent on the enlargement of his kingdom at the expense of the equally land-hungry Boers. For several years he had been importing modern firearms and encouraging Bapedi warriors to acquire guns by working in the diamond fields. The Boers came off worse in the fighting, despite having raised and trained 10,000 black levies and hired mercenaries from the white riff-raff of the diamond fields. This check coincided with a financial crisis in the Transvaal, which had been trying to raise capital on the Amsterdam money markets to fund a railway to Delagoa Bay. The upshot was a deficit of over £100,000, which could not be paid since the Boer farmers refused to pay extra taxes. At the close of 1876 the Transvaal was tottering on the verge of implosion.

Overall responsibility for resolving the Transvaal crisis lay with Sir Bartle Frere, the new High Commissioner for South Africa, whose job was to implement Britain's grand design for the region. He was a dedicated imperial servant: a lad from the provincial middle classes who had learned the duties of Empire at Haileybury and the East India Company's Imperial Service College and undertaken them successfully in India. Frere's Empire was liberal and progressive, as he explained at a banquet in Pietermaritzburg in 1878. His long experience of native peoples had taught him that 'there was every reason to hope that they were capable of being raised from a state of barbarism' in the same way as the English had been over the past thousand years.[13] Frere could not permit the Bapedi to fill the vacuum in the Transvaal, the collapse of which he feared would be a severe blow to European prestige throughout the region. Early in 1877 Shepstone was authorised to annex the Transvaal, take over its debts and promise military help. In the meantime, British in the eastern Cape and the Zulu kingdom in Natal waged a ruthless war in which 4,000 were killed and many deported to the western Cape for forced labour on public works.

Frere's Indian experience dictated his reactions to these crises. Imperial authority needed a monopoly of power: if potential rivals refused to submit and cooperate then they had to be overthrown. The current wisdom was that the Indians revered hard power and, Frere assumed, the Africans would do likewise. His analysis of the current regional balance of power convinced him that Cetshwayo's Zulu kingdom was the chief obstacle to British supremacy and, it went without saying, progress. Shepstone, now installed as administrator of the Transvaal, agreed; he saw Zululand as a Sparta in which every male was 'a celibate man-destroying gladiator'. A signal victory over the Zulus was the only guarantee of permanent British domination of South Africa.

Both men had been misled by military intelligence, which alleged that Cetshwayo was a bloodthirsty tyrant with 40,000 warriors on a permanent war footing. This was wrong, since the Zulu state was a nation in arms rather than a nation with a vast standing army. Cetshwayo's impis were a militia of unmarried young to middle-aged men who, on completion of their service, were rewarded with young brides by the king. The Zulu army also included three women's regiments which guarded the royal kraal.

Cetshwayo did not want a war with Britain. He had enjoyed British sponsorship and sincerely hoped that through conciliation he could maintain friendly relations. Frere and Shepstone were resolved on a trial of strength. Potential objections from Disraeli's Cabinet were smothered by disinformation. Through minatory diplomacy, attempted subversion of prominent Zulu nobles and calculated provocation, Frere and Shepstone forced Cetshwayo's hand. During the winter of 1878 to 1879, as British forces converged on the frontier with Zululand, the fearful and bewildered monarch began to mobilise his army. By January he had about 29,000 warriors under arms.

The king had played into Frere's hands, for he interpreted the massing of the impis as a declaration of war. Early in January 1879 the British invaded with an army of nearly 8,000 (half of whom were native levies) which was supported and supplied by 30,000 black porters, 27,000 oxen and 5,500 mules. This cumbersome force was split into five columns which advanced simultaneously into Zululand.

Frere and Shepstone were taking an enormous gamble, but they felt confident that the odds were in their favour: a modern army would quickly overthrow the Zulu state. They had, however, reckoned without the blunders of its commander-in-chief Lord Chelmsford, a luckless booby whose misjudgement led to the central column being overwhelmed by a surprise Zulu attack at Isandlwana. Over a thousand imperial troops were killed and Zulu losses were at least twice that number. It was a Pyrrhic victory, as Cetshwayo acknowledged when he spoke of the battle as an assegai thrust into the belly of his people. Despite his orders, one impi attempted to enter Natal but was repelled by a small detachment of the 24th (Warwickshire) Regiment at Rorke's Drift. It was a heroic contest for which eleven of the defenders received the Victoria Cross.* Chelmsford scurried back to Natal and ordered other units to do likewise.

It took twenty days for the news of Isandlwana to reach London. The official post-mortem of the disaster revealed not only Chelmsford's unfitness for command, but how Frere and Shepstone had engineered an aggressive war and deceived the British government as to their

---

* This action was vividly portrayed in the 1964 epic film *Zulu*.

intentions. Both were discreetly sacked, Chelmsford was superseded by Sir Garnet Wolseley and reinforcements were rushed to Natal.

Meanwhile, Chelmsford endeavoured to salvage his reputation with a second invasion. Luck was now on his side and compensated for his shoddy generalship. Cetshwayo's commanders overruled his sensible suggestion of waging a guerrilla war against the extended and friable British lines of communication; they stuck to the traditional tactic of an encircling attack by massed impis armed with assegais. The Zulus charged at Ulundi, where Chelmsford's troops were drawn up in a square. Experienced onlookers noted that the Zulu offensive was half-hearted and it was, literally, blown to pieces by artillery, rifle and Gatling gun fire. After the battle Cetshwayo fled, but was pursued and captured. He was deposed and his kingdom annexed.

It was left to Wolseley to clear up the mess. He was an icy, arrogant and self-seeking general with a reputation for efficiency – the 'modern major-general' of Gilbert and Sullivan fame. Wolseley also possessed the ruthless mindset of his French contemporaries: on disembarkation he contemplated the extermination of the Zulus and the unleashing of the pro-British Swazis on their hereditary foes, the Bapedi. He sullenly admitted that he was constrained by 'the howling Societies at home who have sympathy with all black men'.[14] Orthodox warfare sufficed to defeat the Bapedi and secure the Transvaal.

In Zululand Wolseley opted for political fragmentation, creating twelve chiefdoms under puppet chiefs, which led to petty wars. Cetshwayo was briefly restored as a British client in 1882, but he was expelled and died soon after. Those who met him, including Queen Victoria, were impressed by his regal bearing. Occasional disorders in Zululand over the next few years were a small price to pay for the removal of the Zulu army. Moreover – and both Frere and Shepstone would have seen this as a benefit – the Zulus were now part of the pool of labour that was vital for economic growth.

The political future of the Transvaal was settled by another short war. With the Bapedi and Zulus no longer a threat, the Boers wanted their independence back. British prevarication led to an uprising in which British forces confronted a Boer militia armed with breech-loading rifles. Restoring order was the task of General Sir George Colley, Wolseley's pet and successor. He was an even greater muff than Chelmsford, for in February 1881 he deployed nearly 500 unsupported infantrymen in an untenable position on Majuba Hill, which Boer fire-power turned into a killing zone. Colley was shot down and over half his force were killed, wounded or captured. Soon afterwards a truce was agreed.

British voters had already settled the Transvaal question when they elected Gladstone and the Liberals into power in the 1880 general election. Gladstone had campaigned against expansionist imperial frontier wars lightly undertaken by 'prancing proconsuls'. Frere and Shepstone had tarnished Britain's moral reputation and squandered lives and treasure; the Zulu war had cost £4.9 million, most of which had been spent on logistics.[15]

Gladstone's government restored the independence of the Transvaal, which took back its debts and conceded Britain an ill-defined suzerainty over the republic.

The wars of 1877 to 1880 had established a dispensation of power that would endure for the next hundred years. South Africa's most powerful native polities had been extinguished, its black population was in a state of submission, and the white man remained their undisputed master.

6

'Un vaste plan d'occupation': Exploitation and Exploration

━━━━━━

I

The final entrenchment of white supremacy in South Africa began a period of extraordinary and far-reaching change in the rest of Africa, although its direction and scale were unclear at the time. Within the next twenty years, nearly the entire continent would pass under direct or indirect European control. Such a transformation could not have been predicted in 1879 although, as I shall explain, the historical forces that drove what was afterwards called the 'Scramble for Africa' were already in existence and gaining impetus. For the moment they were confined to France and, to a lesser extent, Britain.

Both powers were fast acquiring the technical, medical and logistical capacities needed to send white troops deep into the African hinterland. In 1867 a 13,000-strong Anglo-Indian army had invaded Abyssinia to rescue European hostages, mostly missionaries, who had been imprisoned by the Emperor Tewedros. His fortress at Magdala was stormed, he shot himself, his prisoners were released and the British departed.

Another demonstration of Britain's extended reach occurred in 1874 after the Asantehene Kofi Karikawi had tried to convince the Fanti that he and not the Governor of the Gold Coast was their overlord. His capital, Kumasi, was captured by British and West Indian soldiers, he was deposed and was replaced by a compliant successor. Britain would not be flouted by truculent rulers, under the illusion that distance and impassable terrain gave them immunity from retribution.

What was significant about these operations in the wider context of African history was the low death rate from disease and fevers. Less than 1 per cent of white soldiers died from local distempers in Abyssinia and just forty out of 2,000 in the Gold Coast. These encouraging survival rates were the result of methodical medical preparation, including water purification systems. Nonetheless, tsetse flies, mosquitoes and microbes remained a hazard. In 1878 over half the white and black soldiers ordered to prove that France's chastising arm extended from Senegal to the Upper Niger died from yellow fever.[1]

II

During the previous twenty-five years the unexplored area of Africa had shrunk dramatically. A succession of explorers had traversed and charted most of eastern and Central Africa, including the 700,000 square miles of the Congo basin and the hinterland of the Great Lakes. The new wave of explorers captured the public imagination with colourful and sometimes lurid accounts of whom and what they had discovered. Europeans were fascinated by the revelation of a primordial world full of natural marvels, strange races such as the pygmies and exotic animals, in particular the gorillas of the Congo forests. Many readers wondered whether they were being transported back in time, if not to the Garden of Eden then to the world in its infancy. In terms of stirring the imagination, mid-Victorian exploration in Africa was similar to space travel a century later.

Explorers wrote their own histories and their books, coupled with multiple public appearances on lecture tours (with lantern slides and specimens), made them international celebrities. They enjoyed their fame, for in varying degrees all of them were supremely egotistical and jealous of their reputations. They concurred on one thing: marching across Africa or being carried by palanquin stimulated their adrenaline. On the eve of his trek to uncover the source of the Nile in 1856, Richard Burton trembled with sheer excitement: 'The blood flows with the fast circulation of childhood . . . A fresh dawns the morn of life.' For his companion, John Hanning Speke, trekking through Africa was an antidote to world-weariness: he once confessed that 'being tired of life he had come to be killed in Africa'. Sir Samuel Baker, another seeker after the headwaters of the Nile, felt like an Arthurian knight errant on a quest for the Holy Grail. As he approached Lake Albert he was overcome by an almost ecstatic sense of fulfilment. Through 'hard work and perseverance' his search had succeeded and soon 'I was to *drink* at the mysterious fountain before another sun should set.'²

Obsession and vanity obviated the mental and physical distress of travel. Explorers endured the extremes of fatigue, were debilitated by agues and pestilences, confronted belligerent natives and animals and were maddened by what Henry Morton Stanley called the 'unwhipped insolence' of guides, porters and bodyguards. All this contributed to recurrent bouts of exasperation and melancholia that they overcame and later described, adding to their public stature as brave men of iron will.

Livingstone was sustained by his faith. As he explained to Stanley at their famous encounter at Ujiji in 1871, he was the servant of divine Providence and, therefore, his 'exile' was 'God's doing'. He was briefly cheered by reading copies of *Punch*, which Stanley had thoughtfully delivered, but chose to stay close to Lake Tanganyika and continue searching for the source of the Nile. He died two years later and his body was returned to England for a state funeral. *The Times* declared that wherever he went in Africa, 'he had made the English name not only respected but beloved'. Selections from his writings soon became set as texts for pupils in the new elementary schools in the hope that they would enkindle an imperial spirit among the children of the poor.

Stanley was an explorer whose activities and thoughts were unsuitable material for filling young minds with the imperial ideal. Finding Livingstone had been his debut as an explorer and his apotheosis as a journalist who could make as well as report news. Stanley craved fame and adulation. His illegitimacy, his childhood in a Welsh workhouse, his crass social manner and his career as a reporter for the 'yellow press' were stigmata that could only be erased by spectacular achievements and headlines across the world.

Another scoop beckoned. Stanley turned to exploration and led a second expedition, sponsored by James Gordon Bennett of the *New York Herald*, which crossed Africa from Dar-es-Salaam in the east to the mouth of the Congo in the west. He set off in 1874, took a detour around the shores of Lake Victoria and then descended the Congo, often fighting his way down the river. Stanley returned home in 1877 and set down his adventures in *Through the Dark Continent*, which was an immediate bestseller. It was an epic of endurance in which Stanley, elephant gun at the ready, swept aside all obstacles, physical and human. His treatment of the natives prompted Burton to remark that 'he shoots negroes as if they were monkeys'.[3]

Pierre Savorgnan de Brazza was the antithesis of Stanley. He was a self-confident, generous-spirited and courteous gentleman, the son of an Italian aristocrat, and a French patriot who served as an officer in the navy of his adopted country. In 1874, when he was twenty-two, he volunteered to lead an expedition to chart the Lower Congo and its tributaries. Admiral de Montaignac, the Minister of Marine, agreed and advanced 10,000 francs to meet de Brazza's expenses.

Unlike contemporary British explorers, de Brazza had a political mandate. He negotiated agreements with the chiefs of the riverine polities by which they agreed to ban taxes on cargoes (mostly ivory) that passed downriver to Ogooué. More trade for the port meant smaller subsidies from Paris. De Brazza was also laying the foundations for future French sovereignty of the region. He promised an end to the slave trade and, whenever he hoisted the Tricolour over his camp, he announced that whoever touched the flag became free. He distributed his stock of gaudy cast-offs from the wardrobe of imperial theatre at the Tuileries to chiefs and amazed their subjects with firework displays.[4]

III

On his return to Paris in 1877, de Brazza was awarded the Légion d'Honneur and lionised by the Société de Géographie. He was welcomed in a city humming with ideas about empire-building in Africa. Notwithstanding the reverse suffered in the recent Senegal campaign, the National Assembly had approved funds for a railway to open up the Upper Niger to French traders and soldiers. In 1880 the deputies assigned further credits for a preliminary survey of an even more ambitious project: a trans-Saharan railway that would connect Algeria with France's West African colonies. An engineer, Colonel Paul Flatters, was instructed to map out a suitable route, but his reconnaissance party was ambushed and all but wiped out by Tuaregs.

Such grandiose and costly enterprises would never have been taken seriously ten years before. They were evidence of what was turning out to be a decisive shift in European attitudes to Africa and its future. The new thinking attracted exponents and followers in France and Britain. It spread to Germany where, in 1882, the Deutscher Kolonialverein was founded to lobby for overseas projects. It soon had over 3,000 members, with businessmen strongly represented. Like its counterparts in France and Britain, it was demanding a new and radical approach to Africa.

At the heart of this intellectual and political ferment was one subjective assumption: Africa was failing. Or, seen from another perspective, Europe had failed Africa. Over the past hundred years the European impact on the continent had yielded few changes for the better, which is unsurprising given that it was patchy and restricted. Traditional Africa seemed unreceptive and immutable: the Arab and indigenous slave trades flourished and explorers' narratives testified to the anarchy they were generating. Missionaries were dismayed by recidivism and slow conversion rates: in 1881 one French cleric claimed that 15 million Africans had embraced Islam over the last century.[5] Christianity had not opened the door to civilisation.

What had gone wrong? One influential body of European opinion blamed the Africans for what they claimed was a stubborn rejection of beneficial change. Older racial theories were revived and developed to support this contention. According to Thomas Carlyle, the philosopher-in-waiting to the Victorian middle class, black men had never grasped the essential truth that 'work' was 'the everlasting duty of all men'. In his *Occasional Discourse on the Negro Question* (1849) he sneered at philanthropists' visions of the regeneration of the black races, and he urged Negroes to 'lay down their pumpkins and labour for their living'. Whether or not they did so was irrelevant, argued the French historian Joseph-Arthur de Gobineau. In his *The Inequality of Human Races* (1855) he alleged that racial pedigree dictated historic destiny. This was proved by the white or Aryan races who, though their superior and creative bloodlines, had been the force behind the great civilisations of the world. Variations on this theme abounded for the next fifty years and became the foundation of Hitler's racial fantasies.

The popular pseudo-science of phrenology was enlisted to substantiate this mumbo-jumbo. Paul Broca, President of the Paris Société d'Anthropologie, examined its collection of Negro skulls and in 1861 announced that they belonged to the lowest of human races.[6] Five years later he asserted that 'Never has a people with dark skin, woolly hair, and a prognathous face [prominent jaw and receding forehead] been able to spontaneously elevate itself to civilisation.' They could have achieved this, Broca thought, but were prevented by persistent and chronic instability.[7] Darwinian theories of natural selection and survival of the fittest were hijacked to reinforce such notions. Africans had made little or no headway in the universal struggle of races to grow strong and master their environment.

Sedentary, academic speculation about the African's flaws was confined to libraries and the shelves of musty ethnological museums, but it drew some support from the experiences of explorers. Burton and Speke (who believed in the myth of Ham) had no faith in the African's potential for improvement. Baker believed that his progress would depend on doing whatever the white man ordered. Stanley agreed: whenever black men refused to obey his commands he flogged and shot them. Reacting to humanitarian outrage at his brutality, the *New York Herald* dismissed his victims as 'human vermin' whose 'savagery' was a barrier to progress.[8]

As a Christian, Livingstone rejected these stereotypes and the scientific gobbledegook that detached Africans from the rest of humanity. They were, he insisted, 'equal in capacity to our uneducated poor' and, like them, were open to regeneration.[9] Likewise, Sir Bartle Frere did not see Africans as handicapped in any way. They were, he argued, a people 'waiting for civilisation and commerce' to make their continent 'one of the richest and most fruitful countries which contribute to the wealth of the world'.[10]

According to men of Frere's optimistic mindset, the present condition of Africa was the result of the inertia and lack of imagination of European governments, businessmen and bankers. Only 2 per cent of Britain's huge international investment portfolio (it earned £75 million in 1875) went to Africa. The continent had remained marginal in terms of global trade, although Stanley and de Brazza were telling anyone who cared to listen that it was brimming with customers and raw materials, and ripe for investment. By the late 1870s they found themselves addressing receptive audiences.

The European economic climate was changing in ways that made industrialists and investors more receptive to the still-nebulous opportunities awaiting them in the interior of Africa. Over the past twenty years Europe's economic growth had been phenomenal: by 1880 it possessed 60 per cent of the world's manufacturing capacity. Output was soaring: during this period Britain's exports rose from £164 million to £223 million and France's from £91 million to £139 million. Both countries were investing capital abroad, principally in the developing modern economies of North and South America, Australasia and Russia.

Growth statistics were deceptive since they took no account of efficiency in production and the application of new technologies and scientific discoveries. These were the strengths of German and American industries and explained why both countries were close on Britain's heels and overtaking France. The Gatling guns that subdued the Zulus were invented and manufactured in the United States; so too were the phonographs and other electrical gadgetry that would soon impress African princes.

The bad news was that after 1879 Europe's economic growth was accompanied by a cycle of alternate booms and slumps that continued until 1896. Periodic recessions generated uncertainty, and governments came under pressure to frame policies that would safeguard producers and exporters. These were protective tariffs on imports and measures to secure captive markets and sources for raw materials. The French Republic and the German Empire adopted protection in 1879 and 1882, but Britain stuck doggedly to Free Trade, which had underpinned its former economic supremacy.

In the past Britain could tolerate foreign competition at home and throughout her empire. Trade treaties agreed with African rulers had always allowed foreign traders to compete with British. In the early 1860s, vodka distilled by Hamburg merchants competed with British gin throughout West Africa, where British consuls had offered assistance to German dealers whenever they had disputes with local traders and chiefs. Twenty years on, British merchants selling cotton goods in the Ivory Coast had to pay a 20 per cent duty imposed by the French government to protect its own manufacturers.[11]

Rising productive capacity made it imperative to make the most of every market, however small. Britain's businessmen were willing to brace themselves to meet the new conditions of global trade. Nevertheless, the commercial mind was aware that there were advantages in keeping as much of the world's trade as possible open to Free Trade, even if this meant permanent occupation of areas not yet under foreign control. In the long term, the people of Africa would benefit from competition and an abundance of goods. During negotiations about Anglo-Portuguese trade arrangements in the Lower Congo in 1880, the British Minister in Lisbon predicted that their success would transform 'what are now malodorous lagoons' into places 'of life, health and wealth'.[12]

IV

By this date, France was showing a strong acquisitive interest in these and other 'malodorous lagoons' and those who lived alongside them. They had suddenly become attractive because France's position in Europe was now one of comparative weakness, for she had been the biggest loser in the dramatic redistribution of power that had occurred between 1859 and 1871. Two new nations, the German Empire and Italy, had been created and France had been relegated to the status of a secondary power after her defeat by Germany in 1871. A humbled France had been compelled to surrender the provinces of Alsace and Lorraine with their 1.3 million inhabitants, a heavy loss for a nation whose birth rate was lower than that of other Continental countries. Germany now dominated Europe and in 1879 consolidated her ascendancy by an alliance with Austria.

Frenchmen of all political complexions passionately desired to retrieve their country's old eminence and glory. But how? As in 1815, Europe was closed to French expansion, leaving Africa as the only area where she could compensate for her losses, restore her standing in the world, grow strong enough to defeat Germany and recover her lost provinces. The road to victory lay through Africa, which would deliver France wealth and status. Or, as one advocate of imperial expansion put it, acquiring colonies was 'a question of life or death', for without them, 'France would sink to the level of Romania and Greece'.[13]

Revanchist patriotism provided both the motive and the catalyst for the new French imperialism that gained political ground during the 1870s. Its most valuable converts were the relatively small body of senior officers and diplomats. They pulled strings and persuaded politicians to adopt expansionist programmes. The Niger and trans-Saharan railway projects were pushed by Admiral Jean Jauréguiberry, a former Governor of Senegal and from 1879 Minister of Marine. He was well placed to influence policy-making for, like others of his kind, he was a permanent fixture in the political hierarchy of France at a time when elected politicians were birds of passage. France had seven ministries between 1876 and 1880, most lasting a few months. Meanwhile the Admiral remained at his desk, gave orders (the Ministry of Marine was responsible for France's West African possessions), pulled strings and counselled politicians. He and others of like mind could rely upon backing from sympathetic editors, businessmen and the Catholic Church, which had always believed that Christianity was integral to the *mission civilisatrice*.

Above all, imperialism was integral to the spirit of the Third Republic. It represented progress and prized what republicans believed to be the unique and superior culture of France. It was right and proper that this was exported to the rest of the world. It was an appealing idea and helped immensely in binding together and, for that matter, putting a gloss on the strategic, political and commercial arguments in favour of expansion. The colonial lobby secured powerful allies within the National Assembly, including the three giants of republicanism and successive Prime Ministers: Charles de Freycinet, Jules Ferry and the radical Léon Gambetta, a recent but enthusiastic convert to the idea of France's imperial destiny.

Ordinary Frenchmen were drawn into the imperial movement through the new and sensationalist mass-circulation press. Its readers' opinions now counted for something, for in 1875 the vote had been extended to all adult males. Ten million of them were illiterate, although literacy levels were rising fast. The pro-expansionist *Petit Journal* had a daily circulation of 350,000 in 1873, and appealed to its largely lower-middle- and working-class readership by arguing that cheap food imported from France's colonies would raise living standards.

Imperial enthusiasts applauded de Brazza's assertion that it was far better that a Frenchman had opened up the Lower Congo than an Englishman or a German.[14] He was stirring up disturbing memories, for in the last century Britain had trumped France in North America, India and the Caribbean. There were deep and persistent fears that 'La perfide Albion' would again frustrate France. Yet that infamously rapacious and cunning power also offered Frenchmen an example: the *Journal des Chambres de Commerce* predicted that 'What the English have done in India, we can do in Africa.'[15]

By the end of 1880 France was mentally primed to begin a programme of expansion in Africa. As the Foreign Minister explained to the Italian Ambassador, 'French influence banished from Europe by Prince Bismarck, has transferred its energy to Africa.'[16] As yet there was still no clear indication of how and where this energy would be directed. Tunis turned out to be France's first target, thanks to a coincidence of local misfortunes that were swiftly and ruthlessly exploited by Prime Minister Ferry.

Tunis was the sophisticated capital of an autonomous Ottoman province with a population of 70,000 Muslims and 40,000 Jews, Maltese, Greeks and Italians, many of whom were recent immigrants. Under pressure from European consuls, successive beys had encouraged foreign investment in a modern urban infrastructure, including railways and a gasworks. A sequence of plagues and famines shook the Tunisian economy and by 1880 its depleted revenues were insufficient to service its debts. The financial crisis undermined a government that had never controlled the tribes of the Saharan hinterland. In April 1881 Tunis showed all the symptoms of what we now call a 'failed state' and was, therefore, ripe for annexation – or, as Ferry would have preferred to call it, a 'rescue'.

Cross-border raids into eastern Algeria by Khoumir tribesmen provided the Ferry ministry with an excuse to invade Tunis: *Le Petit Journal* called the attacks 'a stroke of luck'.[17] Like its British counterpart, the French imperial mind treated all disorder as viral: disturbances on the Algerian frontier could easily spill over into the rest of the colony, which had been convulsed by a major uprising ten years ago. Therefore, just before the assault on Tunis, precautionary measures were taken in readiness for any uprisings in Algeria.[18] British misgivings about the annexation of Tunis were dispelled by a secret pledge not to establish a naval base at Bizerta.[19]

At the end of April 1881 French columns crossed the Algerian border and the Bey, who lacked the forces to resist, ordered his governors to surrender. 'Nous sommes perdus', he declared. The Khoumir tribes were not so easily demoralised and fought back: several thousand held up one column for seven hours. Tunis was occupied after a four-week campaign in which it was noted that French losses from sickness had been small. The Bey was forced to abdicate and France declared that Tunis was her 'protectorate', which meant that French bureaucrats took charge of the administration, whose security rested on a French garrison. This swift and efficiently executed *coup de main* enraged the

Italians, whose Consul in Tunis accused the French army of massacring civilians.[20]

While the Chasseurs d'Afrique cantered into Tunis, de Brazza was quietly engaging in a less brazen form of empire-building on the banks of the Lower Congo. Under the auspices of the Ministry of Marine, he had returned there in June 1880 with 100,000 francs voted by the National Assembly and a mandate to implement what he called 'un vaste plan d'occupation'.[21] He approached chiefs who, placing their hands on his, promised to help France in whatever ways they could. Makoko, a senior chief, swore that all his lands were now at the disposal of his new overlord. As he progressed, de Brazza established small stations on the riverbanks. Every ruler who submitted promised land for future plantations and pledged to trade only with the French.

V

France had, however, a rival for the Congo: King Leopold II of Belgium. He remains one of the most despicable villains of history, whom Kaiser Wilhelm II summed up as 'Satan and Mammon in one person'.[22] Leopold was a slave to avarice, utterly without conscience and callously indifferent to the human suffering created by his ventures in the Congo. Yet, perversely, this monster is still revered in his own country, for there are equestrian statues to him in Brussels and Ostend. In 2004 the Belgian Foreign Minister attempted to bully state television into banning a film that examined the atrocities committed in Leopold's name in the Congo.[23]

Leopold's life was devoted to making money overseas. He toyed with projects in the East Indies and South America, but by the mid-1870s he had talked himself into believing that he could make his fortune in Africa. Leopold proceeded in a devious and circumspect manner, first posing as a friend to scientific inquiry and a philanthropist. Under these colours and using his regal status to gain legitimacy, he summoned a conference in 1876 to discuss the colonisation of Central Africa. The result was a deceptively benevolent front organisation, the Association Internationale Africaine, which soon mutated into the Comité d'Études du Haut Congo, which also claimed bogus humanitarian credentials.

The real purpose of Leopold's puppet organisation was revealed in

1878 when he hired Stanley as its agent for 50,000 francs a year. His instructions were to return to the Congo to build roads and agree treaties
with the chiefs he met which, the king insisted, 'must be as brief as
possible and in a couple of articles must grant me everything'. Four
hundred and fifty chiefs signed with an 'x'; none of them had ever seen
a document, or had the remotest concept of land law as understood in
Europe. As for their subjects, Leopold ordered Stanley to treat them
as future 'soldiers and labourers'.[24] Bribes in the form of flashy trinkets
were scattered among the chiefs, and machine-guns and cannon were
on hand to overawe waverers. Within five years Stanley had acquired
for Leopold a vast and expanding private estate.

De Brazza recognised a rival and relations between his party and
Stanley's were testy. The Frenchman correctly identified Leopold and
Stanley as predatory capitalists out for all they could grasp and utterly
indifferent to the welfare of the Congolese. 'I am a Frenchman and
naval officer and I drink to the civilisation of Africa by simultaneous
efforts of all nations, each under its own flag', he declared in the presence of Stanley during a public meeting in Paris in October 1882.[25] The
partition of Africa would, he hoped, be undertaken by sovereign states
whose sights were set on the melioration of the continent. His high-
minded reiteration of the ideals of the *mission civilisatrice* must have
cheered his listeners who, over the past six months, had impotently and
sullenly watched as Britain seized control over Egypt.

PART TWO
1882–1918

7

'Bring on a fight':
Regime Change in Egypt and the Sudan 1882–1889

|

Depending upon one's prejudices or nationality, the British *coup de main* in Egypt in 1882 was either a consummate political masterstroke or a sordid act of chicanery justified by breathtaking humbug. Speed, audacity and ruthlessness characterised the preparations for the invasion and occupation of Egypt. They were secretly coordinated and supervised by Gladstone, who sincerely believed that he was upholding a vital national interest. Aggression and subterfuge seemed out of character for a prime minister who always looked to God for guidance and was revered for his moral integrity. Moreover, he had previously and with characteristic pulpit vehemence expressed his abhorrence of imperial adventures. During the 1880 election he had declared that it was sinful to violate the peace of the Zulu kraal. Within two years, a flotilla of British ironclads was shelling the tenements of Alexandria.

Egypt had been an African success story: for the last forty years successive khedives had endeavoured to transform an autonomous Ottoman province into something approaching a modern European state. The new Egypt was symbolised by the first performance of *Aïda* in the recently completed Khedival Opera House in Cairo in 1871. Khedive Ismail had commissioned the opera from Giuseppe Verdi and the scenario for the tragic romance was the Egypt of the pharaohs. The sets were stunning, as archaeologically correct as possible, and evoked Egypt's former grandeur. Audiences could have been forgiven for believing that the ancient glories were being revived.

Ismail was a self-indulgent but progressive ruler who was regenerating Egypt and building an empire which, he hoped, would one day extend to the shores of the Indian Ocean. Plans were in hand to consolidate Egypt's authority over the Sudan with a railway running alongside the Nile to Khartoum. Egypt already had a domestic railway network linking its leading cities, a telegraph system and, like the pharaohs, Ismail believed that grandiose architecture was an affirmation of national and dynastic prestige. Cairo was taking on the appearance of a European metropolis with boulevards, squares, commercial offices and a stock exchange, all built in that overblown, Italianate capitalist style favoured in Europe's financial districts. The Cairene bourgeoisie would soon be served by department stores like those springing up in Paris and London.

In 1869 the Suez Canal had been opened; it was funded by the European money markets, designed by a Frenchman, Ferdinand de Lesseps, and dug by forced peasant labour. Egypt was now at the hub of the trade routes between Europe and the East. Four out of every five steamships that passed through the Canal were British.

Foreign capital paid for Egypt's renaissance, but by 1876 the money had run out. The country had raised £91 million from Europe's money markets and dispensed £7.4 million annually in interest from yearly revenues of £9.5 million. Just under half the taxes were paid by the poorest Egyptians, the 4.9 million rural *fellahin*, who comprised nine-tenths of the population.[1] Poor harvests in 1876 and 1877 reduced the capacity of the peasantry to pay their dues.

Egypt was on the edge of bankruptcy and, if it defaulted, Europe's finance houses would face vast losses which could trigger a wider financial crisis. Nervous European governments rallied behind their bankers and *rentiers*, and in 1879 decided that Egypt's finances should be placed in the hands of an Anglo-French commission of technocrats with a mandate to guarantee that its creditors got their dividends, come what may. The new masters of Egypt paid themselves handsomely, collecting £400,000 a year in salaries.

Ismail was forced to abdicate and was replaced by his son Tewfiq, who was expected to be a malleable figurehead for the new regime. The situation in Egypt in 1879 closely resembled that of Greece after its financial crisis at the end of 2009, when its national finances were placed in the hands of Eurozone and International Monetary Fund administrators under orders to impose extreme fiscal stringency. The political outcome in Egypt (as in modern Greece) was anger and simmering unrest which coalesced into a popular national movement. Resentment was deepest in the army, whose budget had been severely cut by the commissioners. Senior posts were the virtual monopoly of Circassian Turks, which had created a frustrated underclass of Egyptian-born officers without hope of promotion. This group provided a leader for the nationalists, Ahmed 'Urabi Pasha, who once called himself the 'George Washington of Egypt'.

Opposition to the new order rallied around the slogan 'Egypt for the Egyptians', and it was strongest among Urabi's brother officers, the middle and junior ranks of the administration and the *fellahin*. In the countryside, Muslim preachers prophesied the downfall of the Khedive, his replacement by Urabi and the expulsion of all foreigners.[2]

European politicians were baffled by the sudden appearance of an Egyptian nationalist movement. Some dismissed it out of hand. Joseph Chamberlain, a former radical Liberal and Gladstone's President of the Board of Trade, wrote off Urabi as 'a military adventurer' and alleged that 'there was no national party' in Egypt, while Léon Gambetta believed that 'le sentiment de la nationalité' was beyond the mental grasp of the Egyptian peasant.[3] Yet France's Consul-General in Cairo warned his government that the Egyptian nationalist passion was deep-rooted and 'well justified' by the recent impositions on the country.[4] General Gordon, who had commanded Egyptian soldiers, identified Urabi as a national leader who 'will live for centuries for the people'.[5] By September 1881 Urabi was a political force to be reckoned with and he felt strong enough to order Tewfiq to sack his ministers, 'who had sold the country to the Europeans'. He also demanded an elected assembly and a purge of alien elements from the army and civil service. Tewfiq knew how to bend with the wind and in January 1882 appointed Urabi Minister of War.

The British and French governments feared that matters were getting out of hand, and in May ordered Tewfiq to banish Urabi and all dissident officers. The diplomacy of threats enhanced Urabi's stature as a leader prepared to call the bluff of foreign bullies. With good reason, Egyptians now feared that their country might be taken over, as Tunis had been a year ago. At the end of May 1882 Urabi was in virtual control of the government, and the British Minister in Cairo suspected that he might soon topple Tewfiq.[6]

Like all nationalisms, the Egyptian thrived on scapegoats and hate figures. These were provided by the country's 200,000 foreign residents, of whom 21,000 were French, Italians, Austrians and British, and the remainder Greeks, Maltese, Armenians, Lebanese and Jews. Most were engaged in commerce and all were exempt from Egyptian jurisdiction: a Maltese charged with a crime was tried and punished by the British Consul.

Tensions broke surface violently in Alexandria on 11 June after a Maltese murdered an Egyptian donkey boy during a street fracas. Spontaneous disorders followed in which Egyptians attacked Europeans and their property, and Greeks and Maltese retaliated by firing on the rioters. The British government blamed Urabi's agitators for the tumult, although he had everything to lose from a breakdown in civil order. Egyptians alleged that British agents had supplied Greeks and Maltese with rifles, which were used by snipers.[7] The British press claimed that Muslim fanatics had egged on the mobs, some of whom had chanted slogans calling for the destruction of 'depraved unbelievers'.

II

The Alexandrian riots were a godsend for the British government, which was becoming increasingly fearful of Urabi. A third of Gladstone's personal share portfolio consisted of Egyptian stock, and he was a champion of fiscal discipline, which placed him in the bondholders' camp.[8] But it was his concern for long-term imperial security that persuaded him and his Cabinet to use the Alexandrian disturbances as an excuse for intervention and, ultimately, the overthrow of Urabi and the occupation of Egypt.

Egypt had to be subdued to secure the Suez Canal, an imperial lifeline that had to be safeguarded whatever the cost. Its strategic importance had been proved during the 1877–8 confrontation with Russia, when a large contingent of Indian troops had passed through the Canal en route to Malta. More recently, the Canal had seen a passage of troopships in the other direction, carrying reinforcements from Britain to the war in Afghanistan. The Canal was also vital for British trade: 21 per cent of her exports and 16 per cent of her imports were shipped through it.[9]

Nascent Egyptian nationalism, Urabi's defiance and the prospect of anti-European disorders in Egypt's cities jeopardised the future safety of the Canal. Gladstone had to pounce quickly, for there was a distinct chance that Urabi might soon gain political legitimacy by securing recognition as the de facto ruler of Egypt from the Turkish Sultan and France. If this occurred, then French influence in Egypt would increase and British would fade.

Gladstone, therefore, moved swiftly. On 20 June, telegrams were sent to Simla for the mobilisation of Indian forces for deployment in Egypt. Between 23 and 30 June the Admiralty ordered units of the Mediterranean Fleet, including battleships, to concentrate off Alexandria and Port Said. On 1 July the First Lord of the Admiralty cabled the commander of the Mediterranean Fleet, Admiral Sir Beauchamp Seymour, with permission to demand the dismantlement of the batteries defending Alexandria so as 'to bring on a fight'. Four days later, and after intelligence had been received that France was edging towards negotiations with Urabi, the die was cast. Ambassadors of the European powers were warned that Britain was about to undertake unilateral action against Egypt. On 9 July Gladstone approved the bombardment of the forts in 'self defence'.[10]

On the next day Seymour issued an ultimatum to the Egyptian authorities to deactivate Alexandria's artillery defences. They refused and bombardment began shortly after sunrise on the morning of 11 July. It lasted for just over ten hours and extended far beyond the coastal forts to the city beyond. Over 3,000 shells were fired and many struck housing and commercial premises: photographs taken shortly afterwards show demolished buildings.[11] Official versions of the action and the British press blamed this destruction on local arsonists acting on Urabi's instructions. It was, however, widely reported in French and Italian newspapers, which insisted that Seymour's ironclads alone were responsible.[12]

The bombardment triggered fresh tumults, looting and attacks on Europeans and led to marines and sailors from British warships being ordered ashore to suppress the disorders. The next day, two infantry battalions were disembarked, having been on standby in Cyprus. The arson and riots were invaluable to British propaganda, which alleged that the suppression of the Alexandrian disorders had arrested the spread of anarchy across Egypt.

British public opinion had been out for blood since the June riots. Then, Sir Charles Dilke, the Under-Secretary of State for Foreign

Affairs, had observed how his fellow MPs were beside themselves with rage: 'They certainly want to kill somebody, they [just] don't know who.' He later remarked that 'The bombardment of Alexandria, like all butchery, is popular.'[13] But so were moral causes, and this was why the country backed Gladstone's declaration that Britain was 'saving Egypt for liberty and from anarchy'.

Egypt's 'deliverance' was accomplished during the next eight weeks. Although Urabi had promised not to interfere with the Suez Canal, its offices in Port Said and the Canal itself were occupied by marines by the end of July. A 40,000-strong Anglo-Egyptian army followed under the command of Wolseley. It defeated Urabi's regular forces, which had been swelled by 20,000 Beduin and peasant volunteers, at Tel-el-Kabir.[14] The Egyptians fought hard for their country: a US army observer praised the 'pluck' of Sudanese soldiers who fought hand-to-hand with British infantrymen.[15]

Wolseley then advanced towards Cairo, where he hoped to 'cut off the tip of Urabi's nose' as a present for his wife. He received a viscountcy and £2,000, which he considered inadequate for his exertions.[16] Urabi surrendered, was tried and then exiled to Ceylon. Hundreds of his supporters, chiefly army officers, were imprisoned or banished. Tewfiq kept his throne, and Egypt received an administration manned by British civil servants under orders to balance the budget and stamp out corruption. British officers took charge of the Egyptian army. According to Gladstone, these measures were part of a programme designed to provide an independent Egypt with a stable, honest and solvent government. Once this had been achieved, Britain would withdraw.

This declaration of intent was repeated sixty-six times during the next forty years. The foreign ministries of Europe were not taken in, but foreigners throughout Egypt were relieved by the outcome of Gladstone's brisk little war. There were premature cheers from the *fellahin*, who wrongly imagined that a British government would end conscription.[17]

III

Historians have speculated on whether the British occupation of Egypt placed the French, Italians and Germans under starter's orders in a race that led to the partition of Africa during the next thirty years. This was only partially true. The Egyptian coup was a bolt from the blue that stunned the rest of Europe at a time when French imperialists were already showing their hand in Tunis and the Congo basin. The German imperial lobby was keeping up its pressure on a lukewarm Bismarck, and its Italian counterparts were urging the acquisition of colonies on the shore of the Red Sea. What the Egyptian coup accomplished was an injection of a sense of urgency into hesitant governments: time lost meant territory forfeited. There is no reason to imagine that the annexationists' clamour would have been diminished if Britain had stayed its hand in Egypt.

The events in Egypt in 1882 represented a very British coup in that it had been driven by a uniquely British obsession: the security of Britain's possessions in India, the Far East and Australia. A stable Egypt equalled a secure canal protected by a garrison of 5,000 British troops and a larger Egyptian conscript army trained and led by British officers. The British people were told that these changes would benefit the ordinary Egyptian; soon after Cairo had been occupied, *Punch* published a cartoon of redcoats marching through the streets with a caption about 'a friendly power' in Egypt. This was a gloss: the Tommies were in what they later named the land of 'sand, shit and syphilis' to protect imperial communications and Britain's seaborne trade in the East and the Pacific.

France was a loser from the Egyptian coup and was bitterly resentful. Its government had been outwitted and outmanoeuvred. National dismay was distilled by Pierre Loti, a naval officer and novelist:

> Alas ! Alas ! a nation which for a century has been our rival and whose unshakeable ideas we can only marvel at in terror, is pursuing at our expense her grandiose and determined aim of becoming the greatest, indeed the only power in the Islamic world, and everywhere she is supplanting us.[18]

In fact the Prime Minister, Charles de Freycinet, had dithered throughout the crisis. The mood of the deputies had not been hawkish, and he had initially hoped for British cooperation, but at the same time contemplated an accommodation with Urabi. Britain snatched and kept the political and military initiative and, thrust aside by events, France became an astonished and angry bystander. Her press denounced British deceit and brutality. The left-wing *Intransigent* blamed the occupation of Egypt on the clandestine machinations of international bankers, which was not too far from the truth.[19] France was proud of its cultural and economic presence in Egypt, which stretched back to Napoleon's invasion in 1798, and Édouard Lockroy, an imperialist deputy, boasted that 'L'Égypte c'est plus française que l'Algérie'.[20] Henceforward, France treated Britain as a wily and relentless rival.

IV

Egypt's internal crisis coincided with a revolution in its dependency, the Sudan. It was led by Muhammad Ahmad al-Mahdi, a messianic Muslim holy man and visionary. As his title proclaimed, he was a prophet sent by Allah to reinvigorate and purify the faith and observances of Muslims. Apostasy, deviation and devotional laxity had proliferated in the Sudan thanks to the 'Turks', as the Egyptians were called, and so a religious revival had nationalist undertones. The expulsion or extermination of the Turks and their accomplices was integral to the Mahdi's spiritual revolution.

Egypt's brutal and detested Sudanese empire fell apart during 1882 and 1883. The Mahdi's jihad swept across the country, picking off isolated Egyptian garrisons and defeating punitive expeditions. He attracted wide support, including Egyptian and Sudanese deserters, the irregular horsemen hitherto employed by slavers, and those tribes like the Baggara that had lost out from the suppression of the slave trade.[21] Mahdist armies fought under banners inscribed with Quranic quotations and, from the Mahdi downwards, they wore the patched *jibbahs* of men who had forsworn the material world. Alcohol, hashish and tobacco were banned and blasphemers were flogged.

Each victory over the Egyptians added to the stock of miracles that vindicated the Mahdi's claim to be the chosen messenger of Allah. The greatest was in November 1883 at El Obeid, where he trounced an Egyptian army commanded by a Colonel William Hicks and equipped with Krupp artillery and machine-guns. These and thousands of modern rifles were added to the Mahdi's arsenal and were deployed in the siege of Khartoum at the beginning of 1884.

Faced with events in the Sudan, the British government prevaricated. Gladstone found himself responsible for a misruled empire on the point of collapse, the safety of its administrators and soldiers, and the European community in Khartoum. Force in the form of Hicks's expedition had failed, and so the Cabinet decided to abandon the Sudan altogether. Nevertheless measures had to be taken to stop Mahdism from spreading into Egypt or across the Red Sea. The experience of the 1857 Indian Mutiny had taught the official mind to be extremely wary of any hint of an alliance between nationalism and militant Islam.

Early in 1884, General Gordon was ordered to Khartoum with instructions for an evacuation. He disregarded them and declared, 'I come without soldiers but with God on my side, to redress the evils of the Sudan.' His bravery, steadfastness and faith impressed even his adversaries and after his death Mahdists observed that 'Had Gordon been one of us, he would have been a perfect man.' [22] All his life Gordon had been a fighter looking for moral battlefields and Khartoum was one. He would defend the city, but as a professional soldier he was aware that British forces would be needed to beat the Mahdi. By staying put in Khartoum he believed that he would stir the British conscience to the point where public opinion would force Gladstone to reverse his policy, relieve Khartoum and save Sudan in the name of civilisation.

British forces were already in the Sudan, for in March 1884 sailors, marines and soldiers began to pour into Sawakin on the Red Sea to defend the port from Mahdists under Osman Diqna. They were joined by Indian detachments, a reminder that, like the Admiralty, the India Office wanted the Red Sea to remain a British waterway. The Mahdists were repulsed in a sequence of hard-fought battles watched by reporters and war artists who thrilled the British public with vivid accounts of combat in the hot, dusty scrubland around Sawakin. Years later, Flora Thompson, a working-class schoolgirl living in remote rural Oxfordshire, recalled what she had read and seen as a child: 'Theirs had been the day of the bayonet and the Gatling gun, of horse-drawn gun carriages and balloon observation, of soldiers fighting in tight-necked scarlet tunics.' The young Winston Churchill envied his fellow schoolboys who had boxes of model soldiers wearing the new khaki uniforms of infantrymen in the Sudan.

But it was Gordon who captured the national imagination. Here was a Christian hero, the hammer of the slave trade, embattled in a distant city calling on his countrymen and women for help. He succeeded: Gladstone unwillingly agreed to send a relief force on a hazardous and gruelling journey up the Nile. Its adventures, including the

Battle of Abu Klea in which the Mahdists broke a British square before being repelled, excited the public. This was the scenario for battle of Sir Henry Newbolt's 'Vitaï Lampada':

> *The sand of the desert is sodden red, –*
> *Red with the wreck of a square that broke; –*
> *The Gatling's jammed and the Colonel dead,*
> *And the regiment blind with dusk and smoke.*

On 26 January 1885 Khartoum was stormed and taken, and Gordon was killed. Wolseley's native spies reported that he died fighting, revolver in hand, and their accounts were later confirmed by eyewitnesses.[23] While this was an honourable death for a soldier, the public wanted him to die as a Christian martyr and this was how his final moments were portrayed by George William Joy in a painting that shows Gordon in uniform facing his assailants on a stairway, a Christian hero in the face of barbarism.

Gordon's death was blamed on the government and an execrated Gladstone was compelled to fight a war to avenge the hero. It was averted by a sudden war scare after a Russian incursion into Afghanistan: every British and Indian soldier was needed to defend India. The British withdrew to the Egyptian frontier, although a garrison remained at Sawakin.

The Mahdi died in June and his successor, the Khalifa Abdullahi, took control of the Islamic state of the Sudan. He was an absolute ruler whose legitimacy derived from his spiritual ancestry. Abdullahi declared: 'The Mahdi is the Khalifah of the Prophet, I am the Khalifah of the Mahdi, and therefore I am the greatest and holiest man on earth.'[24]

Abdullahi continued the expansionist policies of the previous, Egyptian, regime. In the name of Islam he went to war in 1887 against the Emperor Yohannes IV of Abyssinia, who had been imposing Christianity on his Muslim subjects. The Emperor was killed at the Battle of al-Qallabat in 1889, the same year that a Mahdist army attempted to invade Egypt. They were defeated at Tuski where, according to a British officer, the charging dervishes were 'mowed down in hundreds' by rifle and machine-gun fire. Traditionalist in tactics as well as faith, the Mahdists stuck to their customary tactic of headlong charges by spearmen, cavalry and camelry and made very little use of the artillery and machine-guns they had captured a few years before. These seemed unnecessary to warriors who were told that their faith would dissolve bullets.

The Khalifa also turned his attention towards the Nilotic tribes of the south, a region that had never been wholly subdued by the Egyptians and which had sent warriors to join the Mahdists. One harsh master replaced another: the Khalifa's forces penetrated the region, bringing with them forcible conversion, sharia law and taxes collected in the form of boys and girls for the slave markets.[25]

The tribes resisted. In the early 1890s the Bari, who had a historic tradition of female leaders and warriors, were led by Kiden, a prophetess with magical powers. She proclaimed that her god was stronger than Allah and forced the Mahdists to retreat.[26] The Azande, who had held their ground against the Egyptian empire, refused to bow to its Mahdist successor.[27] Mahdist detachments probing southwards also clashed with the troops of King Leopold's Congo Free State.[28]

8

'Will and force':
Partition 1882–1914

—━━▭━━—

The skirmish between Mahdists and troops from the Force Publique of the Congo Free State in 1895 was a minor incident in the partition of Africa. Its first phase began in 1882 and ended in 1914, when the contest for the continent became part of the First World War. The participants were Britain, France, Germany and Italy and each moved at a pace dictated by fears that the tardy and hesitant would be losers. Territories were annexed or declared 'protectorates', which was tantamount to annexation. Some established rulers were overthrown and others were retained as puppets. In West Africa, Sultan Ahmadu of Segu was expelled by the French as an example to other resisters, while the British allowed the hereditary rulers of Northern Nigeria to keep their thrones. Only Liberia, which began life as a sanctuary for ex-slaves from America and enjoyed American patronage, and Abyssinia survived. The latter was, however, living on borrowed time, since in 1906 Italy secured Anglo-French approval for its future dismemberment.[1]

Africa underwent a political revolution that would have immense repercussions for its future history: the new boundaries became permanent. Prevailing social and political structures remained largely untouched by the transfer of power, and for good reasons. 'There is in every society a leadership class born to direct the affairs of the people', wrote the French soldier–administrator General (later Marshal) Hubert Lyautey, and it was therefore imperative 'to use that class in our best interests'.[2] Pragmatic imperialists agreed, but were quick to discard defaulting collaborators.

The new political dispensation in Africa was the outcome of a series of compromises made in London, Paris, Berlin and Rome, under pressure from men on the spot and their political and press allies. What is remarkable is how far the latter were able to get their way: the grandiose fixations of a handful of egoists driven by patriotism and megalomania drew many of the lines on the new map of Africa.

Cecil Rhodes, a knot of French soldier–administrators and the German explorer–coloniser Carl Peters all convinced themselves that they were destined to make history on a grand scale. Each was guided by an idealised vision of a new Africa, pacified, cleansed of slavery and poised for economic progress. Rhodes and Peters looked forward to mass European immigration into Africa's temperate regions, which would be regenerated by the settlers who would farm scientifically, open businesses and maintain transport and administrative infrastructures. 'Africa is still lying ready for us', Rhodes once remarked, 'it is our duty to take it.' To this end he deployed his formidable will, his private fortune, a talent for political intrigue and a passionate faith in the historic destiny of the Anglo-Saxon race. Early successes fed Rhodes's imagination and he planned to construct a railway that would run from Cape Town to Cairo whose tracks would never leave British soil. This was the Rhodes portrayed in the famous *Punch* cartoon of 1892 as a colossus astride Africa. His ventures in southern Africa and their consequences are described in the next chapter.

Rhodes's dynamic spirit inspired Lyautey who, on his posting as an aide to General Joseph Gallieni, the new Governor of Madagascar, in 1897 welcomed a chance to perform what he called 'a bit of Cecil Rhodism'.[3] Its essence also inspired other French soldier–administrators whose imaginations equalled Rhodes's in audacity and magnitude. France would make itself mistress of a huge swathe of territory that extended inland from West Africa across the Sahara as far as the Nile and swung southwards towards the borders of the Congo Free State. It too would have a transcontinental railway.

Carl Peters, the architect of Germany's African empire, also thought big. On the eve of his second expedition to East Africa in 1887, he was in a mood 'close to megalomania' and his mind hummed with fancies of a bloc of German colonies reaching from the Zambezi to the headwaters of the White Nile. Like Rhodes and the French imperialists, Peters believed that his imagination, energy and foresight uniquely fitted him for spectacular achievements. Years later he wrote that 'A combination of will and force constitutes the ideal mind of a successful coloniser.' Such a man, he added, 'is not to be led by any sentimental feelings'.[4]

None of these men got exactly what they wanted. Pragmatic diplomacy intervened and the European powers bowed to the principle of reciprocity. Compromise as well as vision was reflected in the political map of Africa in 1914. A broad, pale-carmine band of British territory bisected the continent south to north from South Africa to Egypt. There was no Cape-to-Cairo railway, for its route was blocked by German East Africa and the Belgian Congo.

Germany did not get as much as Peters would have wished, although she had secured what are now Tanzania and Namibia and Togo, on the eve of the First World War, obtained British permission to purchase Portuguese Angola and Mozambique. According to the *Economist* this was right and proper, for if Germany 'is to go down in history as a Great Power [it] must also have its fair share of the territory'.[5] The journal in addition reported recent plans for the German transcontinental railway from Kamerun (Cameroon) to German East Africa.

France dominated Africa north of the Equator, ruling the Sahara as far as the western frontier of the Sudan, and a huge chunk to the south which today comprises the Central African Republic, the Congo and Guinea. There was no trans-African railway running from the Atlantic to the Red Sea; Britain had seen to that. There were, however, compensations, for France had strengthened its grip on the Maghreb by securing a protectorate over Morocco. Italy's gains were commensurate with her standing as a secondary power: a toehold in Eritrea, Somalia and the still-to-be-conquered Libya.

West Africa was an untidy area, with a bloc of French territory broken up by slices of British and German colonies. Gambia, Sierra Leone, the Gold Coast, Nigeria and Togoland and Cameroon were proof that neither power would forgo its share in the highly profitable palm-oil trade, nor would it abandon its merchants, who were well represented in the Commons and the Reichstag.

II

Apportioning land and drawing Africa's new borders had been a complex and often fraught business which had been conducted at two levels. At the highest, ministers and diplomats locked horns over claims and counter-claims and agreed compromises designed not to unduly hurt the amour propre of the powers involved. This was what happened at the Berlin Conference, held in Bismarck's residence on the Wilhelmstrasse during the winter of 1884-5. He invited not only representatives of the powers hungry for land in Africa, but others such as Russia, the United States and Sweden which had no interests there. The international nature of the conference gave its decisions authority. The delegates' conclusions represented the collective will of the 'civilised' world, which bestowed on them the legitimacy of international law. No African representative participated in the Berlin deliberations.

The Berlin Conference was principally concerned with West Africa and the vexed question of the Congo basin. This was finally allocated to King Leopold's trading company, which infuriated the French but pleased the British who wanted to keep them out and secure the region for Free Trade. The conference also agreed the principle that future claims would be settled on the crucial assumption that 'real sovereignty' over a region was the basis for legal acquisition and occupation. As we shall see, defining 'real sovereignty' turned out to be a contentious business. The exact nature of and evidence for 'real sovereignty' were hammered out afterwards in a series of high-level negotiations which occurred whenever the claims of two or more powers collided. Tit-for-tat diplomacy prevailed. For instance, in 1890 the British Prime Minister, Lord Salisbury, agreed to the French occupation of Madagascar, Timbuktu and Chad, and France accepted British control over the emirate of Sokoto. Salisbury wryly observed that the French had been content with 'what agriculturists would call "very light land", that is to say it is the desert of the Sahara'. The French and later the Italians imagined that they would make the desert fruitful just as the Romans had done.

In the same year, Salisbury agreed an East African settlement with Germany. Its sovereignty over what is now Tanzania was confirmed and it received the crumbling North Sea island of Heligoland in return for recognition of British supremacy in Uganda, Kenya and Zanzibar. In 1902 Italy extracted a secret promise from Britain that it would acquiesce to the invasion of the Ottoman province of Libya, if and when the French secured a protectorate over Morocco. She did in 1911 and the Italians duly landed at Tripoli.

Prior rights of possession, however flimsy or tenuous, were crucial to the diplomatic haggling. Bundles of treaties signed by native chiefs, up-country trading stations, gunboats patrolling rivers and garrisoned frontier forts were trump cards at the conference table.

This brings us to the second level of the partition, which truly deserves the name of 'scramble', for it involved adventurous young men in a hurry rushing across Africa and staking their country's claims. Brazen opportunism and pugnacity were vital qualities for the pathfinders of empire. Insubordination was a common vice. In 1893 the German Chancellor, Leo von Caprivi, insisted that Germany would consolidate its grip on South-West Africa 'without bloodshed'. Captain Curt von François took no notice, and went ahead with an aggressive frontier war against the Witboois. Berlin sent reinforcements, but groused about the bill. Von François was gently eased out of his command, but his career prospered.[6]

There were plenty of high-flying junior officers like von François looking for a career break on the frontiers of Africa. They were more than happy to slip the leash, sometimes with a nod and wink from their superiors. In 1888 General Gallieni, then commander-in-chief in Senegal, told Colonel Louis Archinand to ignore orders from Paris, use his initiative and smash any ruler who impeded French expansion in the western Sahara.[7] The Colonel performed his task with a thoroughness that left even Gallieni astonished. Flagrant disobedience paid off: the French press lionised the impetuous young swashbucklers on its African frontiers and, of course, their recklessness extended French power.

Such men as Archinand were dangerous, thought Colonel Frederick Lugard after his tense confrontations with junior French officers in the Borgu district of the Upper Nile in 1897. 'They are free because they are unscrupulous' and brimming with confidence, since they knew 'that they would have the whole applause of France if they attacked me'.[8] Lugard understood these tyros, for he shared their spirit. During the past decade he had fought slavers on Lake Nyasa and imposed order in Uganda on behalf of the Imperial East Africa Company, riding roughshod over the interests of French missionaries. His hard-man reputation was so strong that the French regarded his appointment to command the West African Frontier Force in 1897 as tantamount to a declaration of war. Lugard's cadaverous features and massive cantilever moustache made him a perfect bogeyman.

British, French and German frontiersmen used terror, or the threat of it, whenever African rulers jibbed at the treaties demanded from them. During his first expedition to East Africa in 1884, whenever Carl Peters extracted an agreement from a native chief he called for a cheer for the Kaiser and then ordered his escort to fire three volleys 'to demonstrate to the blacks what would happen if they broke the treaty'.[9] The techniques of the Algerian *razzia* were applied in West Africa against the villages and crops of resisters.

The Yoruba were coaxed into signing agreements in 1893 by a show of force stage-managed by Sir Gilbert Carter, the Governor of Lagos. He traversed their lands with a column of Hausa gendarmerie, whose band played 'God Save the Queen', and two Maxim machine-guns were carried shoulder-high by bearers. These weapons had inflicted heavy losses on the Yorubas' neighbours the previous year after they had refused to cooperate with Carter. As we shall see in the next chapter, sharp lessons were needed whenever chiefs quibbled over treaties they had signed.

Private enterprise shared in the parcelling-up of Africa, often hiring men like Lugard to do the donkey work of treaty-gathering and pacification. Governments, keen to keep costs as low as possible, were happy to delegate empire-building to corporations – the British called them 'chartered companies'. The companies received administrative and fiscal powers in return for commercial privileges in the hope that they would flourish, as the East India Company had done in the previous century.

These arrangements were a disappointment, largely because nearly all new ventures attracted few investors. The Compagnie Française de l'Afrique Équatoriale and the Compagnie du Sénégal et la Côte Occidentale de l'Afrique quickly foundered for lack of capital. The Deutsch-Ostafrikanische Gesellschaft, founded in 1884, struggled to raise funds and was soon wobbling.[10] Insolvency overtook the Imperial British East Africa Company, which found that the costs of administering Uganda far outstripped its profits. In 1894 its responsibilities were reluctantly taken over by the British government.

Cecil Rhodes's British South Africa Company was one exception because it was kept afloat by injections of capital from his diamond-mining fortune. The De Beers Corporation indirectly financed the wagons and farming implements of the pioneers, as well as the machine-guns and rifles of the gendarmerie which protected them. King Leopold II's Congo Free State barely kept its head above water between 1885 and 1890, when John Dunlop's invention of the pneumatic tyre dramatically increased the global demand for Congolese rubber. A stroke of luck turned a loss-maker into a money-spinner.

By contrast, the United African Company flourished thanks to the business sense, calculated ruthlessness and City and political connections of its founder, Sir George Goldie. Between 1886 and 1899 the company forcefully advanced and defended British interests beyond the boundaries of the Lagos protectorate. The company's operations on the shores of the Lower Niger and Benue rivers simultaneously extended the power of Britain and delivered attractive (6 to 8 per cent) returns to its shareholders.*

Foreign imports, mostly textiles and spirits, were squeezed out, and the company enjoyed a monopoly over exports of palm oil and palm kernels, an ingredient of that unpleasant recent invention, margarine. Obstructive chiefs and native businessmen toed the line thanks to Goldie's armed steamers, Hausa gendarmerie and, in dire emergencies, Royal Navy gunboats.

III

Goldie encountered stiff French opposition. Between the 1882 coup in Egypt and the 1904 Entente Cordiale, Britain and France were bad-tempered rivals, first in West Africa and then on the Upper Nile. Stand-offs occurred against a domestic background of jingoistic posturing by politicians and journalists.

The French felt themselves on the defensive against a cunning power which aimed to thwart their ambitions in Africa. Gabriel Hanotaux, who was several times Foreign Minister in the 1890s, suspected that his country was the victim of a vast conspiracy. Britain was covertly plotting to steal Portugal's possessions, remain permanently in Egypt and overthrow the Boer republics. Worse still, he alleged, was 'A conception, a gigantic formula, worthy of the compatriots of Shakespeare . . . the Cape to Cairo railway.' The English language was an accomplice to duplicity, for, according to Hanotaux, 'Elle affirme, elle n'explique pas'.[11]

---

* This was high by contemporary standards; British railway companies yielded only 2 to 4 per cent.

British ministers, civil servants and journalists took an Olympian perspective, treating the periodic outbursts of Anglophobia as proof that the French were flighty and prone to hysteria.[12] In 1883 *The Times* compared France to an idle and wayward child, who 'sets off to amuse herself in her own fashion in some unoccupied corners of the world'.[13]

The dark imaginings of French imperialists were confirmed by rumours. In 1884 the Governor of Senegal blamed 'British gold and intrigue' for local opposition to France, and there were recurring, unconfirmed tales of British gun-running to local tribes. Most astonishing of all was the allegation made in 1898 that Britain was shipping 2,000 Zulus to Nigeria to help British forces evict France from the Borgu region.[14]

The fictitious Zulus were part of a series of crises between 1896 and 1898 over ownership of a region on the shores of the Niger that was then being vigorously trawled for treaties by young British and French officers. Joseph Chamberlain, the Colonial Secretary, was nervous and ordered an extension of the telegraph line from Lagos to the forward base of Lugard's West African Frontier Force at Jebba. His French counterpart Hanotaux was also jumpy about the possibility that 'the hot temper of any individual officer may precipitate a war'.[15] French officers with Senegalese escorts entered villages, ceremonially hoisted flags, and British officers with Hausa and Yoruba soldiers did the same. All were under orders to stand their ground but avoid a fight.

None occurred, although there was some snarling when patrols confronted each other. The French turned out to be sahibs, as Colonel James Willcocks, an officer imported from India, recalled. 'Notwithstanding the strained relations that existed, and many stormy interviews we had with the French, none of us bore them any ill-feeling. On the contrary, off duty . . . we were always good comrades.' The alumni of St-Cyr and Sandhurst sat together by campfires, smoked cigarettes and raised their glasses to the Union Jack and the Tricolour.[16] While scotch and cognac eased local tensions, the British and French governments agreed the frontier between Nigeria and French West Africa, which now separates Nigeria from Benin.

The 1898 Fashoda incident was a far more serious affair for it was a head-on clash between fundamental British and French strategies. Britain's global security depended on control over Egypt, whose economic survival depended on the Nile. It was, therefore, vital for Britain to acquire sovereignty over the entire river. The upper reaches of the White Nile were also coveted by French expansionists, who wanted it to be the eastern frontier of their growing Saharan empire. Once entrenched in the southern Sudan, France would be free to construct her trans-African railway from Dakar to Djibuti.

Britain would never tolerate a French stranglehold on the Nile, and in 1895 Sir Edward Grey, the Under-Secretary of State for Foreign Affairs, publicly warned France that any incursion into the region would be treated as 'an unfriendly act'. In the following year, a large, well-equipped Anglo-Egyptian army under General Sir Herbert Kitchener began the piecemeal conquest of the Sudan.

A cabal of French ministers, senior army officers and colonial ministry officials secretly decided to call Britain's bluff. They masterminded a coup contrived to assert their country's presence on the Upper Nile.[17] The stakes were high: Britain's plans for monopoly of regional power would be scuppered, and France, astride the Upper Nile, could make life difficult for the British in Egypt.

From the start, the Fashoda project was a gamble with the odds stacked against France. The Mahdist state fielded an army of at least 50,000, Kitchener was grinding his way southwards with 15,000 men, while France dispatched less than 150 men to raise her flag on the Nile and lay claim to thousands of square miles of desert and marshland. This detachment was commanded by Captain Jean-Baptiste Marchand, an officer in his thirties with African combat experience under commanders of the forward-at-all-costs school. He hoped to be joined at Fashoda by an even smaller mission that had been ordered to Djibouti to persuade the Abyssinian Emperor Menelik II to ally himself with France.

What seemed in Paris to be a plan for a brilliant coup was a fiasco waiting to happen. Marchand's column reached Fashoda in July 1898, after a fourteen-month trek from the French Congo in which, for some of the time, he rode a bicycle with solid tyres.* On arrival, the captain undertook the spadework of establishing 'real sovereignty': the Tricolour was hoisted over a hastily rebuilt Mahdist riverside fort, and treaties were agreed with local tribal chiefs. At the end of August Marchand's

---

* It used to be displayed in the museum at St-Cyr.

work was interrupted by two Mahdist steamers, which attacked his fort and were driven off.

On 10 September Marchand found that his game was up. Kitchener had just crushed the Mahdist army at Omdurman, and the British government had informed France that an Anglo-Egyptian administration was now the lawful government of Sudan. The General delivered this message in person to Marchand, dismayed him with copies of French papers describing the latest events of the Dreyfus scandal, and asked him whether he had been ordered to oppose the restoration of Egyptian authority over its former territories. He answered yes, but, faced with the flotilla of gunboats and the hundreds of Sudanese and Highland infantrymen who had accompanied Kitchener, Marchand admitted that he was powerless.

France's 'real' sovereignty evaporated; up went the Egyptian flag and, at Kitchener's polite request, Marchand agreed to proceed by steamer to Khartoum on the first stage of his return to Paris. The Abyssinian mission had also miscarried: Menelik was canny enough to realise that the local balance of power was now in Britain's favour.

Frenchmen of an uncritically patriotic cast of mind exploded in fury at the news of Marchand's expulsion. Forgetting for the moment the sheer recklessness of the Fashoda gambit, patriots protested against their country's humiliation. Hotheads clamoured for a war to assert French honour, and the government satisfied them with warlike gestures: on 17 October the Toulon squadron was mobilised. Britain responded by reinforcing its Mediterranean fleet and the Admiralty prepared war plans, which included the bombardment of French and Algerian ports and seaborne attacks on France's West African colonies.[18]

The political temperature in France cooled. Contemporary headlines explained why: throughout the autumn of 1898 the lead story was the unfolding of the Dreyfus scandal, with Fashoda relegated to second place. Four years before, Captain Dreyfus had been found guilty of espionage and sentenced to solitary confinement on Devil's Island. Now France was in ferment over whether or not to reopen his case: the Left alleged, rightly as it turned out, that he had been framed, while the Right, the army and the Catholics wanted the verdict to stand in order to safeguard the honour and prestige of the army. Tensions gave way to violence; there were riots in Paris in September, and wild rumours of an imminent military coup.

France was in no condition to fight Britain, whose preponderance of sea power meant that she could deliver devastating blows against French colonies, and France had few options for retaliation. Furthermore, the French people were convulsed by a corrosive moral and political crisis that was intensifying and had several years to run. One often over-looked consequence of the Dreyfus affair was that it kept France out of a global war, which she would have lost. Early in November the French Cabinet officially recalled Marchand and so effectively cancelled any claims to the Upper Nile. A diplomatic settlement followed which left Britain master of Egypt *and* the Sudan.

The Fashoda incident and its aftermath had a threefold significance. Imperial rivalries in Africa had not, as anti-imperialists had predicted, led to a European war. Conventional diplomacy had triumphed over populist passions. Yet competition for colonies clearly had the power to inflame nationalists, of which more later. Fashoda also proved that Britain's preponderance of sea power gave it an advantage in any row over colonies: quite simply it could ship armies overseas and isolate the colonies of any rival. This was why during the 1880s and 1890s France, Italy and Germany were laying down more and more warships and Britain was endeavouring to keep ahead of them.

IV

Most significant of all, perhaps, Fashoda was a demonstration of how easy it was for imperial zealots to become intoxicated by their visions. Like Rhodes, Marchand and his sponsors imagined that, through sheer will and audacity and the assistance of a handful of soldiers, they could make themselves masters of vast areas. Grandiose visions clouded judgements, beguiled and sometimes drove their creators to the point of lunacy. 'We have behaved like madmen in Africa . . . led astray by irresponsible people called colonists' concluded the President of France, Félix Faure, after the Fashoda dispute had been settled.[19]

Faure was covering his tracks, for he had once favoured the projects of these 'madmen'. Other political leaders in other countries were will-ing to suppress reasoned judgements and lend a helping hand because they (and many voters) imagined that owning large tracts of Africa would somehow enrich their country and advance civilisation. Rhodes, Goldie, Peters and sundry French soldier–administrators were also able to tap a vein of popular nationalism which was bullish, competitive and obsessed with prestige. Heady notions of national 'destiny' and appeals to the Darwinian concept of the struggle for survival also helped make the imperial package plausible and attractive.

Imperialism had become part of the zeitgeist of the age. It was both a force of history and a national duty. In 1870 John Ruskin had told Oxford undergraduates: 'There is a destiny now possible to us, the highest ever set before a nation to be accepted or refused.' If she side-stepped this choice, Britain would 'perish; if she took up the challenge, annexed lands, and sent out colonists, then her power would grow'. Rhodes was inspired by Ruskin's appeal. His message was repeated in German, French and Italian and won many converts.

Particularly flattering (and enticing) were the underlying notions of national moral superiority and that historic providence favoured certain nations. On the eve of the Italian invasion of Libya in 1911, memories of the grandeur of the Roman Empire were invoked. 'We are returning,' declared the ultra-nationalist and future proto-Fascist poet Gabriele D'Annunzio. Voices like this added to the popular clamour for the partition of Africa and, for a time, proved irresistible

V

Any consideration of the partition of Africa must end with the question: could events have followed a different course? And, more importantly, what would have been the consequences for Africa? Any counter-factual history of the continent would have to acknowledge the fact that on the eve of partition, Africa was already the host to myriad local scrambles. The Mahdist empire was extending itself southwards, and small slaving polities in West, East and Central Africa were fighting minor wars of expansion. Would Egypt's projected East African empire have grown and collided with the expanding Zanzibari polity somewhere in Uganda? How far would the Transvaal and Orange Free State have extended their boundaries northwards into Bechuanaland and the Ndebele kingdom?

All the protagonists in these power struggles were desperate to obtain modern, European weaponry. In 1888 King Lobengula of Ndebele demanded 1,000 Martini rifles (the ones that had defeated the Zulus less than ten years before) and a gunboat on the Zambezi as the price for cooperation with Rhodes. A year later in East Africa, German *Schutztruppen* (colonial troops) found themselves fighting with the forces of a slaving chief who were armed with the same rifles that they were using. Two artillery pieces and a machine-gun defended the fort of Chief Nana of the Brassmen on the Benue in 1894.[20] Over 100,000 rifles were confiscated by the French authorities in Dahomey between 1909 and 1915, most presumably imported by its kings during earlier wars of resistance.[21]

The African arms race predated partition. Had it not occurred, there is every reason to believe that African rulers would have continued to fill their armouries with the latest rifles, machine-guns and artillery. Nana's machine-gun was a pointer towards a future of internal African wars of conquest waged more efficiently. Partition effectively ended Africa's regional struggles for local dominance. If it had not, Africa's subsequent history might have followed the pattern of Europe's in the Dark and Early Middle Ages, with intermittent regional wars for political supremacy and consolidation.

9

'It'll all be pink soon':
The Struggle for Southern Africa 1882–1914

I

The partition of southern Africa was a one-sided affair. Britain wrote the rules, set the pace, and so secured for itself a preponderance of power from the Cape to the Upper Zambezi. Successive Liberal and Tory ministries made it clear that they were prepared to go to any lengths, even war, if Britain was prevented from getting its way. In 1894 the Foreign Secretary warned the German Chancellor that Britain would not 'recoil from war' if her supremacy in southern Africa was challenged. As he explained, the region was 'perhaps the most vital interest of Great Britain because by the possession of it communication with India was assured'.[1] This had, of course, been the reason why Britain had first occupied the Cape eighty years before.

Germany backed off sullenly, but continued to needle Britain by making mischief in the region. There was nothing else the Germans could do, for they then possessed an insignificant navy. If directly threatened, Britain could throttle Germany's seaborne trade, isolate her colonies in Africa and elsewhere, and perhaps seize them. It was the threat of such naval action that forced the French to back down after Fashoda in 1898, the year that Germany belatedly began to beef up its navy.

In the event, Britain's strongest adversaries in southern Africa were the Boers. The old power struggle between Britain and the Boers had entered a new and what turned out to be decisive phase in 1886, when a vast goldfield gave rise to Johannesburg. Suddenly the Transvaal was transformed into the richest independent state in Africa. Hitherto a tiresome irritant for Britain, Boer nationalism was now a force to be taken seriously.

The Witwatersrand goldfields triggered an economic revolution and

changed the balance of power in South Africa. The Transvaal became
a magnet for massive investment (most of it City money) and its treasury collected £4 million annually from mineral royalties. By 1895 it
had secured free access to the outside world through the railway that
ran from Johannesburg to Lourenço Marques (Maputo), where a new
harbour was under construction. The Transvaal's communications and
external commerce were no longer dependent on British-controlled
railways and ports.

Thousands of foreign fortune seekers flocked to Johannesburg. All
hoped to get rich quickly and they included flashy moneymen, mine
managers, engineers, clerks and workers in what are today called the
service industries. Alongside the new stock exchange, banks and hotels
were bars, music halls and whorehouses. The Calvinist Boers found
themselves host to a modern Babylon and treated the incomers (Uitlanders) with open disdain. Brash stock-jobbers swilling champagne
in plush hotels and swarms of rowdy drunks and prostitutes were the
price of the Transvaal's new prosperity and independence.[2]

The Transvaal could now defend itself, for among the imports un-
loaded on the docks at Lourenço Marques were artillery, machine-
guns and rifles from German and French factories. These provided
the Transvaal with a powerful arsenal to equip its 40,000 mounted
volunteers (kommandos). Ninety thousand pounds a year was allocated to the intelligence services, and some of this money was used
to subsidise parties of Boer trekkers heading northwards and eastwards into Swaziland and Bechuanaland and what was then called
Zambesia.[3]

Covert payments to land-hungry pioneers were encouraged by Paul
Kruger, the Transvaal's President.[4] Born in 1825, he was a veteran of the
great treks earlier in the century, and had come to embody the dogged
resilience of his people. Kruger was a curmudgeon who read nothing
but the Bible and lived the Spartan life of a veld farmer. He sat on his
verandah and, between draughts of black coffee and puffs on his pipe,
he dreamed of a greater Afrikanerdom stretching across a South Africa
free of British influence. An enriched Transvaal would unite the Boers
of the Cape and Natal (where they were outnumbered by settlers of
British stock) and the Orange Free State.

II

Kruger's vision of a greater Afrikanerdom was Rhodes's nightmare. As we have seen in the last chapter, he had dedicated himself to the fulfilment of his dream of Britain's historic global destiny. British sovereignty would be extended from the Cape to the borders of the Congo Free State, and in time the newly acquired lands would be settled by British immigrants. The wretched poor of Britain's industrial slums would discover health, prosperity and happiness. A domestic class war would be averted and the Anglo-Saxon race would dominate South Africa as it did North America and Australasia.

Rhodes was instinctively acquisitive: during the 1884 expedition into Bechuanaland he shared a tent and a blanket with Edmund Allenby, and the future Field Marshal noted that every morning he awoke cold, for Rhodes had somehow managed to secure all the blanket for himself. Edmund Maund, who worked closely with Rhodes, found him mercurial and noted that his manner in Africa was 'brusque', but in London he was accommodating and affable.[5] Charm worked in Westminster and Whitehall, but it was money that worked political miracles both in Britain and the Cape. Rhodes had plenty of it and, while never averse to employing force to get his way, cash placed in the right hands was his preferred method of proceeding. Whenever the going got rough or he needed allies, Rhodes sold some shares.[6] His wealth helped him construct a political base in Cape Colony through an alliance between capitalists and the predominantly farming Boer community. He assured them that Britain would always respect their interests and culture and, with Afrikaner backing, he served as Prime Minister between 1890 and January 1896.

Boer goodwill and cooperation would cement a South African federation under the British Crown. Thanks to the Transvaal's new affluence, an alternative now existed: a greater Afrikaner state in which the Boers and their values would be supreme.

Before the Boers could be enticed (or bullied) into a British South Africa, their expansionist ambitions had to be checked. Rhodes's first objective was to get geography on his side by blocking Boer expansion towards the borders of German South West Africa and northwards into the vast and yet unclaimed uplands of Zambesia. This was why he was roughing it in Bechuanaland in 1884. Rhodes had encouraged the British government to approve a protectorate over the region, an easy task since the Foreign Office was apprehensive about a future axis between Germany and the Transvaal.[7] Voices in favour of benevolent imperial rule were raised from the missionaries and their friends in Britain, who feared that the Boers would reduce the native population to helotry. The region was duly annexed in 1885 and its essentially benign administration shared between the Foreign and Colonial Offices.

Once Bechuanaland was in the bag, Rhodes was free to begin the penetration of King Lobengula's Ndebele state, known as Matabeleland. It was a strong kingdom that was enlarging itself, and in an emergency Lobengula could mobilise an army of between 15,000 and 20,000 warriors.[8] Like the Zulus, the Ndebele were a nation in arms. Nonetheless, during the 1880s the king was increasingly disturbed about his state's porous southern frontier, which was being encroached upon by Boer trekkers and Portuguese filibusters. Lobengula's anxieties turned him towards some kind of attachment to Britain. In 1888 he appealed to Queen Victoria for help against the Portuguese.

The response was heartening. Lord Salisbury backed Lobengula, threatened Portugal with the naval big stick (two battleships anchored off the mouth of the Tagus) and the Portuguese backed off.[9] France and Germany offered their impotent sympathy and the imperialist press crowed in triumph. Portugal was 'the very worst white government in the world', declared the *Spectator*.[10]

It was against this background that Lobengula agreed to what he imagined to be a commercial treaty with Cecil Rhodes in 1888. The king was promised an annuity, delivery of 1,000 Martini rifles and a well-armed gunboat on the Zambezi to keep the Portuguese at bay.* In return, Lobengula offered mineral rights to prospectors licensed by the yet to be formed British South Africa Company (BSAC). Rhodes was now adopting the corporate imperialism that was being exploited so profitably by the Royal Niger Company.

Rhodes hurried to London, where he persuaded Salisbury's government to agree to the formation of his chartered company. Cash doled out to the funds of the Conservative, Liberal and Irish Home Rule parties assured that the requisite legislation passed through Parliament without a hitch. The British government was a sleeping partner in this

---

* The guns and the warship never materialised.

enterprise but, as Rhodes was always uncomfortably aware, it retained the right to revoke the charter if the company abused its powers or mistreated the natives. Nonetheless, he was confident that his enterprise would succeed, insisting that 'Britain must do it . . . as a duty to civilisation.'[11]

Civilisation would penetrate Matabeleland without bloodshed, or so Rhodes hoped. In 1889 he declared that 'A company with only a million capital and limited working capital cannot, must not, shall not begin operations by the folly of a native war. It must be by Brick and Shovel and gold prospecting.'[12] Nevertheless, the company's column of 200 pioneers and mounted police escort arrived at Lobengula's capital, Bulawayo, with war rockets and machine-guns. It also possessed a searchlight powered by a portable generator that deeply impressed the Ndebele. Nearly eighty years later one recalled the awesome magic which drove away the darkness.[13]

Economic growth in what, by 1893, was already being called Rhodesia was fitful and discouraging. The diggings yielded a mere trickle of gold, although Bulawayo's blacks looked forward to earning wages without having to trudge to the Kimberley diamond mines.[14] They were disappointed, for there was no instant bonanza, but output gradually picked up; and by 1914 Rhodesian gold exports averaged just under £1 million a year. Further prospecting revealed coal, chrome and asbestos deposits.

Potential was all very well, but the money markets wanted something more concrete and by 1891 the BSAC's share price was flagging. Cash flow difficulties delayed the completion of its lifeline, the Mafeking to Bulawayo railway, and there were unsettling rumours of an impending war with the Ndebele. Official subsidies rescued the railway, and in Rhodesia Rhodes turned to diversification. In November 1891 Lobengula was persuaded to allow white settlers to farm in the areas previously allocated for gold prospectors.[15] This was a gamble, for it increased the chances of land wars between colonists and natives of the sort that had occurred in the eastern Cape and Natal. Perversely, given the risks involved, Dr Leander Starr Jameson, the company's administrator in Bulawayo, believed that a frontier war would boost share prices by proving that the company was in total control of the region.[16]

Jameson got his war. It had been customary for the Ndebele to undertake periodic plundering raids on the villages and livestock of their subjects, the Shona. During one of these excursions in the summer of 1893, Shona fugitives sought refuge in Bulawayo, which led to clashes between the pursuing impis and the company's mounted gendarmerie. The Ndebele came off worse, although they should have known what to expect. Four years previously a party of Lobengula's indunas had travelled to England to petition Queen Victoria and, among other diversions, they witnessed a demonstration of Maxim-gun fire. An onlooker reported that the sight 'made them cry out with an "Ahou" of amazement'.[17]

After the war, Rhodes asked the British government whether the company could take over the administration of the Bechuanaland protectorate from the Foreign Office. Its nominal ruler, Khama III, and his subordinate chiefs objected strongly: 'Is the great Queen not able to protect us from the Chartered Company?' they asked. They hoped so, for its intention was 'to impoverish us so that hunger may drive us to become the white man's servants who dig his mines and gather his wealth'.[18] This candid analysis was very close to the truth and its conclusions were repeated by the missionary and humanitarian lobbies, which had been shocked by reports of mass slaughter during the recent war in Rhodesia. Rhodes's request was rejected.

The short, sharp shock of the 1893 Matabele War was the prelude to a protracted conflict between July 1896 and October 1897 in which the Ndebele and Shona joined forces against the company. This uprising was a delayed reaction against the unsettling changes of the past six years by the dispossessed and frightened. Their aim was to turn the clock back by killing or expelling all Europeans. Lobengula had died early in 1894, and so the insurgents looked to leadership from spirit mediums and witch doctors, some of whom promised magical immunity against bullets.[19] As so often when a traditional social order begins to fall apart, millenarian prophets offered hope. Some predicted that once the company had been destroyed a 'new god' would appear and rule the land.[20]

By October 1897 white casualties totalled 450, which led to a merciless counter-terror. Its cruelty was justified by Frederick Selous, a big-game hunter, who wrote afterwards that the rebels were 'savages eager to spill the life-blood of every white man in Rhodesia, savages in whose vocabulary no such words as pity or mercy are to be found'.[21]

Local forces managed to get the upper hand, but British regulars from the Cape garrison were needed to clinch matters.

The war ended with the company firmly in the saddle and Rhodesia safe for immigrants. The company tempted them with rents of four shillings an acre for virgin land and offered loans for those who lacked the necessary capital to set up farms. The response was tepid: by 1914 the white population of Rhodesia stood at 23,000, the black at nearly three-quarters of a million.

One unlooked-for result of the crushing of the Ndebele and the Shona was the creation of what became the worldwide Boy Scout movement. Guerrilla resistance had been overcome by special units of scouts and some professional hunters like Selous, all skilled in the mysteries and disciplines of bushcraft and tracking. The most celebrated was Major Robert Baden-Powell, an officer distinguished by what his colleagues considered a deplorable tendency for self-advertisement. He distilled into the creed of his Scout movement the physical and moral qualities needed to stalk an African warrior which, he hoped, would promote the spirit of Christian manliness, sexual abstinence and imperial pride among the youth of Edwardian Britain. Baden-Powell dressed his Scouts in khaki and the broad-brimmed hats that had been worn by their counterparts in the Rhodesian bush.

III

Misadventures in Blunderland might be a suitable subtitle for a history of Rhodes's relations with the Boers. Having convinced the Cape Boers that he was a sympathetic friend, Rhodes plotted to make war on their brethren in the Transvaal and seize their country. During the second half of 1895 he devised a plan for a coup d'état in Johannesburg that would topple Kruger and bring the Transvaal under British rule. Operations would start with an insurrection by the Johannesburg Uitlanders, funded by Rhodes and directed by his agents. The rebels would demand political rights and be joined by a force of 600 horsemen raised and paid for by Rhodes and including many British South Africa Company policemen. Overall command was in the hands of Jameson.

The small army set off on 29 December, having heard Colonel Grey of the Bechuanaland police explain their (and Rhodes's) goal. 'I cannot tell you that you are going by the Queen's orders, but you are going to fight for the supremacy of the British flag in South Africa.'[22] Everything went wrong: Transvaal's intelligence services got wind of the plot, the Uitlanders got cold feet and stayed at home, and the column was trapped by superior Boer forces at Doornkop, where the survivors surrendered. The leaders, including Jameson, were shipped off to England, where they received six-month gaol sentences under the Foreign Enlistment Act.*

Rhodes was discredited, and henceforward a broken flush in South African politics. There were strong suspicions that he had been abetted by the High Commissioner in the Cape and even, though this has never been satisfactorily proved, the Colonial Secretary, Joseph Chamberlain. Imperialists in Britain praised the daring of Jameson and his companions. For the Poet Laureate, Alfred Austin, they were paladins on a noble quest in his poem 'Jameson's Ride':

> *There are girls in the gold-reef city,*
> *There are mothers and children too!*
> *And they cry, 'Hurry up! For pity!'*
> *So what can a brave man do?*
> *If we fail, they will howl and hiss.*
> *But there's many a man lives famous*
> *For daring a wrong like this!*

Although officially disowned, the Jameson Raid was seen in the Transvaal as proof that Britain intended to use force to crush the country's independence. By 1897 the military budget had quadrupled to £256,000 and a defensive alliance had been signed with the Orange Free State.[23] Immediately after the raid Kruger received a telegram of congratulations from the Kaiser, but British sea power ruled out any practical assistance to the Boers in the event of war.

Sir Alfred Milner, who was appointed High Commissioner in May 1897, saw himself as a 'civilian soldier of the Empire'. After a year in South Africa he confided to Chamberlain that he was pessimistic about the outcome of the 'great game between ourselves and the Transvaal'. 'I am not indeed sure', he concluded, 'that we shall be masters without a war.' Milner had been an outstanding scholar at Oxford and possessed

---

* This forbade British subjects to enlist in foreign armies; it is still in force.

a methodical, bureaucratic mind and a blend of charm and tact that, it was vainly hoped, might seduce the Boers. His approach was to use the Transvaal's Uitlanders as a Trojan horse: Britain assumed the role of their protector and insisted that Kruger granted them full political rights, including the franchise. Each side assumed that Uitlander votes would elect a government amenable to British interests.

Negotiations broke down in the autumn of 1899. A *Punch* cartoon crudely summed up Britain's reason for fighting. A group of working men are staring at a map of South Africa in a bookseller's window and one explains its colouring: 'See that pink, Bill? That's our'n. See that green? That's there'n. *It'll all be pink soon!*'[24] It took nearly three years to extend the pink portions in a conflict that has been extensively described.[25]

Generalship on both sides was indifferent. The Boers squandered their early advantages by laying siege to Ladysmith, Kimberley and Mafeking rather than using their mobile kommandos to seize strategic railway junctions and ports. This blunder gave the British time to bring in and deploy reinforcements. A growing advantage in numbers did not compensate for bone-headed commanders, and in December Britain suffered three defeats in one week. Reinforcements, including the young and largely middle-class volunteers of the Imperial Yeomanry and dominion cavalry, helped turn the tables. Small numbers of Irish, German and Russian Anglophobes joined the Boers, who received a Confederate flag sent by some Civil War veterans who shared their views on the Negro's place in the scheme of things.

The conventional war ended in February 1900 when the largest Boer field army surrendered at Paardeberg. For the next two years diehard Boers fought a ruthless guerrilla campaign in the hope of wearing down Britain's will. It was met by intensive counter-insurgency operations which included farm-burning and mass internment.

The peace signed at Vereeniging in May 1902 was the first of a series of agreements by which the Transvaal and Orange Free State passed under British rule, received self-government and, in 1910, joined with Natal and Cape Colony to create the dominion of South Africa. Boers formed the majority in the new state, which many secretly hoped would become the foundation for a future Afrikaner nation. The British congratulated themselves on their capacity to conciliate old enemies, while the new parliament in Pretoria framed laws designed to perpetuate white supremacy. Strict property qualifications excluded black voters, who were concentrated in the Cape; there were none whatsoever in the Transvaal and Orange Free State. Among the first acts of the white legislators were laws that commandeered black land. Their enforcement led to the founding in 1912 of the South African Native National Congress. It demanded political and legal rights for Africans and was later renamed the African National Congress.

Black men had been the losers in a white man's war, for the political settlement gave the vote to South Africa's million whites and a trifling number of coloureds and blacks. Yet during the war, both sides had mobilised large numbers of Africans. Over 100,000 served with the British army as spies, scouts, drivers, grooms and labourers and 10,000 as armed auxiliaries.[26] Boer kommandos were accompanied by contingents of servants who undertook camp chores. Wages soared: experienced and competent scouts and transport drivers could earn up to £5 a month, equal to a skilled craftsman's wage in Britain.

Many whites were unsettled by black participation in the war, which was officially denied during its early stages. In Natal, where the blacks outnumbered whites by ten to one, the government feared that the war would give the Negroes a 'false idea of their powers' and encourage a sense of independence. As they marched into captivity, Boer prisoners were taunted by Africans with shouts of 'Pass *baas* [boss]'. The pass was an identity card that every black had to carry and show whenever asked; for the next eighty or so years it was a symbol of subjection and a focus for protest. Black British auxiliaries captured by the Boers were automatically shot.[27]

During the negotiations that preceded the Vereeniging Treaty, Afrikaner representatives insisted that they should be allowed to keep their rifles for protection against the restive blacks. Kitchener, the commander-in-chief, agreed, and assured them that the outcome of the war would not in any way alter the principle of white paramountcy. It would hold sway until the end of the century.

10

'If you strike, strike hard':
Pacification 1885–1914

I

Once the diplomats had stopped haggling and Africa's new frontiers had been agreed, the generals took over. They were ordered to enforce partition, win over collaborators and chastise any Africans who objected. Whatever their nationality, soldiers followed the strategic principle tersely summarised by Rhodes on the eve of the 1893 Ndebele War: 'If you strike, strike hard.'[1]

What Rhodes meant by striking hard was modern total war waged with the latest and most lethal military technology. Firepower cleared the way for the new political settlement: defiant Africans faced bombardment by long-range artillery firing explosive shells, machine-guns and magazine rifles which, together, created a killing zone of over a mile in depth. Recalling this hurricane of missiles, one stunned survivor of a German assault on an East African stockade recalled the moment of terror: 'whenever I put my hand up there is a bullet'.[2] Each new contrivance of death was speedily introduced to the African battlefield; in 1912 the French and Italians deployed aircraft in Morocco and Libya, where Sanussi tribesmen were bombed. Superior weaponry kindled an overweening confidence, such as that of a young trooper who had just joined the British South Africa Company's gendarmerie, whose job it was to turn Rhodes's theory into practice. He told his parents: 'Active service won't be much of a picnic though I reckon the Maxims will make short work of the niggers.'[3]

Of course they did, but superior weaponry never compensated for blundering generals. Occasionally Africans did win battles, most spectacularly in 1896 when a 30,000-strong Italian army – over two-thirds of them Eritrean askaris (native soldiers) – was trounced by the Emperor Menelik II at Adwa. Hubris, poor intelligence and ignorance of the terrain did for the Italians, but heavy Abyssinian casualties ruled out a counter-offensive into their colony of Eritrea. On a smaller scale, Mkwana, an East African chief and slaver, encircled a German punitive column in 1891 and killed 300 *Schutztruppen*. His own losses were three times that number, but he managed to capture two machine-guns. Without ammunition, spare parts and trained gunners they were valueless. Within two years the Germans were back and he was defeated.[4] Rhodes's theory of African warfare was applied throughout the continent. Hammer blows, repeatedly struck, produced the desired result of cowed and biddable subjects. Overawed by the deadly efficiency of the European war machine and demoralised by heavy casualties, Africans submitted and collaborated.* Everywhere, piles of corpses testified to the hopelessness of further resistance, which seemed tantamount to mass suicide.

A few of the defeated did actually choose suicide as an alternative to subjection. In East Africa, large numbers of Hutu took their own lives rather than continue resisting the Germans.[5] After his defeat at Omdurman, the Khalifa Abdullahi fled with nearly 10,000 of his followers (two-thirds of them women and children) and planned a counter-attack on Khartoum. His forces were cornered at Um Debreikat in November 1899 and crushed by an Anglo-Egyptian force. As his army dissolved, he gathered his closest followers together, knelt in prayer and waited until they were shot to pieces in what was a public suicide. Six hundred dervishes died with him; British losses were four dead.[6]

The ability to unleash total war was an essential ingredient for upholding that crucial element in imperial rule: prestige. Africans, it was imagined, respected the iron fist and treated hesitancy or forbearance as evidence of a faltering will. This was the lesson the British had learned in India and the French in Algeria. Ideally, submission had always to be total, although there were many occasions when more than one hard knock was needed to secure it. There were over 300 punitive operations in German East Africa between 1889 and 1903, and it required two campaigns in 1895 and 1900 to bring the Asante of the Gold Coast finally to heel.

---

* In the 1950s, British district officers undertaking tours of duty in remote northern Kenya were under orders to give warning demonstrations of machine-gun fire by using it to cut down trees. (I owe this reference to the late Kay McIver.)

II

It was easy to find pretexts for the minor wars of coercion and retribution that proliferated across Africa between 1885 and 1914. New
regimes brought with them unwelcome and sometimes intolerable
rules. Slave-trading and slavery were outlawed, and the rulers of the
slaving polities in East, Central and West Africa and their Arab accomplices fought desperately to defend their profits. Africa was well
rid of them and their victims welcomed their overthrow. In Baghirimi
(Chad) there was heartfelt rejoicing when the brutal, slaving warlord
Rabah Zubayr was defeated by the French, captured and executed at
Fort-Lamy (N'Djamena) in 1900.[7]

The commonest cause of wars was the belated discovery by chiefs
that the concessions made in treaties coaxed out of them by the likes
of Peters and Rhodes went far beyond what they had intended. Wars
to recover relinquished autonomy were treated as rebellions by treacherous rulers. Another frequent cause of insurrection was the imposition of hut and poll taxes, novelties that were universally detested. At
home, these small wars were celebrated as the victories of civilisation
over barbarism. In 1891 *Le Petit Journal* vilified the Tokolors of Upper
Senegal as a breed of voracious parasites who lived 'solely from wars
and the captives of slave trades. They neglect herding and agriculture,
and feed themselves by extortion, the ransoming of caravans and the
selling of slaves.'[8] The German conquest of Cameroon, as described in
a popular contemporary adventure story, *Kamerun*, was a struggle between civilisation and the Duala, who were 'the worst savages known
to this globe'.

Such creatures exempted themselves from any humane considerations. African armies were torn apart by shells and bullets, the
wounded were bayoneted, villages were burned, wells were blocked,
livestock impounded and crops destroyed as a warning that resistance
was futile and led to nothing but suffering. The man on the spot knew
best, and felt free to choose any corrective he thought necessary to
crush opposition. In 1888 General Joseph Gallieni told his subordinates
to ignore instructions from Paris and go ahead with the elimination
of the Tokolor chiefs, who were stumbling blocks to French rule and,
it went without saying, civilisation.[9] The nomadic tribes who lived by
rustling and raids against their neighbours on the eastern marches of

Chad were officially characterised as 'congenital brigands' in 1909. This was a licence to kill their menfolk, occupy or destroy their oases and kidnap their wives and children.[10]

Extreme severity was justified by each colonial power as a lamentable necessity imposed on the civilisers by the obstinacy of the purblind who clung to the archaic African order. Once it had been swept away or reformed in accordance with European values, then Africans would find tranquillity and opportunities for enlightenment and prosperity. This was the message of the imagery on the obverse of the campaign medal awarded to British soldiers engaged in the pacification of Africa between 1900 and 1914. It showed a serene Britannia holding aloft a laurel garland against the background of a rising sun.

III

Each campaign in Africa, however small, was a magnet for ambitious young officers keen to make a name for themselves and pocket generous campaign allowances. A quarter of the German officers who served in East Africa were allowed to add a talismanic 'von' to their surnames, which officially distinguished them as gentlemen, and all got higher pay.[11] Kitchener and Lugard got peerages for their African exertions, and French veterans of African campaigns like Gallieni and Charles Joffre (who captured Timbuktu in 1893) rose to occupy senior commands in the First World War.

Young, enthusiastic and daring officers keen for a scrap were not the invention of writers of British schoolboy fiction; they were everywhere in Africa. Typical was Lieutenant 'Bobo' Jelfs, an Old Etonian, who found himself besieged in Ladysmith in 1899. Are we 'rotters' or 'heroes', he asked his mother in a letter, adding that he was convinced that 'we have played the game' by keeping the Boers occupied.[12] The games fetishism of Victorian public schools produced a breed of fellows who would man outposts or lead columns into the bush with the same jaunty spirit as they faced leg-breaks or tackled a beefy front-row forward.

These swashbucklers were as addicted to sport as they were to war, and were glad whenever the two could be combined. The result was a ghastly incident during the 1893 Ndebele War when several sport-crazed officers treated one skirmish as a big-game hunt, afterwards each adding up his 'bag' of dead tribesmen. One athletic warrior briefly dodged the fire of four machine-guns and was applauded when he finally fell. An attempt to photograph the corpse of 'so plucky a fellow' failed, depriving his killers of the big-game hunter's object of desire, a trophy.[13] Cries of 'Tally Ho' echoed across the veld as Imperial Yeomanry troopers of the Northumberland Hussars set off in pursuit of Boer partisans in 1900. One huntsman in khaki remembered the 'splendid exhilaration of the charge or the chase with "Brother Boer" as the quarry'.[14]

It was perhaps natural for Africans for whom hunting was an economic necessity to admire sporting officers who stalked big game and were masters of bushcraft. The skills of Nimrod coupled with personal fearlessness won respect and enhanced an officer's standing. British, German and French officers all imagined that they possessed those inner qualities of character that won the adulation and confidence of black soldiers.

Europe's black armies were recruited from what were officially judged to be the most warlike tribes, whose genes and upbringing made them natural soldiers. Colonel Charles Mangin, a veteran of campaigns in West Africa, claimed that 'warrior instincts' remained 'extremely powerful in primitive races', whose peculiar nervous systems made them 'resistant to pain'.[15] Raw, atavistic impulses, tempered by strict discipline, would transform the African recruit into as hardy and brave a soldier as any European. He was conditioned to obey orders instantly through drill, which also taught him the complex manoeuvres that were vital for the most efficient application of firepower.

European officers were proud of their ability to bond with the African soldier. Many talked themselves into believing that they possessed a profound insight into his psyche, which was usually assumed to be wild, childlike and fickle, yet capable of intense loyalty. It was axiomatic that an African recruit with a warrior tradition fought well if treated with a paternal firmness exercised with a blend of astringency and fairness. He also adored and followed officers who showed outstanding bravery. French and Spanish officers who commanded Muslim troops in North Africa prided themselves on possession of the mystic quality of *barraka*, a rare divine favour that spared the lives of the audacious. After seeing him risk death on the battlefield, Moroccan infantrymen imagined that the young Francisco Franco, who served there between 1912 and 1917, was blessed with *barraka*.

With or without supernatural advantages, European officers were expected always to show a benevolent consideration for the welfare of the men they commanded. It was absent in Colonel Burroughs of the Sierra Leone Regiment, whose neglect and callousness provoked a mutiny and mass desertion in 1901. 'He punish too much and flog plenty', complained one soldier. Burroughs's superiors in the War Office agreed, judged him 'unfit to command' and sacked him.[16] The spiritual brotherhood of black *Schutztruppen* and their German officers was vividly expressed in a marching song of the 1890s. 'Here we are marching side by side in the darkness of the night . . . brother and brother slaying beast and foes alike. Officers, askaris, and porters marching all together as one.' According to one of their officers, these soldiers were men reborn as 'Germanised blacks' after having been 'de-ethnicised and de-Arabised'.[17] The Sudanese mercenaries, who made up a fifth of the East Africa *Schutztruppen*, had found a new homeland. Their sons and those of locally recruited askaris were given early training in military kindergarten so that, in time, they would follow their fathers into the army.

France was generous to its black soldiers. Senegalese *tirailleurs* were paid fifteen francs a month and were allowed to have up to four *épouses libres* who accompanied them on campaign and whom they were free to sell if they wished. 'Wives' were also commandeered on campaign. After their discharge veterans received pensions and were exempt from taxes and forced labour, and former NCOs were appointed as trustworthy village headmen.[18] In Nigeria, the neighbours of the Hausa treated them with suspicion because they were the backbone of the colonial army and police.[19]

War was creating a new elite in Africa. Of course, the soldier had always been a man who was respected (and feared) in native communities, and this tradition was turned to advantage by the new regimes. All were hastily assembling armies and gendarmeries, and shrewd and ambitious Africans recognised the benefits that flowed from active collaboration. Local power could be turned to personal profit. Bullying and extortion were applied by native troops serving as tax collectors in Cameroon in 1901. A missionary vainly protested that 'injustice was done' and 'cruelties committed'.[20]

Hausa troops and local levies plundered and fired the town of Satiru after crushing a Mahdist uprising in Northern Nigeria in 1906, killing anyone who got in their way.[21] Operational necessity compelled white officers to overlook such behaviour, which was also common among white troops. African villages provided the Connaught Rangers with 'pigs, potatoes, chickens and raw hides which we used as blankets' as they marched towards the Tugela River in 1900. Boer farms produced better pickings and officers turned a blind eye or, on occasion, joined in.[22]

African muscle powered the machinery of conquest in those malarial regions that were fatal for mules and oxen. On average, each fighting man required one or two porters to carry his food and ammunition, and, in turn, their own thin rations. Tests proved that one sturdy porter could carry forty pounds on his head, which represented 250 rounds of ammunition, and two porters could bear the mounting and barrel of a Maxim gun.

Native labourers laid railway tracks in the Sudan and South Africa and undertook the myriad heavy chores of base camps. They and the porters were paid for their drudgery but when demand outstripped supply, as it so often did, wages soared. During the Boer War, British army rates of pay were higher than those in the goldfields, which led to an exodus of black miners. Desertion was a constant nuisance, which was why, whenever possible, logistics officers imported men from distant areas who could not slip away easily to their homes.

Forced labour was frequently employed. Egyptians convicted of crimes during the Alexandrian riots were shipped to Sawakin in 1885 to unload ships. It was grinding work in oppressive heat, and one labourer tried to murder a British officer so as to get himself hanged. Discipline was harshly enforced with the whip: during the Boer War insubordinate labourers were given twelve lashes.[23] Women were corralled into loading camels during campaigns in Somaliland, for local custom exempted men from such menial work. Their husbands received their wages, again in keeping with local practice.[24]

In non-malarial zones, pack animals bore the brunt of carrying provender, equipment, ammunition and their own fodder. They were fed, watered and tended by locally recruited camel drivers and muleteers. Wastage rates were always shockingly high: during operations on the southern border of Algeria in 1900, nearly all the 35,000 camels commandeered by the French died from exhaustion. Over 400,000 horses, mules and donkeys were casualties of the Boer War.[25] Many had been carried by sea from Australia and the United States.

IV

Big armies stiffened with contingents of white troops were needed to defeat the larger and better-armed African states. France deployed 12,000 men in Dahomey during the 1890s, 18,000 against the Merina kingdom of Madagascar between 1894 and 1905, and more than 20,000 to impose a protectorate over Morocco in 1912. Italy fielded a force of 30,000 for its Abyssinian misadventure in 1896, and 35,000 for its invasion of Libya in 1911. Kitchener, who always erred on the side of safety, needed 15,000 British, Indian, Egyptian and Sudanese troops to reconquer the Sudan.

By far the largest concentration of white troops in Africa assembled in South Africa between 1899 and 1902. Four hundred and forty-five thousand British, Australian, New Zealand and Canadian soldiers and a substantial contingent of Boer turncoats were needed to subdue the Transvaal and Orange Free State and suppress a subsequent guerrilla insurgency.

The dominion contingents were volunteers, as were the Imperial Yeomanry, enthusiastic young horsemen and patriots who were raised in 1899. They were asked to sign a book on arrival at Cape Town and again on departure: one gave his reason for joining up as 'patriotic fever' and his reason for leaving as 'enteric fever'.[26] Death rates from disease among white soldiers fell during the last decade of the nineteenth century thanks to advances in preventive medicine. French troops in West Africa were ordered to drink only filtered water and were vaccinated against smallpox after an epidemic in Dahomey in 1892.[27] Oddly, vaccination was voluntary for British forces ordered to South Africa, where contaminated water produced widespread outbreaks of typhoid and enteric fevers.

The conquest of Africa continued well after 1914 with large-scale French and Spanish operations in Morocco in the early 1920s and the Italian invasion of Abyssinia in 1935. These and the earlier wars of conquest and pacification gave the European powers what they wanted: secure colonies with obedient populations. They also confirmed what earlier generations of Africans had already surmised – that political power came from the barrel of a gun.

11

'White savages':
Hearts of Darkness

━━━

|

During operations against 'the man-eating Maka tribe' of Came-roon, Carl Koch contemplated a prisoner. 'In his eyes I saw the great animal that was suppressed in us and had now taken possession of me.' Over twenty years later, Koch rose to prominence in the Nazi SA. A brother-in-arms of the future storm trooper also underwent the same battlefield metamorphosis, which he recalled in detail. 'First it creeps up slowly to the heart, then faster to the brain, this feeling of the beast, a bloodthirsty beast, greedy for murder.' He was in the grip of 'a magnetic force' that drew on the warrior. 'Each man has only one thought: "kill!".'[1]

On one level, these confessions are unsurprising. Discovering and unleashing the inner feral man has been a constant in war: Shake-speare's Henry V calls on his soldiers at Harfleur to be reborn as tigers, taking on 'a terrible aspect'. On another level the experience of the two German officers was deeply disturbing, for they pointed to what con-temporaries feared was an insidious phenomenon of African warfare. Did its circumstances and the perceived 'savage' nature of the adversary have the power to unhinge the European mind?

A series of appalling events in the Congo, French West Africa and German South-West and East Africa strongly suggested that this was so. In each region there were striking instances of Europeans becoming infected with a mental cancer that consumed their moral sensibilities in the same way that Africa's heat and fevers sapped their physical strength. The British were not immune. During the final phase of the Boer War there was a series of minor atrocities, one of which resulted in the execution of two Australian officers for what we now call war crimes. There was also a non-clinical explanation for the atrocities that marked the partition of Africa. By common agreement, the participating powers treated the continent as an exception to the laws of war that applied, in theory if not always in practice, in Europe.

From the start, it is important to remember that all the atrocities of African warfare were committed in full public view. They were reported in the press and scrutinised and debated in Parliament, the French and Belgian Assemblies and the Reichstag. In each country justifications were offered based on operational necessity which itself was driven by a higher motive, the extension of civilisation. Or, put another way, those who were killed had died because they had wilfully rejected progress.

II

The most notorious and devastating of these atrocities occurred in the Congo Free State between the first exploitation of rubber in 1891 and the beginning of direct Belgian rule in 1908. The region was overwhelmed by a sequence of interrelated catastrophes. Long-drawn-out counter-insurgency campaigns were marked by massacres and the destruction of villages and crops, which created artificial famines. Hunger both killed people and reduced resistance to disease, which accelerated epidemics of smallpox and sleeping sickness. Above all, there were the deaths that were the consequence of that predatory capitalism which was the driving force in King Leopold's private state. Directly or indirectly it killed well over a million of his black subjects – some estimates suggest a total of 10 million.

Leopold ruled without a moral compass. All that mattered to him were steady and rising profits. His servants responded to his demands, and did all in their power to accomplish them, even if this involved the vilest cruelty. The attitude of the white managers of trading stations was transmitted downwards to the native gendarmes of the Force Publique and the collaborators who supervised the collection of rubber, the chief source of the colony's income. They cut off the hands and feet of labourers who returned from the forest with less than the quota of eight kilos of sap a fortnight. Such brutality was integral to an economy that rested solely on forced labour, which required constant terror.[2]

In a world of perpetual violence, the will to live often withered. In 1894 a Swedish missionary translated a native song, which expressed the death wish of the exploited:

We are tired of living under this tyranny,
We cannot endure that our women and children are taken away
And dealt with by white savages.
We shall make war . . .
We know that we shall die, but we want to die.[3]

Unsurprisingly, women refused to have children, a phenomenon that also occurred on the American slave plantations. There was no law. One employee of the Congo Free State who murdered a native boasted: 'I don't give a damn. The judges are white men like me.'[4]

Absolute power rested in the hands of men like Mr Kurtz, who managed the Central Station in Joseph Conrad's *Heart of Darkness*, published in 1899. He was a respected and admired servant of King Leopold, once but no longer convinced of 'the goodness of imperialism', although the spread of civilisation was 'only possible if the white man plays the part of God'. With this in mind, the cultivated Kurtz had written a pamphlet on the civilising of the natives, at the end of which he had scribbled in despair: 'Exterminate the brutes.' When the narrator Marlow, a steamboat captain, finds him, Kurtz is in a terminal decline into insanity. 'His soul was mad', deranged by isolation in a wilderness and by his duties which, like those of his colleagues and subordinates throughout the Congo, were 'to squeeze' its people. Heads spiked on poles surround Kurtz's compound.

When Conrad wrote, the world was becoming aware of the monstrous nature of Leopold's regime. It was exposed by the reports of missionaries, the black American lawyer George Washington Williams and the English reformer Edmund Morel who, as a clerk employed by the Elder Dempster shipping line, had been an eyewitness to some of the horrors. They were also recorded in forensic detail by Sir Roger Casement, the future Irish nationalist, who was appointed as British Consul to the Congo in 1901. His findings provided ammunition for the British Congo Reform Association, which under Morel's direction urged the government to put pressure on Leopold. Its members were the grandsons and granddaughters of those predominantly middle-class humanitarians who had provided the political muscle for the anti-slavery movement a century before.

Leopold countered the growing international protests with a public relations offensive. His propagandists produced a documentary film in

1897 which showed a peaceful, happy colony and, in the same year, set up the Universal Exhibition at Tervuren, south-east of Brussels.* Here, over a million visitors saw the contrived façade of a great enterprise, humanely administered and poised for future prosperity. A mock Congolese village with over 250 inhabitants of all races, huts and livestock attracted the greatest attention. Visitors threw sweets at the natives, which made them sick, and notices were put up to the effect that the natives were fed by the exhibition's organisers.[5]

A human zoo and other public relations stunts failed to dampen or deflect international criticism of the Congo regime. In Belgium, the Catholic Conservatives and the Left combined to censure the king; in 1900 a Socialist deputy declared to the Assembly that 'The cause of the blacks is your cause . . . not only because you are men but because you are workers.'[6] Slowly and with great reluctance, Leopold buckled under the pressure and in 1908 agreed to transfer ownership of the colony to the Belgian government. He had made 47.5 million francs from the region, some of which he squandered on his mistresses and royal palaces crammed with kitsch decorations and furnishings.[7] He never showed even an inkling of shame for his actions.

III

Like the Congo, German South-West Africa was a commercial venture, but with a European administrative and legal system under the control of Berlin. When the region was first annexed in 1884, German imperialists hoped that it would soon be filled with immigrants who would grow food for the Fatherland and enhance national pride. 'Where the German flag flies there are our hearts', proclaimed the *Kölnische Zeitung* on hearing the news of the first occupation of South-West Africa. German emigrants would follow their flag. Wilhelm II, who became Kaiser in 1888, declared: 'I have seventy millions of people . . . and we shall have to have room for them.' This did not happen: in 1896 the colony had a mere 2,000 German settlers. The total slowly rose to 14,000 by 1914, which was to be expected, since the initial cost of setting up a cattle ranch was at least 20,000 marks (£2,000).

* The site was used for Leopold's Royal Museum for Central Africa, which still exists; Tervuren is twinned with Dachau.

A submissive native labour force was vital for the colony to flour-ish and attract outside investment. Assimilation into a new economic system required a new attitude to the resources of the country, as the Governor, Theodor von Leutwein, explained to a gathering of Herero chiefs: 'An ox that dies of old age has missed its vocation', which was to be harnessed, sold or eaten.[8] Von Leutwein hoped that gentle persuasion would pacify the natives and prepare them for their new roles as helots serving capitalist agriculture. The settlers preferred the iron fist and condemned von Leutwein's policy as 'wishy-washy humanitarianism'.

Whatever approach the Governor took towards the natives, a clash was unavoidable. They regarded the colonists as interlopers, chafed against new laws which compelled them to surrender their firearms and cease cattle-rustling, and resented demands for forced labour. There was also a mystical sense of attachment to the land: Hendrik Witbooi, the senior Nama chief, argued that Damaraland belonged to his people and that he was the ruler of an independent state under God just like the monarchies of Europe. One Herero asked a German trader where his father had been buried, and was told in Germany. 'Then that is your home', the native riposted.[9]

These were the ideological roots of the Herero insurrection of Janu-ary 1904. It was a nihilistic explosion of rage that began with attacks on the farms of settlers who, with their wives and children, were slaugh-tered. In some instances the killers were the farmer's domestic servants and labourers, which helped to generate the wave of fear, loathing and panic that swept across the German community.

The local commander and subsequent Governor, General Lothar von Trotha, adopted the techniques he had learned during the suppres-sion of the 1900 Boxer Rising in China and campaigns in East Africa. He summed up his strategy as the imposition of 'sheer terror and cru-elty'; he proclaimed the rebels had forfeited their German citizenship and would be annihilated.[10]

Von Trotha kept his word. After defeating the insurgents at Wartburg in August, he ordered the summary execution of all male prisoners, while the remaining Herero men, their wives and children were driven into the desert where they died from thirst, starvation and attacks by wild animals. The same punishment fell on the Nama, who had first sided with the Germans but then joined Hereros. In all, between 60,000 and 70,000 died. Those who escaped death in the desert were herded into a camp on Shark Island where a regime of maltreatment and forced labour led to an average death rate of 200 a month.

In Germany, early praise for von Trotha's resolve turned to dismay as reports of the near-extermination of the Hereros became public. The Kaiser had misgivings on humanitarian grounds and urged clemency towards insurgents who had surrendered. The Chancellor, Bernhard von Bülow, denounced von Trotha's measures as counter to 'the principles of humanity and Christianity'. They would also, he added, 'demolish Germany's reputation among the civilised nations and feed foreign agitation against us'.[11] German Social Democrats took up the cudgels on behalf of what one of their newspapers called 'our coloured workman' in South-West Africa. Their near-extinction by von Trotha also alarmed the colonists, whose fears of a labour shortage prompted demands for an end to the killings.

From the start until the war's official termination in 1908, von Trotha and apologists had imagined that they were waging a 'race war' in which the survival of the Germans was at stake. An insight into its nature and the mindset of those who fought it surfaced in two popular novels that appeared soon after the uprising. In *Peter Moor's Journey to Southwest Africa* (1906), the hero considers the treatment of the natives: 'They are not our brothers, but our servants, whom we should treat humanely but sternly!' This relationship might change in the future once they had learned how to dig wells, grow crops and build houses and so qualify themselves to be treated as brothers. A *Schutztruppe* officer dismisses this as naive sentimentality:

> These blacks have deserved their death before God and man, not because they have murdered two-hundred farmers and have rebelled against us, but because they didn't build houses, and didn't dig wells. The world belongs to those who are superior, those who are alert. That is God's justice.[12]

This was also the message of a contemporary boys' adventure yarn, *Muhérero rikárera* (Watch out! Herero!), in which the rebellion is treated as a Darwinian racial conflict. 'God allowed us to triumph here because we are the more noble and progressive . . . the world belongs to the most vigorous, the most alert.'[13] Both novels were bestsellers and remained in print well into the Nazi era.

A sense of racial superiority had been quickly implanted into the settler consciousness. Mixed marriages were frowned on in the early days of the colony and were banned in 1905. One opponent called them 'a slap in the face to German pride', while another alleged that they would defile 'the purity of the German race'.[14] The authority of the master race was absolute: one farmer pleaded to a court that he had the legal right to flog a pregnant servant.

Local racial assumptions and von Trotha's attempt to exterminate the Hereros have been historically connected with Hitler's genocidal war against Europe's Jews. The links are tenuous. Both were premeditated, but the circumstances and objectives were different. Von Trotha's massacres were a response to an emergency, and dictated by panic and rage and a wish to end the war quickly and decisively. The slaughter of the Jews had its roots in Hitler's crackpot racial fantasies, and was carefully planned and undertaken in a slow, methodical manner. It had no strategic value and no impact on the outcome of the Second World War.

The most telling connection between the Herero campaign and Nazi racial policies was the common premise that there was an absolute hierarchy of races. An assumed inferiority stripped the African (and the Jew) of his humanity and right to exist. 'Haven't you shot a negro yet?' Carl Peters asked a new arrival in East Africa.[15] There were abundant opportunities in the late 1880s when he and his colleagues were endeavouring to establish plantations for the Deutsch-Ostafrikanische Gesellschaft. The underfunded and mismanaged company was soon in difficulties and resorted to forced labour and terror like its counterpart in the Congo.

Overall direction was in the hands of Peters, who was becoming increasingly deranged. He saw himself as the Napoleon of Africa, fulfilling a personal and national destiny that would transform East Africa into Germany's India and raise his fame as a national hero. At the same time Peters behaved as if he were an African despot, a chief with powers of life and death over his subjects and beyond any moral or legal constraint. A gallows erected outside his compound symbolised his power.

In 1894 one of Peters's subjects had the temerity to break into his harem, sleep with one of his mistresses and steal some cigars. After he was caught, an incensed Peters announced that 'The pig will hang today!' and added, revealingly, that this was what any African chief would do. The burglar had also challenged European prestige, for in Peters's eyes 'Using the woman of *bana mkaba* deserves capital punishment.' The concubines, who fled to the village of a local chief, Malamia, were retaken and flogged in Peters's presence. One, Jagodjo, who had previously been the mistress of Malamia, absconded again and was returned by her former lover. Peters ordered her execution. He excused himself with the claim that he had been married to her by native custom, which also entitled him to order her death.[16]

Peters's sordid tyranny provoked protests from local missionaries and led to the scandal being aired in the Reichstag by a Social Democrat deputy. Peters was recalled to Berlin in 1895 and, after an investigation into his conduct, dismissed. He retired to London, where he became entangled in a hare-brained scheme to discover King Solomon's fabled African mines. Peters died in 1918 and was later reinstated as a national hero by the Nazis, who issued a postage stamp in his honour and produced a film in which he was portrayed as a decent patriot who had been disgraced by false allegations trumped up by the British.

In German eyes, perhaps Peters's worst crime had been to dishonour his country and tarnish its self-esteem. The Germans were proud to be upright, cultured, pious, inventive and industrious people, virtues that uniquely qualified them as civilisers and colonists. Peters had fitted this image perfectly: he was the son of a Lutheran minister, a graduate of Göttingen University and a patriot wedded to the idea of a greater Germany. Yet, after just over a decade in Africa, he had repudiated the virtues of his country to become a brutal, fickle and probably half-mad tyrant.

IV

The same phantoms that had subverted Peters also unbalanced the minds of two French officers, Lieutenant Julien Chanoine and Captain Paul Voulet. The former's background was military and aristocratic, while the latter came from solid, provincial bourgeois stock. Both had shown great promise in Saharan campaigns during the 1890s, where they had absorbed the principles of local warfare and the psychology of their opponents. Chanoine once remarked that 'in a Muslim land submission is made from fear' and that 'in the Soudan we live off prestige alone'. It was also crucial, he believed, to fight the enemy with his own methods.[17]

This pair applied these lessons when, in 1898, they were chosen to command one of three powerful columns with orders to penetrate the western Sahara and beyond, and teach its inhabitants that France was now their master. These missions, together with the Fashoda expedition, were part of a grand imperial gambit that had been hatched by imperialist generals and ministers in Paris. Their eventual goal was sovereignty over a vast bloc of territory stretching as far as the Nile and, if Marchand succeeded, beyond it. Success would bring France about 4 million new subjects and hazy economic benefits. Soaring imaginations were, however, constrained by limited funds, which prevented Chanoine and Voulet from receiving the machine-guns they had requested.

The pair commanded a force of nine French officers and NCOs, 600 Senegalese *tirailleurs*, 800 porters, 200 women (soldiers' wives), 100 donkeys and mules and twenty camels. The column required forty tons of water a day and rations were soon running short, which led to large-scale plundering. Nevertheless, there were heavy losses from dehydration and fatigue and, at various times, all the Europeans suffered from bouts of fever, anaemia and diarrhoea. For the officers and NCOs relief was on hand in the form of an abundant supply of alcohol, including 120 bottles of champagne and twenty of the debilitating absinthe, then much in fashion. The extended, cumbersome column set off in February 1899 and trundled eastwards through what is today southern Niger. A swathe of violence and destruction marked its passage: villages were torched, hundreds of men, women and children were flogged and murdered, and 800 women abducted. The atrocities were calculated; in April, as the corpses piled up, Voulet felt confident that now 'the locals are beginning to take us seriously'. Lieutenant Louis Péteau disagreed, protested, and was ordered home.

News of the column's brutality reached Colonel Arsène Klobb, who was in charge of a smaller unit operating nearby. He rode over to investigate and was intercepted by a detachment commanded by Voulet who shot him dead. Voulet then justified himself to his brother officers and troops in an extraordinary outburst:

Now I am an outlaw, I disavow my family, my country, I am not French any more, I am a black leader. Africa is large; I have a gun, plenty of ammunition, 600 men who are devoted to me heart and soul. We will create an empire in Africa, a strong impregnable empire that I will surround with deserted bush . . . If I were in Paris, I would be Master of France.[18]

Chanoine did not question the aims of this reincarnated Bonaparte, but the remaining officers slipped away the next day. The native troops were unnerved, uncertain of where their loyalties or future lay. The upshot was a mutiny in which Chanoine and Voulet were shot, although for years afterwards there were rumours that they had escaped and were living incognito somewhere in the desert.

By the last week of August news of the incident had reached Paris along with the testimony of the French survivors. Its arrival coincided with the closing stage of Dreyfus's retrial at Rennes, but the press found space to print official accounts of Klobb's murder. One conservative newspaper concluded that the incident had been terrible, untoward and regrettable.[19] At the same time, Péteau's home letters were published with details of massacres and what *Le Figaro* called 'actes abominables'.[20]

A beleaguered and embarrassed military establishment dismissed the incident as exceptional, and some senior officers pilloried Péteau and the officers who had abandoned the mission as disloyal and insubordinate. The army dismissed the incident as 'an isolated instance of delirium' without any significance. There were political repercussions when ultra-right-wing apologists for the army accused the Dreyfusards of using the Voulet–Chanoine scandal to discredit their opponents.[22] Chanoine's father, General Jules Chanoine, was a key witness against Dreyfus.

A lesser scandal became entangled with a greater and was soon lost from sight. What occupied the military mind was the question of whether junior officers were bound to follow their superiors' orders come what may, rather than whether France's imperial mission justified extremes of cruelty. On the whole the public, preoccupied with the high drama of the Dreyfus case, remained indifferent. Nevertheless, some on the Left drew attention to the fact that many senior officers had played an important part in the ruthless suppression of the 1871

Paris Commune in which 15,000 insurgents had been summarily shot. The Third Republic did not confine official violence to Africa.

Voulet and Chanoine and, for that matter, von Trotha were waging war in a legal vacuum. There was a consensus among the European powers that the conventions of war, in particular those concerned with the treatment of prisoners, did not extend to Africa. Moreover, diplomats and soldiers denied native polities in order to enjoy the legal status of sovereign states as understood in Europe.

V

The Boer republics of the Transvaal and the Orange Free State were an exception. During the Anglo-Boer War of 1899–1902, captured Boers were treated according to European conventions, and with much grumbling POWs were sent to camps in St Helena and Ceylon. British attitudes were revised after the summer of 1900, when the nature of the conflict changed radically. For the next two years they faced a protracted war fought by mounted guerrilla bands, sustained by rations and fodder supplied by Boer housewives who had remained on their farms.

Defeating an enterprising and elusive enemy required depriving them of sustenance, and so Kitchener, the commander-in-chief, ordered the demolition of farms, the impounding of livestock and the detention of women, children and native servants. The evictions were 'the most disgusting thing we had to do', wrote one Yeomanry trooper, and another noticed how 'even the hardest soldier turned away from the accusatory and pitiful faces of the Boer women and children'. He steeled himself to his duty, for 'it is the only way to end the war swiftly'.[22]

By January 1902, 117,000 Boer women and children and 119,000 Africans were behind barbed wire in camps where a thin diet and appalling sanitary conditions produced epidemics of intestinal sicknesses, chiefly typhoid fever. Twenty-eight thousand Boers died, 80 per cent of them children, and 14,000 Africans. They were victims of a combination of bureaucratic incompetence and medical ignorance rather than malevolence: 28,000 British soldiers also died from the same infections that killed the detainees.

Accounts of the mortality rates reached Britain and provoked an outcry with questions and protests in Parliament, mainly from radical Liberals. How was it, they asked, that Britain, which prided itself on its humanity and moral rectitude, was waging a cruel war against women and children? There were on-the-spot inspections of the 'concentration camps' (as they were labelled) which confirmed the worst fears of the humanitarians. The most energetic, Emily Hobhouse, returned home in April 1901 with a catalogue of blunders. Lord Salisbury's government squirmed and amends were made, but slowly.

In December 1901 Kitchener ordered an end to farm-burning and instructed officers in the field to leave women and children in their farmsteads. Henceforward, their welfare was in the hands of their husbands, who were fighting on the veld. It was all very frustrating for the commander-in-chief, who had already earned opprobrium for his callous treatment of wounded dervishes after the Battle of Omdurman. Kitchener held the Boers in contempt, once privately telling the Secretary for War that they were 'uncivilised Afrikaner savages with a thin white veneer'.[23] Kitchener's attitude to the methods of his wilder subordinates was ambivalent. Dismissing complaints about the large-scale looting of Steinaecker's Horse, a mixed-race irregular unit operating on the Transvaal–Mozambique frontier, his Secretary, Major Walter ('Squibby') Congreve, remarked: 'No one thinks Steinaecker an angel, but he has his uses.'[24] It was impossible to shrug off the crimes of two Australian volunteers, Lieutenants Morant and Handcock, of another ad hoc detachment, the Bushveldt Carabineers. Their troopers accused them of killing at least twelve named Boer prisoners and a greater number of anonymous blacks during sweeps for partisans during the summer of 1901. The eyewitness evidence was convincing, a court martial sentenced them to death, and they were executed by firing squad. Their plea that they had believed that the killings were somehow officially sanctioned was a fiction.*[25]

* An Australian film of this nasty episode was made in 1973 which portrayed Morant and Handcock as heroic figures who were victims of a conspiracy by the cynical and arrogant British high command. In 2010 the British government rejected demands for the verdict to be overturned.

12

'We go where we are led': Missions and Their Enemies

I

Modern Africa's religious boundaries were drawn during the era of partition. Two competitive faiths, Christianity and Islam, dominate the continent and each claims a monopoly of revealed truth. For this reason alone, coexistence has always been uneasy.

Africa is now bisected by a line that runs across its centre and turns sharply south to encompass the Horn of Africa. Above it are predominantly Muslim lands, to the south Christian ones. The division had been dictated by two factors: the historic dominance of Islam along the Mediterranean coast and inland across the Sahara, and more recent activities of Christian missionaries whose efforts were concentrated in the Congo basin, eastern and southern Africa. There are untidy areas where the two religions coexist in roughly equal numbers: Muslims and Christians rub shoulders in the cities, towns and countryside of West Africa. In both Nigeria and the Sudan the south is mainly Christian and the north Muslim.

Political frontiers often cut through religious boundaries. The administrators who decided them imagined that the adherents of two historically antagonistic monotheisms could live alongside each other peacefully so long as they were firmly governed. It was one of the miracles of imperial government that they did so for so long.

In theory, Britain and France were Christian powers and their elected governments were always under pressure to favour and assist Christian missions. Yet conditions on the ground compelled both nations to tread warily when handling their Muslim subjects, who feared that imperial rule might be a prelude to conversion. Moreover, to them Christians were unbelievers who had rejected Allah and the teachings of Muhammad.

Partition had immeasurably helped the spread of Christian missions, which multiplied and thrived; missionaries of every denomination recognised that their task had been made easier and safer by the new colonial regimes. From an African perspective, the missionaries had been the pathfinders of empire and many Africans would have agreed with the contemporary Asian aphorism: 'First the missionary, then the Consul and then the General.'

It was never as simple as that, since there were divergences of aims and eddies of mutual suspicion between administrators, businessmen and missionaries which sometimes became rancorous. Polarisation never occurred, for in the last resort each needed the cooperation and support of the others, particularly wherever European authority was still fragile. Moreover, the new Africa required a growing number of literate Africans to fill the junior ranks of the civil service and commercial enterprises. Most came from the alumni of mission schools.

II

Disagreements with governments and the nagging fear of Islam, which too was making converts, did not unduly dampen the enthusiasm and optimism of the missionary movement. When, in 1910, over 1,200 delegates gathered in Edinburgh for the first World Missionary Conference the mood was buoyant and celebratory. It was summed up by a Scottish missionary who predicted that a century of progress on every continent was a sign that 'the kingdom of God' was coming to power throughout the world.' Yet the African millennium was still a mirage, for recent evidence of comparative conversion rates justified another delegate's prediction that the continent might swing to Islam.

Nonetheless there was still hope, since paganism appeared to be in terminal decline and the number of African clergymen was steadily rising. Many were questioning Protestant orthodoxies, discarding some and founding their own independent churches. This fragmentation had begun in South Africa, and by 1900 was gathering impetus with the proliferation of tiny Pentecostal sects that identified themselves with the Old Testament Israelites and the early Christian churches. These affinities were reflected in such wonderful names as the Apostolic

Nazareth Jerusalem Corinthian Church.[2] A similar pattern of schism appeared in early-twentieth-century Kenya and was accelerated by the arrival of American revivalists.[3] Africa was well on the way to acquiring its own idiosyncratic forms of Christianity.

Mainstream Catholic and Protestant missions flourished. On occasions, national and sectarian rivalries intruded into the work of conversion. Two Methodist missionaries were deported from Algeria after allegedly telling Kabyle tribesmen that under British rule they would be richer and happier.[4] Yet even the post-Fashoda sulkiness did not prevent French Catholics from welcoming the British conquest of the Sudan as a triumph for Christian civilisation.[5]

European donations were the lifeblood of the missionary movement. In the early 1900s French congregations were giving 3 million francs annually for overseas missions. Generosity on this scale owed everything to a massive publicity apparatus, which extended across countries and denominations. It stirred consciences and spread an awareness of Africa, the daily lives of its inhabitants and the benefits of conversion. Above all, there was a strong emphasis on the fundamental Christian duty to rescue the souls of heathens from damnation. The devout and resolute men and women who were achieving wonders in Africa were following in the steps of St Paul and the Apostles.

Just as the missions brought Christianity to the heathen, they brought Africa to millions of pious middle- and working-class Europeans. Mass-circulation illustrated journals, hagiographic biographies, tracts and children's fiction described both the progress of individual missionaries and the people they encountered. This literature had a vast readership: by 1900 the weekly Catholic magazine *Annales* had a circulation of 1.5 million. The quintessential message of these publications was that spiritual redemption was a crucial part of bringing civilisation and progress to Africa. There were also appeals to the heart: 'Paul Rakoto, a Malagasy Story', which appeared in the *Petit Almanach* in 1890 and described the joyful life of a shepherd boy convert, was puffed as 'a model for our dear children of Europe'.[6]

Extensive coverage was naturally given to the stamina and perseverance of the missionaries in the face of disease, extremes of climate and hostile natives. In 1899 *Les Missions Catholiques* reported the 'treacherous' murder of a missionary father in Ubangi-Shari, a recently annexed

French colony in Central Africa inhabited by 'fierce savages and cannibals'. Soon after, readers were given a first-hand account of locust-stricken villages in Madagascar from a priest who described devastated crops and hungry children pleading for food.

Missionary literature also contributed to Europe's already abundant stock of racial stereotypes. In his *Peril and Adventure in Central Africa: Being Illustrated Letters to the Youngsters at Home* (1886), James Hannington (the future Bishop of Eastern Equatorial Africa and martyr) summed up one tribe he encountered as: 'slimly built, generally intensely cowardly; fractious and more difficult to manage than the most spoilt of spoilt children'. Such surveys invariably touched upon what a Sierra Leone missionary called the 'foolish religion of fear' that shackled the collective African mind.

Revelations of the pagan African mind were published from time to time to show readers what the missionaries were up against. In 1907 *Les Missions Catholiques* issued 'Les Mémoires d'un Sauvage', which was the autobiography of a young Masai warrior as told to Father Joseph Cayrac, a missionary in Kenya. There were lurid accounts of witchcraft, with a sorcerer foretelling the young man's future over the 'steaming entrails' of a slaughtered ram, and of Masai dances and their significance. Alongside superstition were tribal political institutions that Cayrac admired because they rested on 'government of the people, by the people and with the people'.[7] Such praise was exceptional for inevitably, given its purpose, missionary literature dwelt on the darker side of the African's character and customs.

Photographs, first reproduced in journals during the 1890s, showed mission churches, schools, hospitals and converts, who had been instructed to abandon nakedness for European dress. The shapeless white dresses of the women were not just a reflection of prevailing European notions of modesty; they were outward tokens of spiritual rebirth. In the 1880s, the Pondos of the eastern Cape washed the traditional reddish ochre dye from their blankets as a public gesture of their acceptance of Christ. This symbolised the repudiation of what Godfrey Callaway, an Anglican missionary, identified as the vices of their past lives: 'beer drinks, the fights, the heathen rites'.[8] Pondo women completely abandoned their traditional dress in favour of what he described as 'flimsy, European dress, including high-heeled boots and a parasol'.

Callaway approved of the imposition of European fashions and brushed aside allegations that missionaries were destroying 'picturesque' native dress and customs. Their disappearance, he argued, was for the greater, long-term good, for a complete detachment from the past was integral to the doctrine of salvation. Less partial observers wondered whether such dogmatism was harmful. In 1902 one colonial civil servant suggested that it was mistaken to wrench the African from all his previous beliefs and tell him that they were utterly worthless. Was it not, he argued, kinder to allow him the comfort of 'the poorest sort of gods who care for all mortals' rather than leave him with 'nothing at all outside himself?'.[9]

Deaconess Maria Burton would have regarded this notion of a gradual transition from paganism to Christianity as heretical. Attached to a mission in Maseru in the 1890s, she was shocked when she found a young female Basuto convert drinking the local beer and dancing. The girl excused herself, saying she was 'singing with my feet'. The deaconess was unmoved, and warned her that she faced a stark choice between her new faith and alcohol.[10] She renounced beer. The gospel of temperance, relentlessly preached to the poor in Britain, was extended to Africa. Sobriety was integral to 'French civilisation', which Father Joffrey claimed he was cultivating among his congregation in Senegal in the early 1900s. Its other components were wearing European clothes and the adoption of tables and chairs at mealtimes.[11]

III

Father Joffrey had been defending himself against allegations that his patriotism was half-hearted. The missionary movement was regularly embroiled in politics, in particular debates about the aims and moral character of imperialism. The majority of missionaries and their supporters fervently believed that Christianity was the foundation of the humanitarian principles that distinguished European civilisation. This was why, irrespective of creed, missionaries insisted that Africans had the right to just and humane treatment. If Africans were maltreated or exploited, the missionaries spoke up for them and their protests carried considerable political clout. In Britain, missionaries and their allies regularly mobilised the voter in the pew. In April 1893 a Methodist missionary wrote to the Liberal *Daily Chronicle* with a harrowing account of a fugitive female slave who had been seized by policemen of the British East Africa Company and dragged before one of its magistrates. He ruled that she should be returned to her master's harem unless £11 was paid in compensation. Within days this scandal had been raised in the Commons and official redress followed. The woman was liberated and critics of the company were confirmed in their fears that its administration was slack and corrupt.[12]

British politicians were proud of the national conscience. On the centenary of the foundation of the Church Missionary Society, the Prime Minister, Lord Salisbury, described its genesis as the 'awakening of humanitarian enthusiasm'. In the same year, the liberal-inclining *Spectator* analysed this element in the national character and concluded that: 'The average British voter holds, as we do, that the gradations of capacity are almost infinite, but no human being is entitled to hold slaves, or to torture other human beings for gain.' Inhumanity anywhere in the world would arouse him 'in such a way as move the opinion of the Christian world'.[13] Governments recognised this and responded, not always with enthusiasm.

Conscious of their collective responsibility as guardians of the rights of Africans, the missionaries and their domestic allies were alarmed by the motives and behaviour of white settlers and the chartered companies. During a Commons debate on the First Matabele War, a radical Liberal MP, William Byles, contrasted the outlook of the missionaries in Bechuanaland with that of the British South Africa Company. The former 'taught the people the use of the plough and other implements of civilisation' while the latter quarrelled with the natives and used 'the Maxim gun to destroy them'. This remark goaded one Tory, who praised Rhodes's troops as 'gallant Englishmen' who were defending the 'interests of their country'.[14] During a 1906 debate on the horrors of the Congo, another Liberal MP reminded Members of his own country's blemished record. He called the recent massacres of Zulu rebels by the settler militia in Natal a sequence of 'inglorious slaughters – too much like rook shooting to be glorious'.[15]

What turned out to be an enduring rift was opening between the humanitarian lobby and the commercial interests, which treated the African as a consumer and a unit of production. On the whole, the missionaries had no objections to the African earning wages or trading – indeed many missions ran their own farms. An American Quaker mission in the Kavirondo district of Kenya intended to foster 'habits of industry' that would fund a 'self-supporting native Christian church'. A water-driven sawmill was erected and, in 1903, a sympathetic administration allocated 1,000 acres to this enterprise.[16] In 1914 Paul von Lettow-Vorbeck, the newly arrived commander-in-chief in German East Africa, was delighted by ways in which the missions had introduced 'European handicrafts'. 'Everywhere one finds carpenters' shops, shoemakers' shops and brickworks.'[17]

What caused humanitarian disquiet was the widespread assumption that forced labour was essential for the success of cash crops, railway construction and mining. According to Ewart Grogan, an adored luminary of Kenyan settler society in the early 1900s, it was a prerequisite for Africa's economic progress. He was a restless young man unscathed by his education at Winchester and Cambridge who craved adventure and found it by undertaking a journey through Africa from the Cape to Cairo in 1898. Afterwards he published an account of his experiences, which largely consisted of a catalogue of animals (including a porcupine) he had shot whenever they crossed his path.

Grogan found space to damn missionaries and their domestic allies who dared to censure his hero Rhodes and the pioneers in Rhodesia and Kenya. They were brave, far-sighted men who would enrich Africa so long as they could find legions of tractable black workers. These were scarce since Grogan shared the fallacy, common among colonists, that the African was infected by a genetic indolence which could only be cured by compulsory labour.

The whip was, therefore, an essential tool in the new economy and Grogan had quickly mastered its use after practice on under-active porters during his safaris. He noted that men from some tribes succumbed after twenty-five strokes while others endured far more.[18] 'Bwana' always knew what was best, and Grogan railed against the missionary frame of mind that idealised the native as a creature to be protected and pampered. The 'chosen of the negrophile, bread-and-butter of the missionaries' and 'darling of the unthinking philanthropist' needed hard work and harsh discipline.[19] Another prominent Kenya settler and manic big-game hunter, Lord Cranworth, deplored the refusal to work of the 'young able-bodied Kikuyu warrior' and the 'sentimentalists' at home who praised his independent spirit.[20] Such fallacies were already entrenched in South Africa, were taking root in Kenya and Rhodesia and, of course, were commonplace among the European community in Algeria.

IV

Calmer figures were also examining relations between the missions and the secular powers. Edward Blyden, a gifted Liberian African who had been employed by the administration of Sierra Leone, recognised a conflict of aims between missionaries and civil administrators. 'It is not', he wrote in 1902, 'the business of imperialism to make *men*, but to create subjects, not to save souls, but to save bodies.'[21] Ferdinand Brunetière, a missionary in Madagascar, saw no discrepancy. Unlike the British and the Germans, 'The Frenchman converts the *indigène* to the genius of our race to produce a man who is an equal brother.'[22]

Racial equality had always been a sensitive and, for Christians, an awkward subject and will be discussed at greater length in Chapter Fifteen. Suffice it to say that by 1914 there was already unease about presumptions of equality among mission-educated Africans. It was strongest among administrators with a military background, who were conditioned to the unquestioning deference of the native soldier. Sir Frederick Lugard complained about the 'loud and arrogant conceit' of educated Nigerians in his legislative council, and insisted that the new government schools in Northern Nigeria should not promote 'ideas of European dress and habits unsuited to their [the natives'] environment'.[23]

Lugard's distaste for the Westernised African and his pretensions was shared by one of his subordinates, the slightly mad Captain Frank Crozier of the West African Frontier Force. In 1901 he flogged a dozen of what he described as 'English-speaking, highly civilized, Christianized and thoroughly spoilt carpenters from Lagos and other parts of the coast' after they had gone on strike. To Crozier's subsequent horror, these 'cheeky' fellows hired 'a black barrister' to issue a writ for assault.[24] Thanks to a highly placed crony, he managed to get off.*

---

* Crozier was an Ulsterman who, among other things, advocated machine-gun fire as a method of executing criminals. He commanded a battalion on the Western Front, where he admitted to shooting down fleeing Portuguese troops, and then took brief charge of the infamous Auxiliary Police during the 1919–22 Irish Civil War [1919–21 Irish War of Independence?]. Afterwards he converted to militant pacifism.

However much the likes of Crozier deplored their familiarity, educated Africans were necessary for commerce and the new colonial administrations. In 1905 the authorities in the Sudan found themselves faced with the urgent need to expand the school population as fast as possible, for 'Every day shows the necessity for a Sudanese class able to read, write and cipher sufficiently to fill minor appointments in Government.'[25]

Since traditional, Quranic Muslim schools did not impart the knowledge needed for employment as, say, a postal clerk or a telegraphist, the state had to provide a basic education. It was politically imperative to educate the sons of chiefs who were becoming partners in imperial administrations. In 1911 the sons of Northern Nigerian chiefs were learning the three Rs, elementary drawing, hygiene, natural history and the geography of Africa in special, selective schools. It was reported that the 'more enlightened chiefs' applauded this scheme.[26] Commercial needs were catered for by one government school in Kenya in 1914 which ran classes in carpentry, farming, printing and stonework.[27]

African education was following the pattern of contemporary Europe, where governments were taking responsibility for founding and financing universal elementary schools for boys and girls. In Britain the state was willing to subsidise the old church schools and colonial governments followed suit. By 1913 Nyasaland mission schools were receiving an annual official grant of £1,000. Such arrangements would be required in the foreseeable future, for the task of creating a state education system was immense. Progress was slow and hampered by a lack of funds: by 1919 there were just over 1,000 pupils in eighteen schools across Northern Nigeria. By contrast, there were over 30,000 Quranic schools with 200,000 pupils.[28]

Over the past fifty years the missions had made some headway, but their schools were scattered unevenly across the continent, so levels of literacy varied greatly from region to region. They were high in Nyasaland and Uganda, both colonies with a concentration of long-established missions. In 1913 there were 119,000 pupils in Nyasaland's 1,500 schools taught by 130 white teachers and Uganda's school population stood at 83,000. In Kenya there were just over 2,200 boys and girls in schools attached to fifty-nine missions.[29] This was just as well, since the government allocated a little over £1,500 a year for state schools in

1908 in contrast to a military budget of £56,000 and an allowance of £20,000 for medical services.[30]

There was compulsory education for all eight- to eleven-year-olds in Madagascar, where nearly 1,100 schools had a total of 107,000 pupils. Ten thousand (a third of them girls) were being taught in state and mission schools in French West Africa, which had an estimated population of 11 million.

V

Education in the French colonies was impeded by a prolonged and bitter political row over who taught what. This dispute was a direct result of the Dreyfus affair, during which Catholic clergymen had campaigned against him, often viciously and in the teeth of the evidence. Here was proof that Catholicism was and would remain inimical to the ideals of the Republic. Boosted by electoral successes between 1900 and 1905, successive Republican ministries introduced a wide-ranging programme of *laïcisation* designed to curtail the influence of the Church in public life. This policy was applied in the colonies: there was no longer any role for Catholic priests in France's *mission civilisatrice*.

By 1914 all the schools in Senegal were secular, nuns had ceased working in hospitals and some missionaries were forced to become salaried public officials answerable to the governor. Since there was a scarcity of nurses, the nuns showed an impressive sense of vocation by staying on and supporting themselves by working as part-time seamstresses and laundrywomen.[31] Here and elsewhere, pragmatic considerations came into play and local officials adopted flexible attitudes.

The Governor of the Ivory Coast convinced Paris that the mission schools were valuable insofar as they taught French to the natives and, by pleading local conditions, other administrators were able to deflect or bypass *laïcisation*.[32] Many missionaries asserted their patriotism. In Madagascar, Father Delmont told his flock they were building a church 'as a duty to the government'. They clearly understood the Pauline injunctions on obedience to the civil power, for one of Delmont's converts told an official that 'like cattle [we] go where we are led when we are told it is for the government'.[33]

Jean-Victor Augagneur, a Republican Socialist deputy and a freemason who was appointed Governor of Madagascar in 1905, would have preferred the islanders to have been atheists and said so. Protestant missions, he alleged, were a 'danger for French authority', 'native pastors' were cussed and 'imbued with ideas tending towards resistance to our rule'.³⁴ The phenomenon of the African clergyman holding libertarian views and refusing to submit to the imperial status quo was already established in South Africa and would shortly spread to Kenya.

What makes such figures and their congregations important was their assumption that personal freedoms and political rights cherished by Britain and France should be extended to their colonies. During the late 1880s, black, independent congregations in the Cape ran their own newspaper, organised the registration of black voters and petitioned Queen Victoria for an extension of the franchise. Such a gesture, they claimed with a touching loyalty, would be worthy of the spirit of the 'brave and generous British nation'.³⁵ They were disappointed, but churches, in particular those of the Ethiopian sects, persisted and were at the forefront of the opposition to South Africa's 1910 Constitution and the confiscation of tribal lands.

There were signs of active political engagement in Kenya among Pentecostal congregations, which were edging their way slowly towards an African political identity. This was inevitable since independent churches that preached spiritual freedom were the natural incubators for ideas about political liberty.³⁶ They were distorted by John Chilembwe, a Nyasaland Baptist minister who had studied at the Virginia Theological Seminary, where he was influenced by the nascent American black political movements. A radical became a revolutionary early in 1915, when Chilembwe protested against the harsh treatment of plantation workers and the recruitment of Africans into the army for the campaign in German East Africa. He led a brief uprising that had nationalist overtones but was in essence nihilistic: his followers killed a handful of Europeans and destroyed property, including a mission. Chilembwe died in a skirmish, his followers were rounded up and several were hanged. The white community had been terrified; the insurrection had been a bolt from the blue and the murders particularly brutal.

This episode was exceptional, but in an exaggerated way it illustrated the connections between the egalitarian, independent black churches and radical politics. Yet there were plenty of African clergy who urged their congregations to follow Christ's and St Paul's injunctions to Caesar's authority in matters temporal. Even so, it is important to remember that the first challenges to the imperial status quo had come from the churches. There would be more, less violent John Chilembwes.

13

'Toxic is the gift of Christians': Islam and Empires

———

I

The political power of Islam was severely shaken during the nineteenth and early twentieth centuries. With astonishing speed and often in the teeth of fierce resistance, British, French, Russian and Italian armies had conquered and annexed Muslim states throughout Africa and Asia. Their Christian rulers knew that they were unwelcome and were constantly aware of Islam's resilience and capacity as a catalyst for insurrection. Accordingly, they moved warily and promised to treat the Muslim faith with respect and sensitivity. In 1901 the Prefect of Algiers assured Muslims that 'under the shadow of the tricolour you can safely fly your green flag'.[1] Perhaps so, but their faith disqualified them from enjoying the rights of French citizenship, which was open to hundreds of thousands of Christian immigrants.

Such exclusion was justified by the stubborn refusal of the Muslim masses to appreciate what was for their own good. They preferred their own ways to those of the modern world foisted on them by infidels who seemed bent on undermining Islam. Seen from a European perspective, this reaction was wilful obscurantism. In his analysis of the accomplishments of British rule in Egypt written in 1894, Sir Alfred Milner railed against the 'medieval barbarity or absurdity' of sharia law and the sheer bigotry of Muslims who were 'hostile to reform because it came from Christians'.[2] A few years later the Anglican Bishop of Zanzibar insisted that 'the idea of slavery is natural to Islam'.[3] The Muslim mind was closed to scientific discoveries. In 1907 a French doctor in Marrakech was murdered by a mob after he had tried to treat the city's sick with modern medicines. The French Foreign Minister hailed him as 'civilisation's martyr'.[4]

The former African Muslim states had been hierarchical autocracies in which power flowed downwards. Superficially Muslims were, therefore, preconditioned to imperial rule, but obedience to Christian masters always went against the grain. Religious conservatism, strongest among the clergy and the poor, and an antipathy towards all unbelievers made Muslims fearful of change, particularly when it impinged on their faith. Unsettled Muslims were fissile and prone to be swept along by gusts of religious fervour whipped up by jihadist preachers. Sporadic holy wars marked the establishment of British and French rule in North and West Africa. The German Empire was spared such upheavals, for it contained relatively few Muslims.

Wherever feasible, Britain and France left traditional social structures intact. Imperial authority was grafted onto that of cooperative hereditary princes to provide continuity and legitimacy to the new regimes. The khedives of Egypt and the sultans of Morocco kept the façade of power: they undertook their ceremonial duties, prayed with their subjects in mosques and took the salute at parades of their soldiers. But their armies were commanded by European officers and their taxes were collected and spent by European bureaucrats. If they chafed at the bit, these figureheads risked deposition and replacement by more pliant kinsmen.

Egypt and Morocco had been dependencies of the Ottoman Empire, the only Muslim state with great power pretensions. By 1914 these were threadbare: Turkey's African provinces had been engrossed by Britain, France and Italy, and the Sultan had just lost his Balkan toeholds to local nationalists backed by Russia. Worse was to come, for France, Britain and Russia were already contemplating the partition and occupation of Turkey's Middle Eastern provinces. Not since the First Crusade had Islam suffered such reverses.

II

A century of defeats by infidels had not crushed the spirit of Islam. The faith equipped its followers with the spiritual stamina necessary to absorb calamities. They drew strength (and hope) from the central tenet of Islam: 'There is no strength and no power except in Allah.' The Quran gave an omnipotent God mastery over the forces of history which He directed in ways that sometimes baffled and dismayed the faithful. Consolation was provided by the Quranic doctrine of *Dunya*,

by which Muslims were permitted to make terms with hostile unbelievers in order to secure a breathing space in which to recover their
strength. Islam was preserved and, by and by and through dissembling,
would regain its former power.

In the meantime, Muslims had to live under Christian rule. Those
who found this unbearable invoked the doctrine of jihad, which called
on the faithful to wage war against the enemies of Islam. The holy warrior surrendered his fate to Allah and, if he was killed, he died a martyr
with the assurance that he would enter a paradise teeming with sexual
delights. Faith eliminated the soldier's natural fear of death, which
made the jihadi a formidable and terrifying adversary. After several
encounters with jihadic warriors in Senegal during the 1850s, General
Faidherbe concluded that: 'It is in the name of the Prophet that our
worst enemies march against us.' Their morale was indomitable, for
they advanced 'as if to martyrdom'.[5]

Collaboration, as laid down in the principle of *Dunya*, was attractive to the Muslim princes of Africa (and India) for it let them keep
their wealth and prestige even if their political power was curtailed.
Coming to terms with the unbelievers also made sense, since their
victories on the battlefield were clear indications of the will of Allah.
Divine providence explained the multiple defeats suffered by Muslim
armies in Senegal and Northern Nigeria during the late 1890s – or so
it was argued by the theologians who persuaded Sultan Muhammadu
Attahiru II of Sokoto to accept British overlordship in 1903.

Attahiru's flexibility recommended him to Sir Frederick Lugard,
the High Commissioner, who recognised the Sultan as an ideal partner in his scheme for indirect rule over the Islamic states of Northern
Nigeria. Its spirit was secular and was based on a Burkean concept of
organic development: native societies and their forms of government
were the outcome of historic organic growth and deserved to be preserved and cultivated because they satisfied the needs of the people. Old
power structures reflected indigenous values and, with adjustments,
could be fitted easily and advantageously into the imperial scheme
of things. Above all, indirect rule lessened the chances of religious
friction.

Of course, changes such as the abolition of slavery had to be made
to appease domestic humanitarian opinion, but they were a price that
monarchs were willing to pay. Some power was better than none at all.

Moreover, as the Sultan's spiritual advisers reminded him, the arrangement was not permanent: the will of Allah could change.

In Sokoto the transfer of power was performed publicly with the ceremonial instalment of Muhammadu Attahiru II. Traditional rituals emphasised the continuity of dynastic rule, while the presence of Lugard reminded onlookers that their Sultan had a new overlord, King Edward VII. The theatre of succession and the sharing of authority was carefully stage-managed and watched by an audience of the Sultan's advisers, his mailed cavalry, subordinate chiefs, Muslim clerics and people of Sokoto. Close by stood ranks of Hausa infantrymen in khaki uniforms and fezzes, British officers and Maxim guns, the stage props of British ascendancy.

This prominent display of soldiers and weapons was a salutary reminder of the signal defeats recently suffered by native armies, and among the onlookers there must have been survivors of those battles in which the riflemen and 'piss guns' (as the Maxims were called) had shot down hundreds. The finale of this tableau was a speech by Lugard. He noted with satisfaction that a 'murmur of approval' greeted his announcement that there would be 'no interference' with the listeners' religion.[6] Lugard had been selective with the truth. The recent settlement had changed Islamic practices: slavery was banned, jihadic preaching outlawed and the punitive mutilations prescribed by sharia law were, in the words of one British official, modified in keeping with 'modern conditions and religious toleration'.[7] Thieves kept their hands, adulteresses were no longer stoned to death and local Islamic courts were placed under close supervision. In the last resort, British law was always supreme. Muslim purists were appalled; beforehand one had warned the Sultan, 'Toxic is the gift of Christians.'[8]

Throughout Muslim Africa indirect rule also rested on a legion of lesser collaborators. There was no shortage of ambitious professional soldiers, junior officials and technocrats who would serve anyone who could pay their salaries and further their careers. Consider Hasan Ridwan, who was born in 1864, joined the Egyptian army and studied engineering and gunnery. He was one of the young nationalist officers who backed Urabi Pasha, was wounded at Tel-el-Kebir and was subsequently pardoned by the Khedive. He rejoined Tewfik's army, served under British command in the 1885 campaign against the Mahdi, and then turned his talents to civil administration. By his early thirties he was appointed a *mamur* (provincial governor) and became closely involved in town planning.[9]

The lower ranks of the Egyptian and Sudanese administration were filled with Muslims who collected taxes, presided over inferior courts, registered births and deaths, managed postal services, acted as translators and served as clerks. Their rewards were security and good salaries, which was why, according to Milner, 'A place under Government is still the highest ideal of . . . the educated Egyptian.'[10] Copts were strongly represented in the Egyptian and Sudanese bureaucracies, but there were also plenty of Muslims. All became men of substance and standing; one British official warmly remembered these junior servants of empire as 'ample, majestic men, bespectacled, dignified [and] omniscient'.[11]

III

Wherever possible, the French also attempted to adopt indirect rule, employing what one official called 'the useful and necessary aristocracy'.[12] In West Africa some officials went further and tried to enlist the Muslim clergy, but soon found themselves in difficulties. Islam did not possess a clearly defined clerical hierarchy; there were no religious counterparts to the Sultan of Sokoto with whom to strike bargains. Nevertheless, the French government persevered and in 1891 succeeded in persuading the Sharif of Mecca to issue a fatwa (edict) which ordered the Muslims of the Soudan to obey their new rulers. None took any notice, for they were unaware of the spiritual kudos of the keeper of the holiest of Muslim shrines who traced his ancestry back to Muhammad.[13] The Sharif had immense spiritual charisma but, unlike the Pope, he could not define dogma or enforce it.

Rather than take orders from theocrats, Muslims sought spiritual inspiration and guidance from independent preachers and scholars, distinguished by their intense piety, profound understanding of the Quran and asceticism. They were the mullahs, *marabouts* and sufis (mystics, scholars and teachers) who ran schools, attached themselves to shrines, or ranged through towns and villages preaching. Such figures often enjoyed vast local popularity and thrived outside the tidy imperial scheme of things. Republican officials distrusted these free spirits and compared them to the Catholic clergy who gulled the credulous French peasantry. In Senegal, the authorities attempted to license *marabouts* but without much success, treated Islamic schools as a nuisance and closed those with less than twenty pupils.[14] They were tolerated in Egypt, much to the annoyance of Milner, who believed that learning the Quran by heart was a hindrance to literacy.

Both British and French proconsuls hoped that their secular allies would silence what Lugard called 'fanatical preachers of sedition'. These were the jihadists whose potential for disruption made them a constant source of often paranoiac anxiety. Disregarding any sign of Muslim discontent was carelessness, and delay in stamping on it was dangerous folly. 'Shoot down without mercy anyone who shows the least hesitation or reluctance to obey you' were the orders of Sir Evelyn Baring, the Consul-General in Cairo, after disturbances among the Sudanese garrison in Khartoum in 1900.[15] His fears turned out to be exaggerated, for the askaris had not been stirred up by jihadist propaganda but by reports of recent British defeats in South Africa. The mutineers had imagined that they were a portent of the imminent collapse of British rule in the Sudan and Egypt.

Such incidents confirmed prejudices about the credulousness and excitability of the Muslim temperament. Intelligence gatherers always kept an ear open for any rumour that might inflame religious passions and precipitate a jihad. Hearsay was transmitted by word of mouth, often with remarkable speed, across country, and disseminated in caravanserais, market places and mosques. Reports of Italian setbacks in Libya took a few weeks to reach Northern Nigeria in 1912 and were already circulating in French Mauritania. The local authorities were uneasy: Italy's difficulties damaged European prestige and hinted that imperial armies were not invincible. Dangerous thoughts would be implanted in Muslim minds and turn them towards a jihad.[16]

British and French officials had good reason to be jumpy. During the winter of 1905–6 this region had been convulsed by a large-scale jihadic uprising that had appeared suddenly. A charismatic Senegalese *marabout*, Sahibu, had appealed for holy war to expel the Christians and open the way for an Islamic millennium. Thousands joined in and crossed the border into recently pacified Northern Nigeria. They were, thought Lugard, 'like the peasants of Russia' who 'look for a general upheaval which shall abolish taxes and all social distinctions'.[17] In essence this was true. The insurgents were from the margins of society:

former slaves thrown out by their masters who could not afford to pay them wages and impoverished peasant farmers. Like rebels elsewhere in Africa, they had been cast adrift in a disconcerting world of change.

The jihadist horde concentrated at Satiru, sallied out and attacked a detachment of 500 British troops, mainly Hausa, which was approaching the town. The tenacity of the insurgents amazed Captain Crozier: 'These men faced certain death with a fanatical bravery to the beating of drums and tom-toms, the sound of shrill blasts on the horns, and the chanting of extracts from the Koran.'[18] A massacre followed: bows and arrows and spears were no match for artillery, machine-guns and rifles. Six hundred jihadists were killed and the survivors fled to Satiru, which was shelled and then plundered by the Hausa and auxiliaries raised by the Sultan of Sokoto. He had denounced Sahibu as a 'false prophet' and his courts passed death sentences on those of his followers who had been captured.[19] The episode was both a reminder of the ever-present threat of jihadist uprising and a vindication of indirect rule.

Sahibu's warriors had been fighting for their land as well as their faith. The same fusion of patriotism and religion was achieved by Sayyid Muhammad Abdullah al-Hasan, the most persistent and effective leader of a jihadist movement in Africa. Between 1899 and 1920 he waged an intermittent guerrilla war against the British, the Abyssinians and those tribes who had come to terms with the infidels. Contemptuously dismissed as the 'Mad Mullah' of Somaliland by his British adversaries, he was a dynamic and adroit partisan general and propagandist. His poetry paraded his spiritual credentials, vanity and patriotism:

> I, of my own volition, chose to fight the infidels.
> It was I who said to the filthy unbeliever – this
>   land is not yours.
> If the English dogs do not flee in panic
> Then let it be said that I am not a true Muslim.

Sayyid Abdullah likened his warriors to 'an advancing thunderbolt' driven by 'fervour and faith'.[20] Their resolve was stiffened by their leader's magical powers; like other jihadic messiahs, he boasted that he could turn bullets to water and he once told his followers that the searchlights of British warships anchored off the coast were the eyes of Allah observing his victories.[20] By 1908 the British, exasperated by Sayyid Abdullah's hit-and-run tactics and the costs of holding him in check, threw in the sponge. He withdrew to the inland where he ruled over a tiny Islamic state from a string of castles. The Mad Mullah might have achieved more but for his isolation. In 1916 Sayyid Abdullah made tentative approaches to the Abyssinian Emperor Lij Iyasu (who had reportedly converted to Islam) in the hope that he might procure assistance from Germany and Turkey.[21]

IV

Most African Muslims were Sunnis who venerated the Ottoman Sultan-Caliph, a descendant of Muhammad and, in theory, their spiritual leader. Their attachment to a distant figurehead was largely sentimental, but it contained a political element. In 1906 Egyptian Muslims with nationalist sympathies objected to Britain's intimidation of the Sultan in support of claims to the Sinai peninsula. The British responded by sponsoring press articles challenging the Sultan's claim to the caliphate.[22] Behind this move was the ever-present fear that the Sultan might invoke his rarely used authority as Caliph to launch a jihad that would unite all Muslims in defence of their faith.

In British and French official circles there was already much speculation about the threat posed by global Pan-Islamic agitation. Admiral Sir John (Jackie) Fisher, the First Sea Lord, summed it up vividly with a warning that if Islam only raised 'its little finger' there would be massive unrest among the British Empire's Muslim subjects in Asia and Africa. He had served in Egypt and commanded the Mediterranean Fleet so he knew what he was talking about.

Just what form an Islamic explosion might take had been apparent from recent events in Morocco and Libya. In 1907 the French government had used the murder of a French doctor in Marrakech (mentioned at the start of this chapter) as a pretext for the occupation of Oujda and Casablanca. France had long coveted Morocco and had used economic penetration, including loans, to erode its independence. Direct political control followed and, in 1908, Sultan Abdal Aziz was compelled to abdicate and replaced by his more malleable younger brother, Abdal Hafid Aziz, who defected to the resistance movement and was, in turn, eased off the throne in August 1912 when his younger brother Yusuf was installed. He accepted the French version of indirect rule, which was now reinforced by a 20,000-strong army.

This flagrant and cynical infringement of Moroccan sovereignty provoked an uprising that drew support from the rural tribes and the urban professional and commercial classes. The Islamic element was pervasive and strong. The insurgents insisted that their country was inseparable from the wider Muslim world and some formed a Pan-Islamic league with its own newspaper. Sufis were prominently involved and French intelligence was disturbed by reports of Muslim secret societies, including one ominously called 'Maghreb Unity'. Equally worrying was the clandestine involvement of the Turkish government, which sent arms and officer instructors to help rebel forces.[23]

Some of the Sultan Abdal Hafid Aziz's soldiers went over to the rebels. In April 1912 the Fez garrison mutinied, besieged the royal palace, murdered Europeans and looted shops and houses. Order was restored by French troops, who suffered over a hundred casualties, including Algerian Muslim *tirailleurs*. French newspapers blamed Muslim 'fanaticism' for the mutiny and *Le Figaro* alleged that perceived French weakness had emboldened the rebels.[24] Hammer blows were the only remedy and they were vigorously applied over the next few months. Order was restored and the great powers acknowledged France's protectorate over Morocco, but fighting in the Rif region continued for another ten years.

What was significant about the Moroccan insurgents was that they offered something new: a blend of traditional jihadic resistance and modern nationalism. Moreover, the machinery of protest – printed propaganda and underground cells – imitated European nationalist and revolutionary models. The Moroccans also had outside help from Turkey and moral support from Egypt.

Egyptian nationalism, smothered by the British in 1882, was reviving in the first years of the twentieth century. Its most fervent and active apostles were the young: in 1909, a pro-British newspaper blamed the dismal degree results of Egyptian medical undergraduates on their spending too much time meddling in politics. They were abandoning the lecture hall for the more exciting world of nationalist societies (some of them secret, like those in Morocco) with their debates and meetings where a new, free Egypt was discussed. Some wrote pamphlets and held demonstrations which called on all the people of a captive nation to rid themselves of an overbearing and greedy British administration. One of the first demands was the nationalisation of the Suez Canal. From the start Muslim clerics were closely involved in the nationalist movement, although their protests focused on the unseemliness and immorality of the infidels, who drank too much.

This embryonic but vibrant national movement soon stretched out its hands to the urban workers of Cairo and Alexandria and *fellahin* of the countryside. Ibrahim Nasif al-Wardani, a pharmacology student who spent some time in Lausanne, mixed with Anarchists and returned home full of plans to mobilise the masses and form trade unions. Assassination was another Anarchist weapon, and he chose to use it in Egypt: early in 1910 he shot dead the Prime Minister, Boutros Pasha Ghali, whose collaboration with the British marked him out as a traitor. Ibrahim was hanged and, as reported in the nationalist press, his final words were 'God is great, and it is he who grants freedom' or, in another version, 'Liberty and Freedom were granted by God.'[25] Islam was integral to the new secular nationalism.

V

Paradoxically, just as Egyptians and Moroccans were exploring and adopting European political ideas and methods, General Lyautey, who was Resident-General of Morocco between 1912 and 1925, was embarking on what he called the 'pénétration pacifique' of the country. It was driven by the progressive spirit of the Republic and designed to apply all the benefits of modern science and technology to the Moroccan people. It went without saying that in the process Islam's power over the masses would wilt as they came to appreciate the blessings of the scientific enlightenment.

Lyautey's brand of benevolent imperialism embraced road-building and ambitious public health programmes run by French military doctors and funded from local taxes. By 1922 the annual health service budget was 12 million francs. Pure water and precautions against bubonic plague, typhoid and cholera were, Lyautey believed, the right of every Moroccan subject.

Ignorance and ingrained religious prejudices hampered Lyautey's work in a country where a mixture of a holy man's urine and water was considered an efficacious antiseptic. In rural areas, mobile hygiene units had to use force to delouse the unwilling and vaccinations were performed at gunpoint.[26] French physicians overcame many of their problems by making accommodations with indigenous medicines. They adopted harmless Muslim placebos to calm nervous patients before applying modern therapies, and hospitals and dispensaries were built in the style of Muslim shrines. Uncertain patients hedged their bets by accepting modern cures and simultaneously making animal sacrifices and undertaking pilgrimages to shrines.[27]

The latter reinsurance was and still is popular among some Christians in Europe. Muslims were gradually converted to the white man's medicine, but they remained hostile to his religion. Christianity and Islam were competitors in many parts of Africa and Christian missionaries often found themselves handicapped in the struggle for converts. Islam's most powerful appeal was its racial and social inclusiveness: the Quran stressed the essential brotherhood of all believers. In the words of a West African Christian, 'Islam . . . makes room for all', so a Muslim from Sierra Leone would find himself welcome in a mosque in Liverpool.[28] Furthermore, conversion to Islam was an easier process than to Christianity. All that was required of the former was an assertion of Allah's supremacy and there was no requirement to abjure all their former beliefs and practices. Unlike Christians, Muslims were permitted to retain a sentimental attachment to what one missionary called 'their old charms and superstitions'.[29] The white man's God allowed no such latitude, nor did His priests mingle freely and familiarly with their black congregations.

In 1906 the Bishop of Nyasaland noticed that the rate of conversions to Islam tended to rise during periods of popular native unrest. Turning to Allah was the equivalent of a protest vote against imperial rule. Sir Harry Johnston, the High Commissioner in Nyasaland, detected this trend and drew sinister conclusions: 'Men who have never been able to unite in the past have a very possible bond in the future in Mohammedan freemasonry.'[30] Imperial rule, still fragile and shallowly implanted in much of Africa, sat uneasily alongside an alternative source of authority with a mass appeal.

14

'Palm trees, enormous flowers,
Negroes, animals and adventures':
The Impact of Africa on Europe

I

By 1914 the histories of Europe and Africa were entwined and the people of each continent were becoming more conscious of each other and the lands they inhabited. This awareness was complex and took many forms. There was the Africa of the missionary, the politician, the investor and businessman, serious figures concerned with the continent's future in the global religious, political and economic order. Then there was the Africa of the masses, which was a source of wonderment and entertainment. This was the strange, romantic continent of popular novelists such as Rider Haggard and Pierre Loti, the great commercial and cultural exhibitions, advertisements, children's toys, pretty postage stamps and thrilling stories and pictures in the newspapers and illustrated journals. The appeal of this empire of recreation was naturally strongest in those countries with colonies in Africa: news reports of skirmishes in the Sahara did not cause much of a stir in Vienna or Athens.

The glamour of the romantic Africa was a magnet for restless young men, hungry for adventure. During his boyhood in the 1860s, Pierre Loti had felt drawn towards a 'far-off tropical land, with its palm trees, enormous flowers, Negroes, animals and adventures'. He trained as a naval cadet in the hope that he would experience these wonders at first hand. Later generations of young men followed Loti, including some who had been inspired by his romances and the adventure stories of Jules Verne.[1] Thrilling newspaper reports of Omdurman and the confrontation at Fashoda fired the imagination of Ralph Furse, setting him on a course that would end at a junior but sedentary post in the Edwardian Colonial Office. His heroes were the contemporary administrators of Empire: Cromer, Milner and Lyautey.[2] It was just as well that these dreamers were young, for they could cope with the shocks of reality. A French journalist who visited Madagascar during the 1896 campaign noted: 'You have to have the ingenuousness of youth to imagine that you can succeed.'[3]

The intrusion of Africa into the European consciousness had coincided with profound political and social changes in the four principal imperial powers. Britain, France, Germany and Italy had become democracies served by modern political parties with mass membership. Political allegiances tended to follow class lines: in general, the upper and middle classes were inclined towards conservatism and liberalism, while the working classes were attracted to the infant Socialist parties whose complexions ranged from rose-pink to deep crimson. Public debate on every political subject was more informed than it had ever been, for official educational policies were creating a literate electorate, although Italy had lagged behind: only 38 per cent of Italians could read in 1914.

Questions about the desirability and usefulness of empires were contentious political issues. As a general rule, British, French and German conservatives and liberals supported and took pride in imperial expansion. A thriving and expanding empire enhanced the status of the nation and, the more high-minded imperialists argued, united its people in a collective sense of duty to extend civilisation. In 1898 one of them, the young Winston Churchill, insisted that his countrymen of every class were the trustees of the lands and subjects of the British Empire, which he described as an 'imperial democracy'. Contemporary French imperialists justified their colonies on the altruistic grounds that their inhabitants were exposed to the blessings of Republican enlightenment. France's Moroccan gambit in 1911 was celebrated by *Le Petit Journal* with a cover which showed an ample-bosomed female wearing the cap of liberty, stepping from the sea and pouring gold coins from a golden cornucopia on crouching Moroccans. One clasps her robe and the caption announces that his countrymen are about to receive 'la Civilisation, la Richesse et la Paix'.

Turn-of-the-century popular imperialism was a heady brew that stimulated extremes of chauvinism and flights of fancy that bordered on the absurd. After a visit to Italian forces in Libya in 1912, the Futurist poet Filippo Marinetti fell into a delirium in which he imagined that the neighs of the cavalry chargers sounded like the word 'Italia'.[4] A more measured triumphalism was expressed in the ode written for the coronation of Edward VII, which was set to Elgar's stirring music:

Land of Hope and Glory, Mother of the Free,
How shall we extol thee, who are born of thee?
Wider still and wider, shall thy bounds be set;
God, who made thee mighty, make thee mightier yet.

Rodomontade went hand in hand with the denigration of rival empires. Still smarting from the humiliation of Fashoda, the French popular press never missed a chance to vilify Britain during the Boer War. Kruger was lionised, British troops accused of mass rape and the murder of prisoners ('Barbarie Anglaise') and British reverses were magnified.[5] It was all too much for the *Daily Mail*, which declared in February 1901 that if its French counterparts persisted in their calumnies, then France would be 'rolled in mud and blood' and stripped of its colonies, which would be given to the Italians and the Germans. Playground cat-calling may have embarrassed politicians (Lord Salisbury damned the *Mail* as a paper written and read by 'office boys'), but they were acutely aware that voters were swayed by the populist ranting of the 'yellow press'. Imperialist politicians and lobby groups targeted working-class voters, now a majority in Britain, France and Germany. Far from being, as socialists suggested, a cynical instrument of the greedy capitalist bosses, empire-building benefited the working classes. Properly managed expanses of fertile land in Africa could provide cheap food and their populations were consumers who would snap up the products of Europe's factories, and so prevent overproduction and its consequence, unemployment. 'Virgin territory of admirable fertility and enormous markets' was how *Le Petit Journal* described the recently annexed Upper Niger in 1891.[6]

The Left was not taken in. Its theorists saw imperialism as a desperate measure to avert the implosion of capitalism as predicted by Marx. Flag-waving and newspaper bombast were devices to dazzle the workers and distract them from their struggle against the bosses and the politicians who danced to their tune. The patriotic revels which marked victories during the Boer War prompted the trade unionist Peter Curran to comment: 'And if the "Jingoes" rejoice in the fact that

England has been a great country on which the sun never sets, then I say that in England there are thousands of homes on which the sun never rises.' The intellectual Left was ambivalent and imagined that imperialism in the abstract offered opportunities for social experimentation. Beatrice Webb thought that the colonies and their passive populations might provide laboratories for enlightened social engineering. George Bernard Shaw welcomed the Boer War as a means to chastise the Afrikaners, whom he loathed. French socialists regarded imperialism as a divisive ideology which would fuddle the minds of the workers and distract them from the class struggle. In August 1912 Jean Jaurès, the leader of the French Socialist Party, denounced 'l'aventure Marocaine' and the 'force brutale' of the military occupation as contrary to republican ideals. A month later, French trade unionists protested against the deployment of young working-class conscripts in Algeria and Morocco.[7] They risked their lives for capitalism and were becoming subverted by militarism, which eroded class solidarity and the international brotherhood of all workers. Some socialists believed that this fraternity of the exploited extended to Europe's colonies; Belgian and German Socialist deputies condemned the atrocities of the Congo and the suppression of the Herero uprising.

II

Africa offered a solution to Europe's demographic problems. Emigration, mostly to the United States, had gained an enormous momentum by the turn of the century. Mass exoduses reduced unemployment numbers, but governments feared that the permanent loss of workers, consumers and conscripts might prove debilitating. In 1902 the *Spectator* was worried about the consequences of 'the drain of our best material', although there was consolation in the fact that a good proportion of British emigrants went to the white dominions of Canada, Australia and New Zealand and remained emotionally attached to their motherland. In the same year, the South African Colonisation Society was founded under the chairmanship of Milner, who hoped that a steady influx of British immigrants would eventually lead to people of British stock outnumbering the Boers.[8]

The need for colonial settlement was more urgent in Italy. Count Francesco Crispi, the dominant figure in Italian politics from 1870 onwards, regretted that what he called 'the overflowing fecundity' of his country was heading for the United States and the Argentine. The annual rate of emigration had risen steeply from 200,000 in the 1880s to 800,000 in 1912. Crispi hoped that the total would fall as Italian families began to colonise the yet to be conquered Libya, where they would be given fertile land. Above all, these pioneers would remain Italian subjects and transform the colony into a second Algeria, which was now home to three-quarters of a million European *colons*.

Africa had little to offer poor and unskilled immigrants, while American industries could not get enough of them. Crispi's pioneers were destined to run farms, which required hard graft and capital. Investment hurdles meant that Britain's African colonies were attracting a trickle of immigrants. In 1914 there were 23,000 white Rhodesians and about 3,000 white settlers in Kenya, most of them farmers. All needed capital: a Kenyan coffee planter required £1,670 to cover the costs of his passage, tools, seeds and twenty oxen, together with a further £150 to pay the wages of a headman and twenty 'boys' (labourers) for eight months. A bank clerk or a railway manager also had to pay his fare out and, on arrival, had to show the authorities that he had £50 in cash and proof of an offer of permanent employment.[9]

Kenya's farmers were, therefore, predominantly from the younger sons of the aristocracy and upper-middle classes. Backed by family cash, the ex-public-schoolboy growing coffee enjoyed status and a chance for betterment. Their counterparts were present in Rhodesia. In 1897 these public-school and university men and ex-officers were characterised by the *Cape Times* as 'men of a well-known English type . . . rather tough customers, but gentlemen' who 'dealt toughly with the natives'.[10]

Beyond the settler colonies, Europeans were birds of passage employed by governments, engineering contractors, banks and trading and shipping companies. The largest concentration was in Egypt, where there were over 13,000 resident Britons in 1914, a tenth of them army and police officers. The rest were administrators and all were well paid, enjoyed generous pensions and an agreeable tempo of life. In 1901 Cecil Spring-Rice, a diplomat and future Ambassador to the United States who was then one of the commissioners in the Egyptian Public Debt Department, told his family: 'I am enjoying the heat here — it isn't bad but tends to uncontrollable laziness.' He dozed and read during the afternoon and, once the temperature had fallen, he played a round of golf and dressed for dinner.[11] Whether in Kenya or Egypt, the European enjoyed an abundance of servants – as, for that matter, he did at home.

Everywhere, European communities clung tenaciously to the rituals and pastimes of their homelands. Captain Boisragon, who was stationed at Old Calabar on the Nigerian coast in the 1890s, recorded that every Sunday the British civil and military community enjoyed a cricket match, and listened to the band of the native constabulary play numbers from the musical *A Gaiety Girl* while ladies from the hospital and the mission served tea.[12] During the Boer War officers stationed at Pietermaritzburg played polo and tennis, attended tea parties and held balls. The hoi polloi were unwelcome, as Private Rutland of the Middlesex Regiment noted enviously, although his kind were catered for by a passable music hall in the town.[13] Like its entertainments, Europe's social order was imported into Africa.

III

Boisragon and Rutland were two of the thousands of Europeans who produced a vast published and unpublished literature of Africa. There were the reminiscences of soldiers, missionaries and pioneers, travellers' narratives and private diaries, fiction with African scenarios and the home letters of expatriates, willing and unwilling. During the Zulu and Sudan wars soldiers' letters to their families were passed to local newspapers for publication. All this material was awash with graphic accounts of the incredible and the dramatic. There were accounts of blood-curdling native customs, bloody engagements in the bush and the desert, and the inevitable recitals of the thrills of big-game hunting. What emerged from these impressions of Africa was a world in which long periods of tedium were punctuated by short spells of excitement and danger.

War and Africa became inseparable in the public mind. Wherever European armies conquered, they were accompanied by war correspondents, artists and, from 1898, film cameramen. An attempt to film Omdurman miscarried, but soon afterwards English audiences were watching footage of the Boer War, and in 1911 Italians saw flickering newsreel images of dreadnoughts off the Libyan coast and boatloads of soldiers coming ashore.[14]

Imperial campaigns caught the public imagination. Like other newspaper tycoons, the proprietors of the imperialist *Petit Parisien* (its weekly circulation stood at 400,000 in 1890) noted that wars boosted sales, and responded accordingly.[15] Its rivals followed suit with graphic coverage of French African campaigns in the 1890s and 1900s. There was even space for the exploits of rivals: in 1891 *Le Petit Journal* published a dramatic image of the last-ditch stand of a German column in East Africa.[16] French readers were thrilled and shocked by images of vultures feeding on corpses, human sacrifice, a fetish house and stirring pictures of the raising of the French flag over conquered cities watched by disciplined ranks of native infantrymen and French officers. Perhaps the most striking was a spirited image of an officer of the Chasseurs d'Afrique galloping alongside the fleeing and wide-eyed resistance leader Samory Touré and seizing him.

Advertising copywriters and designers, who made their living from recognising the prevailing temper and tastes of consumers, believed that Africa was capturing the public imagination. African motifs, indeed anything connected with the new overseas empires, possessed positive patriotic associations which boosted sales. The endorsements of soldiers and pioneers had the same influence as those of celebrities today. In 1885, advertisements for Camp coffee essence showed an Egyptian orderly bringing cups of coffee to a group of officers in tropical uniforms seated outside a tent.* Bovril ('A Factor in our Empire's Strength') beefed up hungry Tommies during the Boer War. The 1904 South-West Africa campaign was exploited by German companies, who were confident that their customers were untroubled by reports of mass murders. Images of *Schutztruppen* appeared on cigarette and cigar packets, and one cigar manufacturer used a naked Herero girl as its brand image.[17]

Trampler chicory went a step further and printed an advertising card which showed German troops shelling a native village. In 1912 the distillers of the aperitif Byrrh appealed to the patriotic drinker with an image of a French officer sharing a glass with a Moroccan sheik while an aeroplane flew overhead. Another puff showed French soldiers,

---

* A later version showed an Indian orderly serving a British officer; recently the distinctly imperial relationship has been changed to one of equality, with the pair drinking their coffee together.

presumably fortified by Byrrh, charging fleeing Arabs. It is of more than passing interest that images of empire were preferred for such 'manly' products as tobacco and alcohol: a picture of a British tar with an ironclad in the background remains on packets of Player's Navy Cut cigarettes.

IV

If a nation was to fulfil its imperial destiny, it had to convert the young and make them aware of lands they would inherit and teach them the moral qualities required to govern and guide their inhabitants. Imperial propaganda was blatant, diverse and, wherever possible, blended instruction with entertainment. Insofar as it penetrated school syllabuses, it was official. An 1899 textbook for English elementary schools informed their mainly working-class pupils that 'our race possesses the colonial spirit which the French, Spaniards and Germans do not possess'. Its ingredients were 'daring' and 'doggedness', a 'masterful spirit' and a 'sense of justice'. In 1913 French children were taught that France 'wants the little Arabs to be educated as little French children' because she 'is generous towards the people she has conquered'.[18]

The schoolrooms in which British virtues were taught were decorated with coloured maps of the world with British possessions marked in red. Colourful colonial postage stamps found their way into children's stamp albums; imperial postage stamps were not only for communication, they were political statements. Britain may have been the predominant power in Egypt, but France maintained post offices in Alexandria and Port Said which sold overprinted French stamps. Similar issues, overprinted for use in Morocco, were an early indication of France's presence in the country and its interests there. Britain and Germany quickly established post offices and issued appropriately overprinted stamps.

Stamp-collecting was a fad of the late nineteenth and early twentieth centuries, particularly among the middle classes. Selling stamps to philatelists was a welcome money-spinner for colonial administrations; Kenya reported a windfall after a new issue in 1907 and the Seychelles education system was funded solely by the sale of stamps. By the 1900s the French, the Portuguese, the Congo Free State and Rhodesia were issuing pictorial issues: those for French West Africa showed a pouncing leopard, palm trees and the features of General Faidherbe, who had pushed back the frontiers of Senegal in the 1850s. In the same vein, issues for Djibuti showed a gunboat. The cheap, *centime* values were marketed in penny packets for children. Canada trumped everyone with an 1898 issue that showed a world map with the British Empire in red with the inscription, 'We Hold a Greater Empire than Has Been'.

For the schoolboy, Africa was a battleground of the imagination where brightly coloured, mass-produced toy soldiers waged war against plumed warriors with shields and spears. The manufacturers judged their market well and were quick to bring out ranges that covered contemporary wars. In the early 1900s German lads played with *Schutz-truppen* and askaris, equipped with machine-guns, and with their native adversaries. British and French toy makers offered *spahis* in Arab robes, Tommies in khaki and camelry wearing tarbooshes. My father fondly remembered a Christmas present of a box of British Camel Corps. Infants in the nursery took comfort from that universally loved and cheery playmate, the Golliwog, now reviled as a racist icon.

There was also a more serious empire for the young which was found in magazines and schoolboy adventure stories. The titles of the former evoke their spirit and content. The earliest was the *Boy's Own Paper*, founded in 1879 and supported by the Religious Tract Society and the Sunday School Union, which explains why an early edition contained instructions on how to take a cold bath.[19] Within twenty years *Union Jack*, *Pluck*, *The Captain* and *Chums* were thrilling the middle- and better-off working-class lad. The last included advertisements for emigration to the dominions and stories about big-game hunters and frontier campaigns. The Boer War yielded plenty of yarns, told in a virile and jaunty style. Their titles say it all: 'Veldt-Scouting by Colonial Scouts', 'Canadian Comrades at the Cape' and 'Through Fire for the Flag'.[20]

The master wordsmiths of boys' literature, G. A. Henty and Captain Frederick Brereton, turned out a stream of fast-moving, action-packed yarns in which plucky and resourceful young fellows found themselves fighting and winning the wars of Empire. Fiction was blended with history and propaganda. In Brereton's *In the Grip of the Mullah* (1903) the Governor of Somaliland tells the two heroes that 'we are known the world over as a fighting race who love freedom and hate the oppressor' who, in this case, is that 'unscrupulous ruffian', the Mad Mullah. At the conclusion of Henty's *Through Three Campaigns* (1901), the author justifies the 1900 expedition to Kumasi by claiming that 'The Ashanti and the surrounding tribes have received a lesson that will not be forgotten', and that 'civilisation' can now advance, bringing peace.

Rider Haggard, who had served on Shepstone's staff in the 1870s and had witnessed the changes that were overwhelming southern Africa at that time, questioned the nature of the civilisation they represented. In *Allan Quatermain* (1887) the hero denounces 'the greed, drunkenness, gunpowder and general demoralisation which chiefly mark the progress of civilisation amongst sophisticated peoples'. Rider Haggard's heroes are, in Quatermain's words, in Africa 'to hunt and seek adventures and new places'. Yet they are also searching for instant wealth (*King Solomon's Mines* and *Benita*) in the form of treasure houses hidden deep within the continent. Africa will yield its wealth to determined and daring adventurers; we are in the world of Cecil Rhodes.

Racial stereotypes abounded in popular fiction. Rider Haggard describes the fictional Wakwafi as 'a fine manly race, possessing many of the good qualities of the Zulu, and a larger capacity for civilisation'. Brereton's Somalis were 'cruel and capricious' and Henty warned his readers that in West Africa the 'light-coloured children' of 'mixed marriages uniformly died', a sign that such unions were unnatural. All three writers produced bestsellers and copies of Henty's and Brereton's books were distributed as prizes by elementary and Sunday schools – understandably so, for their content was wholesome and their sentiments patriotic.

The popular theatre of empire complemented juvenile fiction. In 1885 Berliners were diverted by a brightly lit panorama that showed a scene of recent events in Cameroon. German soldiers were fighting tribesmen 'under a panoply of palm and banana trees'.[21] Events in Rhodesia were the scenario for the 1895 melodrama *Cheer, Boys, Cheer* whose cast included cruel and treacherous natives, Boers ('cowardly hounds') and City slickers manipulating shares.[22]

Elements of the theatre were an integral part of the empire of public instruction promoted by the great international exhibitions held in Europe's major cities and in numerous smaller, private-enterprise shows often held in provincial cities and towns. To make money, these were advertised by striking, gaudy posters: that for the *Le Continent*

Noir display at the 1896 Swiss National Exhibition showed a warrior with a bow and white-robed Africans worshipping some unseen god or spirit. Much of what was on show was blatantly sensationalist, like the display in Berlin's Panopticon in 1893 where visitors saw the 'Amazons', the mythical female royal bodyguard of the kings of Dahomey. They were waxwork figures, but real Amazons – that is to say, imported black women carrying spears – appeared at exhibitions in Paris, Hamburg, Prague, St Petersburg and Chicago.[23] Those unable to see such curiosities for themselves viewed them in cinemas: during the 1890s the Lumière brothers filmed scenes from a mock village at a Lyons exhibition which showed African men and women bathing and working.[24] These scenes appeared with footage of African animals.

The great civic exhibitions of the period celebrated national achievements, industries and empires, were vast in scale and attracted millions of visitors. They experienced Africa at first hand, displayed in pavilions filled with trees, plants, animals and imported African people in their everyday dress (bosoms were exposed) undertaking their daily tasks in mock villages. These exhibits were human zoos and critics complained that there was something deeply repellent and degrading about African men and women being treated like caged animals.

Such exhibitions were staged for profit by impresarios with a knack of knowing exactly what the urban working- and lower-middle-class families expected from a day out. One, Imre Kiralfy, a Hungarian immigrant, created the Greater Britain Exhibition, an extravaganza based at Olympia. In the spring of 1899 200 Zulus and a handful of South African soldiers and policemen were hired and shipped to Southampton, where their disembarkation was filmed to make a one minute publicity short for a show that was a huge success. It transferred to Shepherd's Bush, where it attracted crowds for the next eight years.

The Zulus provided the star attractions: some performed dances twice daily and others played 'howling' warriors in a re-enactment of the battle from the recent Matabele War in which they were overcome by imported soldiers and policemen. Others played passive roles as the inhabitants of a 'Kaffir Kraal'; it was darkly rumoured in the scandal sheets that white women had entered the native huts with gifts for the Zulu men and received favours in return.[25] Suggestions of similar indecorum at a Hamburg exhibition appeared on a German comic postcard of 1912 on which a fashionably dressed lady is forbidden to approach a native village by a policeman who warns: 'Familiarities are forbidden.'[26]

The great international exhibitions were more serious affairs insofar as their prime purpose was to inform, and many exhibits were officially sponsored. Their scale was vast: the 1900 Exposition Universelle occupied 200 acres of central Paris and drew 50 million visitors in seven months. The colonial pavilions reproduced the towns and landscapes of Africa and filled them with Africans. The future novelist Paul Morand, then aged twelve, was entranced by a recreation of Algeria that exuded the exotic and sensual: 'All this hillside exhaled perfume, incense, vanilla and the smoke of pastilles that are burnt in seraglios', and in the background was the 'thin wail of Arabian flutes'. Curiosity and national pride were evoked by the replica of a Dahomey village. It was crowded with 'great negroes, still savages' who 'strode barefoot, with proud and rhythmic bearing' while women pounded millet. These creatures had been 'our old and recent enemies', but now they were 'our liegemen'.[27] By contrast another future writer, Boris Pasternak, was saddened by the 'Amazons' he saw in a St Petersburg show in 1901. He discovered female nakedness for the first time, but was upset by the suffering of the captive women.[28] Such humane feelings were rare among the sightseers at the human zoos.

15

'The honour of the ruling race':
Racial Attitudes, Sexual Encounters and
Africa's Future

I

The message of the human menageries was stark: Africans were a backward and primitive species which had failed to rise beyond the lowest rungs of the evolutionary ladder. Visitors who stared at them had been preconditioned to think in this way, since for the past hundred years scientists and philosophers had been evaluating the world's races according to inborn intellectual and moral capacities in order to produce a global racial hierarchy. The scientific element in this taxonomy gave these racial theories a persuasive legitimacy, which made it easy for them to gain general acceptance. Assumptions based upon this genetic determinism that are now discredited, abandoned and condemned as racism were taken for granted, and would remain so well into the twentieth century.

In 1900 Europeans placed themselves at the apex of a racial pyramid while Africans, Asians and Pacific Islanders filled its lower levels; their position was the consequence of genetic flaws of character and cultural traditions which had impeded their progress. The chief defects of Kipling's 'lesser breeds' were indolence, sexual promiscuity, cruelty, superstition and cannibalism. Allegations on this score were still commonplace. In 1902 a French geographer, writing about the inhabitants of the Ivory Coast, remarked that 'all the people of the tropical forest were cannibals, but they are nevertheless more civilised than their neighbours'.[1] Their redeeming virtues were weaving cloth and laying roads. The German government protested in 1915 that one of their NCOs had been eaten by African soldiers under British command during operations in Togoland.[2] A contemporary French patriotic postcard showed a German prisoner with a grinning Senegalese soldier who mocks him as one 'who would devour Europe'.[3] The cartoonist and his audience implicitly accepted that the Africans ate people.

Cannibalism was perhaps the most shocking excess of degeneracy. Its forms and its impact on the European imagination were starkly revealed by the episode of the Benin bronzes in 1897. They were the spoils of a British punitive expedition against Benin City in south-west Nigeria, undertaken after its ruler had murdered several British officials. As the column advanced through the bush it passed the corpses of hundreds of human sacrifices, killed by the Ebo in an attempt to invoke supernatural assistance. 'Human sacrifice, cannibalism and the tortures of fetish worship' were the evidence of a truly barbaric people, thought one British officer, and grisly photographs taken during the campaign supported his conclusion.[4]

Yet the thousand or so bronze statues and plaques suggested otherwise. Experts were astonished by their sophisticated craftsmanship and a German scholar likened them to the work of Cellini.[5] Other art historians were in a quandary: how could such wonderful creations be the work of a tribe who, in the opinion of one, ranked low in the evolutionary scale? Another thought that the bronzes were beyond the capacities of the Ebo and that they had been imported from either Egypt or Abyssinia.[5] Seen through the contemporary racial prism, whatever aesthetic merit the bronzes possessed was diminished by the perceived degeneracy of their makers.

Sweeping and dismissive racial generalisations were taken for granted even by men and women who were sympathetic towards the people of Africa and believed in their latent capacity for improvement. In 1905 the Belgian commission that had exposed the brutalities in the Congo concluded that forced labour remained the 'basis' by which its inhabitants 'can enter into the pathway of modern civilisation' and be 'reclaimed from [their] natural state of barbarism'.[6] In 1907, a missionary discussing plans for the future running of Anglican missions in Uganda insisted they included arrangements to preserve 'the positions and rights of the superior race'.

Current racial dogma complemented the Darwinian view of history as a prolonged struggle between races for global domination. This parallel between the animal and human universes chimed with those politicians and intellectuals in the English-speaking world who boasted that the innate genius of the Anglo-Saxon race destined it to dominate the world. Rhodes, Joseph Chamberlain, Churchill and Theodore Roosevelt thought this way. With equal vehemence, the French and the Germans insisted that the inborn and self-evident virtues that were the essence of *civilisation* and *Kultur* qualified them for world domination.

Conceits about superior national identities fused with racial pride and fuelled the chauvinistic nationalism that gripped Europe during the period of imperial rivalries and ran wild after the outbreak of war in 1914. One offshoot of this mixture of racist conjecture and nationalism was a morbid obsession with racial 'purity', which was why early-twentieth-century Germans were agitated by the influx of Polish immigrant workers and eugenics societies were formed in Britain and the United States. Anxieties about contaminated bloodlines, coupled with religious mania, led to the pogroms of Russian Jews in the 1890s and the slaughter of Muslims by Serbs during the Balkan Wars of 1912 and 1913. Paranoia about racial purity and the enforcement of white supremacy explained the hideous frequency of lynching in the southern states of America from the 1880s to the 1950s.

Given the insidious value judgements implicit in the classification of the world's races, it was inevitable that some would be dehumanised to the point where their lives were deemed worthless. In Chapter Eleven we have already encountered British, German, French and Belgian commanders in Africa who thought along these lines. In the middle of the First World War, the Liberal MP (and former South African magistrate) Colonel Josiah Wedgwood urged the mass recruitment of black soldiers to offset the losses of white men so as 'to eke out the finest race on earth'.[7]

II

There was some virtue in savagery: certain Africans made excellent soldiers. Native troops had been employed at every stage of the continent's subjugation and remained vital for the survival of imperial government, particularly in areas such as East and Central Africa where the climate and indigenous diseases were too much for Indian and white troops. Naturally resilient black men took their place and European officers were quick to pinpoint those tribes with a warrior culture that prized courage and aggressiveness. It was the same process by which the British had singled out Gurkhas and Sikhs in India as instinctively warlike and, for that matter, the Russians and Austrians had identified Cossacks and Croats as nature's fighting men.

Ferocity was not universal among Africans. When asked by Whitehall in 1903 what manpower was available to defend Lagos against a French invasion, the Governor replied that 'the Haussa is a better and more effective soldier than the Yoruba or indeed any other race'.[8] Lord Lugard, who commanded them in many battles, rejected demands for Hausa porters in 1916 because they were 'a combative race' and therefore too precious to be employed carrying supplies. These chores were better undertaken by the placid Mende and Temne of Sierra Leone.[9]

Another experienced Africa commander, Colonel Charles Mangin, argued that the African soldier would be vital for France in a European war. Sluggish population growth had placed her at a disadvantage against Germany, but the imbalance in manpower could be rectified by African conscripts. In his *La Force Noire* of 1911, Mangin argued that the 'warrior instincts . . . remain extremely powerful in primitive races'. 'Their nervous systems were less developed than Europeans'', which made them resistant to pain, they came from hierarchical societies which meant that they were amenable to military discipline, and they fought like lions. Moreover, in Mangin's opinion, the black soldier would be glad to risk his life in the cause of French civilisation, which was changing his people's lives for the better.[10] His views were echoed by a British officer during the 1914–18 East African campaign who had observed that the black soldier was 'temperamentally disposed to attack by rush with the arme blanche'.[11] Men used to hurling themselves at their foes with spears would be happy to do so with bayonets.

In 1912 and in line with Mangin's proposals, France extended conscription to Algeria and West Africa as the first stage of creating a mass African army for service in Europe. Within two years Arab and black conscripts would be fighting Germans on the Western Front and Turks in the Middle East. French socialists were concerned that African soldiers would be deployed to crush strikes, and the *colons* of Algeria feared for their lives. Their newspaper *La Dépêche Algérienne* howled with rage: 'You are going to teach every *bicot* [wog] how to use a rifle.'[12] Among Algerian Arabs and the more enlightened colonists there were hopes that peacetime conscription would accelerate assimilation and the granting of political rights on the grounds of moral reciprocity. This did not happen. Nonetheless, the decision to conscript Africans to fight in Europe did have enormous repercussions. The mass armies created a new elite of disciplined men trained in arms, conversant with European technology and, as NCOs, familiar with exercising authority. France's pre-war crisis of manpower was the beginning of the emergence of Africa's modern military elites whose roots were in the old warrior culture.

France lacked industrial workers as well as soldiers and, again, Africans filled the gap. In 1905 the government acceded to the demands of the *patrons* and agreed to lift the thirty-year-old ban on Algerian immigration. At first, Kabyles from the coastal region were recruited for the most unpleasant and risky jobs in factories, mines and docks. Three famines between 1905 and 1912 speeded the flow of immigrants and by 1914 30,000 were working in France and sending home a proportion of their wages. French trade unions objected to *all* immigrant labour, which they regarded as a device to break strikes and hold down wages.

Algerians were hired as blackleg labour in the 1910 Marseilles oil refinery strike and were attacked by Italian strikers.[13] British seamen's unions shared the anxieties of their French counterparts and were hostile to African and Caribbean sailors who had settled in British ports and were satisfied with lower wages. In both countries the tensions sprang from economic pressures rather than racial antipathy. This would come later when the numbers of black immigrants rose.

Massive immigration later in the century was marked by racial segregation in urban Europe. It was already well established in those parts of Africa where Europeans had settled and was considered natural and desirable. It was bad form to bring Egyptian guests to Cairo's Turf and Gezira Clubs, and there were whites-only churches in South Africa and Lagos. The suburbs of the newly built Port Harcourt were racially segregated along lines already established in Algerian and South African cities and towns.[14] The white bigwigs of Cape Town (including Rhodes) built mansions amid the vineyards at the foot of Table Mountain, which were the counterpart of the large bourgeois villas in the outer suburbs of European cities. By the early 1900s the Johannesburg authorities were already shifting black miners and their families away from the city centre to outlying shanty towns, the forerunners of the sprawling Soweto townships. These were, of course, the racial equivalents of the slums of Europe's industrial cities.

The duality of the new urban Africa is vividly portrayed on picture postcards, a popular novelty of the 1890s. Views of Cairo and Algiers show docks, railway stations, squares and wide streets lined with offices, banks, hotels and apartment blocks and filled with carriages, trams and the occasional motor car. In striking contrast there are depictions of the native quarters with narrow alleys, tenements with projecting balconies, mosques, kasbahs, street markets, coffee shops with customers smoking hookahs, and groups of men, women and children in traditional costumes, often staring shyly at the camera. They and their surroundings were picturesque, which was exactly what tourists had come to see. The author of a French guidebook to Algeria published in 1899 was appalled by the shabby appearance of Arabs who had adopted European fashions. In their 'European rags' and 'formless felt hats and greasy derbies' they were 'ugly and ignoble'.[15] Traditional clothes had dignity, integrity and, when worn by women, romantic allure. Below a 1913 *National Geographic* photograph of a veiled Algerian lady in a 'crown-like headdress', swathed in silk robes and adorned with gold pendants and bracelets, was a caption that described her as 'the personification of the gorgeous East'.

III

Such creatures, hidden within the harem and preferably unclad, had long excited the European sexual imagination. It treated North Africa as an extension of the Middle East, a region that was widely believed to be pervaded by sensuality and permissiveness, despite the severe moral interdicts of sharia law. This image was perpetuated and refined by Delacroix (who visited Algeria in the 1830s immediately after the French invasion) and Ingres with their Romantic portrayals of submissive women from that treasure house of European sexual fantasies, the seraglio. The most striking in terms of pure eroticism were Ingres's *Odalisque* and *Odalisque with Slave*.

These sexual perceptions of the Arab world had some substance, although the reality was often neither romantic nor glamorous. In 1914 a British sergeant was astonished by the abundance of brothels in

Alexandria: 'You can get down street after street with women at every door and window, shouting each other down to get your custom. All sorts and practically every nationality, some not more than children to fat Arabs and coal black Sudanese.'[16] Prostitutes were also found in large numbers in European cities, garrison towns and ports, but they were more discreet. There were also the street pedlars of pornographic postcards, who importuned soldiers with 'dirty postcards effendi'. They and their wares outraged one missionary who, in 1917, protested to the army authorities, who treated the whole business and the man who had raised it as an embarrassing nuisance.[17]

In Europe, analyses of the nature and expressions of human, particularly female, sexuality were rarely publicly aired beyond medical circles before 1920. Defining and regulating what was or was not permissible in sexual behaviour was still a matter for the churches, which exerted a powerful and repressive influence over law-making and the policing of sexuality. In 1879 a London photographer who displayed photographs of bare-breasted Zulu girls in his shop window was unsuccessfully prosecuted at the instigation of a Christian organisation, the Society for the Suppression of Vice. Such bodies proliferated in mid-Victorian Britain, but they faced an uphill struggle: in 1874 a police raid on the premises of a London pornographer uncovered 130,000 lewd photographs.[18]

There were wide national differences in attitudes to sex. In France homosexuality had been legal since the Revolution and it was customary for young men to visit a brothel as a rite of passage towards manhood. Both were unthinkable in Britain and Germany. Zola's sexually explicit novel *La Terre* was published in France in 1887 and banned in Britain the following year by an apoplectic magistrate after he had heard a reading of its opening passage which described a farm girl helping a bull to mount a cow. Police censors kept a strict eye on all public entertainments in Germany. In each imperial power there was a strong sense that sexual excess somehow tarnished national and racial prestige. What disturbed Germans during the Carl Peters scandal (see Chapter Eleven) was not his lust but the fact that it mired their national self-image of an upright, disciplined people. This was certainly how the Germans wished to appear to their African subjects. Candidates for the South-West African *Landespolizei* were expected to be tall, athletic, bright young men with an aura of authority.[19]

Yet the German colonial authorities recognised that such virile fellows had sexual needs, and so they were allowed the indulgence of native mistresses, whose existence had been a fact of life throughout the period of colonisation. Paris tolerated the presence of concubines in the beds of young officers and officials on the grounds that 'a temporary liaison with well-chosen native women' was invaluable for mastering local languages.[20] François-Joseph Clozel, Governor of the Ivory Coast at the start of the century, took his superiors at their word and toured the colony for the 'daily recruitment of women for himself and his staff'.[21] This practice had a long life: in 1942 a Foreign Office agent reported that in the remoter districts of Gabon there were 'men whose administrative talents seem to be concentrated almost exclusively on the more presentable section of the female native population'.[22]

Marriages with native women were exceptional, not least because their children held an indeterminate and therefore troublesome position within colonial society. In 1895 Albert Nebert, an official in the Ivory Coast, ignored convention and married an African woman, Ago, whose father paid the normal bride price and warned his daughter that if she did not 'smile' for her husband she would be killed. The couple had six children.[23] Mistresses were usually the rule, and many French officers found them refreshingly responsive when compared to French women. Robert Altmayer of the Timbuktu garrison thought that the local women were 'cleaner' than those of his native Lorraine.[24] In Pierre Loti's novel *Le Roman d'un Spahi* (1881) the hero, Jean, a conscript and the only son of a peasant couple from the Cévennes, finds his Senegalese mistress as alien as her country. She was the 'highly flavoured fruit of the Soudan . . . precociously ripened by the tropical spring, bursting with poisonous juices, ripe with morbid voluptuousness, febrile and foreign'. She was also an object of brutal contempt: 'an inferior being roughly equivalent to his yellow-haired dog'. Yet she shows Jean love and devotion when, at some risk, she tends him after he has been fatally wounded in a skirmish.

Official toleration of such liaisons did not extend to sexual scandals that detracted from the high-minded ideals of France's civilising mission. In 1905 Marius Leclerc, an officer stationed at Louga in Senegal, was accused of the kidnapping and rape of a local girl. He pleaded that his actions were no more than 'mariage à la mode du pays', which failed to convince his superiors. His commanding officer insisted that such conduct was now intolerable, and Leclerc was demoted and exiled to a remote and unhealthy district.[25] British courts martial were more severe: during the Boer War white soldiers guilty of rape were given sentences of between two and five years, and two black scouts were executed.[26]

Less sexually relaxed Britain was willing to allow its colonial servants to keep mistresses as they had done in India before the influx of European women after 1840. This tolerance was reluctantly extended to Africa, although it was hoped that the young imperial officer and administrator would stay true to the ideals of Christian manliness drummed into him in his public school. Pure in thought and mentally armoured against temptation, he would channel all his physical and emotional energies into the service of his country, and many did. Others found celibacy impossible, as a series of scandals in Kenya revealed in the early 1900s. One district officer maintained a harem of twelve Nandi women and another purchased three girls, one aged twelve, for forty goats.[27]

Reprimands followed, and in London these cases led to a ban on native mistresses in the form of Lord Crewe's memorandum of 1909. It insisted that all officials had to set 'an honourable example' to those they ruled and warned that 'gravely improper conduct' diminished their authority and capacity to work efficiently. The *Church Missionary Review* welcomed a measure that would enhance 'the honour of the ruling race'.[28] Henceforward, men who kept native paramours would find their careers blighted. Nevertheless old habits continued, particularly in remote districts where they were hard to detect. At least one district officer in Tanganyika kept a mistress in the 1940s.[29]

Prostitutes were an alternative and they flourished in ports, garrison towns and communities with an abundance of young unmarried male immigrants. White clients in East Africa were particularly generous and African women could earn up to £5 a week, nearly ten times as much as they could as domestic servants. Some saved their takings to use them as capital for small businesses. In Southern Rhodesia prostitution was segregated by a 1904 law by which a black who enjoyed the favours of a white whore was liable for five years in gaol and she for two.[30]

This legislation reflects dark and fearful European imaginings about the sexuality of the Negro male. This phantasm, based on exaggerated missionary impressions, depicted him as by nature promiscuous and priapic.[31] He was, therefore, an ever-present threat to white womanhood, which was why white settlers were fearful for the safety of their womenfolk – none more so than Ewart Grogan, the President of the Kenya Colonists Association. In 1907, after an incident in which three Nairobi rickshaw boys had manhandled three female passengers, Grogan publicly flogged the culprits in front of the magistrates' court. A crowd of settlers cheered him on and he justified himself with a declaration that: 'white men could not stand any impertinence to their women in any part of the world'.[32] He used a *kiboko*, a hippo-hide whip traditionally used by African chiefs and enthusiastically adopted by settlers. In 1913 the *East African Standard* insisted that 'the rule of the iron hand is still absolutely essential to the very existence of the white man' in the region.[33]

IV

Civilisation in the form of European influences and habits spread slowly and unevenly across Africa during the early twentieth century. It was strongest wherever Europeans were numerous and where their needs were creating an embryonic African middle class. Educated Africans in South Africa's cities and towns attended balls where there was 'dignified dancing', which must have delighted the missionaries. The waltz was infinitely preferable to the uninhibited indigenous gyrations.[34] Ironically, Europeans would soon be dancing to American rag-time bands, whose rhythms had their roots in the music of African slaves.

Members of South Africa's black middle class also enjoyed cycling, rugby, chess and public lectures. Sol Plaatje, a journalist and future nationalist leader, was secretary of the Kimberley Eccentrics Cricket Club, although he was an indifferent but enthusiastic player. Middle-class African families in Lagos celebrated Christmas with turkeys and mince pies.[35] Their Egyptian counterparts also adopted the pleasures of the European bourgeoisie. They listened to records played on American-manufactured gramophones which cost two Egyptian pounds each and came with a five-year guarantee. These were hugely popular and annual imports of records from America, Britain, France and Germany totalled three-quarters of a million.[36]

Novel diversions and tastes were and would remain highly desirable for Africans and their popularity was interpreted as a willingness to embrace European civilisation. Its nature and how it might best be extended were subjects of debate among Europeans and the small but growing number of educated Africans. In 1905 Pixley ka Isaka Seme, a mission-educated Zulu who had recently returned from college in the United States, felt confident that African regeneration was under way and that 'a brighter day was rising'. Revealingly, he cited Egypt and Bechuanaland (both with native rulers under British protection) and the independent monarchy of Abyssinia as beacons for the future.

Richard Beale Blaize, a Lagos businessman and editor of the *Lagos Times*, was more constrained and questioned the wholesale and uncritical adoption of all things European. Interviewed by a British journalist in 1897, he wondered whether civilisation was 'always disadvantageous to the African race' since it was far easier 'to copy the vices [rather] than the virtues of civilisation'. Rather than be suffocated by civilisation, the African should select whatever was suitable for the needs 'of our climate and physique'. Synthesis was better than 'heedless imitation' of European habits and mores.[37]

Ex-President Theodore Roosevelt, who visited East Africa to massacre big game in 1910, thought otherwise. He was pleased to see railway officials 'dressed in fez and shorts and trousers which indicate a coming under the white man's influence' and held strongly to the views of African inferiority outlined at the beginning of this chapter. Most East Africans were 'still wild pagans' who lived in a land which 'they were utterly powerless in any way to improve'. European rule was their only salvation, and there were plenty of remote areas where it was still fragile. During 1910 and 1911 a British official reported that in northern Uganda 'the Turkana and all the tribes around them and their fathers before them now spend their lives raiding their neighbours'.[38] Slave-raiding continued in the inaccessible mountain area of northern Cameroon and would do so well into the 1920s.[39]

Pacification remained essential for the remaking of Africa. Early in 1914 a Senegalese Muslim grandee looked back on the recent past, in which his people were in a state of 'anarchy' and were 'cutting each other's throats'. He publicly thanked France, 'who has made progress from barbarity and savagery towards the light of civilisation'.[40] A few months later, that light flickered and dimmed as Europe's imperial powers went to war.

16

'Lloyd George', 'Kitchener', 'Sambo' and 'Coolie': Africa at War 1914–1918

I

'The British Empire is now fighting for its existence', declared Lord Kitchener, the Minister for War, in November 1914. So too were the French, Russian, Austro-Hungarian, German and Turkish empires. All were engaged in a titanic clash in which the adversaries were fighting not just to protect their possessions, but to enlarge them and acquire new resources and spheres of influence in Europe and overseas. Soldiers were slaughtered in droves so that their countries would become stronger and richer at the expense of their enemies. Russians died in Galicia so that the Tsar could rule over Constantinople; Tommies fell at the Somme so that Britain could become master of the Middle East and the Union Jack would fly over Dar-es-Salaam; and Frenchmen died at Verdun to regain Alsace and Lorraine and secure the Levant for France. Germans died in France and Flanders to make their nation dominant in Europe and a global superpower without equal, and Turks were slain at Gallipoli to save Islam and recover their Sultan's lost lands and influence.

A hunger for land and power drove the Central Powers (Germany, Austria-Hungary and Turkey) and the Allies (Britain, France and Russia), and its scale was exposed by the uncompromising armistice conditions imposed on the defeated. After Russia had been knocked out of the war in 1917, the Central Powers compelled the new and fragile Communist regime to surrender much of Poland and the Ukraine in March 1918. The victors then fell on the undefended rump of the Czarist Empire: German and Turkish armies advanced southwards and eastwards towards the Caucasus. Grain from the Ukraine and oil from Baku would strengthen the economy of the greater European Reich. In October and November 1918, Allied negotiators scotched this enterprise by their insistence that Germany and Turkey disgorged not only their latest conquests but also their pre-war empires in Africa, the Middle East and the Pacific. The next year the terms imposed by the Versailles Peace Conference confirmed the dissolution of the German, Austro-Hungarian and Turkish empires. The winners then parcelled out the spoils.

Throughout the war, imperial geopolitics had swayed strategic decisions. By defeating Germany where it was strongest on the Western Front, the Allies imagined they could dictate a new disposition of world power. Yet victory in the West proved elusive for both sides and during the later phase of the war statesmen and diplomats secretly prepared for the possibility of a negotiated peace. If this came about, there would be horse-trading over post-war allocations of land, resources and spheres of influence. This was why the British Prime Minister, Lloyd George, endorsed offensives against the Turks in Palestine, the German High Command argued for annexations in Russia, and Enver Pasha, the Ottoman War Minister, backed the invasion of the Caucasus. Each was accumulating valuable chips to be exchanged or cashed in at a peace conference.

Such bargains would not have been tolerated by public opinion. National propaganda agencies had done their work too well and aroused a vengeful spirit and a desire for compensation for sacrifices of blood and treasure. The mere reallocation of deserts, rainforests and investment concessions could never satisfy populations that were showing an extraordinary fortitude in the face of privation and mass casualties. Mobilised for total war, the people wanted nothing less than a total victory with the winners taking all. When, during the December 1918 general election, Lloyd George promised to squeeze Germany until the 'pips squeaked', he was saying exactly what British voters wanted to hear. Their vindictive acquisitiveness was shared by the people of France; to understand why, look at the long lists of the dead recorded on French war memorials.

National stamina did not prove limitless: during 1917 Russia collapsed under the burden of defeats and inflation, and France and Italy were flagging. The British War Cabinet agonised over whether its forces could withstand a further gruelling two years in the trenches, although national morale had been buoyed by the United States' entry into the war in April. Fresh and robust young Americans would surely tip the balance, so long as they arrived in time. The outcome of the war remained unpredictable until the autumn of 1918, when the Central Powers keeled over and threw in the towel. Turkey and Bulgaria buckled after a string of reverses and Austria-Hungary and Germany were in the grip of economic crises that sparked off widespread revolutionary agitation. The German army that withdrew from France in November had been ordered home to suppress Communist insurrections and naval mutinies.

Waging four years of total war had required prodigious exertions. It was universally accepted that manpower was the key to victory, for it was vital on the battlefield and for the maintenance of the industries and transport systems that kept mass armies fed and equipped. Europe's empires were, therefore, mobilised. Britain, France and Germany enlisted over 2 million Africans to fight in local colonial campaigns and, in the case of France, stiffen its armies on the Western Front and in the Near East. Senegalese and Algerians fought at Gallipoli and were the backbone of the army that established French rule on the Levant during the winter of 1918–19. Thousands of Egyptian *fellahin* were recruited to maintain British bases and lines of communication in their own country and France, where they were joined by black labourers from South Africa. Huge numbers of Algerians were drafted into French factories, mines and dockyards to release workers for service at the front. The demand for *poilus* turned out to be insatiable as casualty lists soared after the catastrophic, large-scale offensives of 1916 and 1917.

Germany could not tap African manpower because of the Royal Navy's blockade and Anglo-French invasions of its African colonies. Berlin, therefore, applied a colonial expedient, forced labour, to Europe. Frenchmen, Belgians, Romanians and Poles living in areas under military administration were compelled to work in German factories just as Africans had been press-ganged to lay roads and tend plantations. Germany revived this expedient on a far greater scale during the Second World War.

II

Africa was a theatre of war as well as a reservoir of blood and muscle. Turkish war aims included turning the British, French and Italians out of North Africa and restoring nominal Ottoman sovereignty over Egypt, Libya, Tunisia and Algeria. Germany was strongly supportive and devoted much energy and cash to foment Pan-Islamic subversion in British and French colonies in Africa. Allied sea power in the Mediterranean ruled out any direct military intervention in North Africa, although the Turks twice made half-hearted attempts to invade Egypt. From the start, Britain and France set out to conquer and occupy German colonies. During the first fortnight of the war British warships were shelling German wireless stations on the African coast and within three months Anglo-French forces were engaged in every German colony.

Germany could not defend its empire. The Kaiser's naval strategy required its fleet to remain intact and concentrated in the North Sea as a permanent threat to Britain, which left the Royal Navy free to blockade Germany's colonies. Denied reinforcements and munitions from the Fatherland, they were left to fend for themselves, and by 1916 Cameroon, Togoland and South-West Africa were in Allied hands. Nevertheless, Germans believed that these losses would prove temporary since they would be returned after a German victory in Europe and be augmented by confiscated British and French possessions. After giving Anglo-French forces a good run for their money, the remnants of the German army in Cameroon retired to the tiny Spanish colony of Rio Muni (now Equatorial Guinea), where they drilled and prepared themselves in readiness for a revival of German power in Africa.[1] As late as September 1918, a right-wing German newspaper looked forward to a victory that would mean the return of occupied colonies and the acquisition of new ones, prised from France and Britain.[2]

Colonial inducements lured Italy into the war on the Allied side in 1915. The Italians also touted for Anglo-French support for a future partition of Abyssinia, a neutral state, but were cold-shouldered. Britain and France were unwilling to jeopardise their profitable concessions, although the prospect of an eventual division of Abyssinia prompted the government in Nairobi to propose that Britain should annex lands adjacent to the Kenyan frontier. It was a 'wonderful country in which you sow two crops every year' – 'Including dragon's teeth', minuted a sceptical Colonial Office official.[3] Some in South Africa saw the war as a chance to grab South-West Africa, a step towards a greater South Africa that one day would include Southern Rhodesia and Nyasaland. Belgium and Portugal expected slices of German East Africa in return for their efforts in Europe and Africa.

Ironically, in the months before the outbreak of the war, the British and German governments had been discussing the division of the fly-blown Portuguese colonies. Portugal joined the Allies in 1916, but its efforts were puny and incompetent. In the words of a British officer who served alongside it in East Africa, the Portuguese army 'was a shame to a colonial nation'.⁴ Everywhere there was a lack of 'preparation and method', and Portuguese native troops were wretched starvelings casually led by officers whose watchword was 'be it as God pleases'. Thus it was that Mozambique could muster twenty-six lorries but only six drivers. Ashamed of his army's performance, one officer apologised for 'our decadence, indifference, [and] apathy'.⁵ All in all, the Portuguese were a liability to their ally.

The campaigns in Africa have been well written up. In each of its colonies Germany's forces put up a tough resistance. Intelligent command compensated for the lack of reinforcements and munitions. German troops, mostly native *Schutztruppen*, were led by bold and flexible commanders who were adept at improvisation. British and French generalship was at best indifferent.

In East Africa, General Paul von Lettow-Vorbeck waged a brilliant campaign of fluid and audacious movement and guerrilla attacks and, by 1916, had fought the British to a standstill. A former guerrilla General, Jan Smuts, was summoned from South Africa to inject some ginger into operations but, despite favourable odds of twenty-five to one, he found it hard going. In the final year of the war, von Lettow-Vorbeck still held the initiative and his columns invaded Mozambique and Northern Rhodesia. After the war he attributed his triumphs to his troops' 'conviction that Germany could not be beaten in this war' which, together with a 'strong sense of duty' and 'spirit of self-sacrifice', kept morale high among his askaris and their white officers.⁶ On his return to Germany von Lettow-Vorbeck was lionised, and he concluded his memoirs with the prophecy that: 'the healthy spirit of our German people will prevail again and once more tread the upward path'. He did not, however, back the Nazis.

III

White soldiers fared badly in the white man's African campaigns. Endemic fevers, dysentery, cold nights and hot days spent marching through the bush laden with heavy kit sent sickness rates soaring. The 832-strong Loyal North Lancashire Regiment which landed in East Africa in November 1914 spent most of the next six months at half strength, and during the rainy season the numbers fit for duty fell to 352. Hardy white Rhodesian settlers succumbed as easily as did working-class lads from Britain's industrial cities: after three months in the East African bush, over 100 of the 500 men of the Rhodesia Regiment were in hospital. Sickness rates were even higher among South African troops. Three years into the war, the director of the British army's local medical services concluded that 'The European infantry soldier cannot cope with the climate.' Neither could his Indian counterpart, for many sepoy regiments were reduced to a third of their strength by indigenous distempers.[7]

Africans, therefore, had to bear the brunt of the fighting in Africa. Over 2 million were drawn into the war and 200,000 of them died in battle or from sickness and exhaustion. France raised 535,000 Senegalese and Algerian soldiers, mostly by conscription, of whom 140,000 were destined for the Western Front. The remainder were deployed in Africa, the Gallipoli campaign and operations in Palestine and Syria during 1918. Britain's African soldiers fought only in Africa, although South Africa and Egypt supplied labourers for British forces in France and the Middle East.

Over a million Africans served in Africa, nearly all of whom undertook the donkey work in labour-intensive campaigns. Porters carried their own and soldiers' rations and ammunition, and their numbers often equalled those of fighting men. One howitzer needed at least 100 carriers and each officer required at least eight or nine servants; von Lettow-Vorbeck, always stretched for men, considered five bearers the bare minimum for an officer. Wastage rates from sickness and desertion were greater than those among soldiers and so replacements had constantly to be found. Four-fifths of the adult male population of Nyasaland volunteered or were drafted to join hundreds of thousands from Kenya, Uganda and West Africa, territories taken from the Germans, and the Congo yielded over a quarter of a million for Belgian operations in East Africa.

Enlistment on this scale was only possible thanks to the cooperation of tribal and village chiefs and elders. A porter from Southern Nigeria recalled afterwards how 'The chief called us and handed us to the government messenger saying that the white man needed us.' The draftees were then conducted to a depot, where their names were written in a book, and then each received a blanket, food and a ticket inscribed with his name. Only then did they discover that they 'were going to a war to help the King's soldiers who were defending the country against the Germans'.[8] Clerks flummoxed by local dialects invented droll names for some conscripts; among them were 'Lloyd George', 'Kitchener', 'Sambo' and 'Coolie'.[9]

Such renaming had been common during the slaving period, and the relatives of some of the draftees likened the methods of enlistment to the slave trade. Nigeria became the host to Yorubas who had fled across the border from Dahomey to escape French recruiting officers. Sympathetic chiefs built camps for them and one Colonial Office official condemned the French system as 'a peculiarly objectionable form of slavery'.[10] Nevertheless, and at the insistence of Britain's ally, some of the fugitives were returned.

The demand for porters was insatiable, with death rates of up to 30 per cent. Evasion of the call-up was common: a mass levy of 160,000 in British East and Central African colonies in 1916 yielded only two thirds of the total. Porters raised in Nyasaland called their duties *thangata*, that is, labour without benefit. It was different for soldiers: many years later, a former askari from that colony remembered that he and his fellows joined 'because we were men'.[11] A Masai soldier may have spoken for many others when he told von Lettow-Vorbeck that 'It is all the same for us whether the English or the Germans are our masters.' His remark confirmed the General's impression that the African 'has a fine sense of the transfer of real power from one hand to another'.[12] In Mozambique the change was well received, for German forces were welcomed early in 1918.[13] The inhabitants of Togoland were glad to see the back of the Germans, and hoped that they would be replaced by the British rather than the French.

The war accelerated the exodus of Algerians to France, where they replaced migrant workers from Belgium, Italy, Spain and Poland and, of course, Frenchmen conscripted for military service. Over 220,000 Algerians were recruited and they settled in ghettoes on the outskirts of towns and cities, where they kept to themselves, congregating in cafés. They were kept under close police surveillance and were disdained by the French, who stigmatised them as a threat to women, carriers of syphilis and child molesters.[14]

Workplace regimes were strict (foremen were often former Algerian NCOs), although efforts were made to ensure that Muslim dietary taboos were observed in canteens. Unrest over pay and conditions was crushed with maximum severity: in 1917 five strikers were shot by troops at Brest.[15] The British military authorities also enforced discipline with lethal force. Twenty-eight Egyptian labourers were shot down by troops during a series of strikes and disturbances in Calais and Boulogne in September 1917. The chief grievances were about terms of service and the labourers' recent exposure to German bombardment.[16] Similar measures were used whenever Chinese indentured labourers rioted in protest against mistreatment.

IV

The war in North and West Africa had a strong ideological element. In November 1914 the Ottoman Sultan Mehmed V had used his spiritual authority as Caliph to declare a global jihad against the British, French and Russian empires. Henceforward, it was the religious duty of every Sunni Muslim to rise up against his infidel rulers and, if he was a soldier, to mutiny and murder his officers. Control of the jihad was in German hands: German money funded bribes and propaganda, German agents fomented subversion and, wherever possible, jihadis were provided with German guns. The directors of the jihadic movement believed that their best chances of success lay in regions with a tradition of Islamic resistance. Geography, however, frustrated these schemes, since most potential African jihadis lived in remote areas under Anglo-French rule. If the Sultan's jihad was to avoid the fate of its recent smaller predecessors in the Sudan, Somaliland and West Africa, its holy warriors needed smuggled modern weapons.

The exception was the Libyan coastal littoral between Benghazi and Tripoli where, since 1911, the Sanussi had kept the Italians at bay with the help of Turkish officers and small detachments of soldiers. Twenty thousand Turkish and irregular troops held out for the duration of the war, assisted by supplies shipped in U-boats, including a few aeroplanes and armoured cars.[17] This isolated and largely inert force was the last

Left: Great white queen: a West African wood-carver's image of Queen Victoria.

Below: Sir Harry Smith, Governor-General of Cape Colony (1847–54) and hammer of the Xhosa.

Sir Frederick Lugard, Governor of Nigeria, 1914.

Marshal Hubert Lyautey.

The Governor of German East Africa comes ashore with missionaries
in attendance, 1890.

Reluctant imperialist: cavalry charger hauled on to a train during the war in Sudan, 1898.

British troops with Maxim gun. This weapon underwrote the conquest of Africa.

Below: Alexandria in ruins. This photo shows clearly the damage done to the city by the British bombardment, 1882.

Britain's imperial lifeline: European warships attending the opening of the Suez Canal, 1869.

Below: Instant fortunes: Kimberley diamond diggings, *c.* 1871.

KIMBERLEY MINE 1871

Left: Abd al-Kadir, leader of the Algerian resistance, photographed in exile *c.* 1860.

Below: High adventure in the Sahara, 1898: a French *chasseur* captures Samory Toor, a ruler who had defied France for over twenty years.

Abd el-Krim, 'The Lion of the Rif' who fought Spanish and French armies in Morocco in the 1920s.

Left: Egyptian women demonstrate in Cairo in support of the *Wafd*, 1919.

Above: An Italian colonist breaks new ground in Eritrea, 1910.

Right: Airpower: Italian aircraft over Libya, 1912.

Below: Imperialism in the nursery: a children's book shows Abyssinians worshipping the flag of Italy, 1936.

Sharing power: a Basuto chief and his sons in European dress, *c.* 1890. His top hat and epaulettes indicate his authority.

New fashions: nuns teach West African women the art of dressmaking, 1910.

A German askari learns to operate a heliograph, East Africa, 1914.

The perils of exploration: Dr Livingstone attacked by a lion, *c.* 1850.

Riding for a fall. A German official in practice for a zebra race; East Africa, *c.* 1910.

Modern Africa: Inter-war and post-war colonial stamps advertised progress
in commerce, industry and communications.

Defending *La Patrie*: Moroccan cavalrymen on patrol in north-eastern France, October 1914.

Spanish Civil War Regulares, recruited from Morocco to the side of General Franco, wait for their flight to Spain, July 1936.

Above: An Ethiopian
salutes the Italian troops
with a white flag, *c.* 1930.
The Italians will go on to
surrender in Ethiopia in
1941.

Right: Round-up: British
troops guard Mau Mau
suspects, Kenya, 1953.

Above: Members of the
FLN (National Liberation
Front) captured by the
Foreign Legion during
the Algerian War of
Independence, 1954–62.

Right: The Empire strikes
back: helicopters prepare for
the assault on Suez, 1956.

The battle for Algiers: a still from Gillo Pontecorvo's 1965 film *La battaglia di Algeri*.

Lumumba taken: the Congo, 1960.

Egypt's strongman premier Muhammad Naguib (left) talking with Lieut. Col. Gamal Abdel Nasser, *c.* 1950.

Power transferred: Dr Kwame Nkrumah and the last governor of the Gold Coast Sir Charles Arden-Clarke and Lady Clarke, Independence Day, Ghana, 1957.

Our man in Africa: President Kennedy
and General Mobutu, 1963.

Comrades: Fidel Castro (centre) and the Ethiopian dictator
Mengistu Haile Mariam (right).

Above: Everyday apartheid: white and black South Africans occupy separate benches.

Right: Idi Amin of Uganda.

Below: Emperor Bokassa of Central Africa in coronation regalia.

Bush war: Rhodesian army officers at firing practice in Gwelo, 14 June 1977.

Cuban and Angolan troops in Angola, *c.* 1975.

outpost of Ottoman power in Africa, a forlorn hope perhaps, but one that might have had exchange value in a peace settlement.

Popular sympathies in Egypt lay with Turkey and its protective ally, Germany. Nonetheless, Egypt was frogmarched into the war by Britain: in December 1914 the obstreperous Khedive Abbas Hilmi was briskly deposed (he decamped to Constantinople) and his country was formally annexed and placed under virtual martial law for the next four years. Nationalist and Pan-Islamic agitation was suppressed, but there was disturbing intelligence that there were cells of Turkish sympathisers among army and police officers.[18] During the winter of 1914–15 the military authorities feared that, if the Turkish army broke through the defences of the Suez Canal, the Egyptians would rebel.

National humiliation was accompanied by personal at the hands of an enlarged British garrison. At the end of 1914, British and dominion troops were posted there to meet an expected Turkish offensive against the Suez Canal. One of them, Bert Smythe, an Australian, soon became aware that it was customary for Europeans to mistreat the natives, and his countrymen followed suit. Once off duty in Cairo, Australians 'forget their uniform [and] their self-restraint' and plunged into 'the lowest lives and pleasures', which led to street brawls and an epidemic of syphilis.[19] The last was blamed on Egyptian prostitutes, and early in 1915 Australian and New Zealand troops took revenge by beating up pimps, destroying brothels and burning down part of the red-light district of Cairo. The term 'Ozzy' entered Egyptian slang as a term for a hooligan. During the next four years, Egypt was the sullen host to an enlarged garrison that first defended the Canal and then, during 1917 and 1918, expelled the Turks from Palestine and Syria. Thousands of conscripted *fellahin* toiled behind the lines and, ironically, detachments of Egyptian camel fought alongside Arab forces in the campaigns to 'liberate' Palestine and Syria.

Pan-Islamic agitation in the rest of Africa scared more than it killed. British and French generals and proconsuls were jittery to the point of panic at even the slightest intimation of Islamic subversion. This made sense insofar as one of the prime aims of the Sultan's jihads was to foment mutinies among Muslim troops and sabotage recruitment. Aware of this, the military authorities in Senegal preferred Christian recruits.[20] Expressions of anti-Christian feelings and the ostracising of soldiers in one Algerian village in 1916 were taken very seriously by the army authorities. Their investigation uncovered the source of the agitation as the ingrained prejudices of local women rather than the Sultan's holy war.[21]

Far more alarming was a leaflet that was circulating in Nigeria which promised that any Muslim 'who helps the English, when he dies, he dies a kaffir [unbeliever]'.[22] A similar one turned up in the Upper Volta during 1915, predicting the imminent 'triumph of the cause of Muhammad and the certain annihilation of the French'. It had been handed to the authorities by a local chief and suspected jihadists were subsequently interrogated and tortured to discover the extent of what turned out to be an imaginary conspiracy.[23]

No chances were taken early in 1916, when there were jihadic disturbances on the borders of Nigeria and Chad (the area where Boko Haram is now causing havoc) and the possibility that the region would be penetrated by the Turkish-backed Sanussi from the north. An Anglo-French expeditionary force, well primed with Maxim guns, was assembled at Lagos and rushed northwards along the lately completed railway to Kano.[24] From there it entered Chad and scattered the insurgents.

In the Sudan, where memories of the Mahdi were still fresh, Khartoum's intelligence services picked up rumours that the semi-independent Sultan Ali Dinar of Darfur had been in contact with Enver Pasha, the Turkish War Minister, and was about to make common cause with his Sanussi neighbours.[25] Ali Dinar had been a nominal British client since 1900, when an intelligence assessment indicated that there were limits to his cooperation. 'He should', the report ran, 'be allowed to carry on his own mode of government, paying such taxes as the Government may impose; by these arrangements he will remain quiet and agreeable, but if otherwise he will oppose the Government.'[26] After wavering, the Sultan threw in his lot with the Turks in April 1916. His forces were swiftly overwhelmed: dervish spearmen and cavalry were no match for the aircraft which Khartoum had prudently imported from Egypt. Further south in Abyssinia, the accession of the Emperor Lij Iyasu, a Muslim convert, in 1916 raised the hopes of a new jihadic front. Italian intelligence fabricated the unlikely story of a U-boat that had somehow entered the Red Sea and landed German agents on the Abyssinian coast, which caused tremors in Cairo.[27] Khartoum launched a propaganda offensive that included the circulation of faked pornographic postcards which showed the new Emperor enjoying his wives. He was overthrown by a coup in Addis Ababa engineered by the British and Italian consuls at the end of the year, and replaced by the reliable young Ras Tafari (later Haile Selassie) under the tutelage of the Empress Zauditu, the daughter of the Emperor Menelik and the first female ruler of Abyssinia since the Queen of Sheba.

Cloak-and-dagger operations in Abyssinia coincided with a masterstroke of British military intelligence which blunted the ideological edge of the jihad, the Arab Revolt. In mid-1916 Hussein, Sharif of Mecca and ruler of the Hijaz, joined the Allies and for the next two years Arab regular and irregular forces fought the Turks in Arabia and Palestine. Thanks to the Royal Navy, his followers were equipped by sea with armaments and, later, were supported by Allied troops, artillery and aircraft. Operations were overseen, and in some cases personally commanded, by T. E. Lawrence. Such a formidable and well-armed uprising had, of course, been the dream of the Turkish and German architects of the Sultan's jihad.

The Arab Revolt had enormous propaganda value. Hussein's spiritual prestige was high and news of his defection to the Allies was officially circulated among Muslims in French North and West Africa.[28] Anglo-French propaganda made much of the fact that since Mecca and the Arabian Red Sea ports were now under direct Allied protection, African Muslims were free to make the annual Haj. Underpowered and hampered by geography and good Allied intelligence, the Sultan's jihad had failed.

V

From the beginning of the war, there had been misgivings about the effects it would have on the African mind. Would the conflict become a catalyst for change, most importantly in the ways in which Africans saw themselves and their relations with their white rulers? News of the outbreak of war had aroused fears of native unrest, and Germans in East and South-West Africa hoped their colonies might somehow remain neutral. The Royal Navy's shelling of Dar-es-Salaam on 6 August 1914 blew away all such fancies. In South Africa, where a minority of Boers were at best lukewarm to fighting on Britain's side, a ban was placed on raising black soldiers.[29]

Apprehension about the impact of a war in which blacks helped white men to kill other white men was justified. Towards the end of the war, a military intelligence analysis of the temper of servicemen in East Africa revealed disquieting signs for the future: 'Round the camp fires there had been much talk – in the lingua franca which never fails the African – starting from stomach and wife, and the distance which they themselves have brought from home to hardship, and touching on the killing of white by black, as illustrated before eyes.'[30] This mood lingered, for in 1922 resistance to recent tax increases in the Kavirondo district of Kenya was attributed to a widespread resentment that fresh burdens were being placed on Africans after their 'great sacrifices . . . in the war'.[31]

· Educated Africans looked for reciprocity. In May 1918 the *Gold Coast Leader* claimed that 'never before in modern history has the black man had a better opportunity for his uplift than in the present war . . . we shall not be left out of the reckoning at the last day'.[32] Nigerian newspapers followed the same line, arguing that participation in the war had increased African self-esteem and that loyalty and sacrifice should be rewarded by greater engagement in government.[33]

The declaration in 1917 by President Woodrow Wilson that the war was being waged to secure rights of self-determination to peoples under alien government aroused great hopes among Africa's nascent nationalist movements. Nationalists in North Africa appealed to the French government for representation at the Versailles Peace Conference, for 'The Algero-Tunisian people had abundantly poured out its blood in this war to the deliverance of the invaded lands of Belgium and France.' Egyptian nationalists also asked to lay their case for independence before the conference and were rebuffed. At Versailles, the right to self-government was strictly rationed: it was available for Poles, Latvians, Lithuanians and Estonians, but not for Egyptians, Algerians and Tunisians.

PART THREE

1919–1945

17

'Contagious excitement':
The Rise of Nationalism

I

The end of the war marked the beginning of what turned out to be a twenty-one-year truce in Europe. New ideologies emerged, seduced nations and generated the tensions that led to the Second World War in 1939. Communism, Fascism and Nazism required submission to a totalitarian state which, in return, promised stability, security and an end to recurrent economic crises and mass unemployment. The new charismatic rulers of Communist Russia, Fascist Italy and Nazi Germany set about rebuilding their countries from scratch. There was no place in the new orders for pre-war liberalism, parliamentary democracy and laissez-faire capitalism, none of which seemed to offer remedies for new sicknesses.

The new parties thrived on latent hatreds and violence. Mussolini, who came to power after an armed coup in 1922, later told Italians: 'Every society . . . needs a certain proportion of citizens who had to be detested.'[1] The Duce also expected the reborn Fascist man and woman to be ready to fight for their country and Fascism, for 'war alone can carry to the maximum tension all human energies and imprint with the seal of nobility those people who have the courage to confront it'.[2] Tumults and bloodshed marked Hitler's coming to power in 1933, and his vision of Germany's past, present and future was one of an endless life-or-death struggle for survival between the superior Aryans and the rest of the world. Europe's radical Right had nothing to offer Africans: Nazi racial ideology relegated them to the lowest level of humanity and Mussolini's racial pundit Lidio Cipriani insisted that all Africans suffered from 'an irreducible inferiority'.[3]

Soviet Communism treated the African as a potential revolutionary, as yet unaware of his historic destiny in the global struggle against capitalism and its servant, imperialism. Russia was the powerhouse of world revolution and its propagandists endeavoured to foment it in the capitalist states and their Asian and African colonies. In 1920 they were predicting imminent uprisings by the downtrodden masses in India, Persia, Egypt and Algeria. There was spasmodic unrest which was suppressed by the authorities and in none of these countries did local Communist parties make much headway. No African delegates appeared at the first and second Comintern Congresses in 1919 and 1920, and it was only in 1923 that a Comintern Black Bureau was established in Hamburg specifically for black workers in Africa, Latin America and the United States.

Communist parties in Britain and France toed the Moscow line, denounced their countries' empires and called for the militant solidarity of all races. In 1927 the Communist newspaper *L'Humanité* reminded the French workers that the labourers of Paris, the miners of the Moselle and the poorly paid dockers of Tunis shared a common cause.[4] The same paper used the death in 1934 of the imperial hero Marshal Lyautey to denounce the French Empire and its rulers. He was 'un Coloniste et Fasciste', and an 'ultra réactionnaire', whose Jesuit education and military service had convinced him that it was the duty of soldiers like himself to crush the workers and peasants of France in the same way as he had the people of Morocco. His funeral was a chance for the French workers to show solidarity with peoples ground down by 'l'impérialisme'.[5]

When, in November 1932, the Kenyan nationalist Jomo Kenyatta addressed a London meeting of the Council of Action Against War, he declared: 'Members of the Working Class, the Workers of Kenya Colony greet you. We are workers like you. The capitalist system chooses to kill you . . . Although we look different we are the same.'[6] His words were taken down by a Special Branch officer, for the Communist affinities of early African nationalists meant that they were kept under close surveillance by the British and French intelligence services.

II

Europe's new ideologies intruded on an Africa that had been given a new map. In 1919 Germany's colonies were confiscated and shared out among the victors. Britain and France divided Togoland and Cameroon, Britain secured German East Africa (renamed Tanganyika) and South Africa was allocated South-West Africa. Each territory was administered under a League of Nations mandate, a formula that required the new rulers to govern humanely and promote the welfare of their subjects. Portugal and Belgium were given consolation prizes in the form of small slices of German East Africa.

Italy got nothing beyond a British gift of Jubaland on the southern border of Somalia. Mussolini was galled; he wanted more than Britain's leftovers and he soon gave notice that Italy would fight to engross more of Africa. Imperial conquest was integral to the Fascist image of Italy as a virile, warlike nation. Within a year of coming to power, Mussolini stepped up operations to consolidate control over Libya. As in all things, the Duce wanted quick results, ruthlessly pursued, and so Italian forces used phosgene and mustard gas on the Sanussi tribesmen.[7]

Europe's political extremism flourished against a background of intermittent booms and slumps in the 1920s, and the deeper and longer recession that followed the 1929 Wall Street crash and subsequent American and European bank failures. Penniless banks brought industries to their knees, millions of workers were laid off, production dropped and markets shrank. British exports dropped from £791 million in 1930 to £435 million in 1934 and France's fell from £515 million to £379 million over the same period. South Africa, Africa's only industrial power, suffered similarly, with its total exports falling from £37 million in 1930 to £24 million in 1934. This loss had been made worse by Britain's abandoning the gold standard in 1931.

Those regions of Africa already integrated into the global economy felt the aftershock of Europe and America's economic earthquake. The demand for Egyptian cotton and the minerals mined in South Africa, Northern Rhodesia and the Belgian Congo fell, as did that for cash crops such as palm oil, tobacco and cocoa. Stagnant production led to wage cuts: in Lagos a dock labourer's pay dropped from a shilling a day to between eight and ten pence, while the daily cost of living remained at one shilling and sixpence for a single man and twice that for a family.[8] Traditional husbandry that fed local communities was unaffected, and so food prices remained stable.

African repercussions of the world slump dealt a blow to the old imperial assumption that, as more and more of Africa's people entered the wage economy, they would become consumers of imported manufactures. Moreover, the British were discovering that Africans with money in their pockets were spending it on imported foreign goods. The Ford Model T was the most popular motor car in the Gold Coast and the total sales of Japanese imported cotton in Kenya, Uganda and Tanganyika were nearly nine times those for Lancashire products. Ramsay MacDonald's National Government responded in 1933 by replacing Free Trade with Imperial Preference in the hope that Britain would consume more Gold Coast cocoa and that its growers would buy bicycles made in Birmingham.

For the moment this was wishful thinking, for in some areas Africans were barely able to pay their taxes.[9] In 1933, when the Kenyan authorities appealed to London for funds for social and economic projects that could not be supported by local taxes, they were told that there was nothing in the kitty. The British and French governments had little spare capital for colonial development since their budgets were circumscribed by welfare payments to the jobless and, after 1936, the costs of rearmament. Investment dried up and colonial economies languished.

III

As we have seen, politically aware Africans had treated the First World War as a stepping stone towards political freedoms and responsibilities that would lead to future self-government. African soldiers and workers had contributed to the victory of Britain and France, and they expected something in return. The continent's war effort and casualties had fostered a sense of moral reciprocity, which was why Algerian and Egyptian nationalists had – vainly – requested invitations to plead their countries' causes at the Versailles Peace Conference. In May 1919, the Egyptian Association of Great Britain appealed to the British conscience when it asked Lloyd George's government to give independence to Egypt in the name of 'the glorious dead' who had been slain in defence of liberty and the British sense of 'fair play'.[10]

Egypt took the lead in and set the pattern for Africa's national movements between the wars and after. Students, like those who joined the Egyptian Association of Great Britain, provided the drive and sometimes the muscle for the national cause. They were the inheritors of a political tradition that extended back to the late 1870s, when Urabi Pasha had unsuccessfully attempted to release Egypt from the stranglehold of foreign bankers. Britain's occupation of the country in 1882 gave a fresh impetus to the nationalist movement, which had more than recovered its former strength by 1914. Its growth was made easy by official tolerance of political associations and an absence of press censorship, although police surveillance of political meetings and demonstrations was tight. By 1911 the French Sûreté was lending a hand by keeping an eye on Egyptian students in Paris.[11] Official attitudes to dissent hardened after November 1914 when Britain took direct control of Egypt, which was euphemistically called a 'protectorate'. Four years of virtual martial law followed.

The nationalists were not overawed. Within days of the November 1918 armistice Saad Zaghlul, the leader of the Wafd (Delegation) Party, demanded the immediate restoration of self-government. A lawyer of humble origins and graduate of the Muslim Al-Azhar University, Zaghlul had held ministerial posts before the war and was regarded by the British as a cooperative 'moderate', which then and afterwards signified a nationalist willing to compromise. His demands were rejected by the High Commissioner, Sir Henry McMahon, who, together with his superiors in London, blamed Egyptian restlessness on sinister 'foreign influences'.[12]

McMahon had the support of Lloyd George's coalition government, which believed that the Egyptian movement was unrepresentative of national feeling. Rather, it was the product of external influences, of which the most pernicious were President Wilson's pronouncements about universal self-determination. Equally insidious was Moscow's propaganda, which promised that Russia would do all in its power to assist nationalist movements in Asia and Africa. Hot air generated by Moscow's propagandists was about all they got, but this did not prevent the British and French ministers from interpreting every colonial nationalist movement as evidence of a worldwide Communist conspiracy.

It was British intransigence rather than Soviet sedition that sparked off an insurrection that convulsed Egypt during March 1919. There were strikes, riots, terrorist attacks on British servicemen, arson and sabotage of communications. Urban insurgents plundered property: the Greek commercial community, always scapegoats for the Egyptian mob, claimed losses of £600,000.[13] The extent and ferocity of the uprising momentarily stunned the authorities: one British official described Egypt as in the grip of a 'contagious excitement' that had made its people 'mad'.[14] Shock was followed by fury. The rebellion was savagely crushed: over 1,000 Egyptians were killed and many more arrested, gaoled and flogged. In one army camp, suspected agitators were interrogated by a sergeant-major who extracted confessions with a rhinoceros-hide whip.[15]

All classes joined in the revolt. Lawyers went on strike, and of the 670 rioters held in the Citadel gaol in Cairo at the end of March, nearly a third were workers and the rest university and high school students.[16] In the countryside the *fellahin* joined in, attacking trains and murdering British officers. Middle-class support for the uprising was strong – understandably so, for educated Egyptians felt frustrated by a system that favoured Europeans in the public services. Muhammad Mahmoud, a civil servant who had a Second in History from Balliol College, Oxford, considered himself passed over for promotion and quarrelled with a junior British official 'to whom he was systematically rude'. He was sacked for his impertinence in 1917 and two years later was a prominent member of the Wafd.[17]

Having restored order, the British government had somehow to cope with a national movement that had proved its capacity to make Egypt ungovernable. The stiff-necked McMahon was replaced by a pragmatic imperialist, Field Marshal Viscount Allenby, who balanced British strategic needs (as ever, the safety of the Suez Canal) with the wishes of the Egyptian people. Negotiations were opened with Zaghlul, who had been briefly banished to Malta, and in 1922 Egyptian independence was restored and a constitutional monarchy established.

The Wafd secured 169 of 232 seats in the 1924 parliamentary elections and in 1936 received over 90 per cent of the popular vote. Relations with Britain remained vinegary as the party pressed for the abolition of capitulations, which granted foreigners immunity from prosecution by Egyptian courts. They went in 1935, but Egyptian sovereignty remained diluted.[18] During the negotiations for a new Anglo-Egyptian Treaty in 1936, British battleships had anchored off Alexandria, a visible reminder that Egyptian independence was still conditional.

Nevertheless, the importance of events in Egypt cannot be overstated, for they had set a precedent and example for the rest of Africa. Concessions had been gained by a single highly organised party, the Wafd, with a convincing claim to represent the national will. Britain had to accept the party as the authentic voice of Egypt which, of course, enhanced its prestige and popular backing. Democracy, insofar as it was about choices between parties, was not the automatic outcome of popular, liberation politics. Minority parties did surface, such as the Young Egypt Party, or Greenshirts. They were radicals who received covert funding from Italy and brawled with the Blueshirts, the youth wing of the Wafd.[19] Uniforms and street fights were features of Fascism, which appeared to many frustrated young Egyptians as a dynamic alternative to the turgid conventional politics of their elders.

Other Egyptians looked inwards to find an authentic national identity. Urban middle-class nationalists endeavoured to draw the masses into politics by going into the countryside and enlisting support from the *fellahin*. They were romanticised as the 'true' Egyptians, heroic men and women of the soil, untainted by European influences. The suffering of these noble creatures continued since the Wafd favoured capitalism and the social status quo. Landlords still had the right to flog their tenants, and they exercised it.[20]

The recent struggle became implanted in Egypt's national consciousness. School syllabuses included compulsory lessons on the 1919 rebellion that emphasised the bravery and suffering of Egyptians in their battles for liberty.[21] Egypt's example inspired Indian nationalists: in 1921 a group visited Cairo and praised Egyptians for proving that a united people could no longer be 'ruled against its wish'. They added, approvingly, that Egypt was now 'a thorn in the back of the British lion'.[22] Yet the beast was still there and periodically reminded its hosts of its strength by minatory RAF air shows that pointedly included demonstrations of bombing. Frequent flights over Cairo punched home the message that an 'independent' Egypt remained an occupied country.

IV

Questions about past and future identity were the impulses behind the fledgling Moroccan and Algerian national movements. At first they were atomised groups united only by doubts about France's policy of assimilation, which seemed hostile to Islam and bent on smothering traditional cultures. Yet innovation was not rejected just because it was French. Abu Ya'la, an Algerian Muslim journalist writing in the 1920s and 1930s, supported education for women as well as championing indigenous religious and social traditions.[23] Like many others from the educated middle classes, he recognised the value of the social and intellectual progress that had resulted from French policies, but he did not want to jettison everything from the past. One of the small political groups that were springing up in Morocco, the Comité d'Action Marocaine, approached the French government in 1934 with expressions of satisfaction about the 'evolution' of their country, but pressed for more Moroccans to become engaged in the process.[24] Other Moroccans believed that cooperation was impossible because the French would never shed their ingrained racial and cultural arrogance. Frenchmen 'think of us as dogs and sneer at us *bicots*', alleged Abd al-Kadir, a student leader.[25]

Ultimately, such attitudes impeded the gradual assimilation that was France's long-term aim, although North Africa's proto-nationalists as yet had no clear concept of their countries' futures. Nonetheless, demands for participation in government assumed a gradual dilution of French authority which, in turn, would lead to independence.

Islam was an ally of national movements so long as they did not push secularism too far. Muslims continued to fear that, despite its outward tolerance and good intentions, Christian rule would undermine the devotion of the faithful. This apprehension was confirmed by the French policy of allowing Christian missionaries into Morocco in contravention of the 1912 Fez Treaty that had established the protectorate. Likewise, Egyptian Muslims were antagonised by an influx of French and American missionaries during the early 1930s and their crass behaviour. Understandably, Alexandrian Muslims were incensed by one hot gospeller's revivalist beach services for local children.[26]

The French long-term aim of cultural integration, together with the libertarian political ideals of the Republic, meant that the authorities in Algeria and Morocco allowed freedom of association and an uncensored press, both essential for the growth of political debate and associations. Strength lay in numbers and unity and, as in Egypt, a single nationalist party emerged in Morocco by 1943, the Istiqlal (independence) Party. Its organisation closely followed that favoured by European parties of the extreme Left and Right: it was tightly run, had a binding programme and ran social amenities that attracted the young. There were football, boxing, basketball and cycling clubs and Boy Scout packs. This fun element provided cohesion: joining the party was an entrance into an exciting social world. Istiqlal also broadened its political appeal by alliances with trade unions and chambers of commerce. Like the Egyptian Wafd, its aim was to become the sole voice of the country and so compel the French to listen to its demands.

Divisions between colonists and Arabs ruled out the evolution of a united national movement in Algeria. Old antipathies festered: in *Les Colons*, a popular novel of 1921, the hero declares: 'I am an African. I am the law. I am neither a lazy Arab nor a Maltese dog. I am a *colon*!'[27] The Arab was not only an inferior being, he was an ever-present enemy, which was how he was portrayed in Camus's *L'Étranger* (1942). 'The Arab threatens you? You believe he threatens you? Kill him.' The gulf between the races was widening and more venomous than ever. The *colons* promoted a self-image of themselves as a tough, determined and virile breed who despised the liberalism of metropolitan France.[28]

In 1934, a Socialist deputy to the French National Assembly warned that Algeria was succumbing to 'un malaise profond' whose symptoms were a decay in the social order, which was reflected by communal tensions in places reserved for whites, the decline of French prestige and the rise of Arab pride in the cultural achievements of Islam.[29] His analysis had been prompted by a recent pogrom in Constantine, in which an Arab mob murdered twenty-seven Jews after a drunken Jew had profaned a mosque. Right-wing newspapers dismissed the atrocity as further evidence of Muslim fanaticism, which confirmed the well-worn assertion that the Arab was mentally incapable of becoming a citizen of France.[30]

Algeria's Arab population had more than doubled between 1870 and 1939, when it stood at 5.9 million. A lopsided economy could not cope with this growth, for there was no compensating increase in the land available for local food production, which was largely confined to inefficient peasant smallholdings. There were famines in 1920, 1922, 1924 and 1926, while vineyards expanded and wine exports soared.

V

Periodic dearths accelerated the flow of migrant workers from Algeria to French cities and towns. By 1939 France was host to 120,000, who continued to undertake the dirty work of French industry and clustered together in outlying urban ghettoes. The immigrants retained their tribal and religious identities, often spoke broken French, and many looked like ragamuffins. They faced the antipathy of the working class, were suspected of eating dogs, cats and rats, and, for the police, were criminals by instinct. A commonplace police assumption was that 'When there is a crime, a rape, a theft is committed tomorrow, don't hesitate, get the Arab.'[31]

Outsiders by birth, immigrants gravitated towards left-wing parties that appealed to the socially and economically excluded. The Communists were particularly welcoming, which was what Moscow wanted, but blacks from Paris and French West Africa who sought to attend the 1930 International Conference of Negro Workers in Hamburg were denied passports.[32] Within Paris, politically conscious immigrants formed small groups like the Comité de Défense de la Race Nègre organised by Lamine Senghor. He had been born in Senegal, served as a soldier in the trenches, contracted TB after being gassed, and worked as a postman in Paris. Senghor was a trade union activist, but his driving passion was a bitter sense of injustice about the compensation for wartime suffering: disabled white veterans got better pensions and medical treatment than did blacks.[33] Helpless anger about racial discrimination and injustice was the catalyst for other small associations of African immigrants in Paris and London. They published leaflets and small-circulation journals which attacked imperialism and championed the cause of downtrodden blacks everywhere.

However small, organisations that promoted an assertive African consciousness and which were cultivated by the Soviet Union were bound to provoke official unease, and British and French intelligence agencies were ordered to spy on them and their members. In 1923 the Service de Surveillance, Protection et Assistance des Indigènes Nord-Africains (SAINA) was set up. Its thirty-two European inspectors spoke Arabic and Berber and were ordered to penetrate the North African community, spy on it, chivvy Communist agitators and compel employers to sack troublemakers who could then be deported. Agents also countered subversion with kindness, running medical centres and hostels for immigrants.[34] Black agents were recruited by the secret service, including a former Senegalese soldier, Ramananjato ('agent Joé'), who was ordered to spy on coloured visitors to the 1931 Paris Colonial Exhibition, where he kept his ears open for any hostile comments, and casually chatted to Africans who were part of the human exhibits. His ostentatious activities aroused the suspicion of the police and he was arrested.[35] Inspector Clouseau would have sympathised.

VI

Like the French security services, MI5 and the Special Branch regarded African nationalists as highly susceptible to Communist indoctrination, and for good reasons. The Comintern sponsored international bodies like the League Against Imperialism and gatherings such as the International Conference in Hamburg, which simultaneously aimed to spread Communist propaganda and convert African nationalists. These were also personally approached by agents operating in London and Paris.

The busiest and most determined was George Padmore, a Trinidadian Marxist–Leninist and Soviet agent who, for a time, was head of the Comintern's Negro Bureau. A free spirit, he refused to toe the Moscow line and was thrown out of the French Communist Party as a Trotskyite deviant. One of Padmore's first targets was Jomo Kenyatta, who had come to London in 1929 to study and represent the Kikuyu Central Association in its struggle against land encroachment by settlers. Within a year, Padmore had persuaded Kenyatta to attend the Negro Workers' Conference in Hamburg and helped with his expenses. MI5 identified Kenyatta as a Communist, which was confirmed by his trip to Moscow in 1935, again with Padmore's funding, where he briefly studied at the International Lenin School. Analysis of his activities indicated that he had been suborned and given the job of bringing all black associations under his control. Kenyatta also had links with French and American black activists. Unsurprisingly, his 'phone was tapped and mail intercepted'.[36]

But Communism had yet to put down roots in Africa. The Comintern gave a low priority to subversion in Africa, and even Padmore felt that, while the African masses had revolutionary potential, they had yet to find the will and organisation to combine. He did, however, reckon that large-scale strikes in Nigeria and disturbances over land in Kenya indicated an awakening of the class-consciousness necessary for revolution. He also noted in his pamphlet *The Life and Struggles of Negro Toilers* (1931) that any popular Marxist movement would be vigorously opposed by the 'chiefs and headmen', who collaborated with the colonial authorities and were ready-made 'counter-revolutionaries'. To be successful, African Communists would need to eradicate tribal structures and loyalties. Nationalist agitation was a counterproductive distraction since it was undertaken by '"left" petty-bourgeois intellectuals'.

Christianity, rather than Marxist theory, was a strong influence on the generation of young nationalists who emerged during the 1930s. Kenyatta, Kwame Nkrumah (Gold Coast), Julius Nyerere (Tanganyika), Lamine Senghor (Senegal), Kenneth Kaunda (Northern Rhodesia), Nnamdi Azikiwe (Nigeria) and Hastings Banda (Nyasaland) were all mission-educated. Missionaries had always tended to take the part of Africans against colonial governments and their pupils continued the tradition. The Kenyan authorities blamed them for protests against increased taxation in 1922. The Deputy Commissioner for Native Affairs reported that 'The Mission boy is an element of unrest in many parts, since he feels himself too advanced and civilised a being to be controlled by his less advanced chiefs.' 'Boys' from the Church Missionary Society and Seventh Day Adventists had been behind the propaganda spread by the Young Kavirondo Association and were undermining the authority of chiefs and headmen.[37]

Collisions between national movements and traditional sources of authority and individual identity such as the tribe and village were inevitable. Both were bound to retreat in the face of ideas that emphasised attachment to a nation, although at this stage most nationalists south of the Sahara were thinking in terms of sharing in government rather than independence. For this to happen, Africans had to find self-confidence in themselves and slough off that sense of inferiority that had been imposed on them during and after the era of partition.

In their search for racial self-confidence, many Africans looked to America for intellectual sustenance and moral stamina. In the past, and with missionary encouragement, a steady flow of Africans had studied in black colleges and seminaries in the United States. They arrived in a country where blacks were treated as helots, held in contempt and suffered legal discrimination, particularly in the southern states, where white supremacy was written into the laws. Between the wars, the black emancipation movements were slowly gaining the momentum that would lead to the Civil Rights campaigns in the 1950s. African students experienced the black resurgence and nationalists in Africa and Europe were quick to find a common cause with the American struggle. In Paris and London, black associations joined the worldwide outcry that followed the 1931 Scottsboro scandal in which eight black youths were sentenced to the electric chair by an Alabama judge for the rape of two white girls on the flimsiest of evidence. Jomo Kenyatta was among the protesters.[38] The death sentences were remitted.

American academe was the nursery of two future national leaders, Nnamdi Azikiwe and Kwame Nkrumah. The former had been a junior clerk in the Nigerian Treasury who in 1929 had gained a missionary scholarship to Lincoln University in Pennsylvania, a black college. He read Anthropology, and was appointed a junior lecturer. In 1934 he began a political career, returning to Nigeria where he became a journalist and founded his own newspaper, the *West African Pilot*, and the Nigerian Youth Movement. Like Kenyatta he mixed with expatriate nationalists in London including Padmore, with whom, in July 1936, he joined other 'Peace Lovers, Enemies of Fascism and Friends of Colonial Peoples' in a rally of the Pan-African Federation. Colonel Vernon Kell, the head of MI5, considered him a dangerous man with 'extreme views' on 'European oppression of Africans'.[39]

Nkrumah followed Azikiwe to Lincoln University and took degrees in Economics and Sociology and Theology, supporting himself with various menial jobs. In 1945 he arrived in London to study for a doctorate in philosophy. Padmore became his political mentor and directed him towards the Communist Party, which he joined at some date during the next three years.[40]

Beyond Egypt and Morocco, African nationalist movements were unrepresentative minority groups principally concerned with securing some say in government. Full independence seemed distant, although nationalists in Paris and London were thinking in terms of future 'liberation' of their countries, taking their cue from their Communist allies. The Red connection had invited surveillance, not so much because nationalist groups in London and Paris threatened the stability of nationalists' homelands, but because they were seen as a small part of a wider and highly dangerous international campaign of Communist subversion.

'Force to the uttermost':
More Wars 1919–1939

I

Just as Africans were taking their first, tentative steps towards nationhood and independence, Spain and Italy launched what turned out to be the last large-scale wars of conquest on the continent, in Morocco and Abyssinia. Both nations were driven by greed and historic grievances which alleged that their legitimate imperial ambitions had been frustrated or overlooked by the great powers. Jealousy and bruised pride were most strongly felt by right-wing politicians, professional soldiers, moneymen and journalists who lobbied for imperial expansion, promising that it would yield prestige and profit. In Italy, aggressive imperialism and an infatuation with the glories of the Roman Empire were central to the ideology of Mussolini's Fascist Party which snatched power in 1922. Like Spain, Italy was a relatively poor country with limited capital reserves and industrial resources, deficiencies that were ignored or glossed over by imperial enthusiasts who argued that in the long term imperial wars would pay for themselves.

In 1900 Spain was a nation in eclipse. Over the past hundred years it had been occupied by Napoleon and endured periodic civil wars over the royal succession; it entered the twentieth century riven by violent social and political tensions. Spain's infirmity was brutally exposed in 1898, when she was defeated by the United States in a short war that ended with the loss of Cuba, Puerto Rico and the Philippines, all that remained of her vast sixteenth-century empire.

National shame was most deeply felt in the upper reaches of a hierarchical society where the conviction took root that Spain could only redeem and regenerate itself by a colonial venture in Morocco. Support for this enterprise was most passionate among the numerous officers of the Spanish army (there was one for every forty-seven soldiers), who found allies in King Alfonso XIII, the profoundly superstitious and obscurantist Catholic Church and conservatives in the middle and landowning classes. The army had its own newspaper, *El Ejército Español*, which proclaimed that empire was the 'birthright' of all Spaniards, and predicted that 'weapons' would 'plough the virgin soil so that agriculture, industry, and mining might flourish' in Morocco.[1]

Morocco was Spain's new El Dorado. In 1904 Spain and France secretly agreed to share Morocco, with the French coming off best with the most fertile regions. Spain's portion was the littoral of the Mediterranean coast and the inaccessible Atlas Mountains of the Rif, home to the fiercely independent Berbers. The war began in 1909 and jubilant officers, including the young Francisco Franco, looked forward to medals and promotion, while investors touted for mining and agricultural concessions. Optimism dissolved on the battlefield and, within a year, the Spanish army found itself bogged down in a guerrilla war, just as it had in Cuba forty years before. Reinforcements were hastily summoned, but in July 1909 the mobilisation of reservists triggered a popular uprising among the workers of Barcelona. Breadwinners and their families wanted no part in the Moroccan adventure, and henceforward all left-wing parties opposed a war that offered the workers nothing but conscription and death. Resentful draftees had to be stiffened by Moroccan levies (Regulares) and, in 1921, the sinister Spanish Foreign Legion (Tercio de Extranjeros), a band of mostly Spanish desperadoes whose motto was 'Viva la Muerte!' These hirelings once appeared at a ceremonial public parade with Berber heads, ears and arms spiked on their bayonets.[2]

Resistance was strongest among the Berbers of the Atlas, who not only defended their mountainous homeland but created their own state, the Rif Republic, in September 1921. Its founder and guiding spirit was a charismatic visionary, Abd el-Krim, a jurist who had once worked for the Spanish, but believed that the future freedom, happiness and prosperity of the Berbers could only be achieved by the creation of a modern, independent nation. It had its own flag, issued banknotes and, under el-Krim's direction, was embarking on a programme of social and economic regeneration which included efforts to eliminate slavery. The Riffian army was well suited to a partisan war. Its soldiers were chiefly horsemen armed with up-to-date rifles, supported by machine-guns and modern artillery. The Riffians also had good luck, for they were pitched against an army with tenuous lines of communications and led by fumbling generals.

Riffian superiority in the battlefield was spectacularly proved in July 1921, when Spain launched an offensive with 13,000 men designed to penetrate the Atlas foothills and secure a decisive victory. What followed was the most catastrophic defeat ever suffered by a European army in Africa, the Battle of Annual. The Spanish were outmanoeuvred, trapped and trounced with a loss of over 10,000 men in the fighting and ensuing rout. Officers fled in cars, the wounded were abandoned and tortured, and their commander, General Manuel Fernández Silvestre y Pantiga, shot himself. The circumstances of his death were ironic, insofar as his manly bearing and extended, bushy and painstakingly groomed moustache so closely fitted the European stereotype of the victorious imperial hero. A post-mortem on the Annual débacle revealed Silvestre's reckless over-confidence, his obsequious desire to satisfy King Alfonso XIII's wish for a quick victory, ramshackle logistics, a precipitate collapse of morale and the mass desertions of Moroccan Regulares.

Spain responded with more botched offensives, but now the deficiencies of its commanders were offset by the latest military technology. Phosgene and mustard gas bombs dropped from aircraft would bring the Riffians to their knees. This tactic was strongly urged by Alfonso XIII, a Bourbon with all the mental limitations and prejudices of his ancestors. Together, his generals persuaded him that, if unchecked, the Republic of the Rif would trigger 'a general uprising of the Muslim world at the instigation of Moscow and international Jewry'.[3] Spain was now fighting to save Christian civilisation, just as it had done in the Middle Ages when its armies had driven the Moors from the Iberian peninsula.

The technology for what are now called weapons of mass destruction had to be imported. German scientists supervised the manufacture of the poison gas at two factories, one of which, near Madrid, was named 'The Alfonso XIII Factory'. Over 100 bombers were purchased from British and French manufacturers, including the massive Farman F.60 Goliath. By November 1923 the preparations had been completed, and one general hoped that the gas offensive would exterminate the Rif tribesmen.

Between 1923 and 1925 the Spanish air force pounded Rif towns and villages with 13,000 bombs filled with phosgene and mustard gas as well as conventional high explosives. Victims suffered sores, boils, blindness and the burning of skin and lungs, livestock were killed and crops and vegetation withered. Residual contamination persisted and was a source of stomach and throat cancers and genetic damage.[4] Details of these atrocities remained hidden for seventy years, and in 2007 the Spanish parliament refused to acknowledge them or consider compensation. The Moroccan government disregarded the revelations, for fear that they might add to the grievances of the discontented Berber minority.[5]

Conventional rather than chemical weapons brought down the Rif Republic. Worrying signs that Spain's war in the Rif might destabilise French Morocco drew France into the conflict in 1925. Over 100,000 French troops, tanks and aircraft were deployed alongside 80,000 Spaniards, and the outnumbered Riffian forces were broken. Newsreel cameramen (a novelty on colonial battlefields) filmed the captive Abd el-Krim as he began the first stage of his journey to exile in Réunion in the Indian Ocean. He was transferred to France in 1947 and was later moved to Cairo where he died in 1963, a revered elder statesman of North African nationalism.

II

Spain had gained a colony and, unwittingly, a Frankenstein's monster, the Army of Africa (Cuerpo de Ejército Marroquí). Its cadre of devout, reactionary officers assumed the role of the defenders of traditionalism in a country beset by political turbulence after the abdication of Alfonso in 1931. Politicians of the Right saw the Africanistas (as the officer corps was called) as ideological accomplices in their struggle to contain the trade unions, Socialists, Communists and Anarchists. The Moroccan garrison became a praetorian guard that could be unleashed on the working classes if they ever got out of hand. They did, in October 1934, when the miners' strike in the Asturias aroused fears of an imminent Red revolution. It was forestalled by application of the terror that had recently been used to subdue Spanish Morocco. Aircraft bombed centres of disaffection and the Foreign Legion and Moroccan troops were summoned to restore order and storm the strikers' stronghold at Oviedo. Its capture and subsequent mopping-up operations were marked by looting, rape and summary executions by the Legionaries and Regulares. Franco (now a general) presided over the terror. Like his fellow Africanistas, he believed that it was their sacred duty to rescue the old Spain of landowners, priests and the passive and obedient masses from the depredation of godless Communists and Anarchists.

Red revolution seemed to come closer on New Year's Day 1936 with the emergence of a coalition government which called itself the 'Popular Front'. It was confirmed in power by a narrow margin in a general election soon afterwards, and the far Left began clamouring for radical reform and wage rises. Strikes, assassinations and violent demonstrations proliferated during the spring and early summer, the Right trembled, acquired arms and covertly sounded out the Africanista generals. Together they contrived a coup whose success depended on the 40,000 soldiers of the Moroccan garrison who made up two-fifths of the Spanish army.

On 17 July 1936 Africa, in the form of Legionary and Regulares units from Morocco, invaded Spain. They were the spearhead of the Nationalist uprising and were soon reinforced by contingents flown across the Mediterranean in aircraft supplied by Hitler. Combined with local anti-Republican troops and right-wing volunteers, the African army quickly secured a power base across much of south-western and northern Spain. From the start, the Nationalists used their African troops to terrorise the Republicans. Speaking on Radio Seville, General Gonzalo Queipo de Llano warned his countrymen and women of the promiscuity and sexual prowess of his Moroccan soldiers who, he assured listeners, had already been promised their pick of the women of Madrid.

The colonial troops fulfilled his expectations. There were mass rapes everywhere by Legionaries and Regulares, who also massacred Republican civilians. Later, George Orwell noticed that Moroccan soldiers enjoyed beating up fellow International Brigade prisoners of war, but desisted once their victims uttered exaggerated howls of pain.[6] One wonders whether their brutality was the result of their suppressed loathing of all white men rather than any attachment to Fascism or the Spain of the hidalgo and the cleric. Muslim religious leaders in Morocco had backed the uprising, which was sold to them as a war against atheism. As the Regulares marched into Seville they were given Sacred

Heart talismans by pious women, which must have been bewildering.

When the Republicans were finally defeated in the spring of 1939, there were 50,000 Moroccans and 9,000 Legionaries fighting in the Nationalist army along with German and Italian contingents. Although necessity compelled him to concentrate his energies on national reconstruction, Franco, now dictator of Spain, harboured imperial ambitions. The fall of France in June 1940 offered rich pickings and he immediately occupied French Tangier. Shortly afterwards, when he met Hitler, Franco named his price for cooperation with Germany as French Morocco, Oran and, of course, Gibraltar. The Führer was peeved by his temerity and prevaricated. Fascist Spain remained a malevolent neutral; early in 1941 the tiny Spanish coastal colonies of Guinea and Fernando Po were sources of anti-British propaganda and bases for German agents in West Africa.[7] Spanish anti-Communist volunteers joined Nazi forces in Russia.

III

Franco's demands had been modest compared to those made by Mussolini, for whom the French surrender was a heaven-sent opportunity to implement his long-term plans for a vast Italian empire in Africa. In 1940 he asked the Germans for Corsica, Tunisia, Djibuti and naval bases at Toulon, Ajaccio and Mers-el-Kébir on the Algerian coast, and he was planning to invade the Sudan and British Somaliland. Mussolini's flights of fancy extended to the annexation of Kenya, Egypt and even, in their giddier moments, Nigeria and Liberia.[8] Hitler's response was frosty, for at that time his Foreign Ministry was preparing a blueprint 'to rationalise colonial development for the benefit of Europe'.[9] An enlarged Italian empire was not part of this plan.

Fascism had always been about conquest. As a young misfit spitefully living on the margins of society, Mussolini had convinced himself that 'only blood could turn the bloodstained wheels of history'. This remained his creed: violence was a valid and desirable means for a government to gets its own way at home and abroad. 'I don't give a damn!' was the slogan of Mussolini's Blackshirt hoodlums, and he applauded it as 'evidence of a fighting spirit which accepts all the risks'.[10] Violence was essential for Italy to attain both its rightful place in the world and the territorial empire that would uphold its pretensions. Yet

Mussolini's projected empire was not just about accumulating power: he promised that it would, like its Roman predecessor, bring enlightenment to its subjects. Italians were fitted for this noble task for, as the Duce insisted, 'It is our spirit that has put our civilisation on the by-ways of the world.'[11]

Cinema informed the masses of the ideals and achievements of the new Rome. A propaganda short of 1937 entitled *Scipione l'Africano* blended past and present glories. There was footage of Mussolini's recent visit to Libya, where he is seen watching a spectacular enactment of Scipio's victory over Carthage with elephants and Italian soldiers dressed as Roman legionaries. It was followed by scenes of a mock Roman triumph alternated with shots of the new Caesar, Mussolini, inspecting his troops. There are also images of babies and mothers surrounded by children as a reminder of the Duce's campaign to raise the birth rate, which would, among other things, provide a million colonists for an enlarged African empire.

Fascism's civilising mission was graphically portrayed in the opening sequence of the 1935 propaganda film *Ti Saluto, Vado in Abissinia*, produced by the Fascist Colonial Institute. Against a soundtrack of discordant music there is grisly footage of shackled slaves, a baby crying as its cheeks are scored with tribal marks, a leper, dancing women, an Abyssinian *ras* (prince) in his exotic regalia, the Emperor Haile Selassie on horseback inspecting modern infantrymen and, to please male cinemagoers, close-ups of naked girls dancing. Darkness and grotesque images give way to light with the first bars of the jaunty popular song of the film's title, and there follows a sequence of young, cheerful soldiers in tropical kit boarding a troopship on the first stage of their journey to claim this benighted land for civilisation. Newsreels celebrated the triumphs of 'progress': one showed a Somali village 'where the machinery imported by our farmers helps the natives to till the fertile soil', and in another King Victor Emmanuel inspects hospitals and waterworks in Libya.[12] In the press, Fascist hacks flattered Italy as 'the mother of civilisation' and 'the most intelligent of nations'.[13]

IV

Progress required Fascist order. Within a year of Mussolini's seizure of power in 1922, operations began to secure Libya completely, in particular the south-western desert region of Fezzan. Progress was slow, despite aircraft, armoured cars and tanks, and so in 1927 Italy, like Spain, reached for phosgene and mustard gas. Under Marshal Rodolfo Graziani, Italian forces pressed inland across the Sahara, herded rebels and their families into internment camps and hanged captured insurgents. The fighting dragged on for a further four years, and ended with the capture, trial and public execution in 1931 of the capable and daring partisan leader, Omar el-Mukhtar. Like Abd el-Krim, he became a hero to later generations of North African nationalists: there are streets named after him in Cairo and Gaza.*

Somalia too got a stiff dose of Fascist discipline. Indirect rule was abandoned, and the client chiefs who had effectively controlled a third of the colony were brought to heel by a war waged between 1923 and 1927. The bill swelled Somalia's debts, which were slightly reduced by a programme of investment in irrigation and cash crops, all of which were subsidised by Rome. Italians were compelled to buy Somalian bananas, but their consumption merely staved off insolvency.[14] The flow of immigrants was disappointingly small: in 1940 there were 854 Italian families tilling the Libyan soil and 1,500 settlers in Somalia.[15]

Having tightened Italy's grip over Libya and Somalia, Mussolini turned to what was, for all patriots, the unfinished business of Abyssinia, where an Italian army had suffered an infamous defeat at Adwa in 1896. Fascism would restore national honour and add a potentially rich colony to the new Roman Empire, which would soon be filled by settlers.

Known as Ethiopia by its Emperor and his subjects, Abyssinia was one of the largest states in Africa, covering 472,000 square miles, and it had been independent for over a thousand years. It was ruled by Haile Selassie, 'Lion of Judah, Elect of God, King of Kings of Ethiopia', a benevolent absolutist who traced his descent to Solomon and Sheba. His autocracy had the spiritual support of the Coptic Church, which preached the virtues of submission to the Emperor and the aristocracy. One nobleman, Ras Gugsa Wale, summed up the political philosophy of his caste: 'It is best for Ethiopia to live according to ancient custom

---

* In 1981 a spectacular Libyan film, *Lion of the Desert*, was released which told the story of el-Mukhtar's heroic resistance, with Anthony Quinn in the title role and Oliver Reed playing Graziani. It was banned in Italy for over twenty years.

as of old and it would not profit her to follow European civilisation.'[16]

Nevertheless, that civilisation was encroaching on Abyssinia and would continue to do so. In 1917 the railway between French Djibuti and Addis Ababa had been opened; among other goods transported were consignments of modern weaponry for Haile Selassie's army and embryonic air force (it had four planes in 1935), and European business-men in search of concessions. The Emperor was a hesitantly progressive ruler who hoped to achieve a balance between tradition and what he called 'acts of civilisation'.[17]

Frontier disputes provided Mussolini with the pretext for a war, but he had first to overcome the hurdle of outside intervention orchestrated by the League of Nations. Abyssinia was a member of that body which, in theory, existed to prevent wars through arbitration and, again in theory, had the authority to call on members to impose sanctions on aggressors. The League was a paper tiger: it had failed to stop the Jap-anese seizure of Manchuria in 1931, and economic sanctions against Italy required the active cooperation of the British and French navies. This was not forthcoming, for neither power had the will for a blockade that could escalate into a war against Italy whose army, navy and air force were grossly overestimated by the British and French intelligence services. Moreover, both powers were becoming increasingly uneasy about Hitler's territorial ambitions and hoped, vainly as it turned out, to enlist the goodwill of Mussolini. An Anglo-French attempt to ap-pease Mussolini by offering him a chunk of Abyssinia (the Hoare-Laval Pact) failed either to deter him or win his favour. Interestingly, this resort to the cynical diplomacy of Africa's early partition provoked outrage in Britain and France.

Neither nation was prepared to strangle Italy's seaborne trade to preserve Abyssinian integrity, and so Mussolini's gamble paid off. The fighting began in October 1935, with 100,000 Italian troops backed by tanks and bombers invading from Eritrea in the north and Somalia in the south. Ranged against them was the small professional Abyssin-ian army armed with machine-guns and artillery and far larger tribal levies raised by the *ras*es and equipped with all kinds of weapons, from spears and swords to modern rifles.

The course of the war has been admirably charted by Anthony Mockler, who reminds us that, despite the disparity between the equipment of the two armies, the conquest of Abyssinia was never the walkover the Italians had hoped for. In December a column backed by ten tanks was ambushed in the Takazze valley. One, sent on a reconnaissance, was captured by a warrior who stole up behind the vehicle, jumped on it and knocked on the turret. It was opened and he killed the crew with his sword. Surrounded, the Italians attempted to rally around their tanks and were overrun. Another tank crew were slain after they had opened their turret; others were overturned and set alight, and two were captured. Nearly all their crews were killed in the rout that followed and fifty machine-guns captured. The local commander, Marshal Pietro Badoglio, was shaken by this reverse and struck back with aircraft which attacked the Abyssinians with mustard-gas bombs.[18]

As in Morocco, gas (as well as conventional bombs) compensated for slipshod command and panicky troops, although the Italians excused its use as revenge for the beheading in Daggahur of a captured Italian pilot after he had just bombed and strafed the town. Denials rather than excuses were offered when bombs were dropped on hospitals marked with red crosses.

Intensive aerial bombardment and gas swung the war in Italy's favour. In May 1936 Addis Ababa was captured and, soon after, Haile Selassie went into exile. He was jeered by Italian delegates when he addressed the League of Nations in Geneva, and was cheered by Londoners when he arrived at Waterloo. He remained in England for the next four years, sometimes in Bath, where his kindness and charm were long remembered. In Rome an image of the Lion of Judah was placed on the war memorial to the dead of the 1896 war; Adwa had been avenged.[19] Mussolini's bombast rose to the occasion with declarations that Abyssinia had been 'liberated' from its age-old backwardness and miseries. Liberty took odd forms, for the Duce decreed that henceforward it was a crime for Italians to cohabit with native women, which he thought an affront to Italian manhood, and he forbade Italians to be employed by Abyssinians.

In Abyssinia Italians assumed the role of master race with a hideous relish. Efforts were made to exterminate the Abyssinian intellectual elite, including all primary school teachers.[20] In February 1937 an attempt to assassinate the Viceroy Graziani prompted an official pogrom in which Abyssinians were randomly murdered in the streets. Blackshirts armed with daggers and shouting, 'Duce! Duce!' led the way. The killings spread to the countryside after Graziani ordered the Governor of Harar to 'Shoot all – I say all – rebels, notables, chiefs' and anyone 'thought guilty of bad faith or of being guilty of helping the rebels'.* Thousands were slaughtered during the next three months.[21]

The subjugation of Abyssinia proved as difficult as its conquest. Over 200,000 troops were deployed fighting a guerrilla war of pacification. Italy's new colony was turning into an expensive luxury: between 1936 and 1938 its military expenses totalled 26,500 million lire. In the event of a European war, this huge army would deter an Anglo-French invasion and, as Mussolini hoped, invade the Sudan, Djibuti and perhaps Kenya, while forces based in Libya attacked Egypt. Viceroy Graziani felt certain that Britain was secretly helping Abyssinian resistance and Mussolini agreed, although he wondered whether the Comintern might also have been involved.[22]

By 1938, his own secret service was disseminating anti-British propaganda to Egypt and Palestine via Radio Bari. In April 1939, alarmed by the flow of reinforcements to Italian garrisons in Libya and Abyssinia, the British made secret preparations for undercover operations to foment native uprisings in both colonies.[23] At the same time, parties of young Italians, ostensibly on cycling holidays, spread the Fascist message in Tunisia and Morocco, and Jewish pupils were banned from Italian schools in Tunis, Rabat and Tangier.[24] Africa was already becoming embroiled in Europe's political conflicts.

V

Outside Germany and Italy, European opinion about the Abyssinian War was sharply divided: anti-Fascists of all kinds were against Mussolini, while right-wingers tended to support him on racial grounds. Sir Oswald Mosley, whose British Union of Fascists was secretly underwritten by Mussolini, dismissed Abyssinia as a 'black and barbarous conglomeration of tribes with not one Christian principle'. Lord Rothermere, owner of the *Daily Mail*, urged his readers to back Italy and 'the cause of the white race' whose defeat in Abyssinia would set a

---

* Graziani was found guilty of war crimes in 1945, but not those committed in Abyssinia. He was let out of prison after two years. In 2012 the Berlusconi government funded a public park and museum in honour of him at Affile, southeast of Rome.

frightening example to Africans and Asians. Evelyn Waugh, who was commissioned by Rothermere to cover the war, confided to a friend his hopes that the Abyssinians would be 'gassed to buggery'.

Such reactions, and the moral insouciance of Britain and France, shocked educated Africans in West Africa. The Abyssinian episode had tarnished the notion of benevolent imperialism cherished in both nations, and seemed to condone views of Africans as a primitive people, beyond the pale of humanity as well as civilisation. In the words of William Du Bois, an American black academic and champion of black rights, the Abyssinian War had shattered the black man's 'faith in white justice'. Harlem blacks had volunteered to fight, but had been refused visas by the American government. Du Bois believed that their instincts had been right, for in the future, 'The only path to freedom and equality is force, and force to the uttermost.'[25]

19

'Unable to stand alone': Africa on the Eve of War

I

In 1939 imperial rule in Africa was secure and seemed destined to last well into the future. Britain, France and Italy congratulated themselves on their enlightened policies and the progress their colonies were making. But the pace of advancement varied and the world recession had placed a brake on economic development which, it was agreed, was key to long-term regeneration.

A handful of pessimists asked whether bringing Africa into the modern world was either desirable or possible. In 1923 Lord Cranworth, the Kenyan settler leader, wondered whether a 'huge majority' of Africans 'would, given the chance, vote to return to their past conditions'.[1] After a visit to the Congo in 1927, the French intellectual André Gide remarked that 'The less intelligent the white man is the more stupid he thinks the black.' But it was a judgement he shared, for he did not believe Africans were 'capable of any but the slightest mental development; their brains as a rule are dull and stagnant – but how often the white man makes it his business to thrust them back into darkness'.[2] Internal opposition to colonial rule was, however, fragmentary, and was either ignored in the case of movements seeking a greater African say in government, or crushed by overwhelming force which now included aircraft.

Yet imperial governments were never omnipotent. Local feelings and cultures had to be accommodated, even when they were odious to Europeans. Marcel de Coppet, the enlightened Governor-General of French West Africa between 1936 and 1938, deplored men selling women to pay their debts, which was 'against French principles', but had to tolerate it because it rested on 'traditional customs'.[3] In 1939, the Governor's council in Kenya advised that when the courts tried witchcraft cases, they had to consider whether the offence 'was in accordance with, or repugnant to . . . Native laws and customs'.[4] In French Morocco the authorities heeded Muslim sensibilities even when they appeared obtuse and obstructive.

Imperial governments justified their monopolies of power with familiar arguments. These had gained a fresh legitimacy through the Covenant of the League of Nations, which was drawn up in 1919. Imperial nations which joined the League bound themselves to promote 'the well-being and development of populations unable to stand alone in the strenuous condition of the modern world' and so fulfil the 'sacred trust of civilisation'. Much had already been achieved. The guidebook to the 1931 Paris Colonial Exhibition declared that France 'had delivered millions of men, women and children from the nightmare of slavery and death, and imposed new values which overturned societies in which the strong oppressed the weak and women and children counted for nothing'.[5] As well as replacing chaos with order, France had, in the words of one visitor to the exhibition, Sultan Muhammad V of Morocco, 'brought to our subjects the science indispensable to understand modern life and to enter on to the path of progress'.[6]

Such self-applause was echoed by African expressions of gratitude. 'We praise the British people in our heart and soul, they have rescued us from woes', declared the members of the Ibadan branch of the National Congress of British West Africa in 1921. They had been delivered from a grisly past characterised by the 'atrocities, cruelties, [and] human sacrifices committed by our ancestors'.[7] Chilling folk memories of past sufferings lingered in nearby villages where, in 1933, Hubert Childs, the Assistant District Officer, heard tales of the ravages of Fulani slavers from Dahomey fifty or so years before. King Gezo's female warriors, some mounted and wielding axes, were vividly recollected.[8] Oral traditions mutate and fade, but it is significant that during the interwar years there were still many Africans who could recall the unquiet and perilous times before the arrival of the colonial order.

II

Comparisons of this kind were grist to the imperialist mill. British and French imperial propaganda repeatedly contrasted Africa's wild and bloody past with its present peace and future prospects. The official version of Africa's progress appeared on colonial postage stamps, which were widely collected throughout Europe and the United States. An African nurse working in a government hospital appears on a 1933 Sierra Leone stamp, one of an issue that celebrated the centenary of the abolition of slavery. Nigeria's economic prospects were depicted on a 1936 set with images of a steamer being loaded with exports, a rubber plantation, a road through a forest and a railway bridge over the Niger. *La mission civilisatrice* was symbolised on a 1931 stamp from the Ivory Coast with the image of a white man, framed against the rising sun, emerging from the sea and greeting a group of natives on the shore. His offerings are revealed on a later issue from French Equatorial Africa that shows a scene in which a French doctor is treating native children.

The cinema was the most influential medium for imperial propaganda. Throughout the interwar years, films were the most popular form of entertainment in Europe and the United States: in 1939 450 million cinema tickets were sold in France and 990 million in Britain. Governments controlled the film industry through licensing films and censoring scripts. Specific restrictions were imposed on films with colonial scenarios, which were forbidden to portray British officers and officials as corrupt, drunken or depraved. Interracial love affairs were taboo in Britain and frowned on in Hollywood. Directors who depicted empires in a favourable light received invaluable assistance from the British and French governments, which loaned soldiers as extras and facilitated filming in African locations.[9] The result was a series of thrilling movies, shot in exotic locations, which played to mass audiences and reinforced the notion that the British and French empires were benign and run by brave and selfless soldiers and administrators.

One such was *Itto* (1934), a French-made romantic adventure set in Morocco twenty years before and dedicated to the achievements of Marshal Lyautey. The heroine Itto is the daughter of Hamou, a Berber chief, and engaged to Miloud, the son of another chief, Hassan. He is at war with the French and his followers shoot down a reconnaissance plane. The badly injured pilot is rescued by the Berbers and, true to the sentimental French image of them as a chivalrous enemy, Hassan sends for a French doctor to treat him. The airman recovers and the doctor discovers anthrax among Hassan's sheep, inoculates them and saves his flock. A grateful Hassan swears never again to fight the French. Miloud fights on and is killed, while Itto, having given birth to her lover's son, dies alongside her father in a dramatic siege. Their deaths are tragic, but they are the victims of a purblind resistance to the forces of civilisation. Unlike Hassan, they have failed to recognise the generous spirit of the new French order which is liberating their country from ignorance and is personified by the doctor.[10] A sour American review of *Itto* noted that it 'contributes more to the cause of French imperialism than it does to entertainment'.[11]

Britain's imperial mission was dramatised by Zoltán Korda's spectacular *Sanders of the River* (1935). Its hero Sanders is a District Officer in Nigeria who personifies the dedication and heroism of the men who were transforming Africa for the better. The virtues of this benevolent autocrat are sung by Paul Robeson, who plays Bosambo, the chief of the Ochori:*

> Sandi the strong, Sandi the wise,
> Righter of wrong, hater of lies,
> Laughed as he fought, worked as he played.
> As he taught, let it be made.

Sanders has taught Bosambo how to rule and his pupil is wiser and thankful. 'I have learned the secret of good government from your lordship. It is this, that a king should not be feared but loved by his people. That is the secret of the British.' As Professor Jeffrey Richards observes, respect was more common than love. Gratitude was another matter, for the film tells us that Sanders is gaining the upper hand against slavers, gun-runners and gin-pedlars. These evils belong to the old Africa, personified by the villainous former king Mofalaba, who deposes Bosambo while Sanders is on leave. He returns and, after a splutter of Maxim-gun fire, Bosambo is reinstated and the imperial peace restored.

Korda, a Hungarian-Jewish Anglophile, had the government's blessing and the right-wing press applauded *Sanders of the River*. 'One cannot be modest about the Empire', declared the *Daily Express*. The Nigerian nationalist Nnamdi Azikiwe denounced the film as propaganda and an 'exaggeration of the African mentality'. In 1957 it had its television debut, which provoked the Nigerian High Commissioner to

---

* To help make ends meet while in London, Jomo Kenyatta worked as an extra in the crowd scenes shot at Pinewood.

protest that Nigeria had been depicted as 'a country of half-naked barbarians'. Meanwhile, *Sanders of the River* was being shown to packed houses in Lagos's three cinemas.[12]

III

Men like Sanders were the backbone of British rule in Africa. There were 1,200 of them scattered across the continent, governing 50 million Africans. They were supported by legions of native policemen, clerks, tax collectors, mechanics and labourers, many of whom were employed in laying and maintaining roads. There were over 120,000 Africans in official employment in the Gold Coast. Whenever coercion was required, it was undertaken by tiny police forces: the proportion of policemen to civilians ranged from one in 1,000 in Swaziland to one in 188,000 in the Gold Coast.[13]

Outside Egypt, soldiers were thin on the ground, with only 5,000 British-officered askaris making up the entire African colonial garrison.[14] France had over ten times that number, a high proportion of them West African conscripts who served in garrisons in Africa, the Lebanon and Syria. In 1923 black *tirailleurs* were deployed during the occupation of the Rhineland, which the Germans treated as a calculated racial insult. In Africa, aircraft were frequently used by the French, Spaniards and Italians and to a far lesser extent by the British. While the RAF was keen to become the gendarmerie of last resort throughout British Africa, many local officials had moral qualms about bombing disobedient tribesmen, their homes and livestock. In 1928, when Whitehall insisted on the deployment of aircraft against the Nuers of southern Sudan, one civil servant in Khartoum complained about a 'highly unwelcome and inopportune' form of correction.[15]

Britain's domestic and international self-image required her to govern humanely and fairly: her colonial servants were kindly but firm schoolmasters who relied on reasoned arguments and example to guide their pupils. They were recruited by examination and those who passed were sifted by interviews conducted by Sir Ralph Furse. He emerges from his memoirs as a thoroughly decent Edwardian sporting gentleman with an instinctive eye for a wimp or a cad. His ideal candidate was an intelligent public-school man who had been head of house, had taken a Third at either Oxford or Cambridge, and whose character had been shaped on the playing field or behind an oar. This paragon had a strong jaw, a firm handshake, made direct eye contact and had gained his Blue by scoring a century in the Oxford–Cambridge match. When offered a cigarette, he chose Turkish rather than Virginia. Furse would have been pleased with the description of the Sudan as a land in which 'Blues ran blacks'.

The men chosen by Furse faced a tough life of mental and physical grind. Appointed to the Colonial Service in 1928, when he was twenty-three, Hubert Childs (Oakham and Oxford) was within five years responsible for 2,000 square miles of bush and savannah with 42,000 inhabitants. Whenever practical, he travelled in a two-seater Morris Oxford or by bicycle over occasionally impassable roads which it was his responsibility to maintain. His other duties embraced the supervision of native judges (one was 'hopeless, characterless, spineless and undignified'), the selection of chiefs and headmen, settling land disputes and compiling on-the-spot reports on local conditions. His and his colleagues' labours were under the constant surveillance of his superiors and Parliament, where MPs, particularly those on the Left, were quick to draw attention to any hint of high-handedness or injustice. In 1934 anxieties were voiced in the Commons about district officers in Somaliland having the power to pass death sentences.[16]

Childs also had to both encourage and reprimand. In October 1934 he was ordered to undertake a survey of villages in British Cameroon, asking questions about local traders and craftsmen, schools and agriculture. When some villagers grumbled about their hunger, he admonished them: 'You have only your laziness to thank for that. God has given you a rich country.' Perhaps so, but he noted regretfully that his male listeners considered sowing, tilling and harvesting crops as beneath them, and, therefore, best left to women.[17] Like many others in similar posts, Childs felt an attachment to what he regarded as natural Africans, like the villagers of Igaugan who were 'simple, friendly . . . unspoilt folk'. Their innocence was threatened, for, as the Balé Okunda Abass of Ibadan told Childs, 'the next generation will see great changes'.[18]

Okunda Abass was one of the thousands of native princes, chiefs and headmen whose active cooperation was vital to the administration at every level. In 1928 the authorities urged a Nyasaland chief and his wife to encourage pregnant women to seek obstetric treatment at a new

local clinic.[19] In essence, the relationship between the district officer
and the chief was that between a public-school housemaster and his
prefects. They kept order and undertook some administrative chores
and, in return, enjoyed privileges and learned to balance firmness with
fair play. Special schools exclusively for the sons of chiefs prepared
them for their future responsibilities and emphasised moral leadership
and participation in the lives of their people.

Constant supervision was essential, especially for the wayward and
idle. Born in 1904, the future Rukidi III Omukama of Toro (Uganda)
entered the Budo college for chiefs, where he loafed about and showed
'no strength of character'. It was hoped that a period serving as a trainee
police inspector would encourage 'discipline and regular exercise', but
it was cut short when he succeeded his father in 1928. Over the next five
years, Rukidi's vices got the better of him and he became an embarrassment to the authorities. He was moody, excitable, neglected such
duties as visiting schools, was a bad landlord, turned a blind eye to il-
licit brewing and drank heavily. In 1938 Rukidi received a remonstrance
from the provincial commissioner, which he may not have understood
fully, for he was losing his command of English.[20] Perhaps the question
of his deposition was raised, for he calmed down for the next few years.
By contrast, a Basuto chief, Theko Makhala, was 'energetic, intelligent
and a man of stout character' with 'advanced' views on 'agricultural
improvements'. He drank moderately, his wife less so, and in 1944 he
came under suspicion of corruptly collecting taxes. A warning followed
and he redeemed himself by helping the army recruitment programme,
which earned him an MBE.[21] The British honours system was an invaluable prop to indirect government.

IV

Men like Rukidi and Makhala, dressed in their flamboyant regalia,
played leading roles in that great set-piece of the British imperial theatre of power, royal tours. Their principal purpose was to tighten the
bonds of imperial unity and strengthen the allegiance of native rulers.
It was imagined that royal progresses in the tropics won the hearts of
peoples who were accustomed to hierarchy and had an inborn love of
ceremony and festivals. Since 1919, and with the encouragement of King
George V, successive governments had projected an image of imperial

monarchy in which the King appeared as an august but humane patriarch, the father of an extended 'family' of dominions and colonies.
Stanley Baldwin, Prime Minister between 1935 and 1937, was the apos-
tle of imperial monarchy and convinced himself that the Empire could
not survive without it.[22] So it was that the King made the first royal
broadcast on Christmas Day 1932 to 'all my peoples throughout the
Empire'; he hoped that, like him, his listeners would be celebrating
with their own families.

The imperial mystique of the monarchy had some bizarre consequences. When a young district officer in northern Kenya reprimanded
Turkana tribesmen for cattle-rustling, he warned them that they had
angered 'King Georgie', who would soon show his displeasure. He
knew that an eclipse of the moon was imminent and it dramatically
proved his point. The cattle were returned to their owners.[23]

The King's African subjects not only heard his voice (the 1932
Christmas message was relayed to South Africa and Kenya), but
they regularly saw his eldest son, their future king, Edward, Prince
of Wales, during his African progresses in 1920, 1925 and 1928, which
both cemented imperial unity and kept him out of mischief. This, in
the words of Alan Lascelles, his Assistant Private Secretary, took the
form of the 'unbridled pursuit of Wine and Women, and of whatever
selfish whim occupied him at the moment'. Duty did not preclude
these pleasures: during his 1928 tour of Kenya the Prince seduced a district commissioner's wife.[24] Like every other royal tourist in the tropics,
Edward slaughtered the wildlife.

Edward's imperial tours were filmed and gave British cinemagoers
the opportunity to see their empire at first hand and in the best possible
light. The 1920 Pathé newsreel showed footage of the Prince travelling
by train from Lagos to Kano, where he held what was billed as 'The
Great Durbar'. Dressed in white and wearing a plumed helmet, he
receives the homage of robed emirs and chiefs who approach the royal
dais and kneel at his feet in submission. There were stunning shots of
mounted horsemen with lances, chiefs carrying ornate parasols, rangy
Fulani cattle wandering through narrow streets and bare-breasted
women dancing.

The Africa portrayed in the fiction of Rider Haggard and *Boy's Own
Paper*-style adventures appears in spectacular footage of the Prince's
1925 tour of southern Africa. In Swaziland he receives gifts of leopard

skins, shields and assegais from furred and feathered warriors who, in return, are handed blankets. Next, an entire impi gives an awesome display of war dances before turning and trotting off across nearby hills. It is magnificent cinema with a powerful message: African potentates and proud warriors welcome and pay homage to the eldest son of the King–Emperor, under whose wise rule they now enjoy peace. Crowds of Africans appear everywhere, cheering the Prince, and shots of local schoolchildren parading before him remind audiences that their empire is bringing civilisation to Africa.

V

France could not compete with royal pageantry. By no stretch of the imagination could a president – a transient politician in a frock-coat, silk hat and sash – have the glamour of a handsome prince in his dashing uniform. Yet the republican ideals of freedom and equality represented by this mundane figure inspired deep affection and loyalty. When, in early January 1939, President Édouard Daladier visited Algiers, he announced that it was the 'destiny' of France to uphold 'the liberties of peoples'.[25] Seventeen months later in Dakar, eleven-year-old Bara Diouf was overwhelmed by despair when he heard that France had just surrendered to Nazi Germany. Years later, he recalled: 'the sentiment we felt for France was beautiful, noble. What was it based on? I do not know, perhaps a myth. Because we were all, more or less, prisoners of a myth of an admired republican France toward which we all felt great esteem.'[26]

Diouf was part of a vast entity which Frenchmen proudly called *La France d'outre-mer*. Quite simply, the colonies were an extension of France and her culture, and, in theory, all their inhabitants could one day become Frenchmen and so enjoy the privileges of citizenship. Yet, for all its noble rhetoric, the concept of assimilation was at variance with the reality of the commonplace racial arrogance that was part of colonial life. Assimilation was also riddled with ambiguities and contradictions. For instance, if taken at face value, the universal equality at the heart of the revolutionary ideal of the *Droits d'homme* could fatally undermine the foundations of imperial government. Did this mean that the assimilated African *évolué* possessed all the rights embodied in the republican principles of liberty, fraternity and equality?

The answer was no, for he had no vote and would have been forbidden from occupying a bed in a hospital ward reserved for Europeans. Were the privileges of the *évolué* hereditary irrespective of whether his offspring had passed the stiff tests for citizenship which required fluency in French and renunciation of a candidate's past cultural identity?[27]

These conundrums did not worry those responsible for carrying out the policy of assimilation. Officials hedged and dragged their heels in the belief that the political implications of assimilation were harmful. In their minds the African *évolué* was not the equal of a citizen of, say, Rouen or Lyons, whatever the idealists in Paris may have thought: the universal Rights of Man were incompatible with colonial government.[28]

This was why the pace of assimilation was slow: in 1939 there were 319 *évolués* in Dahomey out of an African population of 1.3 million, and in French Guinea 233 out of a population of 2 million.[29] There were none at all in the French Sudan, Togo, Niger and Mauritania. Senegal was an exception, with 78,000 assimilated Africans together with 100,000 *originaires*, whose ancestors had been given the vote in 1790 by the Revolutionary government in Paris. Since then, Senegal had sent a deputy to the National Assembly.

The egalitarian spirit of the Revolution was revived by the Popular Front, a coalition of the Left, which came to power in May 1936. Ministers insisted that the ideals of the Republic were absolute and neither to be rationed nor withheld. It proposed the rapid acceleration of the processes of assimilation, and, to bring the colonies in line with France, legalised trade unions and prescribed hours of work for Africans. The upshot was a rash of strikes: there were forty-seven in Dakar during 1937. Marcel de Coppet, the new Governor of French West Africa, wanted to go further and encouraged the *évolués* to become engaged in government. Educated Africans imagined that a new dawn was breaking and that they were now about to become true Frenchmen, equal with their brother citizens.[30] Their dream evaporated when the Popular Front resigned in 1938 and was replaced by a conservative administration that stalled the assimilation programme. Just thirty-two Senegalese were naturalised in 1940.[31]

The departure of the Popular Front delighted the settlers in Algeria, where plans were in hand for the naturalisation of 25,000 Arabs. The enraged *colons* took fright and 26,000 flocked to the local branches of the neo-Fascist Croix-de-Feu movement.[32] Meanwhile in Senegal, *évolués* were forming their own Popular Front to support the government in Paris and resist Fascism, whose contempt for Africans was being revealed in Abyssinia.[33]

One aim of the Senegalese Popular Front was to seek converts among the Africans of the countryside, who were largely strangers to politics. They were, however, integral to day-to-day government, for, like the British, the French depended on indirect rule through loyal and biddable princes, chiefs and village headmen. In the words of one official, these figures represented 'the traditions and habits of their race'. Under French supervision, they undertook the donkey work of administration, overseeing markets and extracting taxes, for which they received salaries: a provincial tribal chief in Porto Novo (a descendant of an old Dahomey ruling dynasty) got 45,000 francs a year, and provincial chiefs between 5,000 and 6,000.[34] Their French masters believed that such figures provided both continuity and stability. They were also conservative by instinct, representing the 'authentic' Africa, unlike the 'Europeanised' *évolués*, who could never speak 'in the name of the native'. Seen from the Governor's residence, the assimilated African was a potential subversive who could turn the heads of simple villagers.[35]

France's clients were encouraged to display all the trappings of their customary authority. In 1930 an American visitor to the French Cameroons was impressed by the dignified splendour of the Sultan Ibrahim Njoya, with his ornate throne, elegant palace (refurbished by the French), which housed his harem, and his mounted bodyguard of 'aristocrats'.[36] This was the façade of power: if he displeased them the French could depose him or any other of their servants. The point was made by one official who had Tricolours painted on the exteriors of chiefs' houses. The African, he explained, had a particular 'sensitivity to such external symbols'.[37]

The flag-conscious official was a graduate of the École Coloniale, which had been founded in 1889 to train colonial administrators. The syllabus concentrated on the abstract, with an emphasis on administrative theory and law. Most students came from upper-middle-class backgrounds and many were driven by a high-minded sense of public service together with a longing for adventure. An interpreter clerk from the French Cameroons recalled a succession of district administrators between the wars with varying attitudes and talents. They ranged from 'a very . . . humane, honest, just and conscientious' paragon to a rascal, who was 'mad' and on his arrival asked what was the 'going rate' for 'the local wenches'. He was mocked by the natives and got the district's finances into a mess. Such creatures leaned heavily on their interpreter clerks, who themselves were thought manipulative and unreliable. Many were or aspired to be *évolués*.[38]

VI

In 1939 it would have been impossible to quantify change across an entire continent or to predict exactly its direction. Certainly only the most daring prophet would have foreseen that an African child born in that year would approach middle age in a continent almost entirely ruled by Africans. Even those Africans who were demanding a greater say in how they were governed would not have imagined this, although some already saw it was an ultimate, if still-distant, goal.

The parents of this child would certainly have been aware of recent changes. Railways and roads made travel faster and more endurable, although there were still a few remote districts that were difficult to reach, such as the interior of Niger, which was still impassable to motor traffic. Yet even this colony possessed a skeletal bus network which included a fortnightly trans-Saharan service which ran to Algiers.[39] Letters to and from Niger and just about every other place in Africa were now carried by aeroplanes, which also conveyed tourists. An Imperial Airways poster showed an airliner on a runway with a lissom, bare-breasted woman in the foreground and a toddler at her feet, playing with a baby antelope. The puff ran: 'Through Africa in Days Rather than Weeks'. Pilots were obliging: one passenger remembered that the flying boat from Lake Victoria to Khartoum flew low so that all on board could get good views of the herds of animals below. Cocktails were served each evening in a small lounge.[40]

Nearly all who travelled by air were Europeans. Those whose ancestors had settled in Africa had no reason to think that their elevated status would not continue, although they were less sanguine than they had been. Rising Arab birth rates and a growing Arab presence in towns and cities perturbed the Algerian *colons*, who were becoming increasingly belligerent in defence of their privileges. Their counterparts in South Africa shared their nervousness, but for different reasons. The recession had hurt the local economy with a falling demand for gold and accelerated the growth of the urban 'poor white' population, which was estimated at at least 300,000 in 1932. It hovered on the breadline, feared competition from black labour and was susceptible to the racial politics of Afrikaner supremacy, which yearned for the old virtues of the *Volk* and distrusted liberalism and capitalism.[41]

Kenya's 21,000-strong white community had been dismayed by the 1923 Colonial Office declaration which insisted that the rights of the black population would dictate future policy towards the colony. London had little patience with the settlers, whom civil servants considered selfish and bigoted. As late as 1941 one official in London wondered whether they should all be bought out and encouraged to return home.[42] A handful were blue-blooded refugees from Britain seeking a life in which servants were deferential and plentiful, and in which they were free to indulge in louche decadence. They clustered around 'Happy Valley' in the Nyeri district, and it was rumoured that one of their number had offered cocaine to the Prince of Wales during a dinner party, which was considered going a trifle too far.

If the sybarites of Happy Valley ever felt homesick, they had the consolation of the BBC, whose programmes were relayed through Nairobi by the Empire Service which had been founded in 1932. Within four years, local transmitting stations had been established in Nigeria, Sierra Leone and the Gold Coast, where there were 300 receivers, nearly all in Accra. Listeners tended to get news bulletins and the staple pabulum of 'light entertainment', which included dance band shows and detective thrillers, although, true to Lord Reith's principles, there was a scattering of highbrow material. In March 1941 Kenyans heard a talk, with musical examples, on madrigals. Cinemas were proliferating across urban Africa: Egypt had the most, followed by South Africa. Hollywood dominated the African film market, as it did Europe's, so that in 1934 three-quarters of the new releases in Egypt were American productions.[43] The Americanisation of Africa had just begun.

20

'Wait and see':
Italian Disasters and French Traumas 1940–1945

———

I

The Second World War was the beginning of the end for Europe's colonial empires. It destroyed one, the Italian, and the French was severely shaken by the division of its colonies into two hostile camps. The larger adhered to the pro-Axis Vichy regime set up after France's surrender in June 1940, and the smaller attached itself to the British-sponsored and funded Free French movement led by General Charles de Gaulle. It prevailed thanks to Anglo-American victories in Algeria and Morocco in November 1942, which reunited the empire. Speaking in the Ivory Coast in February 1944, de Gaulle boasted that France was again 'in the front of great nations'.[1]

And so it seemed, for within six months and with American permission, de Gaulle led Free French units into Paris; but a few hours of triumph could not erase four years of defeats and servile collaboration. France had been repeatedly humiliated, her prestige was in tatters and her imperial kudos had been discredited in the eyes of her subjects.

By contrast, Britain had come out of the war remarkably well, although burdened with a badly mauled industrial infrastructure, a $160 million debt to the United States for war supplies and a further $586 million advanced in 1945 to stave off bankruptcy. The Empire had contributed much to the war effort and displayed an impressive and sometimes moving loyalty. Hundreds of thousands of its African subjects had served in the forces, but, like the British people, they expected rewards for six years of exertion and sacrifice. Uppermost in the minds of educated Africans was a sense of moral reciprocity by which Britain conceded political rights in return for supporting the imperial war effort. Such hopes soared after August 1941, when

Churchill and President Roosevelt announced the Atlantic Charter, which was a draft for the post-war Anglo-American reordering of the world. It promised the universal right of 'self- determination' and pledged that henceforward all people would be free to decide their countries' frontiers.

The Atlantic Charter read like a death warrant for Europe's empires, and Roosevelt hoped that it would prove so. De Gaulle understood this and refrained from mentioning the Charter in his broadcasts.[2] Churchill was also unhappy, and he cavilled over those clauses which threatened the British Empire, but the Labour Party had warmly approved the Charter. In the July 1945 general election it won a landslide victory with a manifesto that promised independence for India, Burma and Ceylon, and 'planned progress' for the colonies. Many Labour supporters believed that this would lead to independence, particularly intellectuals on the party's Left who had always been sympathetic to colonial nationalist movements.

Most significant of all in terms of Africa's future history, the war had seen the debut of a new power on the continent: the United States. In November 1942 there were 378,000 American servicemen deployed in North Africa in readiness for Operation Torch, the seaborne invasion of Algeria and Morocco. Just before they came ashore, propaganda leaflets described them as 'liberators'. Practical politics intervened and the Americans had to make a compromise with the Free French which left the Arabs excluded from government. Wartime expediency had overridden the principles of the Atlantic Charter. Roosevelt acquiesced, but many Americans who shared his animus towards empires were incensed by the knowledge that American blood was being shed to restore repressive colonial regimes in North Africa, South-East Asia and the Pacific.

The Atlantic Charter had also called for an end to the protectionist tariffs that had given the imperial powers trading advantages in their colonies. Much to the dismay of Britain and the Free French, corporate America took the Charter at its word and were soon exploring potential markets and sources of raw materials in Africa. Both were needed: American wartime production levels had rocketed and economists predicted that an inevitable post-war fall in demand might easily trigger a slump. Open foreign markets offered a lifeline that would absorb over-production and, perhaps, stimulate future growth. One group of businessmen calculated that once France had abandoned protection, then exports to Senegal which had stood at $1.2 million in 1938 would rise sevenfold by 1949. Most of the imports would be motor vehicles.

American commercial airlines were also planning ahead. They persuaded Washington to demand that the string of emergency airfields built on British territory and linking the Gold Coast to Khartoum and Cairo would be freely available for civilian flights after the war.[3] America moved quickly to secure the Congo's uranium and, in September 1944, joined with Britain to persuade recently liberated Belgium to give both countries a monopoly. The ore was earmarked for future nuclear projects, both warlike and commercial.[4]

American economic penetration of Africa was the prelude to political engagement. Britain and France were apprehensive, but in no position to object. Since the autumn of 1940, the United States had become the Allies' banker and armourer and, therefore, could dictate strategic priorities and the form of the post-war global political settlement. The proof was self-evident: 46 per cent of all Allied equipment was manufactured in America, and in 1945 the United States became the first and only nuclear power. America had the muscle and Roosevelt and his successor, Harry Truman, provided the will. Both were determined that the United States should play an active role throughout the world, which was only right and proper for a nation that now enjoyed a preponderance of financial, industrial and military power.

The implications of this new imbalance of power were soon apparent. In December 1942, Roosevelt attempted to play kingmaker after the occupation of Algeria by forcefully backing General Henri Giraud as a replacement for de Gaulle as leader of the Free French and de facto ruler of France's restored empire.[5] Some Free French supporters, seeing the way the wind was blowing, imagined that Roosevelt also intended to install Giraud as the puppet President of France after the war.[6] At the same time, the Americans were elbowing aside British and Free French representatives in negotiations over the future of Senegal. The American Consul-General in Dakar was overheard speculating about a post-war American sphere of influence in French West Africa.[7] In 1944, Foreign Office officials expected the restored Haile Selassie to play Britain off against the United States when the moment came to decide which power would play godfather to Ethiopia.[8] Together, these incidents suggested that the United States would henceforward disregard historic Anglo-French interests in Africa and, for that matter, elsewhere.

As the war ended, closer American involvement in Africa became an urgent political necessity. During the winter of 1944–5, British and American strategists and diplomats were disturbed by the rapid extension of Soviet power across Eastern Europe, and they feared that it might be pushed further into other regions. Thus, the Russian request to establish an embassy in Liberia in May 1945 sounded alarm bells in the State Department, which quickly set up a legation in its capital, Monrovia. For over a hundred years the United Sates had taken a desultory paternal interest in this pauper republic, first established for freed American slaves. Now it was about to be a participant in a new and yet to be defined conflict: the Cold War. Liberia's President William Tubman was quick to exploit America's sudden interest in his country and asked for money.[9]

II

The fighting in Africa lasted from June 1940 to May 1943 and, despite a few early shocks, it went the Allies' way. Once it was clear that France would collapse, Mussolini had declared war and presented Hitler with a long list of territories as payment for Italy's future efforts on the battlefield. The African spoils included Egypt, the Sudan, Kenya and Djibuti, and political control over Tunis. The Germans were flabbergasted by the Duce's greed, which would have transformed Italy into the dominant power in Africa.

Mussolini's African empire fell apart swiftly and ignominiously. There were 465,000 Italian troops in Africa in the summer of 1940, half of them in Libya, but they were short of modern weaponry, trucks and aircraft. Moreover, as their performance soon revealed, Italian conscripts were indifferent to Mussolini's claim that it was better to live for a day as a lion than a lifetime as a rabbit. The legionaries of the New Rome chose the way of the rabbit and surrendered in droves. By March 1941, the British had accumulated 80,000 POWs from the fighting in East Africa, a third of them Eritrean askaris. Over 113,000 Italian soldiers threw in the towel during the first month of fighting in Libya.

These numbers reflected the scale of Italian reverses. During the autumn of 1940, a half-hearted invasion of the Sudan petered out, and British forces, backed by local insurgents, liberated Ethiopia and restored Haile Selassie to his throne in May 1941. Thanks to overwhelming numbers, the Italians overran British Somaliland, but it was soon recovered. The invasion of Egypt was repelled and, in November 1940, the British Eighth Army swept into Libya. Mussolini's crumbling empire was rescued the following month by Hitler, who ordered Rommel's Afrika Korps to hold the line.

Rommel was dangerous, but only for a time. His tactical genius could not compensate for an inferiority of numbers, shortages of fuel, spare parts and aircraft, and the ability of British signals intelligence to decipher his wireless communications. In November 1942 his outnumbered and outgunned army was decisively defeated at El Alamein. Beating Rommel, saving the Suez Canal and the oilfields of Iraq and Persia had required a prodigious effort: by 1943 over half a million British servicemen and women, including large contingents from India, Australia, New Zealand, South Africa and the African colonies, were deployed across North Africa.

After El Alamein, the Germans and Italians regrouped in Tunisia, where despite their precarious situation they found time to enforce Nazi racial policies. The Jews of Tunis were forced to wear the yellow Star of David, their assets were commandeered and many were herded into specially built camps, where they undertook forced labour. Radio Tunis denounced 'International Jewry' and blamed local Jews for the Anglo-American seaborne landings in November.[10] The war had brought Europe's demons to Africa.

Once the Allied troops were ashore, the Vichy administrations in Algeria and Morocco caved in and many former Vichy supporters hastily converted to the Free French. The war in North Africa finally ended in May 1943 with the mass surrender in Tunisia of a quarter of a million Axis personnel, half of them Afrika Korps men. The invasion of Italy followed in September, and, within five weeks, Mussolini had been deposed and the provisional Italian government had capitulated.

Italy forfeited all its colonies, which were now under British military occupation, and the majority of Italians appeared indifferent to the loss. The newspaper *Italia Nuova* wondered whether they had ever wanted an empire, forgetting that jubilant crowds had celebrated the conquest of Abyssinia seven years before. The left-wing *Avanti!* looked to the future, and hoped that Italy's 'politically immature' subjects would be guided towards democracy by benign international administrations.[11]

Diehard Fascists battled on alongside the Germans in central and north Italy, and alone in Eritrea. Here Captain Valli and Lieutenant Rapullo waged a partisan war against the British in which the latter was killed. His associate was still at large in 1948, and was believed to be getting secret assistance from Fascist elements in the Italian intelligence services who still believed that Italy might somehow recover its colonies.[12] Across the border in Tigré province there was a brief peasant uprising in 1943 against the reimposition of the former feudal regime, which was crushed by Haile Selassie's forces with the help of three RAF bombers.[13]

III

On the whole Germany had been happy to leave Africa to the Italians and French. Before the war, a handful of ardent imperialists had pressed Hitler for the return of Germany's African colonies. The Führer toyed with the idea and, during the second half of 1940, Nazi officials busied themselves drawing up plans for a 'Euro-Afrika' with strictly disciplined colonies (British methods were considered too soft) that would supply the raw materials for the Pan-European economic union which was one of Hitler's main objectives.[14] There was also a proposal for Europe's Jews to be deported to Madagascar, where they would have been allowed their own state. This was dilettantist empire-building, for Hitler's political, economic and racial ambitions were focused on a Euro-Asian empire, and in December 1940 he began preparations for the invasion of the Soviet Union. What he might have had in store for Africa may be guessed from what happened to the people of Russia, for the Nazis' racial ideology considered all blacks, like Slavs, to be inferior beings genetically predestined to serve the Aryan master race.

Planning for a Nazi empire in Africa turned out to be unnecessary, for France's surrender had delivered Germany a surrogate empire. Hitler had permitted France to keep its colonies but, under the terms of the armistice, he insisted that their economies contributed to the German war effort. French colonial products, including industrial diamonds and graphite, were shipped to Vladivostok and then carried by the Trans-Siberian railway to the Russo-German frontier in compliance with the German–Soviet pact of 1939. This arrangement ceased with the German invasion of Russia in June 1941.[15]

IV

Giving economic support to the Third Reich was a price the collaborationist Vichy government was glad to pay for the preservation of the French Empire. In retrospect, Vichy France was a break with the past and a lurch towards Fascism which the French people would still rather forget. The eighty-four-year-old figurehead of the new regime, Marshal Philippe Pétain, claimed that his government represented a revolution, but, seen from the wider perspective of French history, it was a counter-revolution. Vichy's intention was to uproot those ideals that had been implanted in 1789: Liberty, Equality and Fraternity were replaced by *Travail, Famille et Patrie*. For Vichy's subjects in France and Africa these abstractions meant submission, passivity and piety.

Official propaganda elevated 'family' (i.e. patriarchal) values and idealised the traditional, rural France of the peasant and artisan, each a patriot content with his lot. Secularism was discarded and the Catholic Church became a partner in government. Jews were vilified and ostracised and, between 1942 and 1944, civil servants and policemen cooperated with their detention and eventual deportation to the concentration camps. Official publicity exalted the war hero Pétain as a cult figure who was portrayed as the benign grandfather of an extended family, France. Like Hitler and Mussolini, he was often photographed with children.

The preservation and development of its empire were integral to Vichy's ideology: one propaganda poster showed the heads of an Arab, a Negro and an Indo-Chinese against a Tricolour with the slogan: 'Three Colours, One Flag, One Empire'. Vichy's doctrines chimed with a large body of colonial officials and soldiers who had been horrified by the recent liberalising policies of the Popular Front. In Madagascar the Governor purged the administration of Jews, homosexuals and blacks.[16] Elsewhere, governments felt free to tighten control over their subjects who, like the French, needed lessons in the virtues of subordination and unquestioning patriotism. Africans were also taught how lucky they were in their selfless rulers: one propaganda film followed the fictional struggles of a heroic doctor against leprosy, who injected himself with new vaccines to test their effectiveness.[17] Thankful, healthy natives were essential to Vichy's plans for the dynamic regeneration of the colonies that would enrich France. In 1941, the defunct scheme for a trans-Saharan railway running southwards from Oran was revived. Loans for 2 billion francs were floated and 200,000 Africans were press-ganged for forced labour on this project.

Pierre-François Boisson, Governor-General of West Africa, was perfectly qualified to recast the region in the Vichy mould. He was an Anglophobe who was convinced that Jews, Freemasons and Communists were the cause of everything that had gone wrong with France, and that her African subjects could never become Frenchmen and women. Rather, they needed to think of themselves as Africans, and in order to do so Boisson introduced measures designed to cultivate their sense of identity within the confines of their tribal traditions and communities under the benevolent eye of 'Papa' Pétain.

African schoolchildren were taught to revere him and encouraged to write (in French) stories about their distinctive local culture, their parents and villages. Boisson set up the Gardes d'Empire, a body of young men sent into the countryside to convert Africans to the Vichy view of their place in France's vibrant empire. Assimilation lapsed (there were just five *évolués* in 1942) and Dakar's bathing beaches were segregated.[18] Time was against this experiment in quietism which ended in December 1942 when the Anglo-American occupation of Algiers extinguished Vichy authority in Africa. Like their colleagues in Algeria, Boisson and his fellow collaborators declared themselves for the Free French, not out of conviction but to save their jobs and pensions.

The Vichy revolution also won the approval of most of the white community in Algeria. Many *colons* enlisted in the officially backed Légion Française des Combattants, whose job it was to support the police, spread propaganda and fight 'Gaullist dissidents and the Jewish scourge'. The metropolitan campaign against the Jews was extended to Algeria and Morocco, where they were hustled towards the margins of society. In October 1940 their citizenship was revoked and they were banned from all public offices, and a year later Jewish business and professional activities were severely restricted. One thousand foreign Jews, many of them recent refugees from Europe, were arrested and interned. Just before the liberation of Casablanca in November 1942, there were random attacks on synagogues and local anti-Semites were planning a pogrom.[19] If the Allies had not occupied French North Africa, its Jewish population would have suffered the same fate as that of France.

Arabs had joined in the Casablanca riots. Since the mid-1930s, Nazi propaganda agencies had wooed them as potential allies and collaborators, portraying Hitler as a friend to them and to Islam. Britain was not, for it was allegedly in thrall to the Jews. Proof was provided by her recent policies in Palestine, which allegedly favoured Jewish immigrants at the expense of the indigenous Arabs. They and their brothers in North Africa would be saved by 'Al Haji Hitler' – details of his conversion and pilgrimage to Mecca were withheld by Berlin. Paradoxically, given Vichy's insistence on Arab subordination, the Germans suggested that they were promoted to senior administrative posts in Algeria and Morocco. This advice was rejected, although Vichy was happy for Arab volunteers to join the Wehrmacht's Phalange Africaine, a French-officered unit earmarked for the Eastern Front.[20] On the whole, North Africa's Arabs were not duped by Nazi propaganda. Ferhat Abbas, the leader of the Union Populaire Algérienne, placed his faith in the Allies because, in theory, their liberal and humane values made them sympathetic to Arab political aspirations.[21] Some credulous Arabs imagined that the Americans had a Muslim general whose forename revealed his faith: Omar Bradley.[22]

V

Britain treated Vichy as a malevolent neutral, willing to act as Germany's accomplice on several fronts but always shy of declaring war. Churchill's government had no such inhibition and, whenever Vichy activities jeopardised her strategic interests, Britain struck swiftly and hard. In July 1940 British warships shattered a powerful French squadron stationed at Mers-el-Kébir to prevent it from falling into Axis hands and tilting the balance of sea power in the Mediterranean against the Royal Navy. Several French ships were sunk or crippled, over 1,500 French sailors were killed or wounded, diplomatic relations were severed, and the Vichy press howled with rage. As ever, fumed *Le Matin*, the British behaved as if they were above international conventions and laws.[23] Yet signals intelligence indicated that Admiral Jean Darlan, the Minister of Marine, was about to order his ships to attack

British forces. To appease his countrymen's fury, he ordered air raids on Gibraltar.

The French press aired suspicions that the attack at Mers-el-Kébir had been slyly urged by French exiles in London who were then rallying around de Gaulle who, at the end of the month, declared the birth of *La France Libre*. In August, preparations were in hand for a naval coup de main against Dakar to secure its naval facilities for the Free French. The attack would have a political bonus, for it was assumed that if Dakar fell, so would the rest of French West Africa. As originally planned, the blow was to be struck by a British squadron manned by Free French sailors and flying French flags, but it was abandoned in favour of one in which the armada's ships flew the White Ensign. Seen from the defences of Dakar it looked like a straightforward British invasion, which explained why Vichy forces resisted with courage and tenacity. The operation miscarried and the armada steamed back to Gibraltar. This fiasco forms a hilarious episode in Evelyn Waugh's novel *Men at Arms*, in which the fire-eating Brigadier Ritchie-Hook covertly goes ashore to secure the head of a Senegalese soldier for his collection.

During the bombardment of Dakar, Governor Boisson declared that Britain was intent on the 'dismemberment' of the French Empire and he was widely believed.[24] *Le Matin* denounced de Gaulle as a 'traitor' and a mercenary of Britain, France's historic enemy. Memories of Fashoda were refreshed, and Vichy propaganda predicted that Britain, true to its perfidious instincts, would use the war as a pretext for seizing France's colonies in Africa and the Levant. This charge was apparently confirmed by the British invasion and occupation of Syria and the Lebanon in the summer of 1941. The attack was a response to Vichy's willingness to allow the Luftwaffe to construct airfields for sorties against the Iraqi oilfields and bases in Palestine and Egypt. No permanent occupation was intended, and Britain promised post-war independence to Syria and Lebanon, which incensed both Vichy and de Gaulle.

Japan sought a similar accommodation with Vichy early in 1942 – it had already conceded its control over Indo-China. Recent Japanese victories in the Pacific and South-East Asia had been followed by a naval sortie by the Imperial Japanese Navy into the Indian Ocean. Japanese submarines preyed on Allied merchantmen steaming off the east coast of Africa en route for Egypt: two were torpedoed in sight of Aden. To have an impact, these operations needed local bases, and Vichy was willing to provide them. At the beginning of March, Allied intelligence got wind of Japanese and German officers surveying potential naval bases and airfields on Madagascar.[25] Britain's reaction was rapid and devastating: in May 1942 an amphibious attack was made on the island, where resistance, chiefly by local and Senegalese forces, was stiff. The campaign was over by November, when the British installed a Free French governor. In the same month, landing parties from the destroyer HMS *Leopard* occupied Réunion.[26] In Madagascar, as in Dakar and Syria, Vichy African and Arab troops led by French officers had fought bravely and tenaciously.

Waging war against Vichy had been an unwelcome distraction for Britain, which would have preferred to checkmate the regime by subversion. Immediately after the fall of France, the War Cabinet had hoped that it could somehow exert pressure on French colonial administrators to abandon Vichy for the Free French and place their territories under British protection. There were few turncoats: Félix Éboué, the Creole Governor of Chad, plumped for the Free French and so did the administrations of the French Cameroons and the French Congo, where the Vichy faction briefly resisted. At the same time, British officials made approaches to their counterparts in Guinea, Togo, Dahomey and the Ivory Coast, with guarantees that their salaries and pensions would be paid by Britain if they joined de Gaulle. The result was disappointing: the Frenchmen suspected that Britain's real motives were acquisitive and, not unreasonably given Britain's position at the time, they expected a German victory.[27] A year later, and just after Hitler's attack on Russia, intelligence analysis indicated that the white population of French West Africa regarded a German victory as inevitable.[28] In June 1942 Dahomey's whites were strongly pro-Axis, while apathy prevailed in Gabon. A fatalistic spirit infected the white officers and NCOs of the West Africa garrison, whose attitude was one of 'wait and see'.[29]

Native opinion across French West Africa was deeply hostile to Germany and sympathetic to Britain. This helped British wireless propaganda: Radio Accra, which once called itself the 'voice of fighting France', constantly reminded listeners that Vichy was Hitler's lackey. A similar message was broadcast by Radio Mauritius to listeners in Madagascar and Réunion.[30] Early in 1942, British propagandists had a bonus when King Kwadwo Agyeman fled from the Ivory Coast to the Gold Coast along with his sons, lesser chiefs and 4,000 subjects. Soon after, he spoke on Radio Accra and denounced Pétain and the Vichy administration as liars and 'puppets' of Hitler.[31] Radio Dakar too played on fears of Hitler with allegations that Britain coveted France's colonies and, incredibly, intended to hand some over to Germany.[32]

By the beginning of 1943, the propaganda war had ceased and Vichy's colonies were now governed in the name of the Free French. But what did their new rulers have to offer Africans? De Gaulle was wise enough to realise that the pre-war French Empire could not be revived and the African contribution to the Free French war effort deserved to be rewarded. Just how was outlined in his Brazzaville Declaration of February 1944 which, he explained, represented the will of the true France. Racial discrimination would cease in acknowledgement of the part being played by Africans in the Free French war effort, and assimilation would be encouraged to create an African 'vanguard clearly situated above the masses by their intelligence and knowledge'.[33] De Gaulle was a firm believer in France's *mission civilisatrice* and so there was no question of this elite assisting their countries' evolution towards independence. Far from it, for most Frenchmen were convinced that Africans were not ripe for self-government, and would remain so for the foreseeable future. In the meantime, de Gaulle and his supporters spoke of the empire as a 'community', 'union' or 'federation', terms which indicated that the ties with France would become closer rather than loosen.[34] Stamps issued by the Free French showed a phoenix rising from the flames, symbolising the new empire, and images of a French, an African and an Arab soldier standing together, representing the wartime alliance between France's subjects.

Change was in the air. In Algiers, the provisional Free French government pledged that henceforward Arab policy would be compatible with the Rights of Man, which guaranteed personal freedom and equal rights. Yet there were major caveats: individual rights could never override 'traditional institutions' or challenge the superiority of French culture.[35] Further concessions were, however, in hand, with provisions for extending citizenship and enfranchising women and Arabs in preparation for elections to a conference in Paris that would frame a new constitution for France and its empire once the war had ended.

Native aspirations were rising, but patience was running short. In

January 1944 the Moroccan nationalist party, Istiqlal, demanded immediate independence as a reward for the blood shed by Moroccan soldiers fighting for France's 'ideals and freedoms'.[36] Many were then in action in Italy with Free French contingents, fighting paradoxically for that liberty denied them at home. On 8 May 1945, when France was celebrating Victory in Europe Day, there was an Arab uprising in and around Sétif in which the rebels massacred *colons* and their families. Condign retribution followed, which included air raids on Arab villages, and at least 1,500 were killed, many by Arab and Senegalese units. The British Consul in Algiers investigated the episode and reported that, whatever was said to the contrary, it had been a 'nationalist insurrection'. His colleague in Bône predicted that the Arabs would never forget the ferocity of the French counter-terror.[37] They did not.

21

'Black Tarantulas':
Africans at War

▬▬▬

I

In 1939 Britain and France demanded an equality of effort and sacrifice from all their African subjects in a total war waged against the twin tyrannies of Nazism and Fascism in the name of freedom. This was Africa's war insofar as both ideologies held them in contempt; British propaganda never allowed them to forget that in *Mein Kampf* Hitler had described them as 'half-apes' predestined to servitude. Memories of the horrors of Mussolini's subjugation of Abyssinia were fresh: one can sense the sheer exultation of a West African poet celebrating his defeats.

> *Run, you Italians,*
> *Leave your ill-gotten conquests;*
> *Fly on the wings of defeat*
> *For where Britain stands*
> *Your cowardly armies scatter*[1]

But it was always Hitler who terrified Africans. Throughout the war, intelligence analyses of civilian morale in British colonies revealed a widespread revulsion against him and fears of what might befall Africans if he won the war.

A six-year war transformed millions of lives and was a catalyst for social, political and economic changes. Many were not anticipated and some were potentially dangerous for the future stability of the colonies. By mobilising Africans, Britain and France had created a new conduit for the transmission of ideas. Wherever they were posted, soldiers from different parts of the continent talked to each other in camps and canteens, and conversations often turned to their own aspirations and their countries' futures. Speculation prompted questions: men required to endure hardship and hazard their lives in a war for a free and just world inevitably asked what was in it for them.

After the war, a soldier from Guinea observed: 'If we – the black people – hadn't fought in western wars, and been taken overseas, and demonstrated some ability and human dignity, we wouldn't have been regarded as anything.'[2] In 1946 there were disturbing signs of a similar arousal among the inhabitants of the French Cameroons. They believed that they had played a valuable part in the war effort which entitled them to claim equality with Britain and America. The French official who reported their new temper feared that it would foster ambitions far beyond the Africans' capacities.[3] A self-possessed swagger distinguished many demobilised askaris in East Africa who were no longer willing to render 'semi-feudal honours' to their chiefs.[4]

As well as being a breeding ground for discontents, the war offered fresh and enticing opportunities for Africans. In 1944 a Nigerian government journal published photographs which illustrated the new skills being acquired by local soldiers. There was a truck driver, a wireless operator, a mechanic repairing a motorbike, an army cook presenting a mess of red peppers (a favourite with the troops) and a gunner adjusting a long-range sight.[5] The message was clear and confirmed by intelligence analyses of soldiers' morale: these men hoped to turn their training to advantage when they returned home. Moreover, as *The Times* had pointed out two years before, the Africans' ability to master modern technology gave the lie to the commonplace fable that they were somehow unfit to undertake 'the white man's job'.[6]

Alongside the photos of Nigerian troops were reminders of conditions on the home front. Advertisers urged consumers to be patient when confronted with scarcities and remember that they were a tiresome but important part of the colony's war effort. Razor blades were scarce because steel was vital for the war effort, and a pharmaceutical manufacturer announced that it was now producing 'Medicine for Dictators' in the form of TNT rather than everyday pills and potions.

II

A shortage of aspirins in Lagos chemist shops was a reminder that Africa was engaged in a total war whose essentials were manpower, raw materials and food. Providing them and sending them to where they were most needed required the suspension of former economic systems. In 1939 the British government imposed a command economy on all its African colonies. Henceforward, the laws of supply and demand were suspended, and the state took control over mining, agriculture, manufacturing and shipping. Government agencies became the sole market for all minerals, rubber, sisal, cotton, sugar and bananas and paid officially fixed prices, often with American credit. Nearly all these commodities were exported, like the East African beef which ended up in the cans of bully beef, the staple of the British army in North Africa. Home markets were tightly regulated: faced with a possibility of famine in 1944, the Kenyan government raised subsidies paid to maize growers to increase production. Surpluses were sold to the United States to earn desperately needed dollars. Economies that had withered during the past decade now began to blossom.

Cash crops always took priority: in East Africa farmers were instructed to grow Pyrethrum daisies, whose seed pods were essential for the insecticides needed in malarial war zones. Localised shortages occurred, as they did in Britain. Soaring demand for Pyrethrum during 1944 for the Burma front left Kenya short of supplies for its own pest-control programmes. Cotton disappeared from sale in Tanganyika, where men and women were forced to make their clothes from bark.[7]

The mass redirection of labour created more serious problems. Military service and compulsory war work drew farmers away from their fields while the demands of labour-intensive husbandry remained unchanged. Reduced numbers working the land combined with droughts led to dearths in Southern and Northern Rhodesia during 1941 and 1942, when the latter had to import Argentinian maize to prevent a famine.[8] Famine threatened in the Shinyanga district of Tanganyika after a failure of the rains in 1943, but was averted by a handful of local officials who improvised depots and a distribution system using trains, lorries and donkeys. The food was free, which led some farmers to neglect to plant crops for the following season in the hope that a 'kindly' government would provide. They did so finally after coercion from their chiefs.[9]

German expropriation of Algerian wheat during 1942 created a famine which was exacerbated by a thin harvest the following year. Allied relief supplies saved the situation.[10] Malnutrition weakened resistance to disease and contributed to three epidemics of typhus in

Algeria between 1940 and 1942. Again, the Allies came to the rescue in the form of British and American army medical detachments which undertook a programme of mass immunisation.[11] *La mission civilisatrice* in its Vichy version had failed abysmally in its basic duty of caring for its subjects' welfare.

The war skewed the labour market in British Africa. Forced labour, abolished in 1927, was temporarily reintroduced and reduced the numbers available for subsistence farming. The campaigns in North Africa and the Middle East generated an unending demand for men to load and unload ships, level and maintain airfields and perform all the donkey work needed to support mass armies, navies and air forces. Two hundred thousand local labourers were hired to undertake the chores of the vast military complex in Egypt, where even the smallest detachment had its staff of menials. There were 137 labourers and twenty-three cleaners working for the British army's Blood Transfusion Unit in Cairo.[12] Away from the front line, Africans were drafted to increase production of raw materials needed for war industries. In Tanganyika, 84,500 labourers were conscripted to work on rubber, sisal and Pyrethrum plantations. To offset the loss of the Malayan tin mines to the Japanese in 1942, production was increased in the open-cast works on the Jos plateau, which required the impressment of 100,000 workers from across northern Nigeria. The construction and daily operation of airfields at Takoradi, Kano and Khartoum needed 10,000 labourers.

Many Africans evaded the call-up and skulked in the bush. In Tanganyika, memories of the heavy losses among the labour contingents in the last war were a powerful deterrent. There was also indifference of the sort shown by the Makonde in the coastal region, which was challenged by official recruiters who asked their chiefs whether they had no *haya* (shame) about shirking. They replied that there was no such word in their vocabulary, but they had enough cunning to send off detachments of sick men to the reception centres where they were given free medical treatment. Most were still judged unfit for hard labour and were ordered back to their villages, where their chiefs had the satisfaction of knowing that they had outwitted the government.[13]

Wartime pressures and disruptions provoked much grousing and, occasionally, open disaffection. Cumulative stresses led to a sudden rash of strikes and riots across Uganda during January 1945. The tumults began with strikes by sewing machine 'boys', lorry drivers, 'night soil porters' (who emptied cesspits) and factory workers in the towns. The unrest quickly spilled into the countryside, where there were riots in which 'juveniles' were prominent, and chiefs' appeals for restraint were ignored. Mobs attacked police detachments, hospitals and gaols, releasing prisoners. Criminals used the breakdown of public order to rob individuals and loot property.[14] Troops reinforced the overstretched police, several rioters were shot, and peace was finally restored early in February.

The Ugandan intelligence services had been caught on the hop. An inquest into the disorders revealed that trade union agitators had provided most of the impetus, some travelling around the country in motor cars. One of the firebrands, Ignatius Musaazi, had been a student in London during the 1926 General Strike and had hoped to repeat it in Uganda.[15] He and his comrades had found a receptive audience. For the past six years, Ugandans had suffered from shortages of necessities: the price of cotton had increased sixfold and then supplies disappeared. The overall cost of living had risen by 55 per cent, while pay trailed behind to the extent that workers were demanding monthly wages to be doubled to forty-five shillings.

III

Throughout British Africa the authorities had endeavoured to overcome the effects of wartime astringency by a concerted programme of propaganda. Its objectives were threefold: to keep Africans informed of the war's progress, to remind them of the wickedness of the Nazis and to persuade them to throw themselves wholeheartedly into the war effort. Given often low literacy rates (one in sixty Nigerian children attended a school in 1939), extensive use was made of the radio and cinema and street theatre.[16] Travelling cinemas were rightly considered a powerful medium. In the Gold Coast they moved from village to village and, at each, screens and loudspeakers were set up for silent shorts with an interpreter giving a commentary. A soundtrack was also provided by amplified records of marches and local folk music. Audiences saw newsreels of African soldiers and educational films. In many villages loudspeakers were rented for five shillings a week to relay radio broadcasts.[17] Programmes were in Yoruba, Hausa, Igbo and what the Colonial Office called 'Simple English', i.e. local pidgin.[18]

Between 1942 and 1945 the army's East Africa Mobile Propaganda Unit reached an audience of a million. Its commanding officer, Lieutenant A. G. Dickson, led a team largely made up of Africans – they called themselves 'missionaries'. As well as films, they organised pageants which included old soldiers and askaris driving an armoured car and firing machine-guns, which must have made for a noisy and exciting show. Dickson sought the reactions of members of his audiences: one was unmoved and remarked that 'this war belongs to the whites only'. More encouraging was the comment of another: 'The Europeans (particularly the British) do not make us different from them, but regard us as fellow workers in a common cause.'[19]

How would this common cause benefit Africans? Early in 1941, educated West Africans expected that a British victory would mean 'the promise of a new Africa' that would include new freedoms.[20] Yet there were undercurrents of scepticism in some quarters, with allegations that the war was being fought for big business and that Africans would gain nothing from it.[21] Allied setbacks during the first half of 1942 caused alarm and anxiety: the educated classes were 'somewhat shaken' by the fall of Singapore, and there were brief fears that defeats in North Africa would lead to the war spreading southwards and westwards.[22] Newspaper reports of the growing and violent nationalist agitation in India prompted some to think that the British would only make political concessions if their arms were twisted. The West African Students' Union thought 'liberty' and self-government should be given immediately as rewards for 'the acceptance of the horrors of modern war'.[23]

The war held out no hopes for black South Africans, and there were plenty of whites who wanted their country to be neutral. After two days as Prime Minister, General Smuts declared South Africa officially at war with Nazi Germany and the Axis. His opponents were those Boers who sympathised with the Nazi doctrines of the *Volk* and Aryan superiority. The pre-war recession had helped to push many Afrikaners towards two extreme right-wing movements, the Broederbond and the Ossewabrandwag ('ox-wagon guard'), which had 290,000 followers and were strongly represented among the predominantly Boer police force.[24] During the war both groups were engaged in sabotage, assisting escaped German POWs and intimidating men in uniform.[25] When, in March 1942, the Allies seemed to be on the ropes, Oswald Pirow, a pro-Nazi nationalist politician from the Transvaal, hoped that after he had won the war Hitler would regard South Africa as a friend.[26] In May 1944 the ultra-nationalist newspaper *Volksblad* declared that 'Everywhere the Empire is merely the instrument of providing Britannia military help in her wars.'[27]

German sympathisers remained a clamorous but troublesome minority in South Africa. Over a third of a million whites and 77,000 blacks volunteered for the forces and were deployed in East Africa, Madagascar, North Africa and Italy. Smuts's government recoiled from recruiting and training blacks for front-line service: the spectre of the disciplined black soldier familiar with modern weapons terrified white South Africans. Blacks were, therefore, confined to the Labour Corps. Nevertheless, the warlike Zulus were targeted by the government and an official recruiting film of 1943 assured them that they were 'genuine soldiers'. They would be on the side of 'freedom' and 'fighting together with the three greatest liberty-loving nations in the world', Britain, the United States and the Soviet Union. Recruiting posters showed a Labour Corps man dressed like a white soldier in khaki, but holding an assegai rather than a rifle.[28]

British propaganda that stressed an equality of effort and sacrifice for a common goal of freedom was sometimes challenged by a few educated Africans. There was disquiet in West Africa early in 1942 about America's treatment of its black population, particularly the prevalence of lynching in the southern states. The Colonial Office responded with a campaign to show that many black Americans were prospering and that, bizarrely, southern women no longer felt that they required the threat of the lynch mob to protect their virtue.[29] It did not help matters that American servicemen posted to West African airfields objected to black soldiers as guards.[30] There was also unease about reports of a colour bar operating in Britain.[31] In response, the Colonial Office sponsored a campaign to remind British people to treat coloured servicemen and workers with kindness and courtesy, for they had freely come to help the country in its hour of extreme need.

IV

Britain's black soldiers were volunteers, although chiefs, who acted as the government's recruiting sergeants, were encouraged to exert considerable pressure on their young men. Some younger chiefs set an example and enlisted and were automatically made NCOs. Tribal pride and the old warrior traditions remained strong and helped steer men towards the army. One veteran of the First World War boasted: 'My three grandsons have joined for service in this war . . . they wear the same battle dress as the white people wear. They bear themselves as warriors. They will go where they are told and do what they were bidden.' Thus they enhanced the 'honour' of their family and their clan.[32] Loyalty to the Crown and the Empire also played a part. After hearing a talk in which he had been told that he was part of a war for democracy, one askari insisted that he 'was fighting for King George', adding that he wanted extra pay if he was just risking his life for democracy.[33]

France's black troops were mostly conscripts. Draft-dodging was common: on average one in five evaded the call-up by escaping into the bush or, in West Africa, to British territory. Nonetheless, in May 1940 there were 100,000 African soldiers deployed in France to meet the German invasion. They fought doggedly and with outstanding courage, which was why they were often chosen to spearhead offensives. It was all in vain and they found themselves in a retreating army whose morale was plummeting. This baleful experience shook their confidence in the white man. 'We saw those who considered themselves our masters naked, in tears, some [were] cowardly', one veteran remembered.[34] 'We were stronger than the whites', another recalled: 'That bullet hit my tooth would have killed a white. When the shooting came, the whites ran.'[35]

These hardy soldiers scared the Germans, who accused Africans of mutilating corpses, an allegation that owed its credibility to six years of Nazi racial indoctrination. This explains why fanatic SS units took a prominent part in the murder of between 1,500 and 3,000 African POWs in northern and eastern France before and after the French surrender. During one massacre a soldier cried out, 'May France live!' and another, 'May black Africa live!'[36]

Britain was proud of its black soldiers, whose loyalty, resilient morale and willingness to enlist were a vindication of the Empire. The commentary of a Pathé newsreel of 1941 described new recruits from the Gold Coast as 'bronze giants of nature with muscles that would make Joe Louis look to his biceps'. All were volunteers 'who have found the

Union Jack worth fighting for'.[37] Many were tempted by the prospect of excitement and adventure, and their gamecock spirit was expressed in the words of one of their marching songs:

> *Brown men and warriors let us go*
> *Let us go to East Africa and Burma.*[38]

The 82nd (West African) Division, which saw considerable action in Burma during 1944 and 1945, called themselves the 'Black Tarantulas'.[39] Serving alongside the Black Tarantulas were East African troops with strong attachments to their units and proud of their prowess against the 'yellow bush people', their name for the Japanese.[40]

African soldiers wore khaki uniforms, boots (which they insisted on) and an Australian-style slouch hat, which replaced the exotic tasselled tarboosh. They ate with knives, forks and spoons, were introduced to generously rationed cigarettes, and discovered a taste for mass-produced beer. They also received free and excellent medical treatment, which made a deep and lasting impression: in 1945 African soldiers contemplating their countries' future looked forward to the building of more hospitals.[41] Army doctors were impressed by the African soldier's 'inborn pride, love of cleanliness and discipline', but his virtues were somewhat overshadowed by promiscuity. In spite of repeated lectures by medical officers, a disproportionately large number of African soldiers contracted venereal infections.[42] After hearing the benefits of condoms, one unconvinced soldier asked: 'Do Europeans like wearing shoes in the bath?'[43] His bewilderment was shared by at least one British soldier, who told a medical officer that he saw no sense in 'muzzling a ferret'.[44]

Off-duty hours were partly filled by educational programmes which concentrated on practical subjects such as farming techniques and 'domestic' economy that were intended to prepare the soldier for his life after the war. The army authorities hoped that this instruction would propel men towards jobs as mechanics, clerks and drivers and so generate that 'prosperity' which would accelerate 'the development of the colonies'.[45] Savings schemes were promoted to help ex-soldiers get started in civilian life, and by the close of the war the total of these nest eggs was over £1.25 million. On discharge, the thrifty soldier had not only his savings but also his demobilisation allowance (a corporal received £29), and many used their capital in small businesses.

The shared risks of war did not mean that the African soldier enjoyed equality with his white brothers-in-arms in all respects. In North Africa the army authorities thought it prudent to keep black and white troops apart. It was argued that segregated cookhouses, canteens, sleeping quarters and latrines reduced the chances of friction 'among soldiers divided by race, language, colour, outlook, custom and education'. Racial arrogance existed among junior British NCOs of working-class background who, by 'virtue of some assumed right of colour', tried to lord it over their African counterparts of higher rank.[46] East African askaris accustomed to addressing Indians as 'bwana' were puzzled when they were called 'sahib' by Indians in Calcutta, and some tended to treat them disdainfully.[47]

Soldiers perplexed by the hierarchies of Empire speculated about their place within it after the war. After the defeat of Japan in August 1945, African soldiers waiting for shipment home and demobilisation discussed their futures and their hopes for the post-war world. Some shared their thoughts in letters to families and friends at home, and the army censors were struck by references to more and better schools and hospitals, and opportunities for vocational training. Nigerians were sympathetic towards the demands for higher wages by strikers at home and angered by the suppression of Dr Azikiwe's nationalist newspapers.[48]

The war had widened the horizons of Africans and crystallised their thoughts about their future place in the world. In many ways, African soldiers had been treated as Europeans, and Allied propaganda had set great store by individual liberty and praised democracy as the perfect form of government. Both were conspicuously withheld from Africans and the discrepancy was widely recognised. Writing in 1944, Albert Camus observed that France would have to convince Algerians that 'we do not have two policies: one granting justice to the people of France and the other confirming injustice toward the Empire'.[49]

The new mood and aspirations of demobilised soldiers aroused trepidation among British colonial officials. A district officer in Tanganyika told Lieutenant Dickson that discharged soldiers 'return revolutionaries – all the more dangerous for being without any plans for reform'.[50] An official of the Southern Rhodesia Native Affairs Bureau was similarly perturbed by the temper of newly demobilised soldiers.

They wanted better-paid jobs and improved housing and had developed a taste for flamboyant clothes. Worse still, he thought, these men had assimilated European habits and had their heads turned by 'alien influences' which they would not shed.[51]

PART FOUR
1945–1990

22

'Can Russians speak Swahili?':
Nationalist Agitation and Cold War Phantoms in British
Africa 1945–1957

I

In September 1947 about sixty Africans and West Indians gathered for a rally in Trafalgar Square to air the hopes and discontents of Britain's colonies. Beyond them was a city of blitzed buildings inhabited by people enduring the rigours of austerity which, the Labour government repeatedly told them, was the only way to achieve post-war recovery and regeneration. The speakers were also looking ahead to a better future in a new world without empires. Their mood was optimistic: the forces of history seemed to be mustering behind them since in the last month India, Pakistan, Burma and Ceylon had achieved independence.

All the speakers hoped that the African colonies would follow. One declared that 'democracy' and 'empire' were incompatible, and the far-Left Labour MP Fenner Brockway called for his party to make the choice between 'aristocratic government in Africa or independence'. Kwame Nkrumah, then a research graduate at the London School of Economics and soon to become leader of the newly formed Gold Coast Convention People's Party (CPP), warned the government that 'Africans were getting desperate' and, if their freedom was delayed, they would take it by force.[1]

This impatience was understandable. African nationalism, incubated during the interwar years and strengthened by the anticipation of dividends earned by wartime loyalty, was more optimistic than ever. The educated and politicised classes had become more assertive, assumed the role of tribunes and busied themselves enlisting popular support for disciplined parties that justified their claims that they were the true voice of the people. It was becoming louder and more strident: independence was no longer decades away, but years.

Dr Nkrumah was right about the restlessness of his people. Five months later, the Gold Coast erupted: a mass meeting, held in an Accra cinema, to protest about high prices and a stagnant labour market triggered a fortnight of riots and looting. The authorities there and in London were dazed and full of foreboding. As public order dissolved, jittery officials summoned up two frigates, HMS *Actaeon* and HMS *Nereide*, from Simon's Town 'to show the flag', and troops were flown in from Nigeria. The police opened fire on several occasions, and twenty-nine rioters were killed and 237 wounded. Nkrumah and a handful of leading nationalists were arrested and locked up.

Order was restored within a fortnight and the authorities cast about to find someone to blame. Had there been a conspiracy, and, if so, who had hatched it? One intelligence officer detected the hand of hitherto invisible local Communists, who had urged the rioters to provoke the police into opening fire so that 'some on their side would be killed' to create 'martyrs'.[2] This conjecture was supported by the discovery of a sinister document with references to 'a revolutionary vanguard' ready to undergo 'service, sacrifice [and] suffering' to secure independence.[3] As the tumults gained momentum, Joseph Danquah, a barrister and colleague of Nkrumah's, had declared: 'The hour of liberation had struck.'[4] Fearful speculation mutated into fact: the *Spectator* alleged that the mobs had been seeking a 'Soviet state'.[5]

The Gold Coast riots had a twofold significance. They marked the debut of the Communist bogey in Africa and jeopardised Britain's plans for the political and economic future of its colonies, which had been outlined during the 1945 general election campaign. The future Labour Colonial Secretary, Arthur Creech-Jones, promised that henceforward 'colonial peoples must ultimately determine their own associations and destiny' under Britain's benign and generous guidance. The Conservative spokesman on colonial affairs pledged that Africans would be trained in the 'ethics and honesty of local government' so that 'backward races' could eventually achieve 'the management of their own affairs'.[6]

No precise timetable was ever set for this programme, but the prevailing view in London was that it might take forty to fifty years.

Both Labour and the Conservatives agreed that the end result would be independent democracies with all the checks and balances of the British parliamentary system and an independent judiciary. It was also assumed that the process would be peaceful, gradual and firmly supervised from above. When independence was achieved, it was hoped that the former colonies would follow the path that had been taken by the white dominions in the last century, and would join the existing Commonwealth. Always an abstraction rather than a formal alliance, this association was held together by a shared past, a common language and, above all, emotional ties to the monarchy. Royal visits to old and new members of this 'family' of nations became regular events and were puffed in the media as evidence of unity and goodwill. Sentimental bonds reflected hard economic realities: in 1955, 53 per cent of Britain's exports went to the Commonwealth and the colonies, which provided 43 per cent of the country's imports.

II

Unemployed Gold Coast ex-servicemen (who had been prominent in the disturbances) plundering shops were not part of the official blueprint for decolonisation. Neither was the possibility that this process might be hijacked by local Communists under orders from Moscow, although as early as 1946 the Foreign Office had been nervous about an impending Russian assault on British interests by propaganda and sedition.[7] Subsequent events suggested such a campaign was under way, but in fact it was confined to the Middle East, where British power was decaying fast.

Hitherto, Russia had shown little interest in Africa for ideological reasons. This was to be expected, since after Lenin's death in 1924 Stalin dropped the promotion of worldwide revolution in favour of consolidating the revolution within Russia. The continent lacked a politically aware industrial working class, which was vital for a revolution according to conventional Marxist dogma. In regions where there was a growing African working class and racial tension, Communism had made some tentative progress: the Algerian Communist Party had 12,000 members by 1945 and the South African 2,000.[8]

A trickle of Africans continued to make their way to Moscow to study and be immersed in Marxist-Leninism, but not all succumbed to indoctrination. During his stay in 1933, Kenyatta was rebuked for being 'a petty bourgeois' by a South African Communist. He angrily riposted: 'I don't like this "petty", why don't you say I am a big bourgeois.' Such remarks were dangerous, as Kenyatta knew, for he had seen another African student suddenly arrested by the secret police. He vanished and was probably liquidated in a forerunner of Stalin's purges, whose victims included other African students.[9]

Rather than waste effort and energy on a continent with little potential for revolution, Stalin used the immediate post-war years to tighten his grip on Russia's new puppet states in Eastern Europe. Large Communist parties in France and Italy offered opportunities for further advances through subversion, but they were frustrated by the Marshall Aid programme which, between 1947 and 1951, funded the successful resuscitation of the economies of Western Europe. At a cost of $3 billion, America had preserved capitalist democracy and provided the wherewithal for the growth and prosperity that were so obviously lacking in Stalin's satrapies. Among the beneficiaries were Britain, France and Belgium, whom the State Department was then relying upon to detect and parry Communist infiltration of their African empires.

The need to resist Communist activities everywhere became more urgent during 1948. While mobs were emptying shops in Accra, a coup in Prague established Stalin as master of Czechoslovakia and showed the world the KGB's mastery of intrigue and the manipulation of local Communists. In June, Malaya's leisurely progress towards independence was disrupted by a Communist guerrilla uprising that would after 1949 receive covert assistance from Mao Zedong's China. As in the Gold Coast, the Malayan authorities were caught on the hop, and for a short time were all but overwhelmed by a guerrilla insurgency that would take twelve years to defeat. It was against this background that, in 1949, the capitalist West and the Communist East formally squared up, with the former signing the NATO alliance, and in 1955 the latter the Warsaw Pact. In 1950 and with Stalin's approval, North Korea invaded South Korea.

Vigilance became the order of the day in a world in which the Soviet Union appeared to be in a swashbuckling mood, eager to probe and exploit its adversaries' weaknesses. MI5 hurriedly extended its surveillance throughout British Africa, with an eye to exposing Communist infiltration of local nationalist parties. Special attention was given to Nkrumah and Kenyatta, who had had past connections with Russia and its lackey, the Communist Party of Great Britain. Equally suspect were African nationalist parties with socialist economic programmes such as the Northern Rhodesia branch of the African National Congress, whose constitution promised an end to 'capitalist exploitation' and 'a democratic socialist society'.[10]

III

Communism was blamed for the Mau Mau insurrection in Kenya in October 1952, but the intelligence evidence was laughably thin. The alleged running of pistols paid for by Italian Communists and smuggled from Somalia, the machinations of Soviet diplomats across the border in Ethiopia, and the clandestine intrigues of an Indian diplomat based in Nairobi might have been the scenario for a Buchanesque thriller, but they did not constitute a Soviet plot to overturn Kenya's government.[11] Nor did a secret report of a political meeting held in the Nandi district in 1955 in which international affairs were discussed. One questioner asked 'Can Russians speak Swahili?', while another wanted to know 'What does a Russian look like?'[12] The KGB was clearly making little headway in Kenya. Nevertheless, the colony's Governor, Sir Evelyn Baring, persistently claimed that the war against the Mau Mau was part of the global struggle against Communism, an assumption that satisfied the Americans, who would have been very unhappy about an ally waging an old-style colonial war of repression.

Communist propaganda took this view and it was close to the truth. In November 1952 the Polish newspaper *Życie Warszawy* published a photograph of Mau Mau prisoners who had been captured in a war 'to liberate Kenya from the imperialist yoke' and were now 'manacled like slaves'. More, often lurid, stuff followed, with allegations of massacres and Nazi-style atrocities which drew on reports in the *Daily Worker* and questions in the House of Commons. American newspapers labelled the Mau Mau as 'gangsters', and there were undertones of the Wild West in one story of a Kenyan housewife, armed with a revolver, who defended her isolated farm against 'a gang of Mau Mau thugs led by the ranch's male cook'.[13]

Ideology played no part in the Mau Mau uprising; rather, it was a land war between haves and have-nots. The dispossessed were the Kikuyu, Kenya's largest tribe, who wanted to recover the tribal lands that had been acquired by white settlers over the past fifty years. They were the 'haves', who numbered 30,000 in 1952 and farmed 12,000 square miles of prime land, while over a million Kikuyu got their living from 2,000 square miles of less fertile soil. Land hunger did not, however, dictate loyalties in what became a civil war in which Kikuyu killed Kikuyu. Seventy thousand Africans, three-quarters of them Kikuyu, volunteered for the Home Guard, which accounted for a high proportion of the 20,000 Mau Mau dead.[14]

Taking its cue from Malaya, the Kenyan government adopted the euphemism 'Emergency' to describe the war and provide cover for draconian decrees that suspended all personal freedoms, imposed tight press censorship and gave sweeping powers to the police. A proposal to make the possession of 'incendiary materials' a capital offence prompted the Prime Minister, Churchill, to remark that hanging a man for having a box of matches seemed excessive. Oliver Lyttelton, the Colonial Secretary from 1951 to 1954, disagreed, and strenuously defended such measures and those who enforced them. This was his Christian duty, for he believed that he was at grips with forces of darkness: once, when reading a report of Mau Mau sorcery, he imagined that he saw the horns of the devil on the pages.[15] It was a view prevalent in Kenya and the British press, where grisly details of Mau Mau oaths and atrocities such as the Lari massacre of over a hundred Kikuyu men, women and children were treated as evidence of a collective recidivism. Africans had repudiated civilisation and were reverting to a barbaric and superstitious past.

Hideous, oath-swearing rituals, assassinations and massacres were the key elements of the Mau Mau terror. Desperate measures were necessary to offset the inherent weaknesses of a movement that lacked modern weapons, was outnumbered by the government's forces and soon found itself isolated from the mass of Kikuyu. One answer was to recruit through fear, hence the killings. Military operations were confined to hit-and-run raids by small bands on European farms and uncooperative villages, and the extortion of the food needed for survival in the bush.

An equally ruthless counter-terror was the government's response.

Under the Emergency regulations, over a million Kikuyu were up-rooted from their homes and herded into fenced and overcrowded villages where they endured a regime of forced labour under the super-vision of the Home Guard. Mau Mau suspects were interned in camps, interrogated and made to undergo a form of exorcism to release them from their diabolic oaths. Official mumbo-jumbo proved superior to unofficial, and many were released over the next six years. Flogging and torture were common and officially tolerated, and many of their victims died or were crippled by their injuries.

Among the dead was Elijah Gideon, an elderly, infirm Kikuyu Christian who was clubbed to death by askaris under the orders of two white volunteers from the Police Reserve and the Kenya Regiment, both units with sinister reputations. Details of his murder were revealed in the Commons and Lyttelton promised Members that the culprits would be tried for manslaughter.[16] They appeared before Justice Geof-frey Rudd, who fined them £100 and £50 respectively and expressed the view that their conduct had been justified by the desperate times.[17] Hysteria and dereliction of duty were contagious: soon after taking command of operations, General Sir George Erskine was shocked by the indiscipline of the security forces, who, among other things, in seven months had shot dead 430 suspects attempting to escape.[18] Lyt-telton reassured Members that all had died resisting arrest; strangely, no suspect was ever just wounded.[19]

Bad men did many bad things in Kenya, and in Britain individu-als on the Left of politics protested. Yet on the whole the public was willing to overlook them simply because of what it had heard about the malevolence and cruelty of the Mau Mau. 'The menace of the Mau Mau' was the subject of a frightening 1952 Pathé newsreel. It opened with frightening, discordant music and showed footage of bush patrols, policemen rounding up and interrogating suspects and the funeral of a 'wise and peaceful chieftain'. His murder was one of what the com-mentary called the 'bloody deeds' of the Mau Mau, who were referred to as 'terrorists', 'fanatics' and 'bandits' determined to 'drive all the whites out of Kenya'. Horrific details of Mau Man initiation rites were hinted at in the press and the Commons.

According to one version of the Mau Mau oath, initiates were re-quired to submit to and revere Kenyatta as 'our great leader'.[20] He had returned from England with his English wife in 1946 and become head of the Kenya African Union. Within weeks of the declaration of the Emergency, the Kenyan government arrested him and several other political activists and tried them on charges of instigating and encouraging the Mau Mau conspiracy. This was done in the knowledge of Kenyatta's earlier Communist connections, the implication being that he was a Soviet agent. This canard and his arrest appeased the distraught settler community, which was screaming for blood. The truth was that Kenyatta had no links with Mau Mau, as MI5 knew, but was a conventional nationalist.[21] Nairobi paid no attention: a rigged trial with bribed witnesses and a partial judge found Kenyatta guilty and he was sentenced to six years' hard labour.

By 1956 the Mau Mau were defeated and the Emergency was terminated, although 'hard-core' suspects were detained for a further three years. In 1959 eleven of them were beaten to death by African guards at the Hola detention camp. The moral implications of this outrage were dissected by a Conservative MP, Enoch Powell, who reminded MPs of the traditional ideals to which the Empire aspired. 'We cannot say', he argued, that 'we will have African standards in Africa, Asian standards in Asia and perhaps British standards at home.' Public opinion would not tolerate such distinctions and rightly so, for it expected British values to be absolute. 'We cannot, we dare not, in Africa of all places, fall below our own standards in the acceptance of responsibility.' Questions of responsibility were raised in 2013, when four Kenyans appeared in London to claim civil damages for injuries they had suffered during the Emergency. The often grisly forensic details of official torture and coercion had been exhaustively and calmly revealed by David Anderson's *History of the Hanged* and, less calmly, by Caroline Elkins, an American historian. The lawsuit was settled out of court, with the British government allocating £20 million for compensation to claimants who could prove injuries suffered during the Emergency.

IV

In 1959 Powell had restated the traditional ideals of liberal imperialism. Its latest objective had been confirmed by Churchill's Conservative government, which came to power in 1951. In November, Lyttelton told the Commons that he would continue the policy by which the colonies would achieve independence within the Commonwealth. He added that there would be no self-determination for colonies unable to support themselves, although every effort would be made to encourage and fund economic and social development. Of the 956 appointments made by the Colonial Office in 1953, over two-thirds were engineers, town planners, education officers, geologists, foresters and vets.

Just when the African colonies would be ready for independence still remained unclear. The Gold Coast upheavals had been followed by official inquiries which concluded, hesitantly, that the pace of the colony's progress towards self-government should be quickened. Nkrumah was released from gaol in 1949, and 60,000 members of his CPP held a mass rally in Accra to celebrate. There were prayers for him and his supporters sang 'Lead Kindly Light'. The Christian tone of the meeting inspired confidence, although the intelligence agencies suspected that a flamboyant leader who enjoyed the accolades 'Africa's Man of Destiny' and 'Star of Ghana' was a covert Communist. There were also suspicions that Nkrumah had links with a shady diamond smuggler.[22]

The charismatic cult of Nkrumah provided Britain with what it needed: a popular leader with whom they could do business, and one whose ambition and vanity were far stronger than his attachment to Marxist dogma. Moreover, in 1954 he had declared that he had no plans to nationalise foreign companies. Most important of all, Nkrumah had a cordial working relationship with the Gold Coast's Governor, Sir Charles Arden-Clarke, a steady pragmatist who followed the principle that delaying independence would incur greater risks than procrastination. In 1950 arrangements were made for voter registration – 40 per cent of those qualified did so – and there were official reassurances that the ballot would be secret and warnings against intimidation.[23] The CPP won the election and Nkrumah became interim Prime Minister at the head of a Cabinet which advised the Governor in the final phase of the transition to independence. Given the prevalence of illiteracy, ballot papers showed party symbols. His CPP chose a red crowing cockerel, the appropriate symbol for the breaking of a new dawn.

As that dawn approached, the colony's three political parties remained under close surveillance. One spy penetrated the CPP and helped construct profiles of its leading figures. They included sincere nationalists and men who saw independence as an opportunity to advancement in a country where all the top jobs in government and business had previously gone to Europeans. There were also eccentrics, including the son of a fetish priest who imagined that his inherited supernatural powers might help him influence voters. He was a small man who had spent time in the Accra lunatic asylum, called himself 'The Great Lion of Judah' and was polite towards Europeans, who were intrigued by his mannerisms and 'exaggerated Oxford accent'.[24]

New nightmares blended with old, for in October 1950 the *Daily Telegraph* alleged that not only was Nkrumah Moscow's poodle, but that his party was 'using juju of Darkest Africa'. With or without supernatural help, the CPP won 104 out of 175 seats in the Gold Coast's parliament, and in March 1957 Ghana became an independent republic within the Commonwealth. Despite misgivings, Ghana appeared to be a safe bet in terms of economic viability, for it had reserves of £200 million and debts of £20 million. The new state did, however, have one problem: Nkrumah's ego. He considered independence to be a personal triumph which uniquely qualified him for a new career on the world stage as a Pan-African leader and a scourge of what was already being called 'colonialism'. As for Ghana, he promised Vice-President Richard Nixon (then touring Africa) that he would give 'vigorous' support for free speech and 'democratic traditions'.[25] This was very gratifying for Britain, which had taken a gamble in hastening the transfer of power, and seen from the perspective of 1957, the result appeared to set an example of how decolonisation would be managed smoothly and to Britain's advantage. The terror in Kenya was, however, a warning that Britain would not be coerced in surrendering power.

V

The countdown to Ghana's independence coincided with a spasm of imperial bravado within the Conservative Party, whose stiffer back-benchers were unhappy with decolonisation, however protracted. Their apprehension was regularly expressed in the *Daily Telegraph* and the *Daily Express*. Right-wing foreboding about the future of the Empire coincided with an optimistic spirit that followed the accession of Queen Elizabeth II early in 1952. A 'new' and glorious Elizabethan age seemed imminent, as full of genius and achievement as its predecessor. Later in the year, Harold Macmillan, then Minister of Housing, expressed the new mood when he asked whether Britain should 'choose to slide into a shoddy Socialism' or 'march to a third British Empire?'[26] Churchill also looked forward to a period of imperial consolidation and was delighted by plans for a grandiose development of Parliament Square that would be a 'truly noble setting for the heart of the British Empire'.

Such presumptions appeared to contradict the idea of future decolonisation, but it should be remembered that Ghana had been an exception. Rough projections agreed by the Cabinet in October 1954 set the independence dates for the proposed Central African Federation (Nyasaland and Northern and South Rhodesia), Sierra Leone, Uganda and Tanganyika in the mid-1970s at the earliest. Still-unpacified Kenya might have to wait longer. In the meantime, Britain's African colonies remained an economic and strategic asset that would help Britain withstand the twin threats of global Communist subversion and the aggressive nationalism in the Middle East. A demoted superpower needed all the resources it could muster to fend off its enemies and fulfil its political and military obligations to the United States at a time when the Cold War was intensifying.

Cold War anxieties prompted President Eisenhower to persuade Churchill to accelerate decolonisation. 'We are', he wrote in 1954, 'falsely pictured as exploiters of people, the Soviets as their champions', and it would be politically reckless to ignore the 'fierce and growing spirit of nationalism' that was spreading across Africa and Asia. Nevertheless, he sympathised with British caution and reckoned that the end of colonial rule would take at the least twenty-five years. Churchill was unconvinced. He was a child of the Victorian Empire, proud of what Britain had achieved with 'backward races'. Their recent maltreatment in Kenya had caused him much private distress. Churchill also confessed to Ike that 'I am a bit sceptical about universal suffrage for the Hottentots even if refined by proportional representation.'[27]

Events in Ghana did not dispel the fears of pessimists that the transfer of power in Africa was a leap in the dark that could easily end disastrously. There were plenty of Jeremiahs who feared the worst and said so, often. Herbert Morrison, the Labour Foreign Secretary, had famously compared allowing self-government to the colonies with giving a front door key, a chequebook and a shotgun to a twelve-year-old. In 1951 *The Times* had called the government's Gold Coast policy 'a bold, perhaps hazardous experiment'. In the following year one Tory

MP drew a parallel between the Roman and British empires, and reminded the Commons that when the former dissolved, it 'was followed by something much worse – the Dark Ages'.[28]

Others were disturbed by the potential for trouble of tribal and religious differences and the immaturity and political apathy of people who would soon be asked to decide their own future. For the past fifty years, Britain's African colonies had progressed at different rates, and undesirable customs and behaviour that the authorities had striven to suppress had often proved resilient. In 1954 a Basuto headman, three witch doctors and eleven accomplices were charged with the rape and murder of a woman whose body parts were removed for medicines.[29] Traditional customs flourished alongside 'modern' politics. In 1950 there was a revival of intertribal rustling of livestock along Somaliland's frontier with Ethiopia, while nationalists of the Somali Youth League clashed with police on the streets of Burao. There were also tensions between these young bloods and traditionalist, itinerant mullahs, whose power they challenged.[30]

Nationalist parties that represented themselves as expressions of the popular will inevitably clashed with established sources of authority, secular as well as religious. The wayward King Rukidi III of Toro complained in 1956 that the growing Ugandan Congress Party was making the chiefs feel 'insecure' and that its leaders were self-serving.[31] Elsewhere, Britain's willingness to cut cards with local politicians dismayed and worried princes and chiefs who had hitherto collaborated with colonial governments. There was also that easily overlooked but hard to calculate body of Africans who preferred the status quo, or who were indifferent to nationalist agitation. After the outbreak of the Korean War, an African member of the Nyasaland legislative council assured the Governor that 'African people have always rallied to the Empire', while in neighbouring Northern Rhodesia a district officer reported that only one in every 5,000 Africans in his area was interested in politics.[32] In Whitehall it was assumed that the conservative and the neutral would somehow fall into line with the new dispensation by which power was slowly transferred to native governments-in-waiting.

An empire in transition maintained the old racial hierarchies, which was one reason why nationalists found it easy to make converts. In Swaziland the film censors awarded four types of certificate: A for general showing; B for Europeans only; C for non-Europeans, but excluding natives; and D for everyone over the age of twelve.[33] Male passengers at Mombasa airport were confronted by two types of lavatory, one labelled 'European-Type Gentlemen' and the other 'Non-European-Type Gentlemen'.[34]

23

'Comrade Nasser, don't worry!':
Egypt and the Cold War 1945–1980

━━━ ━━━

I

In 1970 Vice-President Anwar el-Sadat of Egypt told the Soviet Ambassador that he held 'a position comparable to that of the British High Commissioner' thirty years before.[1] This paradox sums up the history of Egypt after 1945, during which the country progressed from being a resentful part of Britain's empire of influence to become a subordinate Cold War ally of Russia and then the United States. This should not have happened. In 1952 the Free Officers Group had deposed King Farouk, who was packed off to Capri to continue his sybaritic life in peace. The coup's leaders, General Muhammad Naguib, Colonels Gamal Abdel Nasser and Sadat, believed that they were the godfathers of a just, progressive and independent Egypt and the heirs of Urabi Pasha, Egypt's lost saviour and, like themselves, a soldier. They also admired and wished to emulate another soldier nationalist, Mustafa Kemal Atatürk, who, thirty years before, had thrown foreign armies out of Turkey and oversaw the construction of a forward-looking, secular and successful state. Some of these goals were achieved in Egypt, but this did not obviate the fact that in 1952 there were 88,000 British troops occupying the Canal Zone and in 1970 there were 20,000 Russian military 'advisers' stationed in Egypt.

What happened in Egypt had a huge significance for Africa, setting a pattern that spread across the continent during the 1960s and 1970s. The retreat of the old empires and the dissolution of old spheres of influence created vacuums that were swiftly filled by America and Russia as part of their respective Cold War strategies. As a result liberation and independence did not mean sovereignty, rather a transfer of patronage and novel forms of dependency. New, invisible shackles brought benefits, since often impoverished states required large-scale investment and their rulers convinced themselves that their survival depended on arsenals of modern weapons. Some Africans were alarmed: in May 1960 the *Ghanaian Times* thought that tractors were more appropriate than tanks, but, the editorial added, modern weapons were necessary to resist 'colonial aggression'.[2]

Where dictatorships replaced colonial government, as they so often did, these arms were essential for the crushing of opposition. They were also vital for the various sub-Saharan guerrilla armies that were beginning local wars of liberation. America and Russia provided warplanes, tanks and guns and were paid in political and economic concessions.

All this lay in the future. In September 1955 Egypt desperately needed arms to fight its neighbour, Israel. To achieve aerial and land superiority its ruler, Colonel Nasser, agreed a deal by which Egypt acquired Czech-manufactured weaponry, including eighty MiG-15 fighters and tanks, in return for cotton. It was a coup for Russia, and John Foster Dulles, the American Secretary of State, gloomily predicted that 'we may lose the whole Arab world and maybe Africa'. Herbert Hoover Jr, his Under-Secretary, concluded that if Russia armed Egypt, then America had no choice but to arm Israel.[3] The precedent had been set for proxy arms races in Africa and Asia.

Nasser's plans to beef up Egypt's armed forces coincided with the new phase of the Cold War during which both sides became increasingly paranoid and provocative. In November 1952 General Eisenhower had won the presidential election with pledges of a more intransigent and aggressive policy towards Russia. It was shaped by Dulles, a Manichaean in his view of the conflict between the West and the East, who wanted the United States to snatch the initiative and roll back Communism. His unbending spirit caught the American mood at a time when the McCarthy witch hunt had yet to run its manic course, and in the Pentagon and State Department the talk was of a possible and desirable preventive war against Russia, which was then lagging behind America in the nuclear arms race. Dr Strangelove was not a creature of fiction.

II

Residual British power was needed to win the Cold War in the Mediterranean and the Middle East. It did so successfully in Libya, which it had taken from the Italians in 1943 and where British officials decided to perpetuate the state recently created by Mussolini. Ten years later the provinces of Fezzan, Tripoli and Cyrenaica were formed into a new federation under the Sanussi Amir Sayyid Idris, a dependable if rather lazy client of Britain. Predominantly, Sanussi Cyrenaica was the keystone of the kingdom, much to the displeasure of adjacent Tripoli, where there was separatist agitation led by Bashir Saadawi with Egyptian support.[4] America warmly approved, for it had airfields and training facilities in Libya, and in return for Libyan cooperation it provided subsidies of $42 million between 1954 and 1974.

A subordinate Libya was essential for the security of the vast British base in the Suez Canal Zone, which was integral to American war plans for a nuclear offensive by USAF long-range bombers against industrial sites in southern Russia. By 1952 the Egyptian base had become a strategic white elephant, for it was itself a tempting target for Russian atomic bombs and both Russia and America were turning to missiles for their nuclear delivery systems. For these reasons the United States urged Britain to withdraw and it did so, sulkily, in June 1955.

Washington was relieved. Britain's recent treatment of Egypt had been viewed with a mixture of anxiety and exasperation. While it could pull strings in Libya, the British government was incapable of handling the increasingly formidable and violent Egyptian national movement. Matters had come to a head five months before the 1952 revolution. A series of skirmishes between British forces and Egyptian policemen near Ismailia had sparked an explosion of popular fury in Cairo and Alexandria: Europeans were murdered and those symbols of alien domination, the exclusive Turf Club, the Cairo Opera House and Shepheard's Hotel, were looted and burned. These outrages were an expression of a universal anger: 30 per cent of the rioters who were arrested were students, 30 per cent were skilled workers and 25 per cent were policemen. There were also opportunists, like the cook and doorkeeper caught stealing whisky from the hotel.[5] They were unlucky, for as the British government noted, the official response to the mayhem had been tardy and half-hearted.

The mood in London was vengeful: the Egyptians needed a hammering to remind them of their place in the world. Within two days of the tumults, the Cabinet, presided over by the Foreign Secretary, Sir Anthony Eden, reached for a cudgel. The 1882 invasion plans were disinterred and updated. There were not enough landing craft for the descent on Abukir Bay; the local commander-in-chief warned ministers about the sheer depth of nationalist feeling in Egypt and predicted that the Egyptian army would fight, as it had seventy years before. Oddly, the blueprint for Operation Rodeo, as it was called, included dropping leaflets telling the Egyptians that Britain was defending them, but with no explanation as to why or from whom they needed protection. On All Fools Day 1952 Rodeo was shelved but not forgotten.[6]

Seen from Washington, Britain's response to the Egyptian problem was a further symptom of a terminal malaise. America's chief ally lacked the wherewithal to sustain its now precarious empire of prestige in the Mediterranean and Middle East, refused to admit its incapacity, and imagined that Victorian nostrums were the only answer to indigenous nationalists. British attitudes were potentially dangerous, for they identified the United States with an archaic imperialism and were a bonus for Soviet propaganda.[7] To prevent Russia from gaining political and moral high ground in Africa and Asia, Britain had to be cajoled into shedding its now threadbare pretensions, retire backstage and allow America to inherit her former role.

Saying goodbye to one and a half centuries of global power was distressful, particularly for a generation of politicians like Eden, born and brought up during the late-Victorian and Edwardian imperial heyday. As an old man, Harold Macmillan delighted in recalling how he had watched Victoria's Diamond Jubilee celebrations in London. Sounding the imperial retreat also grated with middle-aged and older members of the working and middle classes who, as Victor Kiernan reminds us, had grown up with 'the lion's roar in their ears' and wanted to hear it again.[8] Their feelings were summed up when the *Daily Express* declared that the departure of the last British soldier from Egypt had been: 'A Day of Sorrow, a Day of Shame'. More would follow.

Radical new approaches to diplomacy were necessary which Britain found hard to stomach. Washington had reached the conclusion that the West would be wiser to reduce its reliance on traditional sources of authority, such as King Farouk of Egypt, and instead offer patronage to the new generation of popular, nationalist rulers-in-waiting such as the Free Officers Group. Such figures appealed to the romantic American historical imagination, which saw them as patriots in the mould of Washington and the Founding Fathers who stood up to the British

Empire in the name of liberty and self-determination. Yet realpolitik always overrode sentiment, which was why, between 1953 and 1969, the United States spent $147 million on modernising the armed forces of the absolutist but strongly anti-Communist Haile Selassie.[9] As in their past dealings with Latin America, Washington's policymakers would follow the maxim 'he may be a son of a bitch, but he's our son of a bitch'. This would also prove to be Moscow's approach to its collaborators.

III

In 1954 Nikita Khrushchev, the new First Secretary of the Soviet Communist Party, decided that Russia would compete with the United States in filling the growing power vacuum left by Britain and France in Africa and Asia. He resurrected Lenin's strategy of encouraging Communist revolutions in countries outside Europe. Underlying this policy was the assumption that the Soviet Union was the natural ally of every liberation movement struggling against colonialism and its driving force, capitalism. A common enemy provided the opportunity for ideological conversion, a process that would be lubricated by Russian investment and implemented by imported Russian economists. Modern weapons were also made available to assist freedom fighters and help new nations defend themselves against capitalist aggression. The evaporation of British power in Egypt, coupled with Nasser's appeal for arms, gave Khrushchev the chance to apply his doctrine. He was gambling, for the KGB men in Cairo regarded Nasser as ideologically unsound despite his nationalisation policies. They concluded that he was a radical nationalist in the mould of those military strong men of the kind who regularly surfaced in Latin America.[10]

This judgement was confirmed between 1952 and 1954, when Nasser consolidated his power. The Muslim League was banned and its leaders imprisoned along with other opponents: the new Egypt would be a secular state. It would also be a fairer one, for land reforms distributed the estates of the landowners among the *fellahin*, imposed rent controls and set a minimum wage for rural workers. Nasser's propaganda exalted him as a progressive patriot, a national redeemer who was above political factions and devoted to the welfare of the people. An egotist, his ambitions extended beyond Egypt, for he saw his country as the banner-bearer of the Pan-Arabist movement and himself as its champion. Having driven the British from Egypt he would supplant their influence across the Middle East, and he soon found friends by backing anti-French movements in Algeria and Tunisia. In April 1955 Nasser made his debut on the world stage when he attended the Bandung Conference, which had been called to form a loose bloc of African and Asian states, outwardly neutral in the Cold War and dedicated to opposing imperialism.

Over this period Nasser's relations with the United States deteriorated. Dulles interpreted the Czech deal as signal proof that Egypt was now in the Soviet camp. Coercion might possibly change Nasser's mind, and Dulles examined the possibility of blocking the headwaters of the White Nile so as to 'strangle him'.[11] Such a move would have required the cooperation of the British, who controlled the Owen Falls dam on Lake Victoria. The United States did not, however, threaten Egypt with famine, but chose a more conventional form of arm-twisting by refusing a $56 million loan to help fund the new Aswan High Dam, which was designed to provide Egypt with what she had always needed: ample and regular water supplies.

Nasser looked elsewhere for investment, and at the end of July 1956 he nationalised the Suez Canal, whose revenues would fund the Aswan project. The world was taken by surprise. Eden, now Prime Minister, was choleric, but he welcomed the chance to overturn a dictator whom he reviled as an 'Asiatic Mussolini' and, at a stroke, restore Britain's standing in the Middle East. He became feverishly obsessed with Nasser and imagined that he was again embroiled in the diplomatic conflicts of the 1930s. This time there would be no appeasement: during August Operation Rodeo (renamed 'Musketeer') was resuscitated and adapted for the capture of the Canal. France was an enthusiastic accomplice, keen to punish Egypt for the support it was giving the Algerian insurgents. Like their ally, the French were hosts to memories of former days of power and glory. Just before the landings in Egypt, the French commander General Beaufré addressed his troops, recalling Napoleon's victories in Egypt and urging them 'to repeat the exploits of your forebears'.

While British and French staff officers were planning a war, diplomats cobbled together compromises, none of which satisfied the protagonists. MI5 and the CIA contemplated assassinating Nasser, perhaps using nerve gas or poisoned cigarettes: the first James Bond novel had appeared three years before.[12] From the start, the United States feared the worst. At the end of July an exasperated Dulles told Vice-President Nixon: 'The British and French are really anxious to start a war and get us into it.'[13] Such an outcome could jeopardise Eisenhower's re-election campaign, and early in September he considered phoning the Queen in the mistaken belief that she had the authority to rein in Eden or dismiss him.

Meanwhile, Eden was casting about to find an excuse to attack Egypt and occupy the Canal, and by the third week of September he had found one. At a secret meeting in Sèvres, British, French and Israeli ministers hatched a plot to give the war legitimacy: Israeli forces would cross the Sinai peninsula and almost immediately an Anglo-French amphibious force would seize Port Said to 'rescue' the Canal and enforce a ceasefire. Before they came ashore, bombers would knock out the Egyptian air force and, revealingly, one prime target was the offices of Radio Cairo from which Nasser had waged his propaganda war against the allies.

On 29 October the Israelis advanced across the Sinai peninsula and the Egyptian army fled towards the Canal. A week later, British and French forces landed and occupied Port Said, while the Egyptians blocked the Canal with scuttled ships. Within two days the United States, Russia and the United Nations had condemned the adventure and an armistice followed. Eden received what the President called a 'tongue-lashing' from Eisenhower, America combined with Russia to support a United Nations resolution condemning Anglo-French aggression, and its forces replaced British and French troops along the banks of the Canal. Britain had a sharp reminder of its economic fragility with a run on the pound, but a sterling crisis was staved off by American credit. In March 1957 Dulles sourly remarked that 'the British knew they had gotten the last injection of dollars from the US they can get for a while'.[14]

The Suez débacle had brutally exposed Britain's pretensions, the perils of defying the United States and painfully confirmed what Washington had long feared. At the very end of 1956 and looking back at the events of the last six months, Dulles insisted that it was now urgent for America 'to fill the vacuum of power that the British have filled for a century'.[15] For the time being, Russia's client Nasser enjoyed an enhanced reputation in the Middle East and Africa (where he soon met Nkrumah) as a dynamic national leader who had given the 'imperialists' a bloody nose. To celebrate his triumph, he issued a victory stamp featuring soldiers and civilians rushing to the shore to hurl back the invaders, although, ominously, the Egyptian army had revealed that it was no match for the Israelis.

IV

Soviet propaganda exploited Nasser's success for all it was worth. Using the General Assembly of the United Nations as his platform, Khrushchev affirmed his support for colonial liberation movements with his characteristic knockabout rhetoric. There were plenty of receptive listeners: in 1960 a third of the Assembly's ninety-nine representatives came from former colonies and protectorates, a total that rose rapidly over the next decade. At various times they heard Khrushchev's harangues against the colonialist West and promises that Russia would do all in its power 'to bring imperialism to its knees'. To spite the Americans, he hailed the leaders of liberation movements and compared their heroism to that of Washington and Jefferson. Nasser was invited to Moscow in 1958, fêted and treated to a performance of *Swan Lake* at the Bolshoi Ballet. Perturbed by the antics of the Black Swan, he was consoled by Khrushchev, who told him the villainous bird was Dulles. He added: 'Don't worry, Comrade Nasser, don't worry! At the end we will break his wings.'[16]

A strong and well-armed Egypt would help ensure Dulles's fate. Egypt received over 40 per cent of Russia's foreign aid budget, which helped pay for the Aswan Dam. The Egyptians were also given substantial numbers of aircraft, tanks and SAM missile systems, and a complement of Russian instructors to explain how they worked. The returns were disappointing in the extreme. In the Six Day War of June 1967, Israel inflicted a crushing defeat on Egypt in which pre-emptive air strikes destroyed 286 of the 340 Russian-supplied warplanes. Khrushchev had resigned in 1964 and his successor, Alexei Kosygin, shared the general dismay at their client's poor performance. Russia had no choice but to transform its advisers into a garrison; by 1970 they totalled 20,000 and included aircrew and specialists to man the radar installations and anti-aircraft batteries.

Still adored by the masses, Nasser died in 1970 and was succeeded as

President by Sadat, who was endorsed by 90 per cent of the electorate, a result that was then common enough in one-party states. Thirty years before, as a young officer Sadat had hated the British domination of his country, and for the next ten years he worked to remove Russian influence and personnel. It was a tricky task, but Sadat had the requisite ruthlessness and determination not only to edge out the Russians but to stifle opposition from KGB-financed Communists and the Muslim League. The Soviet leadership caved in and withdrew their forces and support, for, unlike Britain twenty years before, Russia had no inclination to get entangled in a struggle with local nationalists, and in any case Egypt had shown itself a military liability. As the Russians left, Sadat discreetly sidled towards the Americans, who offered more for his friendship: by the mid-1980s the United States was paying $1.8 billion a year in aid (including armaments) to Egypt. In return Sadat rid Egypt of the incubus of the intermittent war with Israel. In 1978 he signed the Camp David Accord, which was both a peace treaty and the settlement of boundaries between the two countries.

Sadat was assassinated in October 1981 by Muslim fanatics. The system of government by successive military strong men survived for the next thirty-odd years, with the armed forces continuing to dominate economic and military life, until it was challenged by an alliance of incompatibles: pro-democracy middle-class agitators and religious obscurantists of the Muslim League. Disorders led to a return to Caesarean military rule in 2013. Annual American grants now total $2.7 billion, which it considers a fair price for stability and a reliable Middle Eastern ally in a new war against militant and expansionist Islam.

Egypt's experiences were the result of the new imperialism born of the Cold War. It was a form of indirect rule by which freshly independent states accepted assistance from either the United States or the Soviet Union, and in the process surrendered some of their sovereignty. The agents of control were diplomats, CIA and KGB officers, legions of specialist advisers and, in America's case, the representatives of big corporations. All had large purses and the knowledge that the new nations of Africa and, as often as not, their rulers were hungry for money. A new scramble for Africa was under way.

24

A 'horde of rats':
The Algerian War and Its Memories

I

One million seven hundred thousand French soldiers, nearly all of them conscripts, fought to keep Algeria French. Between 1954 and 1962 they were deployed in what the National Assembly repeatedly proclaimed were 'opérations de sécurité et de maintien de l'ordre'. The enemy was the Front de Libération Nationale (FLN), which fielded an army of 400,000 partisans backed by a larger, semi-visible body of civilian accomplices. All suffered heavy losses: calculations of Arab deaths range from 700,000 to 1 million out of a population that stood at nearly 10 million at the end of the war. A further 2 million were uprooted from their homes and herded into closely guarded internment camps. French losses were considerable in terms of colonial wars: 25,000 servicemen were killed, 65,000 were wounded and 350,000 endured the symptoms of what we now call 'post-traumatic stress disorder'.[1]

Ordinary French people suffered another disorder of the mind: a collective amnesia about what happened during a brutal campaign of counter-terror that upset consciences, tarnished national self-esteem and ended in defeat, civil unrest and humiliation. Moreover, the final phase of the conflict spilled over into metropolitan France, which was convulsed by riots, urban terrorism and the threats of military coups and civil war.

Like the war that triggered them, these events were so painful that they had to be banished to historic oblivion. When I recently visited the Paris Musée de l'Armée, I asked where the exhibits for the Algerian War were and was told that there were none. The attendant was rather grumpy, but a colleague of African descent seemed amused. Yet, just over thirty years before, I had watched a hundred or so Algerian War veterans march through a seaside town during the annual celebration of its liberation in 1944. The band played 'Sambre et Meuse' and the crowd cheered the local boys, now approaching middle age. This was unsurprising, for they, their parents and grandparents had been brought up to believe that Algeria was as much a part of France as their native Normandy. In 1957, a year before the domestic troubles began, just under the half the population were against Algerian independence.[2]

Belatedly and hesitantly, France has confronted its phantoms. In 1998 the National Assembly officially redefined the Algerian campaign as a 'war fought over decolonisation', which effectively demolished previous official claims that Algeria had been inseparable from metropolitan France. Three years later, the Assembly publicly acknowledged France's 'debt of honour' to the *harkis*, those Algerians who fought on the French side.[3] It is unlikely that this admission added much to the lives of those lucky enough to escape the cruel vengeance of their countrymen or their descendants who had gravitated towards the wretched *bidonvilles* on the edge of France's larger towns and cities. Like the national lapse of memory, these slums and shanty towns were part of the legacy of the Algerian War. There were others: in October 1988 the government of Algeria revived methods used by the French thirty years before after riots in the working-class districts of Algiers. A state of siege was declared, troops moved in and opened fire. The official estimate of those shot dead was thirty; unofficial tallies put the total at at least 300.[4]

II

After liberation, France had briefly contemplated the creation of a liberal empire based on the principles of the Atlantic Charter. The old colonies, including Algeria, would form the French Union in which everyone would share the political and social rights of French citizens. This was too much for the French electorate, still recovering from wartime humiliations, which wanted a submissive empire and said so by voting against the proposal in 1946. Algerians did, however, get some say in how they were governed, but on terms devised to limit Arab representation. Their powerlessness and the ascendancy of the *colons* were confirmed by the 1948 elections, which were shamelessly rigged to keep Arab representation to a minimum.[5] Old attitudes remained entrenched both in Algeria and France: President Vincent Auriol told Algerians that their country 'was never a state, you were rescued from slavery as well as tribes fighting each other; without France what would you be or do?'

Albert Camus agreed in principle, but warned that Algeria's essential Frenchness depended on it being ruled in the spirit of French justice.[6] Yet, as he knew, the law was partial, for the Arab's legal disabilities remained. They were summed up by a courtroom exchange in which a witness identified himself as an Arab. A French lawyer corrected him: 'No, you are French.' The Arab reminded the lawyer that if this were so, he was entitled to 'the rights' of a French citizen. He was not, the lawyer riposted, for no Arab enjoyed these rights. This irony would have been lost on millions of Frenchmen, who remained convinced that the Arab's Muslim religion automatically disqualified him from citizenship.

This blatant inequality grated with the many thousands of Arabs who had served with French forces during the war. The future partisan leader Ahmed Ben Bella, who had been an NCO and won the Croix de Guerre, spoke for all veterans when he declared: 'My brother returned from Europe with medals and frostbitten feet! There everyone was equal! Why not here?'[7] One of the main reasons was an educational system which excluded Arabs. In 1960 just under 5 per cent of the students (1,317) attending the *écoles supérieures* were Arabs, among them 172 women.[8]

A growing but still marginalised Arab population continued to seek work in France. By 1955 these economic migrants totalled half a million, of whom 40 per cent were settled in Paris.[9] The FLN treated Algerian expatriates as allies: some engaged in sabotage and all contributed to the nationalist coffers, some willingly and others under duress. In the first year of the war, £600,000 had been raised from this source.[10] Thirty thousand Algerians took to the Paris streets in support of the FLN in October 1961 and were met with police baton charges and revolver fire. The application of Algerian methods of crowd control had been ordered by Maurice Papon, the recently appointed Chief of Police who had formerly been Prefect of Constantine and before that a zealous servant of the Vichy regime. Estimates of the dead, including stunned demonstrators who had been thrown into the Seine and drowned, were between thirty and 300. In 1998 Papon was found guilty of assisting in the deportation of Jews during his administrative apprenticeship under Vichy.

                                III

The immigrants had left behind an Algeria in which French authority was absolute: the police arrested and imprisoned dissidents of all complexions and nationalist groups were driven underground. In the face of French intransigence, it was inevitable that they turned towards violence, arguing that the only way to break France's will was armed resistance. The odds were less formidable than in the past, for in May 1954 a defeated French army had surrendered to Vietnamese Communist guerrillas at Dien Bien Phu, ending a nine-year war of attrition. This boded well, for it was proof that determined armed peasants backed by a friendly population could defeat a modern army and liberate their country. On 1 November the FLN began its armed struggle with attacks on isolated prefectures, police and army posts in eastern Algeria. An attempt to blow up the Algiers gasworks failed, but served notice that the front line would be extended to towns and cities.

A fortnight after, that durable political chameleon François Mitterrand (then Minister of the Interior) assured the National Assembly that 'Algeria is France and who among you . . . would hesitate to employ every means to preserve France?'[11] In the following year, 1957, when France signed the Treaty of Rome, her representatives took for granted the fact that Algeria was part of their country. There were, however, provisions to curtail Algerian immigration into Common Market nations.

                                IV

From the start, the insurgents' strategy and war effort were directed and coordinated by the FLN which, in 1958, assumed international legitimacy by declaring itself the Provisional Government of the Algerian Republic under President Habib Bourguiba. The FLN's overall objective was to make Algeria ungovernable and so compel France to withdraw her soldiers and administrators and concede independence. To this end, the FLN waged war on four closely related levels: military, economic, political and diplomatic. The first was a campaign of terrorism and sabotage intended to exhaust French resources and patience, while strikes and mass boycotts of wine and tobacco hurt the economy and reduced revenues. The FLN's political war was internal and undertaken to enforce solidarity among quarrelsome factions and eliminate deviancy. Like the French, the FLN resorted to torture.

Outside Algeria, the FLN successfully waged a diplomatic offensive to gain international recognition as a government that rested on the popular will, to find friends to plead its cause in the UN and supply it with money and arms. All were offered by sympathetic Arab and Communist states, which were quick to recognise Bourguiba's government in exile and send aid totalling $34 million to the FLN. Practical help also came from Egypt and Tunisia, the first offering weapons and radio propaganda and the second providing training bases and rest camps for the partisans. Armed with a passport supplied by Pakistan, Ferhat Abbas, the veteran moderate nationalist who had once hoped for a peaceful accommodation with France, became the FLN's Ambassador to the UN and its advocate in the independent states of Africa.

The Eisenhower administration watched events in Algeria with a mixture of frustration and apprehension. On the one hand, France had behaved itself by relinquishing its control over Tunisia and Morocco in 1956. Both countries continued to play host to bases for American bombers intended for use in a nuclear offensive against Russia. The Moroccans were particularly cooperative; the Istiqlal nationalist party promised to champion the interests of Coca-Cola against those of local wine producers.[12] Yet on the other hand, France refused to play America's game in Algeria, falsely claiming that it was suppressing a Communist uprising as well as defending a historic province of France. After his return from his African tour in April 1957, Vice-President Nixon had concluded: 'French patronage and influence in North Africa are decreasing at an alarming rate.'[13] France seemed in the grip of the British disease, clinging desperately to powers and pretensions that she lacked the means to uphold and led by men trapped in the world of Marshal Lyautey. This sickness might prove fatal: in October 1957 the National Security Council warned Eisenhower that the Algerian War 'imperils the political and financial stability of France'.[14]

Worse still, France's imperial war was depriving NATO of troops needed to defend Western Europe. Moreover, and greatly to the embarrassment of the United States, the Sikorsky helicopters and many of the jeeps and arms used in Algeria had been supplied by the United States to stiffen France's contribution to NATO. FLN propagandists accused America of equipping the French army for 'the war of extermination against the Algerian people'.[15] France answered such charges by playing on American fears that an independent Algeria might go Communist. After all, the Algerian Communist Party supported the FLN.[16] Caught between fear of Algeria going red and offending a valuable if wayward ally, America abstained from the vote on a UN motion for France's withdrawal.

V

Newsreels of the Algerian War showed French draftees wearing GI-style helmets and performing the day-to-day chores of mid-twentieth-century counter-insurgency operations. Tactics rested on the premise that the front line was everywhere and every Arab was a potential terrorist or his abetter. Soldiers patrolled villages, edged warily along streets and alleyways, stopped and searched Arabs and rummaged around their houses for weapons, explosives and propaganda leaflets. Suspects were detained for interrogation and torture. Conscripts also guarded the Morice Line, a barrier of electrified fences and barbed wire that stretched along the frontier with Tunisia. It hindered the FLN's efforts to deploy reserves, but was not the war winner its architects had hoped for. Offensive operations comprised search-and-destroy patrols that hunted bands of insurgents in the countryside. These were largely undertaken by parachutist battalions and the Foreign Legion, both of which boasted their elite status and cultivated a tough, machismo image. They were greatly feared, and with good reason.

The Algerian War was in part a civil war, for 210,000 Algerians joined the French forces. Just under half of these *harkis* were killed, many as part of the vengeful massacres that followed the French departure. With the connivance of their officers, some escaped to France and settled there to the life of outcasts. 'I would prefer Algerian nationality', one admitted in 1981, 'but it is too late.' His son commented: 'My father is an idiot . . . he chose the camp of the defeated and he was brought up here to live like a dog . . . we are hated more than the native Algerians.'[17]

In what turned out to be a war of attrition, the turning point was hard to detect. Until the winter of 1957 to 1958, the French held their own thanks to superior numbers and sheer ruthlessness. They had won the battle for Algiers, a concerted offensive that began in September 1956 and ended the following September. These operations were intended to evict the FLN from its stronghold in the Casbah and to shatter the civilian support systems that were sustaining the hit-and-run terrorist campaign of assassinations and bombings in the city. Over 10,000 suspects were arrested and interned, a tenth of the Casbah's population.

This struggle to smash the FLN's organisation within the Casbah was the subject of Gillo Pontecorvo's vivid and authentic film *The Battle for Algiers* (1966), which has subsequently become a text for both urban guerrillas and security agencies. It focuses on the network of FLN auxiliaries who served as couriers carrying messages, guns and time bombs, moving undetected through the streets. These tasks were most effectively performed by children and women, whose hijabs were ideal for concealment. The opening sequences show prisoners in the forbidding Serkadji gaol, where they can look down into a yard to watch the guillotining of convicted terrorists. Political detainees are still held in this prison. There is also footage of the torture of suspects, and the bombing of cafés and dance halls where *colons* and their families are enjoying themselves.

As the operations reached their successful conclusion their master mind, Colonel Mathieu, a parachute officer wearing sinister reflective sunglasses and based upon the formidable General Jacques Massu, addresses a press conference. He tells them that if France wishes to remain in Algeria, its people 'must accept the consequences'. A fictional remark was a reminder that the war was presenting the French people with stark choices. How long were they prepared to pour money and blood into a war to hold Algeria against the wishes of most of its inhabitants? Were they willing to tolerate what a former staff officer called the methods 'worthy of the Gestapo'?[18] Despite official censorship, details of the use of torture were leaking out and causing disquiet at a time when German and Vichy cruelties were a recent memory. Yet a war which was beginning to unsettle the French conscience was far from lost. Despite securing temporary control over some remote areas, the FLN was hard-pressed and it had not yet broken France's will to fight on. Suddenly, in May 1958, everything changed: the *colons* rebelled and joined forces with mutinous generals who threatened a military coup in France.

VI

The revolt of the *colons*, now commonly called the *pieds-noirs*, opened the final phase of what was now a three-sided conflict. The new protagonists were the 900,000-strong white community and a clutch of generals who believed that Algeria should never be separated from France. What agitated (and terrified) the *colons* was the possibility that exhaustion might compel their government to negotiate an agreement with the FLN, which would leave them a minority at the mercy of a vengeful Arab majority. To preserve the Algerian status quo (and win the war) a new, determined and ultra-patriotic regime was needed in Paris. The rebels demanded the return of France's former saviour de Gaulle and threatened a military coup. Massu's paratroopers seized Corsica and, for a few days, Parisians nervously expected them to drop from the skies on the city as tanks took up positions on the boulevards. The government caved in, de Gaulle returned as Prime Minister, was elected President in December, and the Fourth Republic gave way to the Fifth.

De Gaulle disappointed those who had helped him to power. He was a pragmatist who at first recognised that concessions were vital if Algeria was to become governable again. The upshot was the Constantine Plan of October 1958 for reform and regeneration, funded by the revenues from the oilfields in the south of the country that had been discovered two years before. Among the proposals was a massive increase in primary school education: within three years the numbers of pupils rose from 690,000 to over a million. Like their parents, all were now French citizens under the terms of a new constitution which failed to satisfy either the FLN or the *pieds-noirs*.

Palliatives would no longer work and there was now a distinct likelihood that the Algerian imbroglio would have dangerous repercussions inside France. Slowly and tentatively, de Gaulle accepted the principle of Algerian self-determination, and he carried the French people with him through emotional television and radio broadcasts in which he outlined his policies and called for national support. In November 1960, viewers and listeners heard de Gaulle pledge the creation of an 'emancipated Algeria in which Algerians will decide their own destiny', and two months later an overwhelming majority endorsed his decision in a referendum.

The *pieds-noirs* and hardline generals again resorted to treason. In April 1961 there was a second revolt in Algiers led by General Raoul Salan, which flopped; French conscripts listened to de Gaulle's appeal for loyalty on their transistors and ignored their commanders. Afterwards, a rearguard resistance continued in Algeria and was extended to France under the direction of the underground Organisation de l'Armée Secrète (OAS). During the rest of 1961 and 1962 there were murders, car bombings and two attempted assassinations of de Gaulle.*

Negotiations with the FLN began in May 1961 at Évian, which led to a ceasefire in March 1962 and Algerian independence the following July. Nearly 70 per cent of the French people approved of this outcome and 99 per cent of Algerians.[19] Algeria secured independence and France lost what had become an incubus that threatened domestic stability.

In the meantime, nearly all the 900,000 *pieds-noirs* abandoned a future in an Algeria where they would no longer be the masters. Domestic public opinion had gradually turned against them, not least because they were increasingly seen as an arrogant, selfish and parasitic class. According to Camus, they were characterised as 'a million settlers each with a whip and cigar, riding in a Cadillac', even though a third of them were farmers. This chimed with FLN propaganda, which depicted the *'gros colons'* as pro-Vichy collaborationists (which many had been) and rich, debauched sybarites.[20] In fact, most were petit bourgeois shopkeepers, businessmen and small-scale farmers and they managed to settle comfortably in France and prosper there despite allegations that they had never been truly French. On the eve of Algerian independence, a writer in *Le Figaro Littéraire* suggested that they had never really been French, but were a distinct 'Mediterranean race, French by language, but not by temperament' since they were 'slaves to racial passions'.[21]

In Algiers, Ferhat Abbas announced a new dawn after the 'nuit coloniale' that had first darkened his country in 1830 and brought with

---

* These events form the background to Frederick Forsyth's thriller *The Day of the Jackal*.

it poverty and genocide. Frantz Fanon, a Martinique-born psychiatrist who had fought with the Free French army and witnessed the early stage of the Algerian War before his deportation in 1957, saw it as a model for resistance movements across Africa. In his *The Wretched of the Earth* (1961), he interpreted the conflict as a struggle against the capitalist world waged by the dispossessed and alienated. Peasants with nothing to lose but everything to gain would combine with the lumpen-proletariat being created by rural immigrants to Africa's growing cities to form guerrilla armies that would fight to win independence. For Fanon, they were a 'horde of rats; you may kick them or throw stones at them, but despite all your efforts they'll go on gnawing at the roots of the tree'. Force was the only legitimacy of all colonial regimes and capitalism was their engine. Arguments that colonial rule brought progress were dismissed: 'If you wish for independence, take it, and go back to the middle ages.' Autarky and austerity were infinitely preferable to capitalist servitude.[22] Independent Algeria experienced neither, but its existence was proof that the armed struggle of the masses, as feverishly depicted by Fanon, could succeed. An era of new colonial wars had begun.

25

'Insatiable greed':
Decolonisation and the Cold War

I

The coincidence of decolonisation and the Cold War was a catastrophe for Africa. The continent was drawn into the global struggle between Communism and capitalism in which the rulers of newly independent states found themselves taking sides because commitment yielded political and private advantages. The result was a continent tormented by intermittent wars, its economic development stalled and it became hampered by vast and corrosive public debts. Between 1973 and 1983 the total borrowing by sub-Saharan states soared from $18.6 billion to $60.5 billion.[1] These misfortunes have not prevented bewildered and bitter Africans from blaming their woes on the earlier colonial era, but many had their origins in the first decades of independence.

At the time, some Africans recognised this, but were either unwilling or powerless to prevent it. In 1963 Julius Nyerere, the President of Tanganyika, alerted his fellow African leaders to a 'second scramble for Africa by Russia and its satellites'.[2] Nonetheless, he was prepared to accept Soviet weaponry for his army, and American help in beefing up his security and police forces. In 1969, as the Nigerian Civil War was nearing its end, the rebel Biafran radio declared that: 'Biafrans are fighting an imperial war waged by Britain and Russia in an unholy alliance' with the approval of the United States. Another scramble was under way which, like the first, was driven by an 'insatiable greed to plunder [and] loot Africa and Africans, and, whenever possible, use African puppets to achieve their selfish ends'.[3]

Similar outrage was provoked in 1975 by Russia's decision to deploy 5,000 Cuban mercenaries in support of its nationalist clients in Angola. The Kenyan *Sunday Nation* denounced 'Cuban troops acting on instruction from Moscow' and the outraged Zambian *Times* warned that

Cuba would reap 'African hatred'.[4] The motives and coercive methods of the new scramble were labelled 'neo-colonialism', an expression that was paradoxically and frequently used by Russian propagandists to demonise America and its allies.

II

Both the United States and the Soviet Union needed the compliant cooperation of the new states of Africa: their votes were valuable in the UN, they offered growing export markets and, above all, they were a source of vital strategic raw materials, such as cobalt and diamonds. Neither power wished to rule African lands directly, but preferred to oversee the affairs of sovereign states through cajolery and enticing offers of assistance. In order to manage Africa, the two superpowers flooded the continent with legions of political, economic and military advisers, technicians and experts in the often sinister mysteries of 'security' that helped keep African tyrants in the saddle. From 1975 onwards Russia deployed Cuban mercenaries, first in Angola to assist its favoured liberation movement, and then in Ethiopia to help the puppet regime repel a Somalian invasion. In all, 400,000 Cuban soldiers would serve terms of duty in Africa fighting the Soviet Union's proxy wars.[5]

Soviet–American chicanery went hand in hand with largely unconvincing attempts to secure the moral high ground. Both powers publicly denounced the old European colonial empires as part of their intensive propaganda campaigns for control of the African mind. Capitalism and Communism were promoted as choices which, if adopted, would bring prosperity and progress to poor nations. Communist ideology would also accelerate the overthrow of lingering white rule in southern Africa. When the ANC (African National Congress) and South Africa's Communists visited Moscow in 1960, in search of advice on how best to wage the 'armed struggle', they received lectures on Marxist–Leninist theory. Only by applying it and 'winning of the masses' would they prevail, and then as part of 'the global struggle of the working class of capitalist countries'.[6] For Moscow, the ANC guerrillas in South Africa and their counterparts in Rhodesia and Portuguese Africa were front-line troops in the Cold War.

Not everyone in Moscow was convinced. Some doctrinaire officials questioned the value of recruiting local nationalists, whom they dismissed as 'national bourgeoisie'.[7] In 1974, when Colonel Mathieu Kérékou, the military strong man who ruled Benin, announced his conversion to Marxist–Leninism, one Soviet official was astonished. How on earth, he wondered, could its doctrines be usefully applied to a country ruled by a military clique, without classes or industry, and in which four-fifths of the population were illiterate?[8] Such ideological objections were overridden, for winning over the likes of Kérékou prevented their countries from falling under American influence. Likewise, similar intellectual gymnastics persuaded Washington that the cause of democracy would be furthered through backing autocrats in Africa. This was, of course, an extension of United States policy in Latin America and Vietnam.

Both sides believed that propaganda was vital in winning friends in Africa. It was imagined in Moscow that Africans could be seduced by propaganda that exalted the 'miracles' that had been achieved by Russia since 1917 and promised that they could be repeated once their countries embraced Marxist-Leninism. They were invited to see for themselves, as generously funded students in Russian and Eastern European universities, what had been accomplished. Once they had understood that this was the future, then students would convert to Communism, and return home as a cadre of future leaders. Young Nigerians were tempted by a country where everyone was equal and nobody went without, and they were given a foretaste of Russian abundance with free cigarettes and alcohol on their Aeroflot flights. Disillusion quickly followed. One student grumbled about the glum 'drudgery' of everyday life, which another summed up as 'No cars, no cafés, no good clothes and good food . . . Nothing but shortages and restrictions.'[9]

There was also racism. African students in Moscow were often asked whether they had houses in their country, which was unsurprising since Russian documentaries portrayed Africa as backward and primitive.[10] Mixed marriages and their offspring were treated icily and casual racial abuse was common. In 1966 the British Consul in Prague reported that it was popularly believed that African students were 'chosen by shaking the trees' and 'giving scholarships to the first that fall out of them'.[11] Political indoctrination was universal. Two Kenyans studying mathematics and engineering in Bulgaria were also forced to undertake military training, during which they were asked whether they wished to learn about guerrilla warfare.[12] The government of Malawi (formerly Nyasaland) refused to recognise degrees from Moscow's Lumumba University, and other states treated graduates from Communist universities with suspicion and disdain.[13]

American propaganda was tainted by the violent progress of the Civil Rights movement across the southern states from 1954 onwards. Newspaper reports and newsreel footage of rabid white mobs, snarling Alsatians and policemen cudgelling black protesters revealed a country where, in the South, the black man's place was at the bottom of the pile, and woe betide him if he objected. It was hoped that these impressions might be balanced by posting more African Americans to African embassies, but there were few qualified for such work. The volunteer Peace Corps, formed in 1961 and the creature of President John F. Kennedy, was one antidote to the 'ugly American' image and it worked rather well. Generations of officially funded, predominantly young American men and women undertook the tasks that had been part of the traditional vision of benign and benevolent imperialism. They taught in schools, worked in hospitals and clinics and helped farmers obtain greater yields. Africans also absorbed another highly beguiling image of the United States through Hollywood movies, which unceasingly promoted America as a land populated by prosperous, happy families surrounded by multiple gadgets, and a world in which any man or woman of talent could get ahead. Capitalism worked, although Hollywood's version of the good life in the 1950s and 1960s seemed confined to the white middle class.

III

Above all, America and Russia needed tractable African leaders. The first generation of African leaders were populists who had risen to power on messianic rhetoric laced with the talismanic catchwords 'freedom' and 'independence'. They relied heavily on the paraphernalia of modern mass politics – open-air rallies, posters and party songs – which elevated them as Mosaic figures who were delivering their people from bondage and guiding them towards a better future. After independence, their heads appeared on coins, banknotes and stamps, they undertook foreign tours and were fêted at international

conferences and the UN General Assembly. National saviours such as
Kwame Nkrumah spoke passionately about non-alignment at the same
time as accepting American and Russian funds.

Africa's first-generation leaders could not have done otherwise, for
they had risen to power through promises that independence would be
followed by economic miracles. These required considerable outside investment and subsidies, which was why, in 1959, the State Department
urged Britain and France to be generous with their assistance to their
former colonies, some of which were becoming hosts to 'unrealistic'
expectations of American funding.[14]

The donation of aid was competitive and, in their rush to give as
much as possible, both the Russians and the Americans seldom paused
to consider what was appropriate or how exactly it would generate
robust and lasting economic growth. Russia sent snowploughs to
Guinea as part of an intensive programme designed to win over Sékou
Touré, who had encouragingly proclaimed himself a Marxist. It was a
profitable conversion, for in the early 1960s the American Ambassador in Conakry reported that Guinea was 'swarming with Soviet bloc
technicians and engineers'. Many were plainly incompetent, since their
efforts had produced a malfunctioning printing plant, a defective radio
transmitter and an incomplete national theatre. A Russian tomato can-
nery had been built in an area without water or tomato plantations.
Efforts to create a prestigious national airline foundered, with its nine
Ilyushin airliners more or less permanently grounded, which was probably for the best since their Russian pilots could not speak French.[15]
Meanwhile, Soviet, East German and Czech secret servicemen played
on Touré's paranoia, and were accomplices in his campaign of terror
against opponents in which torture was commonplace.[16] For the next
twenty years Guinea drifted in the economic doldrums, with one of
the lowest per capita incomes in the world.

Gifts, loans and credit had immeasurable political value since they
created a chain of dependency which made it easier for donors to discipline the recipients. Of equal if not greater value was Russian and
American political support in the form of imported police and security
systems and the experts who knew how to operate them. The apparatus
of the police state particularly benefited dictators. They proliferated
throughout the 1960s and 1970s as former nationalist leaders assumed
despotic powers or were unseated by coups which replaced them with

military strong men such as Idi Amin in Uganda. Irrespective of how they came to power or abused it, Africa's dictators were sponsored by the two superpowers as well as Britain and France, who delivered them the means by which to control their people. Africa's capitals became home to shadowy armies of spies and experts in 'security', which was a euphemism for oppression of one kind or another.

When client rulers attempted to slip the leash or indicated that they might switch patrons, intelligence agencies acted as kingmakers. In the early 1960s the KGB had some success in cultivating Nkrumah, who seemed to be nudging Ghana leftwards with a nationalisation programme and demands that foreign companies should reinvest 60 per cent of their profits in his country. He was also a corrupt client, as the Russians discovered after they broke Ghana's codes and read how Nkrumah and his cronies were taking a cut of Soviet aid and squirrelling it away. The CIA wrote him off as 'a vain opportunist and playboy' and, in February 1966, joined with the British to mastermind a coup which toppled the President, who fled into a comfortable exile. Afterwards he alleged that he was the victim of 'imperialist and neo-colonialist agencies' and that the banners waved on the streets by Ghanaians celebrating his downfall had been manufactured in the American embassy. His exit was followed by that of 1,000 Eastern bloc advisers.[17]

Perhaps the most effective control over African rulers of all political complexions was exercised by the United States through its policy of training, advising and pouring money into local police and security forces. This stratagem had been successfully applied in Latin America and was extended to Africa as part of USAID (United States Agency for International Development), where its application cost $3.3 million between 1963 and 1969.[18] Radios and small-arms were delivered to police forces and there was intensive instruction in investigating sedition, strike-breaking and riot control.

Moral criteria were cast to the wind in the distribution of coercion and its technology. President William Tubman of Liberia, whom the CIA rated as a heavy-handed paternalist, received $500,000 to modernise his prisons, but where exactly the cash went was a mystery, for inmates in Monrovia gaol continued to live in wretched conditions on a pound of rice a day. Surveillance aircraft supplied to Somalia were used to strafe dissident villages.[19] What hardline Cold Warriors might have considered doctrinal waywardness was discreetly overlooked. Julius

Nyerere, a champion of 'African Socialism' who insisted that all his policemen were members of his ruling Tanganyika African National Union, accepted $640,000 in police equipment and weaponry from Washington.[20] He also received a substantial arsenal of modern arms from Russia.

Colonel (later Field Marshal) Idi Amin, who seized power from the leftish President Milton Obote in Uganda in 1971 and promised to support capitalism and oppose Communism, was rewarded with six helicopters by the United States and £1 million to strengthen his police force by Britain. Amin had served as an NCO in the King's African Rifles, which recommended him to London, where 'a good African sergeant' was seen as just the man to stamp out Communism.[21] It was soon apparent that Amin's objective was to establish a personal dictatorship based on fear and a campaign of propaganda contrived to convince Ugandans that he embodied the spirit of the nation and alone could decide its destiny. He was as capricious as he was cruel: in 1977 he responded to Anglican criticism of his methods by arresting Eric Sabiti, the Archbishop of Uganda, and two Cabinet ministers, trying them before a kangaroo court and then shooting them. The official version of their deaths was that they had been killed in a road accident. Once it became clear that Amin was Africa's Caligula, Western aid dried up and he turned to the Russians, who gave him $100 million in arms. They too dropped him, exasperated by his utter unreliability.

The Cold War militarised many African police forces and perpetuated those forms of surveillance that had started under colonial rule in the late 1940s as a response to fears of widespread Communist subversion. Single-party states and Caesarean dictators of the Right and Left had even more need of secret policemen than their imperial predecessors since they were under permanent threat of rebellions and military coups. These conditions and the behaviour of those who thrived in them explained why, in the 1960s, when the Royal Shakespeare Company sent a touring party to Africa, *Macbeth* and *Richard III* were the most popular and easily appreciated productions.

IV

Although Machiavelli was proving a better guide to survival in African politics, many looked to Marx for guidance. His analyses and nostrums presented solutions to the continent's economic problems, which were worsening during the 1960s and 1970s. A population explosion which had been under way during the final twenty years of colonial rule was gaining momentum. Rates of life expectancy at birth varied between countries, but the overall trend was upwards. Three examples of life expectancy rates in years illustrate this pattern:

	1880	1940	1960	1980
Mozambique	30	34	43	52
Botswana	33	36	42	66
Somalia	30	34	45	53

Increased food production was imperative, and so too was the need to raise revenues from mineral and cash crops to fund infrastructure, health services and schools. Outside funding was vital, but the processes of procuring investment and loans were fatally skewed by the Cold War. Both sides treated aid as a device to secure allies, and therefore tended not to examine closely how it was spent or on what. Russia peddled the wholesale application of rigid Marxist–Leninist abstractions, although these would overturn traditional production systems which relied on tribal or village units. Nkrumah recognised this incompatibility and, together with Sékou Touré, Léopold Senghor of Senegal and Julius Nyerere of Tanganyika (which became Tanzania after its union with Zanzibar in 1964), preferred a distinctly African version of socialism founded on traditional organisations. Nevertheless, in 1967 Nyerere embarked on a Five Year Plan which included collectivisation, the nationalisation of banks and a command economy.

Kenyatta's forward economic planning for Kenya rested on an 'African socialism' whose roots lay in the 'mutual social responsibility' that was believed to be at the heart of Kenyan village and tribal societies. The population was to be driven by 'the dynamic of hard work and self-reliance', and government would endeavour to guarantee an 'equitable distribution' of wealth. The blueprint for Kenya's version of African socialism admitted that foreign investment was vital for success and treated nationalisation as a last and desperate resort.[22]

Large injections of capital were essential to economic programmes which nationalist politicians had promised would generate growth and prosperity. Credit and loans were widely offered by government agencies, the World Bank, the International Monetary Fund and private banks in the West, and were welcomed by African rulers. The upshot was that sub-Saharan national debts rose over threefold between 1973 and 1980 to over $80 billion. By 1988 the external debt was $165 billion, and by 1990 it had risen to $190 billion. Many countries were stretched to pay the interest, let alone the capital, so that by 1982 arrears totalled $17 billion.

As the extent of the debt imbroglio became clear, the creditors blamed the borrowers. There were allegations of misgovernment, wars, waste and graft, which had led to advances being plundered by crooked dictators and their underlings. Much of this was true: in 1997 the World Bank looked back and regretfully acknowledged that 'assumptions' had been 'too simplistic', which had allowed governments to pursue 'fanciful schemes'. Investors' confidence withered and 'Corruption became endemic, development faltered, and poverty endured.' The monetarist Professor Peter Bauer identified the underlying fault in funding African development as its relationship with the political ambitions of the continent's rulers and the objectives of the West and Russia, which were to secure allies. Bauer argued that what was really needed was a local impetus for growth rooted in individual effort, thrift, legally guaranteed property rights and productive investment. The debtors exculpated themselves with charges that their creditors had been irresponsible to the point of recklessness. Furthermore, they had compounded their follies by hiking up interest rates to claw back as much as possible: the average increased from 4 per cent in 1972 to 10 per cent in 1981.[23]

External and uncontrollable circumstances worsened the problem. Africa was more closely interlocked in the world economy than it had been during the 1930s recession, and so it was far more vulnerable to its successor in the 1970s. This was triggered by the decision taken in October 1973 by OPEC (Organisation of the Petroleum Exporting Countries) to quadruple the price of crude oil. A global economic crisis followed which dragged on into the early 1980s.* Share values plummeted, commodity prices briefly rose and then fell sharply, which hurt African states dependent upon such staples as coffee, cocoa and sugar. Cotton production in Chad was halved as export markets shrank and

---

* Its members were chiefly Arab states but included Algeria, Libya and Nigeria.

per capita income fell.[24] Nigeria was far better placed, thanks to its nascent oil industry. Oil exports soared from $10 billion in 1976 to $80 billion in 1980, and yearly income rose accordingly from $600 to $900. The demand for oil suddenly dropped, and so did living standards. Countries squeezed by debts, interest payments and dwindling markets were compelled to cut budgets for education and health care.

V

Economic stresses generated political crises. Conventional politicians who had promised much were discredited, and power slipped from their grasp to be snatched by professional soldiers. As early as 1959, State Department officials had foretold the imminent collapse of 'democratic' Africa. Newly independent states would become devilled by corruption, inefficiency and 'political bickering' which would lead to military coups. A year before, General Ibrahim Abboud, the commander-in-chief of the Sudanese army, had seized power and declared himself an opponent of Communism and of his neighbour, Nasser, which was to America's 'advantage'. Similar putsches could be expected and it was in the best interests of America to work with the new autocratic regimes and encourage them to foster economic development.[25] Authoritarian Russia took the same brutally realistic view as democratic America.

The State Department's forecasts had been correct. Power soon gravitated towards a breed of middle-ranking officers who posed as national saviours who would rescue their nations from self-serving politicians. Armies, trained by the colonial powers and loyal to their commanders, became Africa's praetorian guard. From 1960 onwards, coups, often little more than palace revolutions, brought to power Joseph-Désiré Mobutu in the Congo, Muammar Gaddafi in Libya, Idi Amin in Uganda, Major-General Siad Barre in Somalia, Jean-Bédel Bokassa in the Central African Republic (formerly French Equatorial Africa) and Colonel Mengistu Haile Mariam in Ethiopia. Bokassa, who suffered from a Napoleon fixation, spent $20 million on a kitsch coronation ceremony in which he crowned himself Emperor of Central Africa. Venal and vicious, he was a good friend to French interests and, when he was unseated in 1979, his sponsors allowed him to retire to a chateau near Paris.[26] Nepotism was rife in these military regimes:

Amin's nephew ran Uganda's security machine and Barre's son-in-law was in charge of Somalia's external intelligence services.

Mengistu was Russia's pawn, and a vital piece in an ambitious Soviet plan to unite Ethiopia with its puppet regime in Somalia to create an East African satellite which would provide naval bases in the Red Sea and Indian Ocean. The way was opened in 1974, when America's client the Emperor Haile Selassie was deposed in a military coup and later murdered. His successor was the Derg, a cabal of army officers from which the Marxist Mengistu emerged as leader in 1974. He national-ised banks, businesses, imposed agrarian collectivisation, placed food distribution in the hands of the state and crushed all opposition. Russia lent a hand by placing 2 billion roubles at his disposal, most of which had to be written off a decade or so later.[27]

Ethiopia's upheavals were Somalia's opportunity to reconquer its southern province, the Ogaden, which had been lost to its neighbour eighty years before. In July 1977, President Barre defied his Soviet masters and invaded south-eastern Ethiopia. Somali MiG-21s strafed Ethiopian and later Cuban soldiers armed with Kalashnikovs in a gro-tesque war which demonstrated the perils of patronising uniformed despots. Hurried shipments of Russian weaponry and Cuban mercen-aries turned the tide, and the Somalis fell back. Disowned by Russia, Barre found a new and accommodating friend in the United States.

Ethiopia's misfortunes continued. The north suffered a severe famine in 1984 that was alleviated by Western assistance, which contrasted in scale to the meagre offerings from Russia. Within a year, the new General Secretary of the Politburo, Mikhail Gorbachev, had begun a radical reordering of the arthritic Soviet system and initiated a for-eign policy of rapprochement with the West that would end the Cold War. Détente included Russia's gradual disentanglement from Africa: old allies were abandoned, those engaged in proxy wars were urged to make peace, and Russia reluctantly agreed to write off between 40 and 50 per cent of debts owed by its clients.

26

'Maelstrom':
The Congo and Rhodesia

I

During the summer of 1959, the British Prime Minister, Harold Macmillan, was brooding over the future of Africa. The affairs of the continent seemed delicately balanced: nationalist movements were gathering a powerful head of steam and, in principle, the British and French governments were committed to granting independence to their African colonies. Whether this process would go ahead smoothly was a matter of doubt, and events in Algeria were a chilling example of what could go wrong. Macmillan was pessimistic: 'Africa may become no longer a source of pride or profit to the Europeans who have developed it, but a maelstrom into which all of us will be sucked.'[1] In January 1960 the Prime Minister began a tour of British Africa which ended in South Africa, where he distilled his experiences in a speech that ended with a prophecy: 'The wind of change is blowing throughout this continent, and, whether we like it or not, this growth of national consciousness is a political fact. We must accept it as a fact, and our national policies must take account of it.'

Macmillan's words and the warning implicit in them went unheeded in Belgium, where half-hearted and fumbling efforts were being made to prepare the Congo for independence. The deadline was set for the last week in June, and the result was the maelstrom that Macmillan had dreaded. The Republic of the Congo imploded during the first fortnight of its existence and its disintegration immediately drew in the United States and Russia, who hurried to enlist local clients and stake their claims to a country whose southern province, Katanga, supplied nearly all the world's industrial diamonds and a substantial portion of its cobalt, copper and uranium. The crisis that followed was on two levels: there was a brief Cold War confrontation, and afterwards a longer and complex struggle for mastery of the Congo fought by local strong men, their armies and, behind the scenes, their foreign backers.

Belgium had parted from its former subjects on bad terms and the independence day celebrations were a fiasco. On 30 June 1960, King Baudouin formally handed over power in Léopoldville with a speech of breathtaking crassness. The descendant of the infamous Leopold II told the crowds that they should be eternally grateful to Belgium for rescuing them from slavery and giving them the blessings of civilisation. The new Prime Minister, Patrice Lumumba, could not contain his fury. 'We are your monkeys no more,' he raged, 'we have experienced contempt, insults and blows.' Soon his country 'would show the world . . . what the black man can do when he is allowed to work in freedom and we shall make the Congo a shining example for the whole of Africa'.² The king hurried off, mislaying his sword as he went.

Thereafter it was downhill all the way. Four days later the 25,000-strong Congolese army mutinied, raping and killing Europeans and plundering their property. An exodus followed: within a fortnight one-third of the Congo's 600 European doctors had fled.³ Many refugees escaped southwards and reached Southern Rhodesia, where their harrowing tales of atrocities scared a white population already uneasy about the possibility of African rule.⁴

On 11 July Katanga, the Congo's richest province, seceded and declared independence under the leadership of Moïse Tshombe, a nationalist politician who enjoyed the open support of Belgium. At this stage the UN intervened, primarily to restore order and police the country, but also to forestall a clash between America and Russia. Twenty thousand UN soldiers were sent, two-fifths of them from Afro-Asian countries. In a phone conversation with the British representative at the UN, its Secretary-General, Dag Hammarskjöld, confided that the Congo had ceased to function as a nation. The blame, he thought, lay with Lumumba, who was 'a very unsatisfactory figure and playing unscrupulously for high stakes'.⁵

From the beginning of the troubles, Lumumba had been at his wits' end to find a way out that might somehow preserve his government and his country's integrity. As Belgian troops were flown in to help evacuate stranded civilians, he threatened to confiscate all Belgian property and assets. This confirmed the State Department's distrust of Lumumba, who was seen as a demagogue, a socialist and a potential

Russian puppet and whom Secretary of State John Foster Dulles feared was 'another Castro or worse'.[6]

Khrushchev agreed, but for opposite reasons. He welcomed the Congo's misfortunes as an opportunity to extend his policy of penetrating Africa and turning the country into another Egypt. Like Nasser, Lumumba could be lured into Russia's camp, but first he needed the sinews of power. Khrushchev ordered an airlift (via Egypt and Ghana) of arms, trucks and crated warplanes to the Congo. Lumumba was given 2.5 billion roubles and a contingent of Eastern bloc pilots and technical advisers. Their arrival prompted Hammarskjöld to warn the British Ambassador in Léopoldville that, if Lumumba remained in power, the 'communisation of the Congo' would be unstoppable.[7] A week later, on 14 September, a Russian bomber attacked targets in Katanga.[8]

Katanga and its minerals were always the prize. America was its principal customer, with imports that had totalled $200 million in the past year, and Wall Street banks were investing heavily in its mines. Such an asset could never be allowed to pass into the hands of Lumumba and his Soviet backers. This possibility alarmed the State Department, whose analysts already regarded the spreading anarchy in the Congo as conducive to some sort of Communist coup.

To save Katanga for the West, it was first necessary to remove Lumumba. Plans were laid in Washington for his murder by 'biological toxins' and an assassin turned up in Léopoldville with a tube of poisoned toothpaste.[9] His skills were not needed, for on 14 September Colonel Joseph-Désiré Mobutu mounted a coup d'état which unseated the Prime Minister. Army loyalty was secured by payments from the ample war chest of Lawrence Devlin, the CIA's head of station in Léopoldville, and $400,000 delivered by the Belgians.[10] With back wages paid and their future incomes secured, the soldiers rallied behind Mobutu, the man who had made this possible.

At a stroke, Mobutu solved America's problems. Within a few days of taking over Léopoldville, the Colonel closed the Soviet embassy and expelled all Eastern bloc advisers. As a public demonstration of the new dispensation of power, Mobutu ordered the mock execution of the senior KGB man in the capital. Khrushchev had been checkmated and he was furious. 'I spit on the UN' he ranted, and he railed against Hammarskjöld as an agent of American imperialism.[11] Yet his nemesis had been Mobutu who, like Lumumba, had been mission-educated and, like Idi Amin, a former sergeant-major. Henceforward the Colonel (soon to be General) was America's man, although the State Department judged him to be 'childish and easily bought off'.[12] He was indeed eminently corruptible, but Mobutu was also a ruthless chancer with finely tuned political antennae.

II

The events of July and August 1960 had left the Belgian people stunned and mystified. They had been immensely proud of what they had imagined to be a model colony humanely run by 10,000 white administrators. Most important of all, for a small country with thin resources, the Congo had made Belgium rich. Here lay the root of the present crisis, according to Sir John Nicholls, the British Ambassador in Brussels. He told the Foreign Office that it was the insidious, money-making spirit of Leopold II which had persuaded the Belgians to treat the Congo as a business. There had been little preparation for independence, which had left the new state without enough trained and experienced Africans to run the government; there were only 200 Congolese graduates in 1960.[13] Nicholls wondered whether this neglect had been deliberate so as to compel the Congolese to continue to rely on Belgian civil servants. He concluded: 'The loss of the Congo may in the end prove salutary if it jolts them out of the softness induced by easy living.'[14]

Nicholls's analysis chimed with the remarks of Tshombe, made in a conversation with British diplomats early in 1961. Belgium had never cultivated a sense of unity and nationhood in the colony, which was home to 200 tribes and over 300 languages. Soldiers' loyalties were tribal rather than to their officers or the state.[15] Fragmentation had been the inevitable result of Belgian motives and policy.

The funds for 'easy living' had flowed into Belgium through the Société Générale de Belgique. This powerful bank controlled 70 per cent of the Congo's income, nearly all of which was generated by the Katangese mines controlled by the Union Minière du Haut Katanga. In 1959 it had paid $45 million, which made it the mainstay of the Congo's economy. This was why Lumumba was desperate to recover Katanga even if the price was subordination to the Soviet Union, although he hoped the UN forces would retake the province. Whoever attempted the task faced a hard fight, for Tshombe had Belgian funds, a cadre of Belgian officers and, thanks to his anti-Communist credentials, furtive American backing. His patrons made him an honorary white by admitting him to the racially exclusive Cercle Albert Club of Elisabethville.[16]

It took five years of fighting to reunite the Congo. Lumumba was one the first casualties: he was arrested by Mobutu's soldiers, flown to Katanga, beaten and then shot in January 1961 by a Katangese firing squad commanded by a Belgian officer. Almost immediately after Lumumba's imprisonment, his followers had rallied in Stanleyville under Antoine Gizenga. He looked to Russia for help and received $500,000, an airlift of weapons flown via Khartoum, and a unit of Czech specialists in guerrilla warfare.[17] Despite Soviet help, the breakaway state was defeated by the Congolese army and Khrushchev took no further interest in the region.

Katanga fell to the Congolese army, stiffened by UN forces, and was reintegrated with the rest of the Congo in 1963. The retaking of Katanga had been strongly urged by Hammarskjöld, who died in a plane crash close to Ndola airport in Northern Rhodesia in September 1961. Afterwards there were allegations that his plane had been shot down at the instigation of those who stood to gain from Katanga's independence. Anxieties on this score were removed by Mobutu, who was pro-Western and pro-capitalist; in May 1963 he visited Washington and was entertained in the White House, where he was warmly greeted by President Kennedy, who saluted him as the man who rescued the Congo from Communism. In 1965 this national saviour made himself President and remained in power for the next thirty-two years; his critics alleged that he had accumulated a fortune equal to his country's foreign debts.

Stability proved elusive, for in the summer of 1964 there was a widespread insurrection across the eastern Congo by masses of restless and alienated young men who called themselves 'Simbas' (Lions) and, insofar as they had a defined ideology, it was nihilistic and leftish. One observer detected an affinity with contemporary American campus dropouts and called them 'bush beatniks'. Their movement attracted the peripatetic revolutionary and universal icon of the disaffected young, Che Guevara, who spent some frustrating months trying to organise the Simbas. His difficulties were enormous, for an American journalist described them as a 'loose agglomeration of tribal bands, often armed with only machetes, spears and wooden clubs' and led by 'witch doctors' who handed out 'anti-bullet pills' and urged celibacy.[18] The uprising was overcome by better-equipped Congolese troops and a band of white mercenaries who made headlines in November 1965 by the dramatic rescue of several thousand hostages trapped in Stanleyville, the Simbas' stronghold. Meanwhile, another primarily tribal conflict spluttered on in Rwanda between the Hutu and the Tutsi and would continue to do so until the close of the century. Before the Congo's independence, Rwanda had been governed by Belgium, under a League of Nations mandate that had been renewed by the UN in 1945. Like the Congo, it was utterly unready for self-government.

Mercenaries were invaluable to all sides in the Congo's wars, which had repeatedly shown that local forces suffered from low morale and inadequate training. According to the British Military Attaché, one engagement in Rwanda in 1967 was an extended brawl between government soldiers 'filled with drink and dope' and commanded by officers who skulked in the rear. They were 'shot down in heaps' by white mercenaries and Katangese, who were also 'drunken and undisciplined'.[19]

III

The presence of Rhodesian mercenaries in the Congo was a reminder of the increasingly dangerous situation in Northern and Southern Rhodesia, where the white minorities were opposed to Whitehall's plans for future independence. Macmillan privately feared that Kenyan independence, scheduled for 1964, might lead to another Congo with a recrudescence of the Mau Mau uprising.[20] For European settlers in Southern and Northern Rhodesia, the Congo's catastrophes confirmed fears that Africans were unfit to govern themselves. Some Rhodesians, including Sir Roy Welensky, a Southern Rhodesian MP and the future Prime Minister of the Central African Federation, were keen to throw in their lot with potentially stable and prosperous Katanga. Rhodesian mercenaries fought in the Katangese army; there were allegations that the Northern Rhodesian government was turning a blind eye to gun-running and that a Southern Rhodesian air force plane had bombed UN forces.[21]

Within Britain, the mayhem in the Congo confirmed right-wing predictions that premature independence for her African colonies would lead to administrative collapse and tribal violence. In August 1960 a *Spectator* article summed up their nightmares. What was occurring in the Congo was the result of a hundred or so 'little men, mostly unprincipled opportunists, failures in their previous occupations, whose chief talent was the ability to raise a local following by mass hysteria'.[22] A hundred or so Tory backbenchers shared these feelings, which were frequently aired in the *Daily Telegraph* and the *Daily Express*.

Yet putting a brake on progress towards self-government was equally perilous. Proof of this was the Algerian War, and, during the 1959 Commons debate on colonial policy, Conservative and Labour MPs agreed that it was a warning of what could follow the rejection of nationalist demands.[23] Wars of colonial repression found little favour with an electorate that had been brought up to believe that imperial government was benevolent and dedicated to the physical, moral and political improvement of its subjects. Public opinion had accepted national servicemen risking their lives to prevent a Communist takeover of Malaya and to rid Kenya of the sorcery and brutality of the Mau Mau. Whether there would be backing for bush wars in Northern and Southern Rhodesia to uphold white supremacy was another matter.

Since the early 1950s successive Tory governments had pursued decolonisation policies designed to avoid confrontation. Britain would gently steer its African colonies towards independence and create sovereign states which, it fervently hoped, would be capitalist democracies within the Commonwealth 'family'. Achieving this goal involved coming to terms with local nationalist politicians such as Nkrumah and securing their cooperation. The pace of the transition would be a canter and the finishing post would be reached during the early 1970s. Accommodations with new elites meant that old ones were sidelined or abandoned altogether. This was distasteful for the Colonial Secretary Oliver Lyttelton who, in 1953, contrasted the pushy Nigerian politicians with the aristocratic manners and demeanour of the Nigerian princes, who had not been contaminated by 'democracy and the *Daily Mirror*'.[24]

Lyttelton had been in the midst of negotiations for the formation of a Nigerian federation. It was accepted in both London and Washington that federal systems were the solution to the problems of smaller or economically unviable colonies. The prospects of success were good in those colonies with a black population such as Nigeria, but far less so in

Kenya, Southern and Northern Rhodesia where there were white minorities. Nevertheless, in 1953 the British government corralled the two Rhodesias and Nyasaland into the Central African Federation which, if carefully managed, would evolve into a democracy in which Europeans and Africans worked together in harmony. Sir Roy Welensky saw the Federation's white population as 'senior' partners in this enterprise who would 'guide' the black majority towards political responsibility.[25] Oddly for a white African politician, his background was working-class and he had been a trade union organiser and, in his youth, a prizefighter. His paternalism was blended with a sturdy patriotism that was common across the white community; a fellow MP described the Rhodesians as 'protecting the British way of life and civilisation'.[26]

Lofty sentiments in Salisbury and London could not hide the fact that the Federation was a non-starter based on incompatible objectives. The British government repeatedly insisted that at some future, unspecified date there would be universal suffrage. Black nationalists were unconvinced: for them, the Federation was an arrangement that would perpetuate white supremacy and pave the way for an apartheid regime like that recently established in South Africa. The franchise rested on property ownership, income and education, which effectively excluded all but a small proportion of Africans. In Southern Rhodesia, more than half the white population of 223,000 could vote in parliamentary elections and 9,000 of the 2.8 million blacks. The imbalance was even more pronounced in Northern Rhodesia, where there were 19,000 white voters and less than 700 black, and in Nyasaland, where white electors outnumbered black by 2,200 to twenty-eight. Given the vast gap in income (white Southern Rhodesians earned on average £1,100 a year and blacks £80), this political disparity was unlikely to change significantly for generations.

In Britain, one-man-one-vote represented natural justice; for most Rhodesians it was anathema that would overturn their world, jeopardise their land and jobs and place their lives in the hands of Communist demagogues. The Congo crisis and the steady growth of the African National Congress added to white apprehensions. In the early days of the Federation, Welensky was anxious about subversion, police loyalty and Africans buying modern firearms.[27]

Shadowy anxieties assumed a terrifying substance in March 1959 with what with hindsight can be called 'The Great Nyasaland Scare'.

The local branch of MI5 convinced themselves that they had uncovered a plot by local black leaders to massacre officials and take over the government. Contagious panic followed, during which the Governor declared a state of emergency and detained over 1,000 suspects, including Dr Hastings Banda, the local African National Congress leader. Protests and riots followed and twenty-five demonstrators were shot. A subsequent inquiry by Lord Devlin, a senior English judge, concluded that Nyasaland had been transformed into a 'police state' for the flimsiest of reasons.[28] Macmillan was dumbfounded and privately dismissed Devlin's findings as perverse and shaped by his Catholic Irish ancestry.

While the administration of Nyasaland was crying wolf, the 7th Duke of Montrose was explaining to the House of Lords why the white population there and elsewhere in the Federation were so fearful. He had settled as a farmer in Rhodesia after the war and he began his speech by declaring himself to be a Rhodesian. His experiences, he imagined, had given him a 'pretty good insight' into the black mind and he assured his listeners that Africans were loyal, trustworthy creatures at heart, but 'sitting ducks' for agitators. 'With the right amount of beer, the right amount of tom-tom beating, the right amount of witchcraft and intimidation, the right amount of inflammatory speech', these otherwise contented people could be 'whipped up to committing acts of violence'.[29] After the bloodshed, they would return to their normal passivity.

In his characteristic bluff manner, the Duke had summed up the feelings of many of his fellow whites: they understood the nature of the African, and Iain Macleod, the new Colonial Secretary, and his officials did not. In the meantime, Rhodesia gave proof of its attachment to Britain: in 1962 the Rhodesian air force and SAS showed 'great enthusiasm' during training exercises in Aden, where Britain was fighting a guerrilla war against Arab nationalists. The Foreign Office hoped that news of their activities did not leak out, for fear of offending African opinion.[30]

Montrose's overripe pleading had been one episode in the tortuous contest in which the British government attempted to persuade African and European leaders that the imperfections of the Central African Federation could be ironed out. Ministers, civil servants and black and white politicians flew to and fro between London and the Federation capitals to negotiate, and an official inquiry listened to anyone with an opinion. These efforts came to nothing, for the well-gnawed bone of contention remained: the whites refused to accept universal suffrage and the Africans would not settle for anything less. Preserving the Federation by coercion was out of the question, as Macmillan made clear to Welensky in 1962: 'I cannot guarantee that British troops would undertake the kind of duties that would be necessary.'[31]

In the summer of 1963 Britain finally conceded that the Federation had failed. It was dissolved and during the following year Northern Rhodesia gained its independence as Zambia, and Nyasaland as Malawi. These states joined the Commonwealth and their rulers, Kenneth Kaunda and Dr Banda, were considered politically reliable by the Colonial Office and MI5. Rather than become too closely embroiled with America or Russia, Kaunda looked to China for assistance. Chinese capital paid for, and Chinese engineers constructed, the Lusaka to Dar-es-Salaam railway. Work began in 1969 and took seven years; Zambian copper exports no longer relied on lines that passed through Rhodesia and South Africa.

The cleavage between Britain and Rhodesia widened between 1964 and 1966. Power passed into the hands of a new party, the Rhodesian Front, under the leadership of Ian Smith. He continued to prevaricate over majority rule while integrating Rhodesia into a bloc of like-minded neighbours, South Africa and the Portuguese colonies of Angola and Mozambique. Rhodesia's outlets to the sea were guaranteed and it would be part of an unwritten alliance dedicated to stemming the tide of African nationalism south of the Zambezi. Each partner was already engaged in what were still relatively small-scale wars against guerrillas who were being supported by the Soviet Union. The Russian connection meant that Rhodesia, South Africa and Portugal could appeal to the West for diplomatic support and weapons.

In November 1965 Smith took the plunge and declared Rhodesia independent. It was a gamble: Harold Wilson's recently elected Labour government was hostile but, mistakenly as it turned out, Smith thought that British public opinion was wholeheartedly on his side. He played the 'kith-and-kin' card and portrayed the Rhodesians as stalwart patriots who had stood by Britain during the war, in which he had been a fighter pilot. He misjudged the mood of contemporary Britain with its Beatlemania, satirical irreverence, frivolous and flamboyant fashions and unprecedented prosperity. The typical Rhodesian lived in another world, which the satirist Gerald Scarfe portrayed as a sort of suburbia in the tropics.

A British opinion poll taken at the end of 1966 revealed that 49 per cent of those questioned upheld the principle of one-man-one-vote in southern Africa and that 58 per cent favoured Rhodesian independence so long as Smith backed progressive measures. Only a third took the Rhodesian view that Africans were incapable of running the country for at least twenty years.[32] The Rhodesian imbroglio was soon seen as a tiresome distraction from more pressing issues such as a costive economy and entry into the Common Market.

Like Macmillan, Wilson was determined not to use force to impose Britain's will on Central Africa and so he turned to the UN for help in imposing economic sanctions on the renegade Rhodesia. Warships were, however, dispatched to the waters off Mozambique to intercept tankers carrying oil to Rhodesia. It was soon clear that there were plenty of countries willing to trade with Rhodesia and find ingenious ways around the sanctions. In 1967, ten Italian civilian aircraft reached Rhodesia via South Africa which the manufacturers believed were destined for local use.[33]

Rhodesia would soon need all the aircraft it could get. In 1962 the Rhodesian African nationalist leader Joshua Nkomo had secretly approached the Soviet Union with a request for explosives, arms and wireless sets for a campaign of sabotage and terrorism.[34] The response had been tepid. Russia's attitude changed once it was clear that the strongholds of white dominance in southern Africa were under attack by nationalist partisans. The opportunity was too good to be missed, and the Soviet Union moved in to help the insurgents and open a new Cold War front.

27

'They have left us in the lurch':
The Last Days of White Africa

⸻

I

It took over thirty years of intermittent wars to overthrow white supremacy in southern Africa. The struggle began in 1961 with an uprising against the Portuguese in northern Angola and ended in 1990, when the South African Prime Minister F. W. de Klerk opened negotiations with Nelson Mandela. The wars were waged on two levels. The first was a test of will and endurance in which conventional armies with air support engaged mobile guerrillas in a war of raids, skirmishes and ambushes across thousands of square miles of desert and bush. All sides used terror to secure popular support. The second level was an international contest of diplomatic dissembling and intelligence skulduggery that sometimes reads like the scenario of a Cold War thriller in which loyalties are transitory and nothing is as it seems.

The combatants were the guerrillas of the liberation movements of Mozambique, Angola, Rhodesia, South-West Africa (Namibia) and South Africa and the armies and air forces of Portugal, Rhodesia and South Africa. The latter three enjoyed a theoretical preponderance of firepower, but the insurgents had plenty of modern weapons, including anti-aircraft missiles, and latterly tanks and a few warplanes. This armoury was largely provided by Russia, for the struggle for mastery over southern Africa offered rich Cold War dividends. The United States too pumped money and arms into what Portugal and South Africa repeatedly insisted were campaigns to contain and then uproot Communism, and protect millions of dollars of American investment. This was true insofar as the nationalist leaderships expressed socialist sentiments, although, as elsewhere in Africa, they were prone to a regrettable indifference to Marxist–Leninist theories.

II

Angola and Mozambique were relics of Portuguese maritime expansion in the late fifteenth and early sixteenth centuries. Portugal's poverty and backwardness coupled with official inertia impeded progress in colonies that existed solely for the enrichment of the mother country. Life expectancy and literacy levels were among the lowest in Africa. From 1932 Portugal had been ruled by the reactionary dictator António Salazar, whose colonial policies followed the traditional blend of repression and exploitation. He encouraged Portugal's abundant poor to emigrate to the colonies, particularly Angola, which exacerbated racial tensions as the immigrants competed with blacks and mulattos for unskilled and semi-skilled jobs.[1] By 1960 Angola's population stood at nearly 5 million, of whom 320,000 were white and 60,000 were mulattos. The colony was enjoying an unprecedented prosperity, for it had become the world's fourth-largest exporter of coffee, and oil and iron ore production were increasing.

So too was dissatisfaction with Portugal's sterile and oppressive rule. In Mozambique the nationalist movement FRELIMO (Front for the Liberation of Mozambique) was a cohesive and tightly disciplined force with Soviet backing. By contrast, the liberation movement in Angola was divided into three mutually hostile factions: the Popular Movement for the Liberation of Angola (MPLA), the National Front for the Liberation of Angola (FNLA) and the National Union for the Total Independence of Angola (UNITA). The MPLA welcomed support from all races and tribes, although depending heavily on the Ambundu (or nothern Mbundu). Its leader, Agostinho Neto, was a taciturn intellectual whose unassuming manner masked a steely will and canny political instincts. The Portuguese rated him their toughest adversary and the Russians were frequently frustrated by his ideological deviancy. The FNLA was led by Holden Roberto, was hostile to whites and mulattos, recruited from the Bakongo tribes and was susceptible to American and South African manipulation.

UNITA's membership came largely from the Ovimbundu and its leader, Jonas Savimbi, was an able general and an egotistical and cynical chancer. When it suited him he covertly supplied intelligence on MPLA bases to the Portuguese, and afterwards he flirted with the South Africans, who provided him with white officers to train his partisans in camps in Namibia. Discretion required that the instructors darkened their faces with 'Black is Beautiful' face cream. Despite his anti-Communist credentials, the CIA summed up Savimbi as representing 'the very worst of black African nationalism'.[2] Nonetheless, he had his uses.

The Angolan War opened with savage attacks on white settlements and a ferocious counter-terror in which 20,000 Africans were slaughtered. The authorities blamed Protestant missionaries for implanting seditious ideas, or, as President Nkrumah put it, 'for daring to interpret the Bible in non-Fascist ways'.[3] Large numbers of Protestant clergy, including American Methodists, were gaoled and seventeen were killed. The Soviet Union adopted the MPLA, initially offered Neto a paltry $25,000 and, as the war progressed, provided training for 7,000 of his partisans. Some may have been among the guerrillas who were filmed by a Russian television unit as they assaulted a Portuguese position. The footage did not thrill senior Soviet officers, who were warning that local 'inter-tribal contradictions' hindered the efficiency of the guerrillas, whose numbers were falling.[4] Others in the higher reaches of the Soviet hierarchy complained that Russia was gambling recklessly in supporting inefficient and bickering partisans across southern Africa, including the MPLA.

Russian involvement proved to be a trump card for the Portuguese government. Although it was a dictatorship, Portugal had been admitted to NATO in 1949, and found it easy to convince its allies, in particular the United States, to treat its African wars as part of the global anti-Communist struggle. An equally persuasive consideration was America's South Atlantic naval and air base on the Portuguese Azores. Its strategic importance was stressed by Dean Rusk, the American Secretary of State, during a meeting with his French and British counterparts in Paris in August 1962. He also remarked that the free use of Portuguese territories for deploying forces in the Indian Ocean was valuable to NATO.[5] Again Cold War priorities overruled all other considerations, and so French-manufactured armoured cars, German-made napalm and American defoliants were deployed in Angola and Mozambique.[6]

NATO's arsenal equipped the 200,000 Portuguese conscripts who fought the eight-year war to retain Portugal's colonies. As in the United States, then embroiled in Vietnam, many young men evaded the draft, some fleeing abroad. Neither the Portuguese nor the insurgent forces of the four national movements managed to gain the upper hand, and the outcome was finally decided by events inside Portugal. Salazar died in 1970 and was succeeded by Marcelo Caetano, who was unseated by a military coup in April 1974. Among other things, the soldiers wanted an end to unwinnable wars in Africa and, in July, the provisional government announced that Portugal would withdraw from all its colonies, a decision that was endorsed by the leftist ministry elected the following year. Close on the heels of the returning soldiers came 300,000 Portuguese colonists, businessmen and civil servants.

III

By throwing in the sponge, Portugal had transformed the political geography of the region, tilted the balance of power against Rhodesia and South Africa and opened a new phase in the struggle for regional supremacy. Hitherto, Angola and Mozambique had served as a defensive glacis protecting Rhodesia and South Africa and Namibia. Throughout the Angolan and Mozambique campaigns, the insurgents had relied on neighbouring Tanzania and Zambia for refugee sanctuaries and training camps. Henceforward, Angola and Mozambique provided the same facilities for Rhodesian guerrillas, South Africa's ANC and Namibia's SWAPO (South-West Africa People's Organisation). South Africa could not afford to lose Namibia, whose exports annually yielded $250 million and which had replaced Angola as a buffer against armed African nationalism.

Angola was also the weakest link in the axis of southern Africa's black states. Portugal's exodus had been followed by a friable and mutually suspicious coalition of the MPLA, UNITA and the FNLA. In August 1975 UNITA declared war on the government, followed by the far weaker FNLA. President Nixon's Secretary of State Henry Kissinger had already identified the MPLA as Communist and agreed to cooperate with South Africa and UNITA in an underground war to destabilise Angola and overthrow Neto.[7] The war for the Portuguese succession had begun; it would drag on for the next twenty-seven years.

America's decision to fight a proxy war in Angola provided the welcome opportunity for President Fidel Castro to enter the conflict. His motives were altruistic and ideological, since Cuba had little to gain from the extinction of the remaining white regimes in Africa. What seemed a Quixotic gesture was, for Castro, the fulfilment of Cuba's historic destiny as the champion of liberation movements across the Third World. Over the past seventy years, Cubans had toppled their Spanish masters and then overturned America's puppet tyrant, Batista. In 1961 Cuban forces had repelled an American-sponsored invasion by former Batista supporters at the Bay of Pigs. Cuba's history and spirit qualified it as the natural champion of the world's oppressed masses against imperialism and its mainspring, capitalism. Or, in Castro's words, the global 'conflict between privileged and under-privileged humanity'. As for Angola, his representative in Luanda, Jorge Risquet, later declared that the new nation was 'the pillar in the struggle against the racists'. 'The imperialists must know', he continued, 'what Angola is doing for Zimbabwe [Rhodesia], what Angola is doing for Namibia, what Angola is doing for South Africa.'[8] The ultimate objective was the extinction of what Castro called the 'Fascist–Racist' regime in South Africa.[9]

During 1974 and 1975 36,000 Cuban soldiers backed by artillery, anti-aircraft missiles and elderly Russian tanks had arrived in Angola, together with humanitarian assistance. Cuban forces fought UNITA and FNLA units and the South African army, and supervised train-ing camps for Rhodesian and Namibian guerrillas. Over the next ten years, Castro's well-equipped troops more than held in check Angola's internal and external enemies while Cuban civilians replaced Portu-guese administrators, doctors and teachers. Russia footed most of the bill, but not without misgivings. Aggressive gambits in southern Africa could jeopardise the new policy of détente with the United States, and Castro's previous knight-errantry in Central and South America had failed to weaken America's grip over the region.

Neto remained a prickly and wayward partner, although during his 1976 visit to Moscow he had conceded Russia a naval base at Luanda. Nonetheless, the KGB thought it prudent to place a female agent among his senior staff, who, it was hoped, would persuade him to look more favourably on his patrons. Her usefulness ceased after she was arrested for involvement in a plot hatched in May 1977 to replace Neto with the biddable Marxist Interior Minister, Nito Alves. Cuban troops thwarted Alves's coup, which added to tensions with Russia.[10] It was the moment for Neto to hedge his bets, and during 1978 he began to take tentative steps towards the West. In the following year he flew to Havana and asked for the gradual reduction of Cuban forces in Angola. Cuba, now committed to aiding Rhodesian and Namibian partisans, was sympathetic. Yet her mostly reservist soldiers were becoming overstretched in Africa, which increased the vulnerability of the homeland to a further invasion by the United States, ninety miles away.

Neto died in September 1979, and soon afterwards his successor, José Eduardo Dos Santos, made approaches to the newly elected Reagan administration. The upshot was an impasse: the United States wanted the Cubans out while Dos Santos was suspicious of America's backing for his most formidable enemy, South Africa.

South Africa treated Angola as a hostile state. Its borders were porous and impossible to police, which allowed Rhodesian and Namibian guerrillas to come and go as they pleased and establish refugee camps and training bases. These became targets for raids by Rhodesian and South African ground and air forces. In May 1978 South African aircraft bombed and strafed a SWAPO camp at Cassinga, 150 miles inside Angola, prior to an assault by parachutists. They were driven off by Cuban units backed by obsolescent Russian tanks, and the South Africans suffered a bloody nose and a blow to their reputation for invincibility. Six hundred Namibian refugees, including women and children, were killed.

There was international outrage, although interestingly the Western press quickly dropped the story. The United States had secretly encouraged such raids but, when faced with photographs of civilian corpses, denied involvement. The South African Defence Minister angrily claimed that 'they have left us in the lurch'.[11] America was in a quandary: at his inauguration in 1977 President Jimmy Carter upheld the right of Africans to fight for their liberty and independence, but he and his advisers remained fearful that their struggles would prove to be a breeding ground for Communism. Washington, therefore, was prepared to cut cards with two devils, Savimbi and South Africa.

IV

Meanwhile, Rhodesia's efforts to suppress nationalist insurgencies were opening another Cold War front. Since 1975 independent Angola and Mozambique had been providing bases for Rhodesia's two partisan armies, the forces of Joshua Nkomo's ZAPU (Zimbabwe African People's Union) and Robert Mugabe's ZANU (Zimbabwe African National Union). As in Angola, each party had strong tribal affiliations: ZAPU drew strength from the Ndebele and ZANU from the Shona. Both aimed to overturn Ian Smith's Rhodesian Front government and end white minority rule by force, but disagreed over strategy. Mugabe pinned his faith in a bush war of attrition that would slowly undermine their opponent's morale and will. Nkomo favoured Fabian tactics: ZAPU would gradually create a large Soviet- and Cuban-trained and equipped army in bases in Zambia and Angola. When it was strong enough, this uniformed and disciplined army would engage in a conventional war in which Russian ground-to-air missiles would eliminate Rhodesian aerial superiority. Two of these weapons were used to shoot down two Rhodesian civilian airliners in 1978 and 1979.

The guerrillas' external training camps were vulnerable to air raids and surprise hit-and-run attacks by Rhodesian ground forces. They attacked ZANU's training facilities at Nyadzonya in Mozambique in 1976, inflicting heavy casualties, and in 1979 the Rhodesian air force bombed the Cuban-run ZAPU camp at Boma in eastern Angola which, over the past two years, had trained over 6,000 guerrillas. At the same time, the guerrillas began a campaign of urban bombing and mining roads to reduce the mobility of Rhodesian troops.

A specialist unit, the Selous Scouts, had played a key part in the Nyadzonya raid. They had been named after the big-game hunter and hero of the Matabele Wars, Frederick Selous. From the start, Rhodesians had had to fight for their existence and the land originally conquered by Selous and his kind. Their exertions and sacrifices were annually celebrated on the anniversary of the hoisting of the Union Jack over Bulawayo in 1890. Past victories stiffened the will to fight on, and Smith revealingly praised his armed forces as equal in spirit and grit to those of another embattled state, Israel. Yet he also cited the historic Rhodesian willingness to compromise, which had been shown by Rhodes's readiness to negotiate with the Ndebele. So throughout the war, Smith endeavoured to come to terms with Britain and the United States as well as seeking help and guidance from his only ally, South Africa.

The Conservative and Labour governments of the 1970s were pledged to secure majority rule in Rhodesia and support economic sanctions against its government. For a country beset by chronic economic instability, this legacy of an all but vanished empire was a tiresome embarrassment, made worse by constant sermonising by the leaders of new African and Asian Commonwealth countries. Economic sanctions against Rhodesia were a dead letter, simply because South Africa turned a blind eye to infringements. Furthermore, Britain would not fight to restore its authority over Rhodesia, although soon after Rhodesia's declaration of independence a squadron of RAF fighters had been sent to Zambia to calm President Kaunda's jitters. British warships cruised off the Mozambique coast on the lookout for sanction-breaking vessels to no effect.

Futile gestures could not mask the fact that Britain's power in Africa was vanishing. As the Conservative Opposition leader, Edward Heath, told the Commons in March 1968, Britain lacked the men and the money to intervene in southern Africa without American help, which was unlikely to be forthcoming because of the Vietnam War.[12] Impotence was accompanied by a lack of political will. In 1976, as the Rhodesian conflict was escalating, the Russian Ambassador discussed with James Callaghan the pressure on Britain to intervene and was told that nothing would ever be done to protect the white minority from the African majority.[13] The British public did not want to be sucked into another Algeria.

Neither side was winning the Rhodesian war, and by 1978 Ian Smith was seeking a peace through compromise. He therefore discussed peace plans with the British, American and South African diplomats and agreed to limited African participation in government. The franchise was extended to some but not all Africans, who helped elect a new government under Bishop Abel Muzorewa. The CIA noted that white Rhodesians continued to dominate the armed forces, police, judiciary and administration. The fighting continued, and during the second half of 1979 ZAPU's bases were hammered and its offensive capacities crippled.[14] The British and American governments remained committed to the principle of majority rule, but were increasingly alarmed by the likelihood that heavily reinforced Cuban forces would soon become directly engaged in the Rhodesian war in response to the growing number of Rhodesian raids into Mozambique.

To make matters worse, Mugabe was directly pleading for Russian assistance, although so far he had been given a cold shoulder. America was, therefore, under pressure to respond, but it had to tread warily, for it did not want to appear to be openly on the side of apartheid. Within Britain, Tory right-wingers supported Rhodesia with varying degrees of zeal, alternately appealing to notions of kinship and raising the bogey of Communism in southern Africa. Julian Amery went so far as to confide to a Rhodesian newspaper that, once back in power, the Conservatives would jettison sanctions and cease to have dealings with ZANU and ZAPU.[15]

Ian Smith drew false hopes from the election of Mrs Thatcher in May 1979. He congratulated her fulsomely, with a reminder that 'all Rhodesians thank God for your magnificent victory' and the hope that 'you succeed in restoring decency and honesty to the British political scene'.[16] Smith's flattery did not seduce Mrs Thatcher, who followed the line taken by Washington, which was simultaneously to support majority rule and secure a negotiated settlement that would guarantee it. This was finally achieved at the Lancaster House Conference in December. A British interim administration (complete with a Governor-General) took charge of Zimbabwe; ZANU and ZAPU partisans stopped fighting, and their parties put forward candidates for an election in which all Zimbabweans voted. It was held in February 1980 and Mugabe's ZANU won a landslide victory. Much to the satisfaction of Washington, the United States was the first nation to open an embassy in Harare, formerly Salisbury. Since 1980, Zimbabwe's is a multi-party system, albeit a very oppressive one where Mugabe's ZANU-PF has dominated. There have been many opposition political parties since independence, most of whom have contested elections. One of the parties – the Movement for Democratic Change (MDC) – arguably won at least two of these elections, and for a short period formed a 'unity government' with Mugabe's ZANU-PF.

V

The year 1980 marked a turning point in the history of South Africa. It had lost an ally, Rhodesia, and was now hemmed in by hostile African states which provided bases and training camps for the fighters of Umkhonto we Sizwe (the Spear of the Nation), or MK, the armed wing of the ANC. South Africa now faced multiple threats and was compelled to wage war on several fronts. The Soviet Union was both armourer and paymaster for South Africa's enemies and sustained them in what became a war of attrition. It was one which the Russians were confident they could win: in 1980 and less than a year after the invasion of Afghanistan, the Chairman of the KGB, Yuri Andropov, promised that Russia would press ahead with 'world revolution'. Cynics in Moscow were less cocksure; the costs of underwriting global revolution were soaring and the recipients lacked the resources to repay Russia: in 1989 Angola's unrecoverable debt totalled $5 billion.[17] Fighting the Cold War in Africa was becoming a strain on Russia's weakening economy, which also had to shoulder the burdens of the fiercely resisted invasion of Afghanistan in 1979. By contrast, Castro's revolutionary will was unshaken and he continued to send forces to help defend Angola and assist the ANC in toppling the apartheid state.

Russia's proxy war effort justified South Africa's claim that it was part of the front line in the Cold War, which guaranteed a supply of arms from the West and the covert but unenthusiastic backing of the United States and Britain. During the late 1970s and 1980s, South African air and land forces launched large-scale raids into Angola, Mozambique, Zambia and Botswana and stepped up the war to retain Namibia. Death squads regularly crossed borders to abduct or assassinate ANC leaders and activists. South Africa also sponsored RENAMO (the Mozambique National Resistance Movement), which had been created by the Rhodesian intelligence services in 1975 to make trouble for the Russian-backed government of Samora Machel. At home, and with Soviet and Cuban assistance, the ANC was growing stronger and embracing black community groups, students' organisations and trade unionists. Their rallying cry was 'Make apartheid unworkable! Make the country ungovernable!'[18]

Yet the future was not entirely bleak, for embattled South Africa had gained a new, sympathetic friend, Ronald Reagan, who was inaugurated as President in January 1981. His grand design was to 'roll back' Communism everywhere and South Africa would help him achieve it. Reagan had no qualms about the morality of apartheid. In a radio broadcast two years before, he had warned that black majority rule in South Africa would trigger 'outright tribal war'. He also praised Pretoria's attempts to smother African militancy by the establishment of black homelands (Bantustans), a cluster of docile mini-republics which, the President noted approvingly, would be 'pro-Western and anti-Communist'.[19]

The Bantustans were the logical outcome of the apartheid policies of the predominantly Boer National Party that had ruled South Africa since 1948. Its slogan then had been 'die kaffer op sy plek' – which means 'the black man in his place'. Defining it and keeping him there was the fundamental aim of apartheid, a racial doctrine based upon the assumption that the African was genetically inferior and predestined to perpetual helotry. Apartheid was enforced by a cruel police state which constructed a system designed to perpetuate the dominance of 3 million whites over 14 million blacks. There was a tightening of the pass laws which controlled the black man's movements and dictated where he lived, and fresh legislation to enforce racial segregation in public places, transport and education. An individual's race was determined by laws which created seven rigid ethnic categories, including Chinese and Malays. Those who objected could appeal against their classification, but faced close scrutiny: in 1986, of 387 'blacks' who sought to become 'Cape coloureds' (i.e. of mixed blood) and so take a step up the racial ladder, 279 were rejected.[20]

All races were quarantined from morally harmful and seditious outside influences by the censorship of films and books, and special care was taken to isolate the blacks from anything that might lead them to question their hereditary subordination. They were spared Hollywood's depiction of the infectious vices and excesses of Europeans, and the detective thrillers of Mickey Spillane were banned because of their sex and violence.[21] The opening sequence of the film Zulu, in which a Zulu takes a rifle from a dead British soldier, led to an immediate ban. Home-produced films for the African market stressed the virtues of the simple and wholesome way of life of black rural communities which were contrasted with the depravity and alienation of the towns and cities.[22] Sexual relations between whites and blacks were forbidden, which was good news for black prostitutes in the British-controlled enclaves of Basutoland (Lesotho) and Swaziland, where pornography could also be purchased or viewed. Crossing the frontier from Lesotho into South Africa was to enter a country with a disquietingly oppressive atmosphere which permeated every aspect of life. Visitors from Rhodesia, where relations between the races were easier and more relaxed, also sensed this brooding tension.[23]

Apartheid was justified by a blend of Old Testament injunctions and economic necessity. The Dutch Reformed Church had always claimed that Afrikaners, like the Israelites of the Old Testament, had a covenant with God, which gave them mastery over the land, its peoples and its fruits, an arrangement that suited farming communities. South Africa's industrial revolution at the end of the previous century created great wealth, which the Boers welcomed, but also transformed society in ways they deplored. Their inward-looking rural world was confronted by the alien and frightening one of the expanding industrial cities and towns. These had proved a magnet for Africans who, by 1945, already made up 40 per cent of the industrial workforce.

As the numbers of black urban workers rose, the authorities became more and more fearful of the 'rootless masses' who inhabited the vast shanty towns and squatters' camps which were developing a lawless life of their own. Another Afrikaner bogey was the shadowy horde of black 'idlers' who lived on the margins of urban society.[24] Apartheid banished these nightmares and delivered a disciplined and submissive workforce that was essential for future growth and prosperity. The white South African electorate strongly approved; in the 1977 general election the National Party took 134 of the 165 seats, and in 1981 131 of 165.

Successive nationalist administrations presided over a flourishing economy. By 1980, South Africa had attracted $104 billion in overseas investment, mostly by multinational mining corporations. Twenty per cent of this capital was American and Britain too had substantial South African holdings which totalled £656 million in 1969, and during the 1970s South Africa was the third-largest market for British exports. The apartheid regime may have been an international moral outcast, but it was well aware that its allies could not afford to kill or even maim a goose that laid so many golden eggs. Or, as Reagan explained in 1981, South Africa was 'essential to the Free World for its production of minerals that we all must have'.[25] Russia too shared in the bonanza: it secretly agreed with Pretoria to fix world prices of diamonds, gold and platinum to the advantage of both countries, and in the mid-1980s was spending $1 billion annually on South African diamonds for its own use and re-export.[26]

South Africa was also a strategic asset for the West. Time and time again, Pretoria reminded the West that it controlled the seaways between the Atlantic and the Indian Oceans that would become vital in the event of nuclear war, in which the Suez Canal was certain to be an early Russian target. In 1959 this point had been raised by a State Department survey of future relations with South Africa which also stressed South Africa's mineral resources. As for apartheid, there were fears that the 'comparative literacy and sophistication' of the blacks made them susceptible to Communism. Nonetheless, it was felt that America was morally obliged publicly to discourage South Africa's racial policies.[27]

Yet the fact remained that South Africa was run on inhumane principles which were abhorrent to the consciences of a large body of Western Christians, liberals and socialists. The former moderator of the Methodist Church Lord Soper spoke for them all during a Lords debate in 1968 when he declared: 'I could not look a black man in the face again if I were to accept this as an inevitable evil in which I could have no part except to acquiesce to it.'[28] His views were those of the British anti-apartheid lobby, which for the past eight years had been pressing for stringent economic sanctions against South Africa and a boycott of South African imports.

The post-war world viewed racism through the prism of events in Nazi Germany and its European satrapies between 1933 and 1945. Quite simply, racism had led to the systematic slaughter of millions of Jews, Gypsies and Slavs for no other reason than their birth and ancestry. Recent history had proved beyond question that racism was malignant in that it dehumanised people and treated their lives as worthless. Moreover, the South African National Party had a history of sympathy towards Nazism. Two Prime Ministers, John Vorster and P. W. Botha, had been members of the pro-Nazi Ossewabrandwag movement during the war and the former had been interned.[29]

Opposition to apartheid was most deeply felt in those countries that had just emerged from colonial rule, for its racial assumptions were a reminder that they too had often been regarded as somehow racially inferior. South Africa was depicted as the embodiment of colonialism, whose prime ingredients were exploitation and a sense of white racial superiority. For this reason, African and Asian members of the Commonwealth made a great fuss about South Africa, which left in 1961. British governments regarded the Commonwealth as a surrogate empire of influence, bound together by photogenic royal tours, sporting contests and economic aid. There were also shared political values, which were often imaginary, since many of its new member states were corrupt single-party dictatorships with few if any individual freedoms.

In the UN, Commonwealth countries joined with other Afro-Asian ones and the Soviet bloc to vilify South Africa, demand the imposition of economic sanctions against it and chide Britain and America for temporising on this issue. Among those who made the most noise were repressive dictatorships which cared as little about human rights as did South Africa. The West had to appease this clamour, but did so as cautiously as was possible. In March 1960 the State Department succeeded in toning down the forthright language of the UN resolution that condemned the shooting of sixty-nine African protesters against the pass laws by South African policemen at Sharpeville.[30]

British governments faced a similar dilemma at a time when, despite the sentimental talk about the Commonwealth, they were all too conscious that their country's influence in Africa was waning fast. At all levels, the Labour Party had thrown its weight behind the anti-apartheid movement when in opposition, but when it was in office front-bench pragmatism replaced idealism, at least among the leadership. Like America, Britain had to coexist, albeit unenthusiastically, with its ally and customer, South Africa. So it was that in 1976 the veteran Labour firebrand Tony Benn, then Secretary of State for Energy, stoutly defended the purchase from South Africa of uranium mined in Namibia.[31]

Both Labour and Conservatives did, however, attempt to enforce the UN embargoes on arms exports to South Africa, although there were some very odd compromises. While it was illegal to export Saracen armoured cars, which were often deployed for crowd control, it was permissible to sell spare parts for those already in use. Wasp helicopters were supplied in 1962 for anti-submarine warfare, but some were quickly converted for anti-guerrilla operations.[32] Arming South Africa was a profitable business: sales in 1970-1 included a £6 million boom-defence vessel and electronic equipment for corvettes which cost £2.25 million.[33]

There was also a feeling, stronger in Britain than in America, that South Africa might somehow be persuaded to soften its racial policies by demonstrations of cooperation and goodwill. For instance, in 1968 it was seriously argued that sending an MCC cricket XI to play

South Africa might make its people think again about apartheid, since the South Africans set great store by their sporting prowess. They set even greater store by racial exclusiveness and refused to accept Basil D'Oliveira, a player of mixed race, in the team, having already banned a New Zealand XI that included a Maori.[34] Since the MCC would not play by Pretoria's rules, the fixture was called off. Whenever South African teams toured Britain, anti-apartheid groups disrupted their matches, much to the fury of cricket fanatics.

South Africa was remarkably resistant to any form of international disapproval, which intensified whenever its armed forces cracked down on expressions of black discontent. Pretoria was unmoved by the worldwide outrage that followed the 1960 Sharpeville massacre. The government also weathered the storms that followed the bloody suppression of the Soweto insurrections in 1976, which had been triggered by the decision to make lessons in Afrikaans compulsory in all black schools. A year later the torture and death in police custody of Steve Biko, a charismatic leader of the Black Consciousness Movement, provoked further international condemnation. By a grotesque irony, the police acknowledged they 'could not afford another Biko', and so henceforward the bodies of men and women killed in custody were discreetly disposed of.[35] One corpse was placed near a crocodile hole. External pressure from unfriendly and nominally friendly nations did not change the official mind of South Africa or reduce the brutality of its security forces.

VI

Western public and official distaste for apartheid did not override Cold War realpolitik. As South Africa constantly reminded its critics, it was fighting a war against Communism, and its own defeat would be a strategic and economic catastrophe far greater than that recently suffered by America in Vietnam. Moreover, it was enjoying some success. At home, the ANC's 'armed struggle' was being fiercely resisted, the SWAPO guerrillas in Namibia were being held in check, and South Africa had repeatedly shown its capacity to deliver hard knocks to its enemies' bases in Mozambique, Angola and Botswana. Yet by the mid-1980s there was no indication of when and how a total victory might be achieved or, given the nature of the conflict, the form it would take.

One thing, however, was clear: South Africa's survival was tied to the course and outcome of the Cold War. It was entering a new and what turned out to be its final stage during the early 1980s when Reagan pressed ahead with a massive rearmament programme that was intended to swing the balance of nuclear power in America's favour. The Soviet Union could not respond in kind, for it was in the early stages of a chronic and prolonged political and economic crisis whose symptoms indicated that it was in danger of losing control over its subjects at home and in Eastern Europe. Communism was not working, and cynics wondered whether it ever would. Visions of a global revolution were dissolving rapidly. By 1985 the Afghan adventure had become a humiliating débacle, and policies contrived to extend and tighten Russian influence in Ethiopia and southern Africa were now luxuries which could no longer be afforded. As one official remarked of the Angola intervention, 'Why, with all our problems, did we have to get involved? Whether it was just or not, we could not afford it.'[36] There was one compensation: the sparse Russian diet was supplemented by imported fish caught in Angolan waters.

In outline, this was the view taken by Mikhail Gorbachev, who had become General Secretary of the Communist Party in 1985. He quickly appreciated that if Russia was to be rescued from domestic chaos and collapse she had to jettison fruitless foreign adventures quickly and without losing too much face. He secretly signalled his intention to pull back from Africa during his 1986 meeting with Reagan at Reykjavik during arms control talks. Gorbachev had in mind a gradual disentanglement rather than a helter-skelter retreat, and he knew that pledges to disengage from Africa would be valuable bargaining counters in the diplomacy of détente. The United States concurred and welcomed the opportunity to secure regional stability and send the Cubans home.

The Cold War endgame placed South Africa in a vulnerable position. At first its government was sceptical of Gorbachev's promises of withdrawal, which seemed to be contradicted by the reinforcement of the Cuban forces in Angola, which totalled 55,000 in August 1988. America demanded their withdrawal as the price for its support for UN resolution 435, which demanded the evacuation of South African forces from Namibia and its full independence. Both were achieved by a deal struck in New York in December 1988. Castro bowed to Russia's will, but when Gorbachev travelled to Cuba to explain his policy, he got a dusty reception and much growling about the 'betrayal' of Communism.[37] Nevertheless he had to comply, for from the start Cuban engagement in Africa had depended on Soviet airlifts of men and equipment. As the Cubans went home, SWAPO won the elections in independent Namibia.

South African compliance had been in large part the result of American pressure and the anxieties of its powerful business community. Sanctions were beginning to hurt the economy and jeopardise investment, and further difficulties were on the horizon since in 1986 Congress had overridden Reagan's refusal to implement them. Faced with an uncertain and possibly dangerous future, the Afrikaners fell back on their tradition of resilience in the face of reverses, which had enabled them to survive defeat in the Boer War and gradually recover power.

Once again, the Boers would cut cards with their enemy, this time the ANC. President Botha made the first move and opened secret talks with the imprisoned ANC leader Nelson Mandela in July 1989. His aims and those of his successor, F. W. de Klerk, were breathtakingly bold and ambitious and relied on the willingness of Mandela to forgive the past and throw his immense moral authority behind the remaking of South Africa. De Klerk promised to dismantle the apparatus of apartheid, lift the ban on the ANC and extend the franchise to all South Africans. The transition to a multiracial democracy would require patience and forbearance on all sides. This was achieved, for, as de Klerk and Mandela knew, the alternative was a racial civil war and anarchy. This fear concentrated all minds, and Africans responded well to Mandela's appeals for tolerance and forgiveness and his vision of a united, just and prosperous South Africa. In 1994 the ANC won a general election and since then South Africa has enjoyed a fragile stability.

The struggle for mastery in southern Africa was over; henceforward Africans everywhere were in charge of their own affairs. Whether or not this was a happy ending has yet to be seen.

NOTES

CHAPTER ONE
Mission Civilisatrice: Europe
and Africa in 1830

1. Sessions, p. 310
2. Ibid., p. 101
3. Lee, pp. 24–5
4. Cairns, p. 47
5. *Quarterly Review*, 17 (July 1817), p. 305
6. Bassett, p. 331
7. Curtin, p. 21; Cohen, *French Encounter*, p. 255; Brower, p. 48
8. Livingstone, *Narrative of an Expedition to the Zambesi*, p. 598
9. Colson, p. 29
10. Bovill, I, p. 103; II, pp. 159, 282; Price, p. 198
11. Davis, pp. 245, 459
12. Cohen, *French Encounter*, p. 243
13. Bovill, I, p. 103
14. Ibid., p. 679; *Boyden*, p. 20

CHAPTER TWO
'Sold just like chickens':
Slavery and the Slave Trade

1. Zimba, Alpers and Isaacman, p. 272
2. Ruete, p. 217
3. Adams and So, pp. 25–7
4. Klein, *passim*
5. Toledano, p. 56; Mowafi, 15ff.
6. Zimba, Alpers and Isaacman, pp. 257–8
7. Adu Boahen, *Britain*, pp. 128, 153
8. Cohen, *French Encounter*, pp. 141–6, 196
9. Peterson, p. 427
10. Cohen, *French Encounter*
11. Toledano, pp. 116–17
12. Zimba, Alpers and Isaacman, p. 150
13. Toledano, p. 31; Mowafi, pp. 29, 39, 65
14. Hubbell, pp. 39–40
15. Lloyd, p. 83
16. Ibid., p. 84
17. McCaskie, p. 487

CHAPTER THREE
'Ethiopia shall soon stretch out her hands to God': Missionaries

1. *Missionary Career of Dr E. S. Krapf*, p. 25
2. Ellingworth, pp. 212–13
3. Etherington, pp. 116, 146, 173
4. R. L. Watson, pp. 363–4
5. 'Narrative of Events . . ., p. 235
6. McCaskie, p. 487
7. Etherington, p. 81; Bjerk, p. 11
8. Knight-Bruce, p. 55
9. Beaven, p. 430
10. Turpin, p. 315
11. RH, UMCA, Box A1 (IV) A, 232–6 [What is RH?]
12. Etherington, pp. 32, 63–4
13. Vernal, p. 179
14. Etherington, p. 56
15. Cohen, *French Encounter*, p. 276
16. Cohen, *French Encounter*, pp. 122–3
17. Cairns, p. 149
18. Ruete, pp. 207–10
19. Nwoye, p. 7
20. Knight-Bruce, *Journals*, p. 32
21. Cohen, p. 255 [ditto?]
22. Etherington, pp. 62–3
23. *Mission Life*, II, p. 163
24. Etherington, p. 67
25. Beaven, p. 426
26. Axelson, pp. 157–9

CHAPTER FOUR
White Man's Countries I: Razzia: The Conquest of Algeria

1. Kiernan, p. 160
2. Brower, p. 88
3. Kearny, p. 38
4. Ibid., pp. 38–9
5. Brower, p. 48
6. Perkins, pp. 15–16
7. Brower, pp. 23, 25, 33
8. Ibid., pp. 27–48; Sessions, p. 319
9. Brower, p. 69
10. Perraudin, pp. 8–9
11. Perkins, pp. 142–3
12. Sessions, pp. 318–19
13. Verdès-Leroux, p. 191n.
14. Cohen (ed.), p. 12
15. *Le Figaro*, 31 July 1870
16. *Journal des Débats Politiques de Littéraires*, 18 August 1845
17. Verdès-Leroux, p. 75
18. Sessions, p. 313

CHAPTER FIVE
White Man's Countries II: 'I am a chief and master': South Africa

1. Welsh, pp. 9–10
2. Streak, p. 95
3. Ibid., p. 95; Lister, p. 16
4. du Toit and Giliomee, p. 111
5. Boyden, p. 107
6. Stapleton, p. 27
7. Hattersley, pp. 125, 213–14
8. Atkins, pp. 85, 169
9. Ibid., p. 91
10. Martens, p. 122
11. Welsh, pp. 73–4

12. Ibid., pp. 77–82
13. Laband and Knight, p. 9
14. Guy, p. 62
15. TNA, WO 33/236

CHAPTER SIX
'Un vaste plan d'occupation': Exploitation and Exploration

1. Curtin, pp. 41, 52–3, 81
2. Brodie, pp. 171–5
3. Ibid., p. 182
4. West, pp. 80, 85; Nwoye, pp. 27, 38
5. Cohen, *French Encounter*, p. 269
6. Ibid., p. 230
7. Staum, pp. 179–80
8. West, p. 182
9. Helly, p. 168
10. *The Times*, 17 April 1874
11. Falola and Brownell, pp. 150–1
12. Louis, *Ends of British Imperialism*, p. 52
13. Daughton, p. 10
14. Nwoye, p. 15
15. Schneider, p. 65
16. Crispi, II, p. 108
17. Schneider, p. 64
18. *Journal des Débats Politiques et Littéraires*, 22 April 1881
19. Marder, p. 150
20. *Journal des Débats Politiques et Littéraires*, 2 May 1881
21. Nwoye, p. 61
22. Hochschild, p. 340
23. Stannard, p. 267
24. Hochschild, pp. 68, 71
25. West, p. 123

CHAPTER SEVEN
'Bring on a fight': Regime Change in Egypt and the Sudan 1882–1889

1. Berque, p. 173; Robert Hunter, pp. 187–8
2. Cole, p. 263
3. *Le Petit Journal*, 10 July 1882
4. *Quarterly Review*, 155 (1883), p. 236
5. Harrison, p. 139
6. Ibid., p. 103
7. Ibid., p. 93; Cole, pp. 255–6
8. Porter, p. 93
9. Marder, p. 144
10. Harrison, pp. 13, 15, 25, 16, 106
11. Ibid., p. 2; the photos can be viewed on www.levantine heritage.com.htm
12. *Le Petit Journal*, 14, 16, 18 July 1882
13. Holland, p. 114
14. Cole, p. 267
15. Kiernan, p. 77; Harrison, p. 135
16. Harrison, pp. 135–6
17. Schölch, p. 301
18. Hargreaves, p. 39
19. *L'Intransigent*, 19 July, 20 September 1882
20. *Le Petit Journal*, 19 July 1882
21. Poggo, p. 25; Sikainga, p. 273
22. Ohrwalder, p. 50
23. TNA, WO 32/7786; Johnson, *Death of General Gordon*, pp. 294–6
24. MEC, Sudan Intelligence

Report, III, March 1895, p. 4. (debriefing of Rudolf von Slatin, former Governor-General of the Sudan and a prisoner of the Khalifa for ten years)
25. Beswick, p. 95
26. Beswick, p. 26
27. Poggo, pp. 275–6
28. MEC, Sudan Intelligence Report, III, March 1895, p. 81

CHAPTER EIGHT
'Will and force': Partition 1882–1914

1. Bosworth, pp. 328, 334
2. Scham, p. 7
3. Ibid., p. 8
4. Perras, pp. 67, 180
5. *Economist*, 20 April 1912
6. Bley, pp. 3–5
7. Kanya-Forstner, p. 175
8. Perham, p. 661
9. Perras, pp. 57–8
10. Ibid., pp. 75–6
11. Perham, p. 627
12. Chamberlain, pp. 120–1
13. Louis, *Ends of British Imperialism*, pp. 77–8
14. Kanya-Forstner, pp. 101–2, 123, 184, 248
15. Perham, p. 685
16. Willcocks, pp. 101–2
17. Brown, *Fashoda*, pp. 132–3, 139; Anderson, p. 321
18. Marder, pp. 320, 324–5
19. Kanya-Forstner, p. 268
20. Mann, p. 66; *Niger Coast*

Protectorate, Reports and Correspondence, p. 296
21. Clayton, p. 398

CHAPTER NINE
'It'll all be pink soon': The Struggle for Southern Africa 1882–1914

1. Kennedy, pp. 200, 216–17
2. Izedinova, pp. 18, 22
3. Surridge, p. 21
4. RHL, Rhodes, Mss Afr s 228, 3A, 167
5. L. James, *Imperial Warrior: Allenby*, p. 34
6. Newbury, p. 101
7. Schreuder, p. 352
8. Ranger, p. 41
9. Axelson, pp. 244, 299–300
10. *Spectator*, 6 July 1889
11. RHL, Mss Afr s 229, IV, 18
12. RHL, Mss Afr s 229, IV, 316–17
13. I am indebted to Professor John MacKenzie, who interviewed this man.
14. RHL, Mss Afr s 228, 3A, 1
15. Newbury, pp. 99–100; Glass, p. 123
16. Glass, p. 123
17. RHL, Mss Afr s 229, IV, 315
18. RHL, Mss Afr s 228, 3B, 273
19. Beach, p. 390
20. Ranger, 'Connexions', p. 350
21. Selous, p. xvii
22. TNA, DPP1/2/2, 883–4
23. Surridge, pp. 22, 32
24. *Punch*, 8 November 1899
25. The best and most thorough is

Pakenham, *The Boer War*.
26. Warwick, p. 5
27. Ibid. pp. 100–1

CHAPTER TEN
'If you strike, strike hard': Pacification 1885–1914

1. Glass, p. 97
2. Mann, pp. 66–7
3. NA, DPP 1/1/1.665
4. Mann, p. 136
5. Redmayne, p. 431
6. Gleichen, *The Anglo-Egyptian Sudan*, p. 268
7. Horowitz, pp. 393–6, 401
8. Schneider, p. 163
9. Kanya-Forstner, p. 175
10. Vaughan, pp. 181, 185
11. Mann, p. 45
12. NAM, Jelf Letters
13. Donovan, pp. 286, 288
14. Pease, pp. 233, 236
15. Lunn, pp. 324–5
16. TNA, WO 32/4349
17. Mann, p. 233
18. Perraudin, p. 338
19. Osuntokun, p. 124
20. Hassing, p. 120
21. Adeleye, p. 206
22. L. James, *Savage Wars*, pp. 244–6
23. TNA, WO 148/48
24. TNA, WO 106/2738
25. Pakenham, p. 576
26. Ross, pp. 180–1
27. Curtin, p. 105

CHAPTER ELEVEN
'White savages': Hearts of Darkness

1. Harder, pp. 119, 121
2. Hochschild, pp. 35, 172
3. Ibid., p. 172
4. Ibid., p. 254
5. Ibid., pp. 175–7; Stanard, p. 42
6. Renton, Seddon and Zeilig, p. 46
7. Ibid., p. 37
8. Bley, p. 117
9. Ibid., pp. 29–30, 91
10. Zimmerer, 'War, Concentration Camps', p. 46
11. Bley, pp. 163–6; Sarkin, p. 135
12. Lehmann, pp. 115–16
13. Brehl, p. 120
14. Bley, pp. 211–13; Zimmerer, pp. 19–20
15. Perras, p. 118
16. Ibid., pp. 197–8, 216
17. Taithe, pp. 130–1, 135
18. Ibid., p. 131
19. *Journal des Débats Politiques et Littéraires*, 27 August 1899
20. *Le Figaro*, 30 August 1899
21. Taithe, p. 181
22. Miller, pp. 79–80
23. Pakenham, p. 500
24. TNA, CO 291/27/435, 117–32
25. TNA, WO 93/41, 43–4, 68, 86, 234–41; WO 92/91, 16; Transvaal Archives CS 1092 for the depositions against Morant and Handcock

CHAPTER TWELVE
'We go where we are led': Missions and Their Enemies

1. Stanley, pp. 2–3
2. Pretorius and Jafta, p. 211
3. Rasmussen, pp. 17–19
4. *Spectator*, 14 November 1896
5. *Les Missions Catholiques* (1901), p. 2
6. Daughton, pp. 232–3
7. *Les Missions Catholiques* (1907), pp. 16–20, 44, 46
8. Callaway, p. 128
9. Hudson, pp. 454–5
10. M. S. B. Burton, *Happy Days*, p. 36
11. Foster, pp. 95–6
12. Hansard, 4th Series, 11, 205
13. *Spectator*, 19 October 1895
14. Hansard, 4th Series, 22, 408, 419, 427–8
15. Hansard, 4th Series, 166, 306–9
16. Rasmussen, pp. 2–4
17. von Lettow-Vorbeck, p. 14
18. Grogan and Sharp, p. 392
19. Ibid., pp. 340, 360–1
20. Cranworth, p. 65
21. Blyden, 'Islam in Western Sudan', p. 28
22. Daughton, p. 250
23. Osuntokun, p. 11; Umar, p. 56
24. Crozier, pp. 80–1
25. Gleichen, *The Anglo-Egyptian Sudan*, I, 11
26. Colonial Office Annual Reports, 788, *Northern Nigeria Report for 1910–11*, pp. 11–12
27. Colonial Office Annual Reports, 881, *East Africa Report for 1914–15*, p. 30
28. Umar, p. 61
29. The figures are official and appear in *Whitaker's Almanack* for 1913.
30. Colonial Annual Reports, 636, *East Africa Protectorate Reports for 1908–9*, pp. 6, 7
31. Foster, pp. 71–9
32. Ibid., pp. 57–74, 93
33. Daughton, pp. 3–4
34. Ibid., pp. 210–11
35. Mills, pp. 343–4
36. Rasmussen, pp. 26, 28

CHAPTER THIRTEEN
'Toxic is the gift of Christians': Islam and Empires

1. Perkins, p. 64
2. Miller, pp. 313, 328–9
3. Dale, p. 60
4. Amster, p. 4
5. Kanya-Forstner, pp. 37, 45
6. Colonial Annual Office Reports, 409, *Northern Nigeria, 1903*, pp. 24–5
7. Umar, pp. 47–8
8. Ibid., p. 48
9. R. T. Harrison, *Gladstone's Imperialism*, p. 201
10. Milner, p. 313
11. Starkey-Balasubramarian, pp. 28–9
12. Perkins, p. 97

13. C. Harrison, *France and Islam*, p. 19
14. Ibid., pp. 57–8, 94–5
15. TNA, WO 32/6383
16. Osuntokun, p. 16; Harrison, *France and Islam*, p. 95
17. Colonial Annual Reports, 516, *Northern Nigeria Report for 1905–6*, p. 6
18. Crozier, p. 108
19. Adeleye, p. 266
20. M. Lewis, *Somali Poetry*, *passim*
21. TNA, WO 32/5932
22. Meek, pp. 62–3
23. Burke, pp. 105–9
24. *Le Figaro*, 23 April 1912; *L'Humanité*, 19 April 1912; *Journal des Débats Politiques et Littéraires*, 9 September 1912
25. Badrawi, pp. 28–9, 41
26. Amster, pp. 112, 122
27. Ibid., pp. 58–9, 104–96
28. Blyden, 'Islam in Western Sudan', pp. 27–8
29. Bone (ed.), p. 45
30. Ibid., p. 130

CHAPTER FOURTEEN
'Palm trees, enormous flowers, Negroes, animals and adventures': The Impact of Africa on Europe

1. Hargreaves, pp. 23, 82
2. Furse, p. 11
3. Hargreaves, p. 111
4. Kiernan, p. 173
5. *L'Écho de Paris*, 11 December 1899; *Le Petit Parisien*, 20 December 1900, 19 January 1901; *Le Figaro*, 5 February 1901
6. Schneider, pp. 157–9
7. *L'Humanité*, 17 August, 21 September 1912
8. MacKenzie, p. 162
9. Cranworth, pp. 37, 150
10. Ranger, *Revolt*, p. 42
11. Mak, p. 24
12. Boisragon, pp. 37–8
13. NAM, Rutland Papers
14. www.hutleyarchives.com
15. Schneider, p. 81
16. *Le Petit Journal*, 3 October 1891
17. Schneider, p. 81
18. MacMaster, p. 122
19. MacKenzie, p. 524
20. McDonald, p. 531
21. Short, pp. 1–2
22. MacKenzie, pp. 52–3
23. Blanchard, Boëtsch and Snoep, pp. 99, 126
24. Ibid., pp. 276–7
25. MacKenzie, pp. 103–4; www.colonialfilm.org.uk
26. Blanchard, Boëtsch and Snoep, p. 310
27. Schneider, p. 191
28. Blanchard, Boëtsch and Snoep, p. 126

CHAPTER FIFTEEN
'The honour of the ruling race': Racial Attitudes, Sexual Encounters and Africa's Future

1. Rabot, pp. 127–8
2. Shroer, p. 183

3. Fell, p. 227

4. Boisragon, p. 159

5. Forbes, p. 57; Coombes, pp. 55, 178

6. *Spectator*, 11 November 1905

7. Killingray, *The Idea*, p. 425

8. TNA, FCO 141/13572

9. Killingray and Matthews, p. 9

10. Lunn, pp. 224–5

11. TNA, Cab 45/28, 'War and Survival in East Africa, 1914–1918', p. 8

12. MacMaster, p. 59

13. Ibid., pp. 52–3, 121

14. Bickford-Smith, pp. 201, 203

15. Trumbull, p. 40

16. NAM, Horwood Papers

17. TNA, FO 141/466/1429

18. Hyam, p. 30

19. Muschalek, pp. 588, 591

20. Hyam, p. 157

21. White, p. 180

22. TNA, FO 859/18

23. White, pp. 181–2

24. Ibid., pp. 184, 199

25. Ibid., pp. 189, 191

26. TNA, WO 92/4

27. Hyam, pp. 160–3

28. Ibid., p. 169

29. Private information.

30. Hyam, pp. 100, 138–9

31. Jeater, p. 321

32. Anderson, 'Sexual Threat', pp. 49–50

33. Shadle, p. 58

34. Bickford-Smith, p. 197

35. Ibid., p. 198

36. Fahmy, p. 88

37. Coombs, p. 39

38. TNA, WO 106/253

39. van Beek, *passim*

40. C. Harrison, *France and Islam*, p. 119

CHAPTER SIXTEEN
'Lloyd George', 'Kitchener', 'Sambo' and 'Coolie': Africa at War 1914–1918

1. Strachan, p. 541

2. *Daily Review of Foreign Press*, 17 October 1917

3. Yearwood, p. 318

4. TNA, Cab 45/71, 30

5. TNA, Cab 45/71, 3, 12, 16, 27–9

6. von Lettow-Vorbeck, pp. 324–6

7. TNA, Cab 45/28, 2–7

8. Killingray and Matthews, pp. 13–14

9. Matthews, pp. 255–6

10. Osuntokun, p. 137

11. Page, *The War of Thangata*, p. 87

12. von Lettow-Vorbeck, p. 33

13. TNA, Cab 45/71, 14

14. MacMaster, pp. 62–3

15. Ibid., p. 124

16. TNA, WO 95/81 (5 September 1917); WO 95/4018 (10–12 September 1918)

17. Strachan, pp. 730–1

18. Badrawi, *Political Violence*, pp. 114–15

19. www.smythe.id.au

20. Foster, p. 107

21. MacMaster, 237

22. Osuntokun, p. 149

23. Saul and Royer, pp. 91–2, 96–7, 275
24. Osuntokun, pp. 157–8
25. Slight, p. 244
26. MEC, *Sudan Intelligence Reports*, 70, p. 9
27. TNA, WO 157/701; 702
28. C. Harrison, *France and Islam*, pp. 123ff.
29. Nasson, p. 256: Killingray, *The Idea*, p. 423
30. TNA, WO 196/259
31. TNA, FCO 141/5650
32. Killingray and Matthews, p. 15n.
33. Osuntokun, p. 79

CHAPTER SEVENTEEN
'Contagious excitement': The Rise of Nationalism

1. Gillette, p. 57
2. Mack Smith, p. 47
3. Ibid., p. 112
4. *L'Humanité*, 27 December 1927
5. *L'Humanité*, 1, 4 August 1934
6. TNA, KV 2/1787, 7A
7. Balfour, p. 128
8. Anderson and Rathbone, pp. 133–4
9. Lewis, p. 31
10. TNA, FO 608/214, 214, 13
11. Badrawi, *Political Violence*, pp. 81–5
12. BL, Miller, 55, 97
13. TNA, FO 608/214, 8
14. BL, Miller, 13, 97
15. Kiernan, p. 199
16. *Egyptian Mail*, 14, 16, 18, 19 and 22 March 1919
17. TN FO 686/214, 2–3
18. The Wafdist government issued a postage stamp to celebrate this event: it showed an allegorical figure of 'Justice'.
19. MEC, Killearn Diaries, 9 and 24 November, 1936
20. Kholoussi, pp. 277–8, 282–3, 287, 289
21. Ryzova, p. 148
22. *Egyptian Mail*, 15 April 1921
23. Shriner, p. 278
24. Segalla, p. 213
25. Ibid., pp. 203–4
26. TNA, FO 141/752/2
27. Kalman, p. 112
28. Alexander, p. 122
29. *Le Petit Journal*, 8 August 1934
30. *Le Temps*, 8 August 1934; *Le Figaro*, 8 August 1934
31. MacMaster, pp. 78, 100, 123, 127, 129
32. Boittin, p. 99
33. Ibid., pp. 82–3, 87
34. MacMaster, pp. 156–7
35. Boittin, pp. xiii–xiv, 83–5
36. TNA, KV2/2/1787. 1A, 5A, 19A, 26, 29A, 111, 137B
37. TNA, FCO 141/5650
38. Boittin, p. 101; TNA KV 2/1787/9A, 26
39. TNA, KV 2/1817, 23A, 29A
40. TNA KV 2/1849, 1, 2

CHAPTER EIGHTEEN
'Force to the uttermost':
More Wars 1919–1939

1. Balfour, p. 28
2. Ibid., p. 213
3. Balfour, pp. 135–6, 165
4. Ibid., pp. 153–5
5. BBC News, 'You are the World: Africa', 19 January 2002
6. Kiernan, p. 203
7. TNA, WO 106/2866A, Bulletin 5, p. 5
8. Mack Smith, pp. 226–7; Rodogno, pp. 25–8
9. Mazower, p. 116
10. Baer, p. 10
11. Gillette, pp. 56,174
12. Baratieri, pp. 120, 123
13. Mack Smith, p. 71
14. Hess, pp. 161–4
15. Mack Smith, p. 109
16. Haile Selassie, p. 186
17. Ibid., p. 208
18. Mockler, pp. 78–80
19. Falasca-Zamponi, p. 179
20. Mack Smith, pp. 228, 113
21. Mockler, pp. 176–80
22. Ibid., p. 179
23. MEC, Lampson Diary, 28 April 1939
24. Abitbol, p. 38
25. Du Bois, pp. 87–8

CHAPTER NINETEEN
'Unable to stand alone': Africa on the Eve of War

1. Cranworth, pp. 230–31
2. Betts, p. 16
3. Genova, pp. 99–100
4. TNA, FCO 140/5515, 115, 223
5. Evans, p. 17
6. Scham, p. 205
7. Watson, p. 16
8. RHL, Childs, Mss Afr ss 1661, 9 (1) 17 September 1933
9. Slavin, p. 100
10. Ibid., pp. 114–19
11. *New York Times*, 29 January 1939
12. Richards and Aldgate, pp. 25–6, 28
13. Parsons, p. 259
14. Killingray, *Fighting for Britain*, p. 259
15. TNA, Air 20/604, 34
16. Hansard, 5th Series, 288, 207–8
17. RHL, Childs, Mss Afr ss 1861 (3) 20 October 1934
18. RHL, Childs, Mss Afr ss 1861, (1) 20 and 22 December 1933
19. King, p. 165
20. TNA, FCO 141/18139, 1–4
21. TNA, FCO 141/4431–6
22. Williams, pp. 244–5
23. I owe this story to Hector Gordon.
24. Lascelles, pp. 104–5
25. *L'Humanité*, 7 January 1939
26. Ginio, p. xiii
27. Genova, pp. 184–5

28. Ibid., p. 27
29. Naval Intelligence Division, pp. 53, 133
30. Genova, pp. 135–7
31. Ginio, p. 101
32. Kalman, p. 123
33. Genova, p. 126
34. Naval Intelligence Division, p. 60
35. Genova, pp. 58–9
36. *National Geographic Magazine*, 59 (June 1931)
37. Ginio, p. 124
38. Cohen, *Rulers*, pp. 78, 85
39. Naval Intelligence Division, pp. 392–3
40. I am indebted to the late Mrs Betty Blunt for this vignette of the now departed joys of air travel.
41. Elphick and Davenport, p. 134; Shear, pp. 173–4
42. Lewis, pp. 26–7; Lonsdale, p. 101
43. Flibbert, p. 453

CHAPTER TWENTY
'Wait and see': Italian Disasters and French Traumas 1940–1945

1. De Gaulle, p. 152
2. Khenouf and Brett, p. 267
3. TNA, WO 106/2889, 50, 74
4. TNA, Prem 3/239, 3
5. See, *passim*
6. TNA, WO 106/2895, 8
7. TNA, Adm 199/616A, nn; TNA, WO 106/28955, 8; WO 106/28699, 4; TNA 106/2888, nn
8. TNA, WO 193/279, 19 March 1944; Tareke, p. 104
9. LHC, MF 416, 1
10. Abitbol, pp. 122, 133
11. TNA, WO 193/279, High Commissioner in Rome to Foreign Office, 10 October 1944
12. TNA, KV 3/310, 148A–150A
13. Tareke, p. 111
14. Mazower, pp. 115–18
15. Jenkinson, pp. 15–16
16. Ibid., pp. 37, 87
17. Ginio, pp. 91–20
18. Ibid., pp. 47, 50, 56, 101
19. Abitbol, pp. 101, 145
20. Ibid., pp. 54, 101, 118–19
21. Khenouf and Brett, pp. 268–71
22. Ibid., p. 71
23. *Le Matin*, 5 July 1940
24. *Le Figaro*, 25 September 1940
25. TNA, WO 208/928, nn
26. TNA, Adm 199/164A
27. TNA, WO 106/2866A, Bulletin 1, p. 1
28. TNA, WO 106/2866A, Bulletin 9, p. 8
29. TNA, WO 106/2866, Bulletin 22, p. 13; WO 106/2867nn
30. TNA, CO 875/7/5, 65
31. Ginio, pp. 122–3
32. CO m875/7/6, 57
33. Genova, pp. 202–3
34. Betts, p. 227
35. Ibid., p. 161
36. Ibid., p. 63

37. TNA, FO 141/1052, EG/ AMH/ and 33, 89, 96

CHAPTER TWENTY-ONE
'Black Tarantulas': Africans at War

1. Djan, p. 31
2. Echenberg, p. 142
3. Delavignette, p. 152
4. Dickson, p. 14
5. *Nigeria*, 22 (1944), pp. 5–25
6. *The Times*, 23 November 1942
7. Westcott, p. 145
8. Killingray, 'Labour Mobilisation', pp. 86–8
9. Meek, pp. 58–9
10. Khenouf and Brett, pp. 58–9
11. Crew, II, pp. 273–4
12. Ibid., p. 520
13. Meek, pp. 42–4
14. TNA, FCO 1141/18107, 9, 10, 40
15. G. Thompson, 'Colonialism in Crisis', p. 607
16. TNA, CO 875/7/6, A32
17. Wilson, 'Gold Coast Information', *passim*
18. TNA, CO 875/76, 21
19. Dickson, pp. 11–13
20. TNA, WO 106/2866, Bulletin 4, 1
21. TNA, WO 106/2866A, Bulletin 5, App Am 1–2
22. TNA, WO 106/2866, Bulletin 22, 6–7
23. TNA, WO 106/2866, Bulletin 24, 4–5
24. Shear, pp. 173–4
25. TNA, KV 3/100,7
26. TNA, WO 106/4932
27. TNA, WO 106/4921
28. Grundlingh, pp. 183, 188–9
29. BL, Macmillan. C 276, 280
30. TNA, WO 1086/2899, 35–6
31. TNA, WO 106/2866A, Bulletin 24, App A, 1
32. *African Affairs*, 43 (January 1943), pp. 29–30
33. Sabben-Clare, p. 157
34. Killingray, *Fighting for Britain*, p. 147
35. Alexander, pp. 273–4; Echenberg, p. 147
36. Alexander, p. 248; Schalk, p. 2
37. Killingray, *Fighting for Britain*, p. 46
38. Ibid., p. 69
39. TNA, WO 106/5863 nn
40. TNA, WO 203/2355, Report for February–April 1945, 22
41. TNA, WO 203/2855, Report for August–September 1945, 13
42. Crew, II, p. 426
43. Killingray, *Fighting for Britain*, pp. 96–7
44. Private information.
45. TNA, WO 106/5863, 2A, 1–3
46. TNA, WO 106/5863, 5A, 4
47. TNA, WO 203/2355, Report for February–March 1945, 22–3; Report for August to September 1945, 13
48. TNA, WO 203/2355, Report for August–September 1945, 9.13
49. Drew, pp. 133–4

50. Dickson, p. 18

51. NADA, 23 (1946), p. 5

CHAPTER TWENTY-TWO
'Can Russians speak Swahili?':
Nationalist Agitation and Cold
War Phantoms in British Africa
1945–1957

1. TNA, KV 2/1817, 350 B
2. TNA, FCO 141/5089
3. TNA, Adm 1/21117, App II
4. TNA, Adm 1/21117, 1 March
   1948
5. *Spectator*, 18 March 1948
6. *African Affairs*, 44 (April 1945),
   pp. 114–17
7. Taylor, p. 122
8. Drew, p. 148
9. Andrew and Mitrokhin, pp. 4,
   504–5; Walton, pp. 261–2
10. TNA, CO 1015/1758
11. TNA, CO 882/447, 58, 68, 71
12. TNA, FCO 141/6197, 7
13. *Time*, 12 January 1953
14. Walton, p. 242
15. Ibid., p. 241
16. Hansard, 5th Series, 516, 224,
    517
17. TNA, CO 822/471, 33
18. TNA, CO 822/454, *passim*
19. Hansard, 5th Series, 514, 1163
20. Ibid., 537, 151
21. Walton, pp. 261–2
22. TNA, KV 2/1849, 176A; Ghana
    was the name of a medieval
    West African empire.
23. TNA, FO 1110/443, 2

24. Rathbone, p. 113
25. LHC, MF 285, Tab B
26. Ashton, p. 33
27. *Churchill-Roosevelt Correspond-
    ence*, I, pp. 163–4, 167
28. Hansard, 5th Series, 499, 1266
29. TNA, FCO 141/443,135
30. TNA, FO 1110/43, 5
31. TNA, FCO 141/18139, 3,11
32. TNA, FO 1110/443, PR 96/1,
    2–3
33. TNA, FCO 141/17447, 24
34. BL, Lennox-Boyd Mss 3394, 62

CHAPTER TWENTY-THREE
'Comrade Nasser, don't worry!': Egypt
and the Cold War 1945–1980

1. Andrew and Mitrokhin, p. 253
2. W. S. Thompson, *Ghana's Foreign Policy*, p. 247
3. LHC, MF 568, 17 October and
   27 September 1957
4. Louis, 'Libyan Independence',
   p. 167
5. Kerboeuf, p. 203
6. TNA, Defe 4/52, 20–2; Defe
   4/53, 47; BL, Macmillan, D 10,
   76–7
7. Hannington, pp. 77–8; Aldrich,
   pp. 463–4
8. Kiernan, pp. 228–9
9. Kuzmarov, p. 168
10. Andrew and Mitrokhin, p. 146
11. LHC, MF 568, 27 September
    1955
12. Aldrich, p. 480; Walton, p. 296
13. LHC, MF 569, 31 July 1959

14. LHC, MF 570, 19 March 1957
15. LHC, MF 569, 29 December 1956
16. Andrew and Mitrokhin, p. 143

CHAPTER TWENTY-FOUR
A 'horde of rats': The Algerian War and Its Memories

1. Prochaska, p. 263
2. Verdès-Leroux, p. 20
3. *French Encounter*, Cohen, 'The Harkis', p. 279
4. Cole, p. 125
5. Horne, pp. 70–2
6. Schalk, pp. 63–4
7. Horne, p. 77
8. Verdès-Leroux, p. 75
9. Fysh and Wolfreys, p. 32
10. Horne, p. 237; Baer, p. 153
11. Horne, p. 99
12. De Vries, pp. 69–70
13. LHC, FE 2285, Tag A
14. LHC, MF 174, Introduction, p. 1
15. Baer, p. 87
16. Schmidt, pp. 48–9
17. Cohen, 'The Harkis', p. 178
18. Schalk, pp. 66–7, 78–9
19. Verdès-Leroux, p. 20
20. Ibid., p. 23–4
21. Ibid., p. 25
22. Fanon, pp. 76–7

CHAPTER TWENTY-FIVE
'Insatiable greed': Decolonisation and the Cold War

1. Green and Griffith-Jones, p. 228
2. Dallin, p. 42
3. TNA, DO 188/1, 173
4. TNA, FO 45/1886, 108
5. Pascoe, p. 99
6. Shubin, p. 333
7. Mazov, p. 296
8. Andrew and Mitrokhin, p. 428
9. Mazov, pp. 361–3
10. Quist-Adade, pp. 165–6
11. TNA, FO 1110/2123, PR 147/2
12. TNA, FO 1110/2123, PR 174/8
13. TNA, FO 1110/2123, 2, 8, 21
14. LHC, MF 174, 'US Policy Towards South, Central and East Africa', pp. 9–10
15. Mazov, pp. 299–300
16. Andrew and Mitrokhin, pp. 437–8
17. Ibid., pp. 435–7; Mazov, p. 308
18. Kuzmarov, p. 165–8
19. Ibid., p. 172
20. Ibid., p. 184
21. Andrew and Mitrokhin, pp. 185–6
22. *African Socialism*, pp. 4, 9, 17, 27
23. Green and Griffith-Jones, p. 214
24. Ndulu, p. 100
25. LHC, 'Memo on the Political Implications of Afro-Asian Military Takeovers', Summary, p. 3

26. Kuzmarov, p. 175

27. Webber, p. 25

CHAPTER TWENTY-SIX
'Maelstrom': The Congo and Rhodesia

1. Horne, pp. 182–3
2. Namikis, p. 57; Williams, p. 31
3. TNA, FO 371/14663, JB 1015/280
4. Smith, p. 108
5. TNA, Fo 371/146775, JB 22251/1347
6. Kuzmarov, p. 176
7. TNA, FO 371/466634, JB 1015/295
8. Namikas, pp. 92–3
9. Aldrich, p. 612
10. Schmidt, p. 63; Kasminsky, p. 106
11. Namikas, pp. 107–8
12. Andrew and Mitrokhin, pp. 176–7
13. *Colonial Office Africa Report*, August 1965, pp. 14–15
14. TNA, FO 371/146643, JB 1015/285
15. TNA 371/ 154879, 28
16. TNA, FO 371/154879, JB 1018/31
17. *Colonial Office Africa Confidential*, 4 February 1961
18. *Colonial Office Africa Report*, August 1964, p. 20
19. TNA, FO 1100/25, 39
20. W. R. Louis, *Decolonization*, p. 253

21. TNA, FO 371/154885, JB 1081/150; Hansard, 5th Series, 651, 444
22. *Spectator*, 11 August 1960
23. Hansard, 5th Series, 612, 684; 777
24. Lunn, p. 154
25. RHL, Welensky, 75/1, 3–4
26. RHL, Welensky, 84/7, 16
27. RHL, Welensky, 61/6, 23, 34, 26
28. Walton, pp. 280–2
29. Hansard, House of Lords, 5th Series, 215, 268, 269
30. TNA, Defe 25/126, 4, 6, 36
31. Horne, p. 409
32. *Africa Confidential*, 9 December 1966, Supplement, p. 2
33. TNA, Prem 13/1760
34. Shubin, pp. 153–4

CHAPTER TWENTY-SEVEN
'They have left us in the lurch': The Last Days of White Africa

1. Birmingham, pp. 20–1
2. Gleijeses, pp. 39, 65–9
3. TNA, FCO 11/8924, T2994/61
4. Shubin, pp. 9, 25
5. TNA, Prem 11/8924, Minutes of Tripartite Talks
6. Schmidt, pp. 82–3
7. Gleijeses, pp. 28–9
8. Ibid., pp. 22–5, 55
9. TNA, FCO 7/3129, 47
10. Andrew and Mitrokhin, p. 454; Gleijeses, pp. 73–4
11. Ibid., pp. 28–9, 65

12. Hansard, 5th Series, 761, 1579
13. TNA, FO 45/1886, 123
14. Andrew and Mitrokhin, p. 461
15. Hansard, 5th Series, 938, 1086
16. TNA, FCO 3/2411, 1
17. Gleijeses, p. 515
18. *Truth and Reconciliation Commission Report*, II, p. 55
19. Gleijeses, pp. 177–8
20. Guelke, p. 26
21. McDonald, pp. 35–6
22. Tomaselli, p. 72
23. I am indebted to Matthew Parris and Frank Dearden for these impressions of South Africa.
24. Posel, pp. 38–9
25. Gleijeses, p. 324
26. Andrew and Mitrokhin, pp. 468–9
27. LHC, National Security Council, *US Policy Towards South, Central and East Africa*, pp. 13, 16–17, 19
28. Hansard, 5th Series, House of Lords, 293, 453
29. Gleijeses, p. 179
30. LHC, MF 534
31. Hansard, 5th Series, 913, 625; 916, 800
32. TNA, BT 213/245, 5A, 23; Hansard, 5th Series, House of Lords, 330, 1278–80
33. TNA, Cab 148/128, Annex B
34. Murray, pp. 670, 678
35. *Truth and Reconciliation Commission Report*, II, pp. 234–5
36. Gleijeses, p. 516
37. Andrew and Mitrokhin, p. 477

BIBLIOGRAPHY

ABBREVIATIONS
BL: Bodleian Library
LHC: Liddell Hart Centre
JAH: *Journal of African History*
JICH: *Journal of Imperial and Commonwealth History*
MEC: Middle East Centre
NAM: National Army Museum
RHL: Rhodes House Library
TNA: The National Archives

UNPUBLISHED SOURCES.
BL: Bodleian Library, Oxford: Papers of Sir Alan Lennox-Boyd and Harold Macmillan.
LHC: Liddell Hart Centre, London: Confidential US State Department Files, 1945–1959 (Microfilm).
MEC: Middle East Centre, Oxford: Sudan Intelligence Reports and diaries of Lord Killearn.
NAM: National Army Museum: Jelf, Rutland and Harwood Papers.
RHL: Rhodes House Library: Papers of the Universities Mission to Central Africa, Cecil Rhodes, Hubert Childs and Sir Roy Welensky.
TNA: The National Archives, Kew, West London: Adm (Admiralty) 1, Adm 199: BT 20; Cab (Cabinet) 45; Cab 148; CO (Colonial Office) 291, CO 875, CO 882, CO 1015; Defe (Ministry of Defence) 4, Defe 25; DPP (Director of Public Prosecutions) 1; FCO (Foreign and Colonial Office) 3, FCO 11; FCO 141; FCO 1110; FO (Foreign Office) 45, FO 608; FO 686; FO 859; Prem (Prime Minister's Office) 3, Prem 11, Prem

12; WO (War Office) 32, WO 33, WO 92, WO 93, WO 95, WO 106; WO 148, WO 157, WO 193, WO 203, WO 206.

Newspapers and journals are cited in the endnotes by title and date. Hansard references are to volumes with page and line numbers. All books are published in London save where otherwise indicated.

PUBLISHED SOURCES

Abitbol, M., *The Jews of North Africa during the Second World War* (Detroit, MI, 1989).

Aclimandos, T., 'Revisiting the History of the Egyptian Army', in A. Goldschmidt, A. J. Johnson and B. A. Salmoni (eds), *Re-Envisioning Egypt, 1919–1952* (Cambridge, 2005).

Adams, A., and J. So, *A Claim to Land by the River: A Household in Senegal, 1720–1994* (Oxford, 1996).

Ade Ajayi, J. F., and R. Smith, *Yoruba Warfare in the Nineteenth Century* (Cambridge, 1964).

Adeleye, R. B., 'Mahdist Triumph and British Revenge in Northern Nigeria: Satiru, 1906', *Journal of the Historical Society of Nigeria* 6 (1972).

Adu Boahen, A., *Britain, the Sahara and the Western Sudan, 1788–1861* (Oxford, 1964).

—, *African Perspectives on Colonialism* (Baltimore, MD, 1989).

Aldgate, A., and J. Richards, *Britain Can Take It: British Cinema in the Second World War* (2007).

Aldrich, R. J., *The Hidden Hand: Britain, America and Cold War Secret Intelligence* (2001).

Alexander, M. S., 'Colonial Minds Confounded: French Colonial Troops in the Battle of France, 1940', in M. Thomas (ed.), *The French Colonial Mind*, II (2011).

Amster, E. J., *Medicine and the Saints: Science, Islam, and the Colonial Encounter in Morocco, 1877–1956* (Austin, TX, 2013).

Anderson, D. M., 'Sexual Threat and Settler Society: "Black Perils" in Kenya, c. 1907–30', *JICH* 38 (2010).

— and P. Rathbone, *Africa's Urban Past* (2000).

Andrew, C., and V. Mitrokhin, *The World Was Going Our Way: The KGB and the Battle for the Third World* (New York, 2005).

Andrews, C., *The Kafir War of 1834–1835* (1996).

Atkins, K. E., *The Moon Is Dead! Give Us Our Money!: The Cultural Origins of an African Work Ethic, Natal, South Africa, 1843–1900* (1993).

Axelson, P., *Portugal and the Scramble for Africa, 1875–1891* (Johannesburg, 1967).

Badrawi, M., *Political Violence in Egypt 1910–1924: Secret Societies, Plots and Assassinations* (Richmond, Surrey, 2000).

Baer, G. W., *The Coming of the Italian–Ethiopian War* (Cambridge, MA, 1967).

Balfour, S., *Deadly Embrace: Morocco and the Road to the Spanish Civil War* (Oxford, 2002).

Baratieri, D., *Memories and Silences Haunted by Fascism: Italian Colonialism MCMXXX–MCMLX* (Bern, 2010).

Bassett, T. J., 'Cartography and Empire Building in Nineteenth-Century West Africa', *Geographical Review* 84 (1994).

Beach, D. N., '"Chimurenga": The Shona Rising of 1896–1897', *JAH* 20 (1979).

Beachey, R. W., *The Slave Trade of Eastern Africa* (1976).

Beaven, W. H., 'Extracts from the Journal of the Reverend Dr W. H. Beaven', *Mission Life* 3 (1873).

Bediako, K., *Jesus in Africa: The Christian Gospel in African History and Experience* (Carlisle, 2000).

Berque, J., *Egypt: Imperialism and Revolution* (1972).

Beswick, S., 'Women, War, and Leadership in South Sudan (1760–1994)', in J. Spaulding and S. Beswick (eds), *White Nile, Black Blood: War, Leadership, and Ethnicity from Khartoum to Kampala* (Lawrenceville, NJ, 2001).

Betts, R. F., *France and Decolonisation, 1900–1960* (1991).

Bickford-Smith, V., 'The Betrayal of Creole Elites, 1880–1920', in P. D. Morgan and S. Hawkins (eds), *Black Experience and the Empire* (Oxford, 2004).

Bierman, J., *Dark Safari: The Life Behind the Legend of Henry Morton Stanley* (1991).

Birmingham, D., *Frontline Nationalism in Angola and Mozambique* (1992).

Bjerk, P. K., 'They Poured Themselves into the Milk: Zulu Political Philosophy under Shaka', *JAH* 17 (2006).

Blanchard, P., G. Boëtsch and N. J. Snoep, *Exhibitions: L'Invention du sauvage* (XX, Musée du Quai. Branly, 2011).

Bley, H., *South-West Africa under German Rule, 1894–1914* (1971).

Blyden, E. W., 'Islam in Western Sudan', *Journal of the African Society* 2 (1902).

—, 'The Koran in Africa', *Journal of the African Society* 4 (1905).

Bob-Milliar, G. M., 'Verandah Boys versus Reactionary Lawyers: Nationalist Activism in Ghana, 1946–1956', *International Journal of African Historical Studies* 47 (2014).

Boisragon, A. M., *The Benin Massacre* (1897).

Boittin, J. A., *Colonial Metropolis: The Urban Grounds of Anti-Imperialism and Feminism in Interwar Paris* (Lincoln, NE, 2010).

Bone, D. S. (ed.), *Malawi's Muslims: Historical Perspectives* (Blantyre, 2000).

Bosworth, R. J. B., *Italy the Least of the Great Powers: Italian Foreign Policy before the First World War* (Cambridge, 1979).

Bovill, E. W. (ed.), *Missions to the Niger*, 4 vols (Cambridge, 1964–70).

Boyden, P. B., *The British Army in Cape Colony: Soldiers' Letters and Diaries, 1806–58* (2001).

Brehl, M., '"The Drama Was Played Out on the Dark Stage of the Sandveldt": The Extermination of the Herero and Nama in German (Popular) Literature', in J. Zimmerer and J. Zeller (eds), *Genocide in German South-West Africa: The Colonial War of 1904–1908 and Its Aftermath* (Monmouth, 2008).

Brereton, F. S., *In the Grip of the Mullah* (1903).

Brodie, F. M., *The Devil Drives: A Life of Sir Richard Burton* (1984).

Brower, B. C., *A Desert Named Peace: The Violence of France's Empire in the Algerian Sahara, 1844–1902* (New York, 2009).

Brown, W. H., *On the South African Frontier* (Bulawayo, 1970).

Brugger, S., *Australians and Egypt, 1914–1919* (Melbourne, 1980).

Burke, E., 'Pan-Islam and Moroccan Resistance to French Colonial Penetration, 1900–1912', *JAH* 13 (1972).

Burton, M. S. B., *Happy Days and Happy Work in Basutoland* (1902).

Burton, R. F., *First Footsteps in Africa* (1910).

—, *First Footsteps in East Africa*, ed. G. Waterfield (1966).

Cairns, H. A. C., *Prelude to Imperialism: British Reactions to Central African Society, 1840–1890* (1965).

Callaway, G., *Sketches of Kaffir Life* (1905).

Chamberlain. M. E., *The Scramble for Africa* (1999).

Chirol, V., *The Egyptian Problem* (1920).

Ciarlo, D., 'Picturing Genocide in German Consumer Culture, 1904–1910', in M. Perraudin and J. Zimmerer (eds), *German Colonialism and National Identity* (2011).

Cliffe, L., and J. S. Saul, *Socialism in Tanzania*, I and II: *Policies* (Dar-es-Salaam, 1973).

Cohen, W. B., *Rulers of Empire: The French Colonial Service in Africa* (Stanford, CA, 1979).

—, *The French Encounter with Africans: White Response to Blacks, 1530–1880* (Bloomington, IN, 2003).

—, 'The Harkis: History and Memory', in P. M. E. Lorcin (ed.), *Algeria and France, 1800–2000: Identity, Memory, Nostalgia* (Syracuse, NY, 2006).

Cole, J. R. I., *Colonialism and Revolution in the Middle East: Social and Cultural Origins of Egypt's Urabi Movement* (Princeton, NJ, 1992).

Colonial Office Reports: *East Africa Protectorate Report* for 1906–1907 (1910), 1908–1909 (1911), 1914–15 (1916); *Northern Nigeria Report* for 1902 (1904), 1908–1909 (1910), 1911 (1912).

Colson, E., 'African Society at the Time of the Scramble', in L. H. Gann and P. Duignan (eds), *Colonialism in Africa, 1870–1900*, I (Cambridge, 1969).

Coombes, A. E., *Reinventing Africa: Museums, Material Culture and Popular Imagination in Late Victorian and Edwardian England* (New Haven, CT, 1994).

Cowen, M., and N. Westcott, 'British Imperial Economic Policy During the War', in D. Killingray and R. Rathbone (eds), *Africa and the Second World War* (New York, 1986).

Cranworth, Lord, *A Colony in the Making: Or, Sport and Profit in British East Africa* (1919).

Crew, F. A. E., *The Army Medical Services: Campaigns*, 2 vols (1956–7).

Crispi, F., *The Memoirs of Francesco Crispi*, tr. M. Prichard-Agnetti, 3 vols (1912).

Crowe, S. E., *The Berlin West African Conference, 1884–1885* (Oxford, 1942).

Crozier, F. P., *Impressions and Recollections* (1930).

Curtin, P. D., *Disease and Empire: The Health of European Troops in the Conquest of Africa* (Cambridge, 1998).

Dale, G., *The Contrast between Christianity and Muhammadanism* (1909).

Dallin, A., 'The Soviet Union: Political Activity', in Z. Brzezinski (ed.), *Africa and the Communist World* (Stanford, CA, 1963).

Daughton, J. P., *An Empire Divided: Religion, Republicanism and the Making of French Colonialism 1880-1914* (Oxford, 2006).

Davis, D. B., *The Problem of Slavery in Western Culture* (Ithaca, NY, 1966).

de Gaulle, C., *Lettres, Notes et Carnets, Juin 1941–Mai 1945* (Paris, 1983).

de Vries, T., 'Not an "Ugly American": Sal Tas, a Dutch Reporter as Agent of the West in Africa', in L. van Dongen, S. Roulin and G. Scott-Smith (eds), *Transnational Anti-Communism and the Cold War: Agents, Activities, and Networks* (Basingstoke, 2014).

Decker, A., 'Idi Amin's Dirty War: Subversion, Sabotage, and the Battle to Keep Uganda Clean, 1971–1979', *International Journal of African Historical Studies* 43.3 (2010).

Delavignette, R., 'A Letter from French Cameroun', *African Affairs* 46 (1947).

Deng, F. M., 'Abyei: A Bridge or a Gulf? The Ngok Dinka on Sudan's North–South Border', in J. Spaulding and S. Beswick (eds), *White Nile, Black Blood: War, Leadership, and Ethnicity from Khartoum to Kampala* (Lawrenceville, NJ, 2001).

Dickson, A. G., 'The Mobile Propaganda Unit, East Africa Command', *African Affairs* 44 (1945).

Divine, R. A., *Eisenhower and the Cold War* (Oxford, 1981).

Djan, O. S., 'Drums and Victory: Africa's Call to the Empire', *African Affairs* 41 (1942).

Donovan, C. H. W., *With Wilson in Matabeleland* (1894).

Drew, A., *We Are No Longer in France: Communists in Colonial Algeria* (Manchester, 2014).

Du Bois, W. E. B., 'Inter-Racial Implications of the Ethiopian Crisis', *Foreign Affairs* 14 (1935).

du Toit, A., and H. Giliomee, *Afrikaner Political Thought: Analysis and Documents, 1780–1850* (Berkeley, CA, 1983).

E. S., *The Missionary Career of Dr. Krapf* (1882).

Echenberg, M., *Colonial Conscripts: The Tirailleurs Sénégalais in French West Africa, 1857–1960* (Portsmouth, NY, 1991).

Edelstein, M., *Overseas Investment in the Age of High Imperialism: The United Kingdom, 1850–1914* (1965).

Ellingworth, P., 'Christianity and Politics in Dahomey, 1843–1867', *JAH* 5.2 (1964).

Etherington, N., *Preachers, Peasants and Politics in Southeast Africa, 1835–1880* (1976).

Evans, M. (ed.), *Empire and Culture: The French Experience, 1830–1940* (Basingstoke, 2004).

Fabian, J., *Out of Our Minds: Reason and Madness in the Exploration of Central Africa* (Berkeley, CA, 2000).

Fahmy, Z., 'Media-Capitalism: Colloquial Mass Culture and Nationalism in Egypt, 1908–18', *International Journal of Middle East Studies* 42 (2010).

Falasca-Zamponi, S., *Fascist Spectacle: The Aesthetics of Power in Mussolini's Italy* (Berkeley, CA, 2000).

Falola, T., and E. Brownell, *Africa, Empire and Globalization: Essays in Honor of A. G. Hopkins* (Durham, NC, 2011).

Fanon, F., *The Wretched of the Earth*, tr. C. Farrington (Harmondsworth, 2001).

Fell, A. S., 'Beyond the *bonhomme Banania*: Lucie Cousturier's Encounters with West African Soldiers during the First World War', in J. E. Kitchen, A. Miller and L. Rowe (eds), *Other Combatants, Other Fronts: Competing Histories of the First World War* (Newcastle upon Tyne, 2011).

Flibbert, A., 'State and Cinema in Pre-Revolutionary Egypt, 1927–52', in A. Goldschmidt, A. J. Johnson and B. A. Salmoni (eds), *Re-Envisioning Egypt, 1919–1952* (Cambridge, 2005).

Flint, J. E., 'Britain and the Partition of West Africa', in J. E. Flint and G. Williams (eds), *Perspectives of Empire: Essays Presented to Gerald S. Graham* (1973).

Forbes, H., 'On a Collection of Cast-Metal Work, of High Artistic Value, from Benin, Lately Acquired for the Mayer Museum', *Bulletin of the Liverpool Museums* 1 (Washington, DC, 1898).

Foster, E. A., *Faith in Empire: Religion, Politics, and Colonial Rule in French Senegal, 1880–1940* (Stanford, CA, 2013).

Frankema, E., and F. Buelens, *Colonial Exploitation and Economic Development: The Belgian Congo and the Netherlands Indies Compared* (2013).

Furse, R., *Acuparius: Recollections of a Recruiting Officer* (Oxford, 1962).

Fysh, P., and J. Wolfreys, *The Politics of Racism in France* (Basingstoke, 2003).

Gavois, M.-O., 'La perception du pouvoir métropolitain par les Européens d'Algérie', *Cahiers d'histoire* 85 (2001).

Genova, J. E., *Colonial Ambivalence, Cultural Authenticity, and the Limitations of Mimicry in French-Ruled West Africa, 1914–1956* (New York, 2004).

Gillette, A., *Racial Theories in Fascist Italy* (2002).

Ginio, R., *French Colonialism Unmasked: The Vichy Years in French West Africa* (Lincoln, Neb, 2006).

—, '"Cherchez la femme": African Gendarmes, Quarrelsome Women, and French Commanders in French West Africa, 1945–1960', *International Journal of African Historical Studies* 47 (2014).

Glass, S., *The Matabele War* (Harlow, 1968).

Gleichen, Count (ed.), *The Anglo-Egyptian Sudan: A Compendium Prepared by Officers of the Sudan Government*, 2 vols (1905).

Gleijeses, P., *Visions of Freedom: Havana, Washington, Pretoria, and the Struggle for Southern Africa, 1976–1991* (Chapel Hill, NC, 2011).

Green, R. H., and S. Griffith-Jones, 'External Debt: Sub-Saharan Africa's Emerging Iceberg', in T. Rose (ed.), *Crisis and Recovery in Sub-Saharan Africa* (1985).

Grogan, E. S., and A. H. Sharp, *From the Cape to Cairo: The First Traverse of Africa from South to North* (1900).

Grundlingh, L., 'The Recruitment of South African Blacks for Participation in the Second World War', in D. Killingray and D. Rathbone (eds), *Africa and the Second World War* (New York, 1986).

Guelke, A., *Rethinking the Rise and Fall of Apartheid* (Oxford, 2005).

Guy, J., *The Destruction of the Zulu Kingdom: The Civil War in Zululand, 1879–1884* (Pietermaritzburg, 1964).

Haggard, H. R., *Allan Quatermain* (1887).

Haile Selassie, *The Autobiography of Emperor Haile Selassie I: 'My Life and Ethiopia's Progress', 1892–1937*, tr. and ed. E. Ullendorff (Oxford, 1976).

Hannington, J., *Peril and Adventure in Central Africa: Being Illustrated Letters to the Youngsters at Home* (1886).

Harder, C., 'Schutztruppe in Cameroon', in M. Perraudin and J. Zimmerer (eds), *German Colonialism and National Identity* (2011).

Hargreaves, A. G., *The Colonial Experience in French Fiction: A Study of Pierre Loti, Ernest Psichari and Pierre Mille* (1981).

Harrison, C., *France and Islam in West Africa, 1860–1960* (Cambridge, 1988).

Harrison, R. T., *Gladstone's Imperialism in Egypt: Techniques of Domination* (Westport, CT, 1995).

Hassing, P., 'German Missionaries and the Maji Maji Rising', *African Historical Studies* 3 (1970).

Hattersley, A. F., *The British Settlement of Natal: A Study in Imperial Migration* (Cambridge, 1950).

Helly, D. O., *Livingstone's Legacy: Horace Waller and Victorian Mythmaking* (Athens, OH, 1987).

Henty, G. A., *Through Three Campaigns* (1901).

Hess, R. L., *Italian Colonialism in Somalia* (Chicago, 1966).

Hochschild, A., *King Leopold's Ghost: A Story of Greed, Terror, and Heroism in Colonial Africa* (New York, 1998).

Holland, R., *Blue-Water Empire: The British in the Mediterranean since 1800* (2012).

Horne, A., *Harold Macmillan*, II: *1957–1986* (1989).

Horowitz, M., 'Ba Karim: An Account of Rabeh's Wars', *African Historical Studies* 3 (1970).

Hubbell, A., 'A View of the Slave Trade from the Margin: Souroudougou in the Late Nineteenth-Century Slave Trade of the Niger Bend', *JAH* 42 (2001).

Hudson, A., 'The Missionary in West Africa', *Journal of the African Society* 3 (1903).

Hyam, R., *Empire and Sexuality: The British Experience* (Manchester, 1990).

Illingworth, P., 'Christianity and Politics in Dahomey, 1842-1867', *JAH* 5

Isaacman, A., and B. Isaacman, 'Resistance and Collaboration in Southern and Central Africa, c. 1850–1920', *International Journal of African Historical Studies* 10 (1977).

Izedinova, S., *A Few Months with the Boers: The War Reminiscences of a Russian Nursing Sister*, tr. C. Morby (Johannesburg, 1977).

James, L., *The Savage Wars: British Campaigns in Africa 1870–1920* (1985).

—, *Imperial Warrior: The Life and Times of Field-Marshal Viscount Allenby, 1861–1936* (1993).

James, W., 'The Black Experience in Twentieth-Century Britain', in P. D. Morgan and S. Hawkins (eds), *Black Experience and the Empire* (Oxford, 2004).

Jeater, D., 'The British Empire and African Women in the Twentieth Century', in P. D. Morgan and S. Hawkins (eds), *Black Experience and the Empire* (Oxford, 2004).

Jenkinson, J., '"All in the Same Uniform"? The Participation of Black Colonial Residents in the British Armed Forces in the First World War', *JICH* 40.2 (2012).

Johnson, F. E., 'Here and There in North Africa', *National Geographic Magazine* 25.1 (January 1914).

Kalman, S., 'Fascism and Algérianité: The Croix de Feu and the Indigenous Question in 1930s Algeria', in M. Thomas (ed.), *The French Colonial Mind*, II (Lincoln, Neb., 2011).

Kanya-Forstner, A. S., *The Conquest of the Western Sudan: A Study in French Military Imperialism* (Cambridge, 1969).

Kearny, P., *Service with the French Troops in Africa* (New York, 1913).

Kennedy, P., *The Rise of the Anglo-German Antagonism, 1860–1914* (Dublin, 1993).

Kerbœuf, A.-C., 'The Cairo Fire of 26 January 1952 and the Interpretations of History', in A. Goldschmidt, A. J. Johnson and B. A. Salmoni (eds), *Re-Envisioning Egypt, 1919–1952* (Cambridge, 2005).

Khenouf, M., and M. Brett, 'Algerian Nationalism and the Allied Military Strategy and Propaganda during the Second World War: The Background to Sétif', in D. Killingray and R. Rathbone (eds), *Africa and the Second World War* (New York, 1986).

Kholoussi, S., 'Fallahin: The "Mud Bearers" of Egypt's "Liberal Age"', in A. Goldschmidt, A. J. Johnson and B. A. Salmoni (eds), *Re-Envisioning Egypt, 1919–1952* (Cambridge, 2005).

Kiernan, V. G., *European Empires from Conquest to Collapse, 1815–1960* (1982).

Killingray, D., 'The Idea of a British Imperial African Army', *JAH* 20.3 (1979).

—, '"A Swift Agent of Government": Air Power in British Colonial Africa, 1916–1939', *JAH* 25.4 (1984).

—, 'Labour Mobilisation in British Colonial Africa for the War Effort, 1939–46', in D. Killingray and R. Rathbone (eds), *Africa and the Second World War* (New York, 1986).

—, *Fighting for Britain: African Soldiers in the Second World War* (Woodbridge, 2010).

— and J. Matthews, 'Beasts of Burden: British West African Carriers in the First World War', *Canadian Journal of African Studies* 13.1–2 (1979).

— and R. Rathbone, *Africa and the Second World War* (New York, 1986).

King, M., and E. King, *The Story of Medicine and Disease in Malawi: The 150 Years Since Livingstone* (Blantyre, 1997).

Kinghorn, J., 'Modernisation and Apartheid: The Afrikaner Churches', in R. Elphick and R. Davenport (eds), *Christianity in South Africa: A Political, Social, and Cultural History* (Cape Town, 1997).

Klein, H. S., *The Atlantic Slave Trade* (Cambridge, 1999).

Knight-Bruce, G. W. H., *Memories of Mashonaland* (1895).

Kuzmarov, J., *Modernizing Repression: Police Training and Nation-Building in the American Century* (Amherst and Boston, MA, 2012).

Laband, J., and I. Knight, *The War Correspondents: The Anglo-Zulu War* (Stroud, 1996).

Laband, J., and P. Thompson, 'African Levies in Natal and Zululand, 1838–1906', in S. Miller (ed.), *Soldiers and Settlers in Africa, 1850–1918* (Leiden, 2009).

Langbehn, V., and M. Salama (eds), *German Colonialism: Race, the Holocaust, and Postwar Germany* (New York, 2011).

Larguèche, A., 'The City and the Sea: Evolving Forms of Mediterranean Cosmopolitanism in Tunis, 1700–1881', in J. Clancy-Smith (ed.), *North Africa, Islam and the Mediterranean World: From the Almoravids to the Algerian War* (2001).

Lascelles, A. F., *King's Counsellor: Abdication and War: The Diaries of 'Tommy' Lascelles*, ed. D. Hart-Davis (2006).

Laumann, D., 'Narratives of a "Model Colony": German Togoland in Written and Oral Histories', in M. Perraudin and J. Zimmerer (eds), *German Colonialism and National Identity* (2011).

Lee, D., *Slavery and the Romantic Imagination* (Philadelphia, 2002).

Lehmann, J., 'Fraternity, Frenzy, and Genocide in German War Literature, 1906–36', in M. Perraudin and J. Zimmerer (eds), *German Colonialism and National Identity* (2011).

Leonard, D. K., and S. Straus, *Africa's Stalled Development: International Causes and Cures* (Boulder, Col., 2002).

Lewis, J., *Empire State-Building: War and Welfare in Kenya, 1925–52* (Oxford, 2000).

Lewis, M. and B.W. Andrzejewski, *Somali Poetry* (Oxford, 1968).

Livingstone, D., and C. Livingstone, *Narrative of an Expedition to the Zambesi and Its Tributaries and of the Discovery of the Lakes Shirwa and Nyassa, 1858–1864* (1865).

Lloyd, S., *Suez, 1956: A Personal Account* (1980).

Lonsdale, J., 'The Depression and the Second World War in the

Transformation of Kenya', in D. Killingray and R. Rathbone (eds), *Africa and the Second World War* (New York, 1986).

Loti, P., *The Sahara: Le Roman d'un Spahi*, tr. M. Larne (1930).

Louis, W. R., 'Libyan Independence, 1951: The Creation of a Client State', in P. Gifford and W. R. Louis (eds), *Decolonization and African Independence: The Transfer of Power, 1960–1980* (1988).

—, *Ends of British Imperialism: The Scramble for Empire, Suez and Decolonization* (2006).

Lucking, T., 'Some Thoughts on the Evolution of Boer War Concentration Camps', *Journal of the Society for Army Historical Research* 82 (2004).

Lunn, J., 'French Race Theory, the Parisian Society of Anthropology, and the Debate over *la Force Noire*, 1909–1912', in M. Thomas (ed.), *The French Colonial Mind*, II (Lincoln, Neb., 2011).

McCaskie, T. C., 'State and Society, Marriage and Adultery: Some Considerations Towards a Social History of Pre-Colonial Asante', *JAH* 22 (1981).

McDonald, P. D., *The Literature Police: Apartheid Censorship and Its Cultural Consequences* (Oxford, 2009).

Mack Smith, D., *Mussolini's Roman Empire* (1976).

MacKenzie, J. M., *Propaganda and Empire: The Manipulation of British Public Opinion, 1880–1960* (Manchester, 1984).

MacMaster, N., *Colonial Migrants and Racism: Algerians in France, 1900–62* (1997).

Mak, L., 'More than Officers and Officials: Britons in Occupied Egypt, 1882–1922', *JICH* 39 (2011).

Mann, E. J. *Mikono ya damu: 'Hands of Blood': African Mercenaries and the Politics of Conflict in German East Africa, 1888–1904* (Frankfurt, 2002).

Marder, A. J., *The Anatomy of British Sea Power: A History of British Naval Policy in the Pre-Dreadnought Era, 1880–1905* (Hamden, CT, 1964).

Martens, J., 'Enlightenment Theories of Civilisation and Savagery in British Natal: The Colonial Origins of the (Zulu) African Barbarism Myth', in B. Carton, J. Laband and J. Sithole (eds), *Zulu Identities: Being Zulu, Past and Present* (Scottsville, 2008).

Matthews, J. K., 'Clock Towers for the Colonized: Demobilization of the Nigerian Military and the Readjustment of Its Veterans to Civilian Life, 1918–1925', *International Journal of African Historical Studies* 14 (1981).

Mazov, S., 'Soviet Policy in West Africa: An Episode of the Cold War, 1956–1964', in M. Matusevich (ed.), *Africa in Russia, Russia in Africa: Three Centuries of Encounters* (Trenton, NJ, 2007).

Mazower, M., *Hitler's Empire: Nazi Rule in Occupied Europe* (2008).

Meek, C. I., *Brief Authority: A Memoir of Colonial Administration in Tanganyika*, ed. I. Meek (2011).

Mille, P., 'The "Black-Vote" in Senegal', *Journal of the African Society* 1 (1901).

Miller, S. M., 'Fighting the Other Enemy: Boredom, Drudgery, and Restlessness on the South African Veld, 1900–1902', in I. F. W. Beckett (ed.), *Victorian Wars: New Perspectives* (2007).

Mills, W. G., 'Millennial Christianity, British Imperialism, and African Nationalism', in R. Elphick and R. Davenport (eds), *Christianity in South Africa: A Political, Social, and Cultural History* (Cape Town, 1997).

Mockler, A., *Haile Selassie's War: The Ethiopian–Italian Campaign, 1935–1941* (Oxford, 1984).

Morsy, M., *North Africa, 1800–1900: A Survey from the Nile Valley to the Atlantic* (1984).

Mowafi, R., *Slavery, Slave Trade and Abolition Attempts in Egypt and the Sudan, 1820–1882* (Malmö, 1981).

Murray, B. K., 'Politics and Cricket: The D'Oliveira Affair of 1968', *Journal of Southern African Studies* 27 (2001).

Muschalek, M., 'Honourable Soldier-Bureaucrats: Formations of Violent Identities in the Colonial Police Force of German Southwest Africa, 1905–18', *German Colonialism* 41.4 (2013).

NADA: The Southern Rhodesia Native Affairs Dept. Annual (XX).

Namikas, L., *Battleground Africa: Cold War in the Congo, 1960–1965* (Washington, DC, 2013).

'Narrative of Events in the Life of a Liberated Negro, Now a Church Missionary Catechist in Sierra Leone', in Church Missionary Society *Missionary Register* (1837).

Nasson, B., 'War Opinion in South Africa in 1914', *JICH* 23 (1995).

Naval Intelligence Division (US), *French West Africa*, II: *The Colonies* (1944).

Ndulu, B. J., *Challenges of African Growth: Opportunities, Constraints, and Strategic Directions* (Washington, DC, 2007).

— et al. (eds), *The Political Economy of Economic Growth in Africa, 1960–2000*, 2 vols (Cambridge, 2008).

Newbury, C., 'Cecil Rhodes, De Beers and Mining Finance in South Africa: The Business of Entrepreneurship and Imperialism', in R. E. Dumett (ed.), *Mining Tycoons in the Age of Empire, 1870–1945: Entrepreneurship, High Finance, Politics and Territorial Expansion* (Farnham, Surrey, 2009).

Nicolini, B. (trans. Watson, P.-J.), *Makran, Oman and Zanziba: Three-terminal Cultural Corridor in the Western Indian Ocean, 1799-1856* (Leiden, 2004).

Nwoye, R. E., *The Public Image of Pierre Savorgnan de Brazza and the Establishment of French Imperialism in the Congo, 1875–1885* (Aberdeen, 1984).

Ohrwalder, J., *Ten Years' Captivity in the Mahdi's Camp, 1882–1892* (1892).

Oliver, R., and A. Atmore, *Africa Since 1800* (Cambridge, 1994).

Omu, F. I. A., 'The Dilemma of Press Freedom in Colonial Africa: The West African Example', *JAH* 9 (1968).

Osuntokun, A., *Nigeria in the First World War* (1979).

Page, M. E., 'The War of *Thangata*: Nyasaland and the East African Campaign, 1914–1918', *JICH* 19 (1978).

—, '"With Jannie in the Jungle": European Humor in an East African Campaign, 1914–1918', *International Journal of African Historical Studies* 14 (1981).

Pankhurst, R., 'The Russians in Ethiopia: Aspirations of Progress', in M. Matusevich (ed.), *Africa in Russia, Russia in Africa: Three Centuries of Encounters* (Trenton, NJ, 2007).

Park, M., *Travels in the Interior of Africa* (Stroud, 2005).

Parsons, T. H., 'African Participation in the British Empire', in P. D. Morgan and S. Hawkins (eds), *Black Experience and the Empire* (Oxford, 2004).

Pascoe, W. W., 'The Cubans in Africa', in D. L. Bark (ed.), *The Red Orchestra*, II: *The Case of Africa* (Stanford, CA, 1988).

Pease, H., *The History of the Northumberland (Hussars) Yeomanry, 1819–1923* (1924).

Perham, M., *Lugard: The Years of Adventure, 1858–1898* (1965).

Perkins, K. J., *Qaids, Captains and Colons: French Military Administration in the Colonial Maghrib, 1844–1934* (New York, 1981).

Perras, A., *Carl Peters and German Imperialism, 1856–1918: A Political Biography* (Oxford, 2006).

Perraudin, M., and J. Zimmerer (eds), *German Colonialism and National Identity* (2011).

Peterson, B. J., 'Slave Emancipation, Trans-Local Social Processes and the Spread of Islam in French Colonial Buguni (Southern Mali), 1893–1914', *Journal of African History* 45.3 (2004).

Pirouet, M. L., *Black Evangelists: The Spread of Christianity in Uganda, 1891–1914* (1978).

Poggo, S. S., 'Zande Resistance to Foreign Penetration in the Southern Sudan, 1860–1890', in J. Spaulding and S. Beswick (eds), *White Nile, Black Blood: War, Leadership, and Ethnicity from Khartoum to Kampala* (Lawrenceville, NJ, 2001).

Porter, B., *The Lion's Share: A Short History of British Imperialism, 1850–1970* (1975).

Porterfield, T., *The Allure of Empire: Art in the Service of French Imperialism, 1798–1836* (Princeton, NJ, 1998).

Posel, D., *The Making of Apartheid, 1948–1961: Conflict and Compromise* (Oxford, 1997).

Pretorius, H., and L. Jafta, '"A Branch Springs Out": African Initiated Churches', in R. Elphick and R. Davenport (eds), *Christianity in South Africa: A Political, Social, and Cultural History* (Cape Town, 1997).

Price, R., *Making Empire: Colonial Encounters and the Creation of Imperial Rule in Nineteenth-Century Africa* (Cambridge, 2008).

Prochaska, D., 'The Return of the Repressed: War, Trauma, Memory in Algeria and Beyond', in P. M. E. Lorcin (ed.), *Algeria and France, 1800–2000: Identity, Memory, Nostalgia* (Syracuse, NY, 2006).

Quist-Adade, C., 'The African Russians: Children of the Cold War', in M. Matusevich (ed.), *Africa in Russia, Russia in Africa: Three Centuries of Encounters* (Trenton, NJ, 2007).

Rabot, C., 'Recent French Explorations in Africa', *National Geographic Magazine* 13.4 (April 1902).

Ranger, T. O., *Revolt in Southern Rhodesia, 1896–7: A Study in African Resistance* (1967).

—, 'Connexions between "Primary Resistance" Movements and Modern Mass Nationalism in East and Central Africa. Part I', *JAH* 9.3 (1968).

Rasmussen, A. M. B., *Modern African Spirituality: The Independent Holy Spirit Churches in East Africa, 1902–1976* (1996).

Rathbone, R., 'Police Intelligence in Ghana in the Late 1940s and 1950s', *JICH* 21.3 (1993).

Redmayne, A., 'Mkwawa and the Hehe Wars', *JAH* 9.3 (1968).

Renton, D., D. Seddon and L. Zeilig, *The Congo: Plunder and Resistance* (2007).

Richards, J., *Visions of Yesterday* (1973).

Robert Hunter, F., *Egypt Under the Khedives, 1805–1879: From Household Government to Modern Bureaucracy* (Pittsburgh, PA, 1984).

Robinson, P., 'The Search for Mobility During the Second Boer War', *Journal of the Society for Army Historical Research* 86 (2008).

Rodogno, D., *Fascism's European Empire: Italian Occupation During the Second World War* (Cambridge, 2006).

Ross, P. T., *A Yeoman's Letters* (1900).

Ruete, E., *Memoirs of an Arabian Princess from Zanzibar* (Princeton, NJ, 1996).

Ryzova, L., 'Egyptianizing Modernity through the "New *Effendiya*"', in A. Goldschmidt, A. J. Johnson and B. A. Salmoni (eds), *Re-Envisioning Egypt, 1919–1952* (Cambridge, 2005).

Sabben-Clare, E. E., 'African Troops in Asia', *African Affairs* 44 (1945).

Şaul, M., and P. Royer, *West African Challenge to Empire: Culture and History in the Volta-Bani Anticolonial War* (Athens, OH, 2001).

Schalk, D. L., *War and the Ivory Tower: Algeria and Vietnam* (Oxford, 1991).

Scham, A., *Lyautey in Morocco: Protectorate Administration, 1912–1925* (Berkeley, CA, 1970).

Schmidt, E., *Foreign Intervention in Africa: From the Cold War to the War on Terror* (Cambridge, 2013).

Schneider, W. H., *An Empire for the Masses: The French Popular Image of Africa, 1870–1900* (1982).

Schölch, A., *Egypt for the Egyptians!: The Socio-Political Crisis in Egypt, 1878–1882* (Oxford, 1981).

Schreuder, D. M., *The Scramble for Southern Africa, 1877–1895: The Politics of Partition Reappraised* (Cambridge, 1980).

Schroer, T. L., '"Racial" Mixing of Prisoners of War in the First World War', in J. E. Kitchen, A. Miller and L. Rowe (eds), *Other Combatants, Other Fronts: Competing Histories of the First World War* (Newcastle upon Tyne, 2011).

See, K.-Y., 'The Downfall of General Giraud: A Study of American Wartime Politics', *Penn History Review* 18.1 (2010).

Segalla, S. D., *The Moroccan Soul: French Education, Colonial Ethnology, and Muslim Resistance, 1912–1956* (Lincoln, NA, 2009).

Selous, F., *Sunshine and Storm in Rhodesia* (1897).

Sessions, J. E., *By Sword and Plow: France and the Conquest of Algeria* (Ithaca, NY, 2011).

Shadle, B., 'Settlers, Africans, and Inter-Personal Violence in Kenya, ca. 1900–1920s', *International Journal of African Historical Studies* 45 (2012).

Shear, K., 'Tested Loyalties: Police and Politics in South Africa, 1939–63', *JAH* 53 (2012).

Shelford, F., 'On West African Railways', *Journal of the African Society* 3 (1903).

Sheriff, A., and E. Ferguson (eds), *Zanzibar Under Colonial Rule* (1991).

Short, J. P., *Magic Lantern Empire: Colonialism and Society in Germany* (Oxford, 2013).

Shubin, V., *The Hot 'Cold War': The USSR in Southern Africa* (2008).

Sikainga, A. A., 'Military Slavery and the Emergence of a Southern Sudanese Diaspora in the Northern Sudan', in J. Spaulding and S. Beswick (eds), *White Nile, Black Blood: War, Leadership, and Ethnicity from Khartoum to Kampala* (Lawrenceville, NJ, 2001).

Slavin, D. H., *Colonial Cinema and Imperial France, 1919–1939: White Blind Spots, Male Fantasies, Settler Myths* (Baltimore, MD, 2001).

Slight, J., 'British Perceptions and Responses to Sultan Ali Dinar of Darfur, 1915–16', *JICH* 38.2 (2010).

Smith, I., *The Great Betrayal: The Memoirs of Ian Douglas Smith* (1997).

Stanard, M. G., *Selling the Congo: A History of European Pro-Empire Propaganda and the Making of Belgian Imperialism* (Lincoln, NE, 2011).

Stanley, B., *The World Missionary Conference, Edinburgh 1910* (Cambridge, 2009).

Stapleton, T., '"Valuable, Gallant and Faithful Assistants": The Fingo (or Mfengu) as Colonial Military Allies During the Cape–Xhosa Wars, 1835–1881', in S. M. Miller (ed.), *Soldiers and Settlers in Africa, 1850–1918* (Leiden, 2009).

Staum, M. S., *Labeling People: French Scholars on Society, Race, and Empire, 1815–1848* (Montreal, 2003).

Strachan, H., *The First World War in Africa* (Oxford, 2004).

Streak, M., *The Afrikaner as Viewed by the English, 1795–1854* (Cape Town, 1974).

Sudan Intelligence Reports, 3 vols (Cairo, 1905).

Surridge, K. T., *Managing the South African War, 1899–1902: Politicians v. Generals* (Woodbridge, 1998).

Taithe, B., *The Killer Trail: A Colonial Scandal in the Heart of Africa* (Oxford, 2009).

Tareke, G., *Ethiopia: Power and Protest* (Lawrenceville, NJ, 1996).

Taylor, P. J., *Britain and the Cold War: 1945 as Geopolitical Transition* (New York, 1990).

Thompson, F., *Lark Rise to Candleford* (Oxford, 1965).

Thompson, G., 'Colonialism in Crisis: The Uganda Disturbances of 1945', *African Affairs* 91 (1992).

Thompson, W. S., *Ghana's Foreign Policy, 1957–1966* (Princeton, NJ, 1969).

Toledano, E. R., *Slavery and Abolition in the Ottoman Middle East* (Seattle, 1998).

Tomaselli, K., *The Cinema of Apartheid: Race and Class in South African Film* (New York, 1988).

Trumbull, G. R., *An Empire of Facts: Colonial Power, Cultural Knowledge, and Islam in Algeria, 1870–1914* (Cambridge, 2009).

Truth and Reconciliation Commission of South Africa Report, II (Cape Town, 1998).

Turpin, J., 'The Pongas Mission', *Mission Life* 5 (1874).

Udal, J. O., *The Nile in Darkness: Conquest and Exploration, 1504–1862* (Norwich, 1998).

Umar, M. S., *Islam and Colonialism: Intellectual Responses of Muslims of Northern Nigeria to British Colonial Rule* (Leiden, 2006).

US Naval Intelligence Division, *French West Africa, II: The Colonies* (1944)

van Beek, W. E. A., 'Intensive Slave Raiding in the Colonial Interstice: Hamman Yaji and the Mandara Mountains (North Cameroon and North-Eastern Nigeria)', *JAH* 58 (2012).

van der Poel, J., *Railway and Customs Policies in South Africa, 1885–1910* (1933).

van Onselen, C., 'The 1912 Wankie Colliery Strike', *JAH* 15 (1974).

Vaughan, C., 'Violence and Regulation in the Darfur–Chad Borderland c. 1909–56: Policing a Colonial Boundary', *JAH* 54.2 (2013).

Verdès-Leroux, J., *Les Français d'Algérie de 1830 à aujourd'hui: une page d'histoire déchirée* (Paris, 2001).

von Lettow-Vorbeck, P. E., *My Reminiscences of East Africa* (1920).

Walton, C., *Empire of Secrets: British Intelligence, the Cold War and the Twilight of Empire* (2013).

Ward, G., *The Life of Charles Alan Smythies, Bishop of the Universities' Mission to Central Africa* (1899).

Warwick, P., *Black People and the South African War, 1899–1902* (Cambridge, 1983).

Watson, R., 'Literacy as a Style of Life: Garveyism and Gentlemen in Colonial Ibadan', *African Studies* 73 (2014).

Watson, R. L., 'The Subjection of a South African State: Thaba Nchu, 1880–1884', *JAH* 21 (1980).

Webb, J. L. A., 'The Horse and Slave Trade between the Western Sahara and Senegambia', *JAH* 34 (1993).

Webber, M., 'Soviet Policy in Sub-Saharan Africa: The Final Phase', *Journal of Modern African Studies* 30 (1992).

Werner, A., 'Native Affairs in Natal', *Journal of the African Society* 4 (1905).

West, R., *Brazza of the Congo: Exploration and Exploitation in French Equatorial Africa* (1972).

Westcott, N., 'The Impact of the Second World War on Tanganyika, 1939–49', in D. Killingray and R. Rathbone (eds), *Africa and the Second World War* (New York, 1986).

Whidden, J., 'The Generation of 1919', in A. Goldschmidt, A. J. Johnson and B. A. Salmoni (eds), *Re-Envisioning Egypt, 1919–1952* (Cambridge, 2005).

White, O., 'Conquest and Cohabitation: French Men's Relations with West African Women in the 1890s and 1900s', in M. Thomas (ed.), *The French Colonial Mind*, II (Lincoln, Neb., 2011).

Willcocks, J., *The Romance of Soldiering and Sport* (1925).

Williams, S., *Who Killed Hammarskjöld?: The UN, the Cold War and White Supremacy in Africa* (Oxford, 2014).

Wilson, J., 'Gold Coast Information', *African Affairs* 43 (1944).

Yearwood, P. J., 'Great Britain and the Repartition of Africa, 1914–1919', *JICH* 18.3 (1990).

Zimba, B., E. Alpers and A. Isaacman (eds), *Slave Routes and Oral Tradition in Southeastern Africa* (Maputo, Mozambique, 2005).

Zimmerer, J., 'War, Concentration Camps and Genocide in South-West Africa: The First German Genocide', in J. Zimmerer and J. Zeller (eds), *Genocide in German South-West Africa: The Colonial War of 1904–1908 and Its Aftermath* (Monmouth, 2008).

Zimmerer, J. and Perraudin, M. (eds), *German Colonialism and National Identity* (2011)

ACKNOWLEDGEMENTS

My greatest thanks are to my wife Mary for her encouragement, assistance and forbearance during the writing of this book. Invaluable suggestions, advice and information have been provided by my sons Edward and Henry James, Andrew Lownie, Lucinda McNeile, Andy Paul, Innes Meek, Andrew Williams, Susan Osman, Robert Steedman and Michael Rudd. I must also thank Hector Gordon, Matthew Parris and Frank Dearden for sharing with me their experiences and knowledge of Kenya, Rhodesia and South Africa. I am also grateful across the years to my father, who introduced me to the world of empires through their postage stamps, and to Peter Hodgson, a former district officer, who took time off from teaching Mathematics and Classics to tell us about the peoples of West Africa. I am also indebted to Andy Joyce for his help in unravelling the mysteries of computers, and to my editor Linden Lawson for wisdom and patience beyond the call of duty. I am also grateful to Alan Samson for his generosity, good sense and inspiration.

Further praise for many kindnesses and help is due to Valerie Dickson of the University of St Andrews Library, the staff of the National Archives, the Liddell Hart Centre, Rhodes House Library, the Middle East Centre and the Bodleian Library.

INDEX

NOTE: Personal ranks and titles are generally the highest mentioned in the text